TEACHERS DOING RESEARCH

The Power of Action Through Inquiry

Second Edition

TEACHERS DOING RESEARCH
The Power of Action Through Inquiry
Second Edition

Edited by

Gail Burnaford
Joseph Fischer
David Hobson

LEA

LAWRENCE ERLBAUM ASSOCIATES, PUBLISHERS

2001   Mahwah, New Jersey   London

Lawrence Erlbaum Associates, Inc., Publishers
10 Industrial Avenue
Mahwah, New Jersey 07430-2262

Cover design by Kathryn Houghtaling Lacey

Library of Congress Cataloging-in-Publication Data

Teachers doing research : the power of action through inquiry / [edited by] Gail
Burnaford, Joseph Fischer, David Hobson.—2nd ed.
   p.   cm.
   Includes bibliographical references and index.
   ISBN 0-8058-3589-X (pbk. : alk. paper)
   1. Action research in education—United States. 2. Teaching—
United States. I. Burnaford, Gail E. II. Fischer, Joseph, 1926–
III. Hobson, David.
   LB1028.24.T4263 2000
   371.102—dc21
                                         00-042653
                                          CIP

Printed in the United States of America
10 9 8 7 6 5 4 3 2 1

CONTENTS

PREFACE

Teachers Doing Research: The Power of Action Through Inquiry is a book that describes the processes of doing teacher action research. But it is more than that. It is also a text filled with examples of teacher action research projects, provided by teachers themselves. In this second edition, we have developed many more specifics and provided a variety of methodological options for teachers who do research in their classrooms and schools (chaps. 1–5). That is a major focus of the book. We have broadened the context for teacher action research, by discussing its influence in school reform both in the United States and internationally (chaps. 6, 7, and 9, and Senese's teacher research essay). We have also expanded our discussion of teacher action research with preservice teachers, especially in chapter 6. Finally, we have examined the connections between teacher action research and the larger arena of educational research (chap. 8). There are three sections we have titled In Practice that provide readers with opportunities to respond to the reading and try out related activities.

Following the preface, Part I is the primary "methods" section, titled Ways of Doing Teacher Action Research. Chapter 1, Action and Reflection: Narrative and Journaling in Teacher Research, by David Hobson, introduces teacher action research as a means of reflecting on one's own personal journey through teaching. He describes strategies for journaling to evoke ideas for more intentional research that grows from this personal dimension of teaching.

Joseph C. Fischer's chapter 2, Action Research Rationale and Planning: Developing a Framework for Teacher Inquiry, furthers the discussion by helping the reader develop research questions and a plan/proposal for doing systematic research. Fischer provides two formats for a research proposal in the chapter; another format is provided for readers' application in the In Practice section following chapter 4.

Chapter 3, Teachers' Work: Methods for Researching Teaching, introduces resources and methods descriptions for teacher action researchers. Methods for collecting and interpreting data have been organized to respond to the context of schools and classrooms. Author Gail Burnaford then discusses how research can be an integral part of curriculum development, as exemplified in the work of two teacher researchers, Bonnie Anastos and Craig Hill.

This volume also has attempted to make an intentional contribution to teacher action research by engaging in an analysis and discussion of how technology can play a part in the work. As we go to press, many teachers are utilizing technology in their preparation for teaching and in their classrooms; they are also beginning to tap into the potential of technology for their own classroom research. In chapter 4, Teacher Researchers Go Online, David Hobson and Louanne Smolin balance their detailed introduction to technology for novice researchers with a discussion of the issues and questions related to technology-based teacher research as this field progresses. We have also integrated a series of web sites throughout the book related to the topics and issues described in the chapters and the teacher research stories. As we prepare for this second edition, we are also planning for a *Teachers Doing Research* web site (teachersdoingresearch.com), where readers, teacher research participants, preservice candidates, and teacher educators can participate in dialogue with the authors, editors, and each other.

Chapter 5, Hobson's Learning With Each Other: Collaboration in Teacher Research, begins Part II of this volume, School and Professional Contexts. With this second edition, we have become more intentional about regarding the work of teacher researchers as part of a professional community. Hobson's chapter describes ways in which teachers and teacher leaders can utilize that community meaningfully to further research.

Burnaford's chapter 6 extends that notion of collaboration to the school environment, with particular attention on how preservice teachers can collaborate with school partners to engage in research that is mutually beneficial. This chapter, School and University Teacher Action Research: Maintaining the Personal in the Public Context, also discusses how university researchers and teacher researchers can and do collaborate. (This is elaborated further in Judith Lachance Whitcomb's teacher research project story after chap. 7.) Chapter 7, Linda S. Tafel and Joseph C. Fischer's Teacher Action Research and Professional Development: Foundations for Educational Renewal, provides reflections from experienced teachers on how teacher action research and staff development can and should be related.

Part III, titled The Larger Arena, is just that. Susan Jungck's chapter 8, How Does It Matter? Teacher Inquiry in the Traditions of Social Science Research, provides a background history for teacher action research and the strands of social science research that have contributed to its current status in education. Chapter 9, written by Fischer and Norman Weston, focuses on contexts for teacher research that range from the U.S. metropolitan city of Chicago to two cities in South America. This chapter, Teacher Research and School Reform: Lessons from Chicago, Curitiba, and Santiago, raises the questions about the larger influence that teacher action research can have on the political landscape of challenged school districts.

There are 11 examples of teacher action research in two sections of the book titled, appropriately, Teachers Doing Research. The teachers and administrators represented in these projects reflect a range of work that we have seen. We have worked with each of these researchers, and we have learned from the contributions they have made to the field. There are high school teachers doing research, as noted by foreign-language teacher Emmerich Koller in his project, and school administrator Joe Senese in his reflections on educational change in his building. Middle school teachers, including Wallace (Chip) Shilkus, who teaches industrial arts, Richard Moon, who teaches physical education, and Judith Lachance Whitcomb, a science teacher, are also engaged in teacher action research. Martha Stephens contributes a detailed description of her research with special education students; Vida Schaffel, Susan Sheldon and Jackie Samuel, and Judith Lachance Whitcomb explain how they have been researchers in urban K–8 settings.

Elementary teachers Nancy Brankis, Kelli Visconti, and Nancy Hubbard utilized the methods of action research to strengthen their peer and personal relationships as well as their interactions with their students. Visconti and Hubbard, both contributors to the first edition of

Teachers Doing Research, have continued to shape and reshape their understanding of practitioner research, introducing it to colleagues, presenting at conferences, and pursuing other avenues to support their work as researchers.

We invited Owen van den Berg to write an afterword to this edition because we believed that his perspective on teacher action research captured the progression that we hoped to offer in this book. The title of the afterword, The Three P's in Teacher Research: Reflecting on Action Research From Personal, Professional, and Political Perspectives, describes what we have written about in *Teachers Doing Research: The Power of Action Through Inquiry*.

ACKNOWLEDGMENTS

We thank those who have offered comments and insights to the creation of this edition, including Arnold Aprill, Christine Miller, Janet Miller, and Cynthia Weiss. We also appreciate the patience and support of Naomi Silverman, our editor at Lawrence Erlbaum Associates, who had faith that the first edition of this book was timely and that we had much more to say in this second edition. Two reviewers provided helpful feedback as we developed the second edition: Evelyn Jacob at George Mason University, and Mary Manke at Minnesota State University, Mankato. Finally, we thank the contributors to this book, who have taught us much about researching *and* teaching.

About the Contributors

Nancy Brankis is a Lincolnshire-Prairie View District Gifted/Enrichment Coordinator. She earned a master's in education in curriculum and instruction from National-Louis University and a master's in education in administration from Northern Illinois University. Nancy inservices educators across all disciplines on the highly effective use of implementing journal writing with students. She has received a fellowship in gifted education for her graduate work, which focused on the integration of journaling across the curriculum. She has also conducted staff developing workshops at her school concerning the development of reading strategies, Odyssey of the Mind, and the value of journaling with students. E-mail: Nbrankis@district103.k12.il.us

Gail Burnaford is associate professor and Director of Undergraduate Teacher Education and School Research Partnerships at Northwestern University, where she teaches courses on action research for preservice teachers. Before coming to Northwestern, she taught at National-Louis University where teacher action research is a centerpiece of the master's program. A former middle and high school English/Language Arts teacher, Dr. Burnaford's research interests include teacher action research, arts/curriculum integration, and adolescent literacy. Her previous book, *Images of Schoolteachers*, is in its second edition with Lawrence

Erlbaum Associates. Her newest book, *Renaissance in the Classroom: Arts Integration and Meaningful Learning*, coauthored with Arnold Aprill and Cynthia Weiss, is also in press with Lawrence Erlbaum Associates. E-mail: G-burnaford@nwu.edu

Joseph C. Fischer is a professor at National College of Education, National-Louis University in Chicago. He is one of the founding instructors of the field-based master's of education program in which teacher action research is a primary component of professional development. Since 1975, he has worked in school improvement, action research, and curriculum integration programs in Chicago Public Schools. He received his doctorate from the University of Chicago in 1972, majoring in comparative and international education. Dr. Fischer has taught action research courses in Germany, Brazil, and Chile. His research interests include school reform, democratic education, teacher development, and the role of schooling in advocating for human rights and social justice. E-mail: Jfis@wheeling1.nl.edu

David Hobson is a professor in the Interdisciplinary Studies Department of National-Louis University in Evanston, Illinois. He was a founder and long-time director of the Graduate Center for Human Development and Learning at Fairleigh Dickinson University. As a former middle and high school social studies teacher, he taught psychology and sociology to adolescents. Dr. Hobson has conducted numerous workshops throughout the country on journal keeping and collaborative professional development. His research interests include teacher action research through collaboration, journals as tools for writing, and self-study for teacher educators. E-mail: Dhob@evan1.nl.edu

Nancy Hubbard has been involved in education for seventeen years as a teacher and counselor. She received both her master's in education and her doctorate in instructional leadership from National-Louis University. Her dissertation was entitled "Exploring the personal intelligences: An interpretive study with first-year teachers." Dr. Hubbard was a multiage teacher in Batavia, Illinois, at McWayne Elementary School, an open-enrollment school where multiple intelligences are the basis for learning. She has also been an instructor for National-Louis University's field-based master's program. Currently Dr. Hubbard teaches in Cameroon, Africa in a one-room school house. E-mail: Nhubbard@inil.com

Susan Jungck is a professor in the Foundations and Research Department at National-Louis University in Evanston, Illinois. Her doctoral work at the University of Wisconsin-Madison focused in curriculum theory as informed through anthropological, critical, and interpretive research traditions. She has worked for many years with teachers and college faculties conducting research in both the United States and Thailand. These experiences have contributed to her appreciation of how teacher researchers effect critical change. E-mail: Sjun@wheeling1.nl.edu

Emmerich Koller teaches German at Glenbrook South High School in Illinois and at Northwestern University's Center for Talent Development. Mr. Koller earned degrees in philosophy, German, and education from New York State, Roosevelt, and National-Louis Universities, respectively. In 1989, he was the recipient of the Certificate of Merit from the Goethe House, New York, and the National German Teacher's Association for outstanding achievements in furthering and encouraging the study of the German language and culture in the United States. In 1993, he received the Distinguished Teacher Award from the White House Commission on Presidential Scholars.

Richard Moon is a physical education teacher for Grades 3 through 8 at Fremont Middle School in Mundelein, Illinois. A 20-year veteran, Rick taught P.E. at the Diamond Lake Migrant School. He coaches boys' and girls' basketball, track and field, and boys' volleyball. He completed a teacher research project focusing on gender relationships and competition/cooperation in physical fitness in 1992. This topic is of special interest to him as he is the father of two girls, Amy, age 9, and Kelsey, age 7, who feature in his project. E-mail: Rmoon@mail.fremont.lake.k12.il.us

Jackie Samuel is a Chicago-based professional actress, director, storyteller, and arts educator. She has been an arts educator for more than 10 years in the Chicago public schools. Her expertise and affiliation with the Chicago Arts Partnerships in Education has afforded her the opportunity to tour Manchester and London, England, to observe arts practices in schools and art organizations. As an actress, Ms. Samuel received a Chicago Jeff Citation for her performance in the critically acclaimed *The Good Times Are Killing Me*. She has also appeared in films such as *Losing Isaiah, Blankman, Blink*, and *Love Your Mama*. Currently, she is artistic director of the Bethel Cultural Arts Center in Chicago. E-mail: CHATTYJACK@aol.com

Vida Schaffel (Cookie) has been teaching in Chicago since the early 1960s. She left the profession to raise her family and returned in the mid-1980s, after which she earned state certification in the field of English as a second language. She received her master's of education in curriculum and instruction in 1993 and conducted a teacher research project in her classroom involving literacy and language learning. She is currently a preschool teacher at Falconer School. E-mail: CookieSch@aol.com

Joseph C. Senese has been Assistant Principal for Curriculum, Instruction, and Staff Development at Highland Park High School in Highland Park, Illinois, for the last 8 years. He initiated the Action Research Laboratory in 1995. He has presented the work of the Action Research Laboratory at national and international conferences, including the American Educational Research Association's annual meetings. E-mail: Jsenese@ d113.lake.k12.il.us

Susan Sheldon received her bachelor's degree in finance from Indiana University in 1990. Upon graduation, she joined the Northern Trust Company in its Corporate Lender Training Program. After 3 years in the banking and trust industry, Ms. Sheldon decided to change her career to one that would involve more creativity—education. She attended Loyola University's School of Education and received a master's degree in curriculum and instruction in January 1996. She has been a teacher with the Chicago Public Schools since September 1996. She has taught fourth grade, fifth grade, and eighth grade. She is currently a seventh-grade teacher of Mathematics and Literature at Washington Irving Elementary School. E-mail: Scssheldon@juno.com

Wallace Shilkus (Chip) has taught industrial arts for 12 years at Elm Place Middle School in Highland Park, Illinois. Prior to that, he taught at S.E.D.O.L. in Lake County, Illinois, for 5 years, where he focused on woodworking, drafting, and architecture classes for behaviorally disturbed children. He received his BA from Winona State University in 1982 and his master's of education from National-Louis University in 1999. E-mail: Cshilkus@d113.lake.k12.il.us

Louanne Smolin is an assistant clinical professor in the Department of Curriculum and Instruction at the University of Illinois in Chicago. In addition to teaching courses related to the integration of technology in classroom settings, she creates workshops and seminars to ensure that all students enrolled in teacher certification programs meet national technology standards for teacher education. Dr. Smolin's research interests include human–computer relationships and the relationship between gender and technology. E-mail: Louanne@iceberg.org

Martha Stephens is a teacher of students with learning disabilities at Clarke Middle School in Athens, Georgia. She earned a doctorate in the field of learning disabilities from the University of Georgia. During the past 32 years of teaching, her career has included 10 years of university teaching, 10 years of administrative work, and more than 10 years of work in the classroom, including the instruction of both regular education and special education children, ages 6 through 16. She looks forward to several more years of writing and working in the public school classroom setting. E-mail: Msteph@negia.com

Linda Tafel is Provost of the National College of Education of National-Louis University. She had previously served as a professor in the College of Education in Interdisciplinary Studies and Educational Leadership and Dean of the College of Education. She has been an active consultant in school reform initiatives in the Chicago area and teaches in the doctoral program in instructional leadership with particular interest in staff development and related issues. Dr. Tafel holds a doctorate in curriculum and supervision from the Northern Illinois University. E-mail: Ltaf@wheeling1.nl.edu

Owen van den Berg is a native of South Africa, where he established a master's program in action research at the University of Western Cape in 1987. Since 1995, he has been living in St. Louis, Missouri, where his major work has focused on supporting teachers doing action research, both in the DLAR (Developing Leadership in Action Research) project and in work at Maryville University and National-Louis University. His current position is as associate professor at the National College of Education at National-Louis University in St. Louis. E-mail: OWENV@worldnet.att.net

Kelli Visconti has been a fifth-grade teacher at Jane Stenson School in Skokie, Illinois, for most of her career. Her undergraduate work in elementary and secondary education with a major in English was completed at Concordia University, River Forest, Illinois, in 1987. She has a master's degree in curriculum and instruction from National-Louis University, 1993. Teacher research has become an interest of hers through her curiosity about the teaching profession. Her master's thesis on teacher burnout and its particulars led her to seek renewal by starting and leading a teacher research group at her school. Attending and presenting at conferences on teacher research, including her presentation at AERA in April 1999, furnished her with many opportunities to expand her interest and understanding of teacher research. E-mail: Kvisconti @sd68.k12.il.us

Norman Weston is an assistant professor in the Interdisciplinary Studies Department at National-Louis University. Before receiving his doctorate in curriculum design from the University of Illinois at Chicago, he taught in public and parochial elementary schools for 10 years. In 1980, he was awarded a Fulbright–Hays fellowship for exchange teaching. Dr. Weston is research advisor for the Action Research in Learning Communities Project, sponsored by the Chicago Annenberg Challenge and the Illinois Alliance for Achievement Network. E-mail: Nwes@whe2.nl.edu

Judith Whitcomb notes that after 29 years of teaching in the Chicago public schools, she still gets the rush of excitement every fall when she enters her classroom on the first day of school. Driven by her students' need to know, she has become involved in many educational initiatives through the years, including work on Bill Kurtis' New Explorers curricula and serving as a master teacher for teacher workshops at Argonne National Laboratory. Currently a middle school science teacher at Sauganash Elementary School in Chicago, Ms. Whitcomb also teaches science methods courses at North Park College and Northwestern University. She has been the recipient of the Ellis P. Steinberg award for precollege science teaching and was named to the Association of Science/Technology Centers Honor Roll. She has also received the Illinois Science Teachers Association Award for Excellence in Secondary Science Teaching. E-mail: Jwhitcomb@kiwi.dep.anl.gov

INTRODUCTION

About 8 years ago, when we began preparing the first edition of this book, a colleague announced without hesitation, "A book about teacher research? Why bother? That's just a flash in the pan." We didn't heed his warning, because we believed that teacher research was much more than a temporary phenomenon. We knew that we as teachers and teacher educators had something to say about how to look at one's own practice and make change.

Now, as we prepare the second edition of *Teachers Doing Research*, we read about the "movement" that Cochran-Smith and Lytle (1999, p. 15) noted is "little more than a decade old," and we reflect on what we have learned and where this movement has taken us. For us, teacher research is much more than a decade old. We, the editors of this book, have been working in a program that has teacher research as a center-piece for more than 25 years. The master's program in curriculum and instruction at National-Louis University is based on a genuine dedica-tion to graduate education that is focused on teachers' needs and inter-ests. The master's project, which is always grounded in the teaching experience of the candidate, is a reflection of that dedication. We have also worked in schools, in this country and in other countries, in which teacher research has been a venue for personal and professional re-newal and reform. We have engaged in self-study and curriculum in-

1

quiry on our own practice, and we have supported the writing, publication, and presentation of teachers' research among our colleagues in public schools.

Although our experience and interest in teacher research have stood some test of time, as we prepared a new edition of this text, we had to ask ourselves, *Is* this just another book on teacher research? What does this volume contribute to the dialogue around this "movement"? What do we have to say that is keeping pace with the continuing interest in this phenomenon?

The second edition of *Teachers Doing Research* has a new subtitle: *The Power of Action Through Inquiry*. The new title was chosen to more forcefully convey our belief that teachers must be at the center of the action research process. What do we mean by the phrase "the power of action through inquiry"? In our work with teacher researchers, we have found at least four types of actions involved in this professional work: (a) critical reflection on classroom practice that provides a foundation for improving learning and instruction; (b) engaging in research that helps teachers play a more active role in their professional development; (c) designing more effective curriculum and authoring better school improvement plans using action research frameworks; and (d) supporting teachers who advocate for the larger issues of democratic education, human rights, and social justice.

The second edition of *Teachers Doing Research* continues to place teachers at the heart of the action research process, while more explicitly delineating how such research powerfully helps teachers make informed and wise decisions as they try to improve schools for all learners. Ultimately, the "action" in teacher action research entails moral decisions about what it means to educate young people, and how to create safe and democratic schools for learning and inquiry. Most chapters in this new edition address in some way this central issue of teacher action research.

The second edition is, in part, a book about the process of researching. We have learned more about the methods for collecting information and analyzing it in ways that make sense for teachers. Although we have borrowed from qualitative research traditions, we are also suggesting that the paradigm may indeed be different for teacher research. We are exploring the ways in which teacher research methods may be of teachers' own making, and not simply an adaptation of those used by qualitative university researchers.

We have also raised issues about how the processes of teacher research are being adapted to larger arenas of collaboration—across classrooms, districts, and universities. We examine the ways in which teacher research has been embraced by these communities, while cautioning, as others have done, about the danger of coopting a viable tool for teachers in the service of larger, external goals. In this edition, we have tried to articulate the various bridges needed to acknowledge the larger forums for teacher research, but with wariness of the potential for diffusing the power of teachers in the process. We are aware of the shift in terminology assumed by school systems who have embraced the term *action research*, but omit the term *teacher* from the title. We see the need for continuing dialogue on how the term *teacher* can remain—and *action* can then follow.

It is this power—of individual teachers and teachers in collaboration with others—that we firmly underscore in this volume. Last year, a graduate student at Northwestern University said to Gail Burnaford, one of the editors, "I didn't know you could do both. I thought you had to choose—you could either be a researcher or a teacher. The profession is much more appealing to me now that I know I can—and should—do both." Our conception of teacher research challenges the traditional role of "teacher" and suggests a new agenda for the profession that includes the creation of knowledge and the advocacy for change. With this expansion of the role of teacher comes the redefinition of the role of teacher educator as well. We who are university faculty members are learning to work differently with teacher colleagues who are also researchers.

Our interest in technology further underscores our belief in the potential for a recasting of the role of teachers as they pursue research in and on their practice. Using the tools of technology has the potential to recast roles of creator, dispenser, interpreter, and organizer of knowledge. Teachers have new access to information and can make decisions that are not dependent on their own immediate district guidelines or university-based research. In the next decade, we hope to see more teacher research that is grounded in inquiry beyond the individual classroom and taps into experiences across cities and countries, courtesy of the Internet. Teachers can work with other teachers in ways we have not yet imagined. Collaboration will take on new meaning for research in this context. Our second edition has helped us look into that vision for the future.

Finally, this second edition has raised our own awareness of the various purposes, procedures, and avenues that teacher research may take. As Cochran-Smith and Lytle (1999) noted in their assessment of the teacher research movement, it is not a monolith (p. 22), and faces the danger "of becoming anything and everything" (p. 17). We see teacher research as growing in stature *because* it is flexible and powerful in the hands of teachers, but we acknowledge the need for systematic and intentional monitoring by the profession and the advocates of such inquiry in order to maintain its integrity and usefulness.

This edition, like the first edition, is replete with teachers' own writing about their work and their research questions. It is also a work that attempts to help professional development leaders, university faculty, and others interested in promoting teachers' own legitimacy as researchers do their work. We believe that teacher research, as a factor in professional teachers' practice and preparation, is here to stay. We welcome your response.

The Editors

REFERENCE

Cochran-Smith, M., & Lytle, S. L. (1999). The teacher research movement: A decade later. *Educational Researcher, 28*(7), 15–25.

I

WAYS OF DOING
TEACHER ACTION RESEARCH

1

ACTION AND REFLECTION: NARRATIVE AND JOURNALING IN TEACHER RESEARCH

David Hobson

The personal is most universal.
—Carl Rogers (1961, p. 3)

ONE STARTS WITH ONESELF

Researchers have been accustomed to distancing themselves from their work as if such separation would somehow render the work more plausible, credible, perhaps even more "scientific." We teachers often possess narrow notions about doing research from our university experiences where use of the word "I" was forbidden and we were taught that such expressions as "the researcher noted . . ." and "the investigator found . . ." were more appropriate. Happily, times have changed, and today the idea of "teacher-as-researcher" has gained greater value, not only in the educational research community, but also among classroom teachers who realize that investigations conceived, implemented, and evaluated by actual teachers in real classrooms among live schoolchildren promise to better stand the tests of practicality and personal relevance. This is research to be used by teachers, not merely displayed for purposes beyond the classroom.

Sometimes we are so close to a subject or an activity we can scarcely see it. One of the fundamental benefits of doing teacher research is the opportunity it affords us for perceiving our world a little more freshly. One of the purposes of the research process is to render the familiar a little strange. We want both things at once, to be close to the matter at hand, but also to develop the perspective that comes from a degree of distance. This is especially problematic in the world of the classroom teacher where what one *does* is so close to who one *is*.

Kurt Lewin (1948) asserted that the *person* stands at the center of his or her own life space, and that an understanding of that life can only be accomplished by beginning with the perspective of that individual. Lewin is also remembered for bringing the *action* into action research. Through action, teachers come to understand what is really happening in their classrooms. If you want to understand something, try to change it. This matter of change, of actually doing something even as one is studying it, is central to classroom-based teacher-conducted research. The teacher researcher is not just standing back and observing some pristine phenomena from a distance. No, the teacher is in the midst of a group of children, and is doing: taking action, making things happen. Both of these ideas are central to teachers conceiving and implementing their own research among the students in their classrooms. One starts always with the person, student or teacher, exactly where he or she is, and tries to *do* something.

Many teachers are interested more in the doing than the saying. So much is said about good practice, but teachers tend to be very concerned with what is done. Argyris (1982) brought considerable attention to this seeming dichotomy when he described the differences between theories-espoused and theories-in-use. The first is comprised of what we think and say about what we do, whereas the latter must be constructed directly from observing our behavior, from what we actually do.

This kind of work is personally grounded in a teacher's own experience and is expressed in his or her own voice. Reflection is a process of making sense of one's experience and telling the story of one's journey. A teacher's current research possesses a history with stepping stones that have led to the present and constitute a path of inquiry that can bridge the gap between teaching and researching. In order to bring the two more closely together in the minds of teachers, teacher research needs to be thoughtful and intentional. Vida Schaffel feels it is important to situate her research in her own life. As a teacher who left the profession for a few years to raise children, she brings a real-life perspective to her research writing (see Vida Schaffel's Teacher Research). For Nancie Atwell, the shift toward greater reflection occurred when she began writing: "Writing fuels my best insight. It makes me understand things I did not know before I wrote," she explains (Atwell, in Patterson, Santa, Short, & Smith, 1993, p. ix). Our experience tells us, however, that finding the time to write is difficult during a typical school day and that it helps to match the rhythm of school life to the schedule of writing up one's research. As one teacher commented to us, "Writing up research is a summer job!" Some of the practical ways teachers have found to write even as they teach are described in this chapter. Writing is a valuable tool for reflection.

Schon (1983, 1987) carried this line of inquiry further and developed some ideas about reflective teaching, a concept that includes both *reflection-in-action* and *reflection-on-action*. The first of these is "reflection on one's spontaneous ways of thinking and acting, undertaken in the midst of action to guide further action" (1987, p. 22), whereas the second consists of reflection after the event, and includes a kind of metacognition, or thinking about the thoughts and reflections gathered during the action. A teacher who reflects *on action* after a lesson is over might consider: What kinds of decisions did I make during the lesson? What responses and reactions from the students affected those decisions? What was I thinking about and feeling during the lesson? That's what Schon refers to as *reflection-on-action*.

It is thought, of course, that reflection leads to better action (Schon, 1983) and that the reflective teacher is a more effective teacher (Grant & Zeichner, 1984). The point of all this is obvious; we teachers benefit from paying more careful attention both to what we say and do, and how these two elements work together. Teacher inquiry helps a teacher practice both *reflection-in-action* and *reflection-on-action*; both are really forms of research.

In his work on identifying the various intelligences, Gardner (1983) provided a framework for considering how human beings, including teachers and their students, learn and grow. He named six basic types of intelligence: logical–mathematical, linguistic, bodily–kinesthetic, musical, spatial, and naturalistic (Shores, 1995). Beyond these six, Gardner suggests two "higher intelligences," called "*inter*-personal" (the ability to notice and make distinctions among others, to look outward—see chapter 4 on creating a community for teacher research) and "*intra*personal" (relating with oneself, looking inward). These two forms of intelligence are intimately intermingled, neither able to develop without the other, and each dependent on the other. Gardner (1983) saw the sense of self as the balance struck by the individual between the prompt-ings of inner feelings and the pressures of other persons. A developed sense of self is seen to be "the highest achievement of human beings, a crowning capacity which supersedes and presides over other more mundane and partial forms of intelligence" (pp. 242–243). These higher forms, put most simply, are "the capacity to know oneself and to know others" (p. 243). It is through use of these higher aspects of the self that we manage *how* we learn.

Here, of course, is an essential link with teaching and teacher re-search. Teachers are perfectly positioned at the intersection between these two domains, the inner and the outer. Teachers are very impor-tant factors in classrooms and much of what they know and think and do in their classrooms is dependent on their knowing of themselves, al-most as, if you will, finely tuned and deeply resonating instruments. Each teacher brings a lifetime of experience, as teacher and student, in a variety of schooling environments, to the present situation. Even if new to the profession, teachers carry their experience of schooling to the present tasks. Teachers take in a multiplicity of stimuli continu-ously; they select and sort and make meaning all day long; they act on what they learn and "know" with those around themselves. Teachers are continually researching, working from the outside and the inside; looking outward and inward, perpetually moving back and forth be-tween these two higher intelligences: the inter- and intrapersonal di-mensions of human knowing.

It is especially important for a teacher to develop a deep under-standing of how these dimensions develop because it is the teacher who has responsibility for facilitating such development in students. The teacher is a very visible model whom students watch carefully. A most obvious place to begin developing such an understanding is with oneself.

> The most meaningful image of action research derived from our teaching is a continuous, conscious attempt to seek increased meaning and direc-tion in our lives with students, and in our own personal lives. (Schubert & Schubert, 1984, p. 5)

One of the primary teachings of Piaget was simply that knowledge is constructed by the learner and that new experience must be assimi-lated by the learner in ways that make sense to the learner. Teachers everywhere know this to be true, whether describing themselves or their students: One learns oneself. "All genuine learning is, in the last analysis, self-learning, self-discipline" (Cantor, 1953, p. 67). Knowledge must be constructed by the individual. Rogers (1961) put it this way: "The only learning which significantly influences behavior is self-discovered, self-appropriated learning" (p. 455). Allport (1955) suggested that it is the process of becoming that determines what is real for the person, and that self-awareness plays an important role in the drawing along of this becoming. Often, such self-awareness exists in the form of intuitive knowing, a sense of rightness and congruity, an emerging gestalt, or a growing sense of what "wants" to happen.

If we consider what this could mean with respect to teacher research, we might take a closer look at exactly how a research idea comes to mind. A teacher observes the classroom, the students, and himself or herself for a few weeks, asking the question: What wants to happen here?

Gail Burnaford tells a story about her early teaching days that demonstrates this notion of research based on observation. Sometimes, "what wants to happen" is unexpected and unplanned, as Burnaford's experience illustrates.

I began teaching high school English in 1973. It was a time of student rights, choice and autonomy in curriculum, and attention to the interests of the individual child. Consequently, our department offered students a smorgasbord of possible electives which they could apply toward their English requirement. One such minicourse stands out in my mind.

It was the last period of the day, and I was aware that those who would be sitting in my class for the course *Biography and Autobiography* would be the ones who had failed to sign up for any other course; they would be the students who attended school only sporadically and found little relevance in what was going on there for their own lives. Sure enough, when I walked into the room that day, I saw 37 adolescent bodies, all but four of whom were male, and most of whom could not comfortably fit into the chair-desks provided for them. There I was with my syllabus neatly typed and duplicated under my arm and a collection of biographies/autobiographies of famous people ready to roll. We would be reading about people such as Benjamin Franklin, Thomas Jefferson, Clara Barton, and, yes, Florence Nightingale. After all, that's what the course outline prescribed and I was ready and willing!

When I looked out on that sea of faces, I can remember thinking, "Gail, you'd better think again." I asked the class if they knew what the terms "Biography" and "Autobiography" meant. A few hands passively went up in the air. Then, with a definite sense of trepidation, I seized the pile of carefully crafted syllabi, dropped them into the metal trash can beside the desk, and asked, "So, who do you want to learn about?"

With that, the room began to come a bit more alive. We brainstormed people they had heard something about during this turbulent time in their own history. They wanted to know what this guy Cesar Chavez was all about and what did he have to do with grapes? They wanted to learn more about Martin Luther King, Jr., Bobby Kennedy, and Malcolm X. They wanted to find out about Billie Jean King and what happened to Karen Carpenter. I asked them whether they thought they could write the story of their own lives so that they too would have an autobiography to add to the bookshelf and some hesitantly said, "Yea, that might be a good idea." With that, we were on our way. (Burnaford, personal communication, 1973)

I recently began working with two groups of preservice teachers. On the night before class, I had a dream that took me back to my days as a student teacher. Memories of these students flashed into my consciousness. All through the next day, those memories kept surfacing. When I got to class, I told the teachers of this experience. "It may not seem so to you right now, but these beginning experiences of teaching may stay with you all of your lives. You may forever be learning from them, as I have. These are precious years, so give them much attention. Write descriptions, take photos. Collect artifacts, develop maximum awareness of these situations—start becoming teacher researchers."

One never learns it once and for all, as every teacher knows: "The discovery is never made; it is always making" (Dewey, 1929, p. 76). Working classroom teachers know that inquiries into practice are continuous and engage us in daily ways. It's especially important that preservice teachers realize that the discovery is never complete; we are constantly learning throughout our careers from our students, colleagues, and from our own experiences. Dewey (1929) counseled that the practical inquiry of teachers should be the *substance* of educational research. It is the "knowledge that enters into the heart, head, and hands of educators" that should be the material of our study, and that renders the educative process "more humane, more truly educational than it was before" (pp. 76–77). Today, as classroom research conducted by teachers in their own classrooms becomes more pervasive, Dewey's vision is even more compelling. His was "unmistakably a vision of the teacher continuously pursuing self-education in the course of the act of teaching" (Schubert & Schubert, 1984, p. 12). As Dewey (1929) put it, "each day of teaching ought to enable a teacher to revise and better in some respects the objectives aimed at in previous work. ... Education is a mode of life, of *action*. [It] renders those who engage in the act more intelligent, more thoughtful, more aware of what they are about" (pp. 74, 75–76, italics added).

Asserting one of the great ideas from the social sciences, field theorist Lewin (1948) found that decision is the link between motivation and action. Participation in the *decision* to take some action makes a difference in how invested one is in actually carrying the action through. To modern educators, this concept provides an essential linchpin to the practice of involving learners (including teacher researchers) in the planning of their own learning.

Schubert (1992) told the story of how he got his first teaching job. He recalled his interview where, when asked how he would develop a program with a "multitext approach," he answered smoothly, despite the fact that he had never heard the term before. After securing the job, he did indeed use a multitext approach to teaching and became committed to multiple perspectives in his teaching—a commitment that was also shared by his young students. Schubert now describes his multitext approach as a form of teacher lore that he has to share with other teachers. Similarly, he has accumulated a wealth of teacher lore from other teachers he has known throughout his life who have influenced him.

Teacher lore, Schubert (1992) explained, "portrays and interprets ways in which teachers deliberate and reflect and it portrays teachers in action" (p. 9). He continued: "Teacher lore refers to knowledge, ideas, insights, feelings, and understandings of teachers as they reveal their guiding beliefs, share approaches, relate consequences of their teaching, offer aspects of their philosophy of teaching, and provide recommendations for educational policy makers" (p. 9). Schubert's story of his first job interview reveals one piece of the larger story of his view of learning and the practice of effective teaching. His story prompts other teachers to tell their stories about how they learned to do what they do.

AUTOBIOGRAPHICAL NARRATIVE (TELLING STORIES)

Teachers can almost always be found sharing anecdotes about their experiences with children. This telling of stories can become a vital part of doing teacher research. According to Schubert (1992) it seems "that telling anecdotes ... enables the teller to bring experience into language. In this way, we can come to terms, as teachers, with something significant, something worth telling, something important ..." (p. 204).

The parallels between teacher stories and teacher action research seems clear from Schubert's explanation. As teachers share their beliefs and approaches and as they reflect and act upon their reflections, they are engaging in a form of teacher action research. Their actions may have influence and impact, not only upon students, but also on policy makers and others who study teaching praxis.

One way our mind makes sense of the world is through narrative. Our narratives include our insights, searches for meaning, and the connectedness we find in the world. We tell stories in order to see how others conceive of the world, and to share the journey of storytelling with others. Jalongo (1992) described a teacher story as a metaphor for change; teacher action research grasps that metaphor, brings it to life, then perhaps creates a new metaphor that enriches his or her teaching. Autobiographical narrative could be construed as the conceptual center of teacher action research. Narrative asks the question: What does this research have to do with me?

The telling of stories as a framework for teacher research also provides a context for viewing the teaching and learning that occurs in schools through a critical lens. One reason for conducting educational research is to "illuminate discrepancies or inequities or silences within aspects of teaching, curricular, and learning processes" (Miller, 1992, p. 166). Looking at our own autobiographies, reliving our own experiences with inequity, power, and authority in schools, offers us the opportunity to inform ourselves further and move forward to change situations in which today's students experience injustice. This aspect of educational research can be the work of teacher researchers who look at the world of teaching critically. Apple (1993) noted that "critical work needs to be done in an 'organic' way." He said, "the role of the 'unattached inteligentsia' seems a bit odd ..." (p. 7). Teachers are "attached" in the most immediate way to the real issues surrounding justice and pedagogy. Teachers can examine the lives they live in schools and the experiences children encounter each day in their classrooms in an "organic" way, stemming from their own histories and the histories of their students. Then, critical perspectives become more than theory. In a way, an autobiographical approach is a means of taking stock, of reassessing your knowledge and beliefs about the teaching of reading, for example. Action research becomes more than a means of adopting a teaching technique; it becomes "transforming," as Freire (1985) suggested. It becomes an avenue for constructive change which is personally meaningful and deeply felt.

Dan Lortie (1975), in *The Schoolteacher*, suggested autobiography as a way to increase awareness of one's views about teaching and "to expose them to personal examination" (p. 231). Grumet (1978) held that autobiography allows teachers to ask their own questions, articulate their own stories, explore their own memories, and strongly affirm the legitimacy of their own real experiences. Her way of going about teacher autobiography is close to the matter at hand: immediate, alive, fresh, and yet is simultaneously analytic, thoughtful, viewed from a distance. This storytelling is not without risk, however, and should be approached respectfully:

> And yet, even telling a story to a friend, is a risky business, the better the friend, the riskier the business. How many of you would like to get your own story back from a certain person? Do you remember how her eyes were glazed, how she didn't really listen, only waited for you to finish so her own turn to tell would come? Do you remember how she asked the wrong questions, appropriating only those parts of the story that she could use, ignoring the part that really mattered to you? (p. 321)

> So if telling a story requires giving oneself away, then we are obligated to devise a method of receiving stories that mediates between the self that tells, the self that is told, and the self that listens: A method that returns a story to the teller that is both hers and not hers, that contains her self in good company. (p. 323)

One way to open up fresh possibilities for storytelling is to shape the context so that the storyteller makes several passes at the telling, going at it from various vantage points, perhaps at different times.

Grumet (1987) asked for three separate narratives rather than for one longer, continuous account, having learned from Pinar's approach to educational autobiography that such a "triple telling" could usefully sort reflection into *past* experience, *present* situation, and *future* images. Multiple tellings, according to Grumet (1987), "splinter the dogmatism of a single tale" and free the teller from "being captured by the reflection provided in a single narrative" (p. 324). This technique may be especially useful for pre-service teachers as they work to integrate coursework, classroom experiences, and reflections about who they will be in their own classrooms someday.

A K–8 physical education teacher and coach, Rick Moon, is one whose teacher research had a very personal, autobiographical connection, and that was part recollecting the past, part examining the present, and part imagining the future (see Rick Moon's Teacher Research). He worked back and forth between these three perspectives, gaining much knowlege from perceiving his work from the different vantage points.

Moon's inquiry arrived with the birth of his daughter, Amy. Suddenly, this physical education teacher began to observe the girls and boys in his classes a little more closely. He noticed girls "holding back" because they were not "supposed to be so good." He discovered that not one girl thought herself more athletically skilled than *all* of the boys and not one boy rated *any* girl superior to himself, even though Moon was sure that several of the best athletes were in fact girls. When casting his net into the past, seeking the autobiographical connections that might inform his current research, Moon remembered his mostly male "methods" teachers in college having very firm beliefs about gender roles; beliefs to which he also subscribed, including the view that boys needed to learn combativeness "in order to prevent women and sissies from taking over society." A few years later he looked into the eyes of Amy, his newborn daughter and wondered what the future might hold for her. The possibilities, he thought, seemed limitless. As a teacher researcher, he decided to study the matter of gender equity in his own classroom. "To be a man today and to be married, and to be a father, requires rethinking the images one holds."

Again and again in teacher research, we are confronted with the primacy of the teacher. It is the teacher who is at the center of action in the classroom; it is the teacher who is trying, in real life and real time, to understand what is going on in the classroom and to make a difference.

Ayers (1993) employed the metaphor of the highly personal, idiosyncratic journey:

> Much of what I know of teaching is tentative, contingent, and uncertain. I learned it by living it, by doing it, and so what I know is necessarily ragged and rough and unfinished. As with any journey, it can seem neat and certain, even painless, looking backward. On the road, looking forward, there is nothing easy or obvious about it. (p. xi)

Teachers can begin to connect their own autobiographies with classroom research by recalling elements of their own schooling and by thinking about their years as teachers. These "prompts" may help you get started:

FIG. 1.1. "The things I could have written if I had a good pen!" Reprint by permission of Joe Martin.

- Discuss or write about the great (and not so great) teachers you have had in school. What were your experiences in those classrooms?
- Who were three of your "best" students? Why do you consider them "best"? What do your choices say about you as a teacher?
- What was one of your best moments as a teacher? As a student?
- What is a "good day" like for you?
- If you had a gift of 10 hours extra in school each week—just for you— how would you spend it?
- Describe yourself as a teacher. How would one of your average students describe you as a teacher?

Putting ourselves at the center of inquiry grounds the action in who we are; it relates the professional to the personal through teacher research (see Fig. 1.1).

JOURNAL KEEPING

I am a long time journal keeper. I believe it to be a wonderfully rich and evocative teaching and learning tool. Keeping a journal has been a practice in both my teaching and my learning. As a way of developing a reflective ongoing relationship with oneself and one's work, a personal journal is hard to beat.

> The future enters into us, and transforms itself within us, long before it actually happens. (Rilke, 1934, pp. 64–65)

Teacher research represents a forming up of developmental reachings that have often been a long time in coming. A journal can be a means by which we bring into fuller awareness, both for the student and for ourselves as teachers, some of the deeper processes through which we make meaning. Sometimes we realize this when we reread the journal and realize that we've been working on something for a long time without knowing it. But once the lightbulb goes on, and we read our journal writings with the new insight in mind, we see Rilke's point come home; that the new development was there all the time, perhaps incubating, finding form, growing—what took us so long to see it? Our developmental reachings seem so obvious in hindsight. We see this very clearly in our students, but less quickly in ourselves. The journal can help to reveal the organic nature of development.

As part of her association with an ongoing group of teacher researchers, Nancy Brankis realized how her own discoveries of learning seemed to be "connecting" and "weaving" together in the journal she kept (see Nancy Brankis' Teacher Research). Perhaps this is an illustration of Schubert's (1990) observation that journal writing can be helpful in developing the "organizing center of what it means to be a good teacher" (p. 218). Brankis also realized that she "had tapped an inner motivation and sense of connection from within." It was this experience that led her to wonder about possible implications for her own second-grade class and eventually to create a classroom research project collaborating with them.

Many teachers do this continually—use themselves and their own experiences as means for doing personal and practical research. The journal is a place where much of that very important research process can be described, drawn, reflected on, analyzed, and put back into use in the classroom. Each teacher's journal can become the textbook of emergent practice, ongoing research, and as such may be the most important book a teacher can fully write and read.

The experience of working with a journal, though, is far from cut and dried; it can require a considerable tolerance for ambiguity, uncertainty, and not knowing. I think of journal keeping as a form of active listening. Carl Rogers (1961) put it this way:

> It seems to mean letting my experience carry me on, in a direction which appears to be forward, toward goals that I can but dimly define, as I try to

understand at least the current meaning of (my) experience. The sensa-tion is that of floating with a complex stream of experience, with the fasci-nating possibility of trying to comprehend its ever changing complexity. (p. 275)

Fulwiler (1987b) conceived of journals as assignments given by teachers to their students and, having consulted with numerous such teachers, identified a number of common features that characterize such journals:

They tend to be conversational, colloquial, first-person, informally punc-tuated, experimental, and expressed in the rhythms of everyday speech. They contain observations, questions, speculations, digressions, synthe-ses, revisions, and are full of information. They are self-aware. The entries tend to be frequent, long, self-sponsored, and chronological. These char-acteristics separate them from more formal assignments and make them especially fun to both write and read. (pp. 2–3)

Another kind of teacher journal, identified by Lytle and Cochran-Smith (1990), describes classroom life. Such journals are often kept by student teachers and are important means of dialoguing with cooperat-ing teachers and university supervisors. In it, teachers describe their observations, make analyses of their experiences, reflect on their prac-tices over a period of time, and make interpretations of what has tran-spired.

They intermingle description, record keeping, commentary, and analysis. Similar in some ways to ethnographic field notes, they capture the imme-diacy of teaching—teachers' evolving perceptions of what is happening with the students in their classrooms and what this means for their con-tinued practice. (Lytle & Cochran-Smith, 1990, p. 86)

Such writing is especially helpful when it comes to reading the jour-nals because the entries form a *written record of practice* over a period of time that teachers can use to evaluate their experiences. Such ac-counts provide a means by which teachers can construct and recon-struct interpretive understandings using data from their classrooms.

Teachers' journals can become repositories in which anecdotal re-cords and chronological accounts of classroom activities are stored. Or, they may be more narrowly organized as very intentional and sys-tematic inquiries, ones that can open up windows to show what teachers see going on in schools as perceived through their own eyes and written in their own voices. Such journals can also show how writing is used to illuminate and inform their work lives. Journals are the necessary link between action and reflection in a teacher researcher's work.

After more than 30 years of experience of working with journals, I am sure of one thing: each person's journal is unique. The only real way to explore the experience of journal keeping is to give oneself the experience—to actually begin writing one's own. Each journal is a uniquely personal tool, which is best individually tailored to fit each person's special requirements. The most effective approach to understand journal keeping is simply trying it and discovering what works. Still, from watching myself and others experiment with creating our own forms of journal keeping, I have observed a few practices that seem to make the process more workable. You may want to try some of these to see how they fit you, and maybe rework or revise them to suit your needs.

Formats

I use an $8\frac{1}{2}$ 11 page format, placed in a three-ring binder. This has the advantage of allowing you to remove pages, perhaps to show them to others, or to rearrange them in other sections. The page is large enough to tape or staple notes and jottings or photographs into your journal. The pages are easily printed from a computer or word processor on three-ring paper and slipped into the notebook.

A large notebook, though, can be somewhat unwieldy for carrying around, so some teachers prefer a smaller, 6 9 format. This kind of notebook can be slipped into a purse or carryall and is more easily transported. Some teachers advocate using a blank lesson plan book to make quick reminder notes for entries to be written later. Others keep a post-it note pad on the desk for easy access. John Edgcomb, a high school art teacher, asks his students to inspect their academic notebooks for doodles and then to expand upon them in art class. He and his students use a spiral-bound journal, which is printed with lines on only half the page, leaving some unencumbered space for drawings. In any case, it's important to use a format that is comfortable and convenient for you.

Date Entries

This simple convention yields many dividends. It allows you to view developmental process over the continuity of time. The fact that the journal is sequential and chronological gives it the ability to provide material from which recurring patterns can be found, generalizations drawn, and hypotheses formed. Also, because entries can be moved around if you're using a loose-leaf format, the dates on the entries will allow you to reconstruct sequences if need be. It's a good idea to date and time your entries and to use a new page for each one.

Time

Many teacher researchers express frustration with the time constraints that seem to prevent them from keeping copious notes on the events in their classrooms. A teacher wonders, "I'll need to make my own journaling more a part of my life. But how?" Although there are no easy answers to this dilemma, there are solutions devised by teachers who realize the importance of capturing the data as it happens. Of course, tape recorders, video cameras, and invited observers can assist a teacher researcher by gathering one kind of information that can be processed at a later time. Using post-it notes, index card files, and brief notes on a lesson plan book may be sufficient for in-class reminders of events and thoughts.

Eventually, though, it will be the teacher researcher's task to debrief what has been collected in writing. One idea is to write while students are writing. Some teachers have discovered that an early morning hour is the best time to find a word processor and write freely without interruption. Researchers generally suggest that it is best to write about an event or a time period as soon as possible and before discussing it with anyone; oral expression appears to change what has occurred as the speaker shapes the conversation for its audience. Individual journal writing offers a teacher the time necessary to process it independently first.

Teacher researchers who are desirous of specific and practical suggestions for using journals with their students would do well to look for the following books: Holly's (1989) *Writing To Grow* is a resource for adult journal-keepers. Fulwiler's (1987b) *Teaching with Writing* and (1987a) *The Journal Book* are indispensable. Zemelman and Daniels' (1988) book, *A Community of Writers* addresses journal writing with junior and senior high school students. Daniels' subsequent book with Marilyn Bizar (1998), *Methods That Matter*, described the process of "representing to learn" and enumerated 23 ways to use a notebook. Routman's (1991) *Invitations* and Isaacs and Brodine's (1994) *Journals in the Classroom* include helpful advice on journal writing in the primary grades.

Descriptive Writing

With experience, many journal keepers come to value the usefulness of descriptive writing. Description is more than a transcription of reality. It is not just a tape recording. Rather, description recreates one's own perception of an event. Trying to describe a complex experience is very demanding. The act of describing an event makes one look more carefully, more discriminatingly, more thoroughly. Faithful description helps one to actually see more.

For example, I am doing classroom reseach on evaluation. I may want to write in my journal about seventh-grader Josh's conference with me about his progress report. Describing that interaction fully—in order for it to be significant for my research—I will want to include the following: My attitude toward Josh and his achievement, Josh's attitudes and feelings, my approach to the conference, how I heard and listened to Josh, how I believe he heard me, what was accomplished during the conference, and what was not. Direct quotes and an account of body postures and facial expressions would be valuable to a thorough, rich description as well. Later, when we want to read and work with our journal writing, we will want to read what is written there, to structure it in a variety of ways to reveal meaning, to reflect on it, to learn freshly from previously rendered experience. If, when the time comes for such a reading, all we have are a series of nondescript writings, there will be little information with which to work (i.e., "had progress report conference with Josh").

Reflective Writing

Here is another kind of journal writing. Following a period of describing experience, journal writers often find themselves reflecting on the experience just described. Reflection is a standing back, a pausing to re-read, to mull things over and search for connections, associations, significances, and possible meanings not noticed before. Reflective writing comes more from a distance; from a certain perspective. One moves from a description of experience to a sort of commentary on it. Perhaps you have a dim glimmering of a recurring pattern. Maybe you see a possible motivating dynamic and want to phrase a hypothesis. An association to another event bubbles up to consciousness. You're reminded of something you read last week. You're reminded of another student you had last year. When writing reflectively, the teacher researcher's mind can be given free reign as it seeks to make meaning.

Double-Entry Journal Writing

One way to make a more workable distinction between descriptive and reflective writing is to distinguish between them in the pages of the journal by using facing pages. On the right-hand page, write the descriptive account of a given experience, including its subjective aspects. On the left-hand facing page, reflect on that experience (see chapter 3 for a sample double-entry journal format).

Daily Log

This is an attempt to describe the essence of a particular day: You woke up this morning, and then what happened? And then what happened? An accumulating collection of such entries can reveal, from a daily perspective, just what is occupying your mind, as well as be revealing of your activity. Done late in the evening or on the morning of the following day, an accumulation of daily logs can reveal what sorts of things absorb your attention, what continuing issues predominate, or what your priorities appear to be.

Steppingstones

Developed by Progoff (1975), this technique is very helpful in discovering the continuity and exploring the meaning of remembered experiences a teacher brings to a particular subject or concern. Earlier, I mentioned the possibility of listing the great (and not so great) teachers you have known. Think about it this way: Name the first important teacher you knew. Write a few descriptors. Name the next important teacher in your life. And the next. And the next. You may come up with a dozen or so. Then, write a sentence or two about each of the teachers identified. These small descriptions can be viewed as forming the steppingstones by which you traveled to your present understanding of what it means to be a teacher. What do these persons have in common? From what contexts do they come? Which are role models you now use to shape your practice? Which of these remembered images do you wish to avoid? Identifying, and describing in writing, the step-

pingstones of one's experience is a powerful way of exploring and reflecting on one's development over time.

Dialogue With a Person

Perhaps you realize from the previous exercise that one particular
teacher had importance for you. Imagine yourself having a conversation with that person. Try to write down in your journal how the dialogue unfolds. Perhaps you will start with a question: What do you
think of my teaching now? Then, as a playwright, you write down what
that person says in your imagination. You reply. The other responds,
and the written dialogue gradually unfolds. Such dialogues can be constructed with persons who have long ago passed away, people who are
active in your life today but unapproachable, or people who are public
or even fictional figures with whom you cannot interact directly.

Underlinings

Everyday, all day long, our attention is drawn on by various objects.
We are continually engaged in the activity of searching, scanning, noticing; our eyes are endlessly moving. It is very easy and often quite helpful to make an effort to consciously notice *what* has been drawing our
attention, almost unaware. One obvious place to look is in the pages of
what we've recently been reading. There is much to be discovered by
searching a little more methodically for artifacts of "researching" that
we have already been collecting and bringing the results of that investigation into the pages of one's journal. One needn't always start over
from scratch; often we are ahead of ourselves, already producing evi-
dences of an inquiry in progress.

Journal of the Journals

A journal is not just for writing, of course; it is also for reading. If kept
over a long enough period of time, a journal can be viewed as a reposi-
tory for a teacher's observations, stories, insights, and wonderings.
One way to help reclaim various renderings of such a story or a developing theme from journal material is to create what I call a "journal of
the journals." The teacher researcher reads a series of entries, seeking
a theme, a recurring pattern, or a story often told. Once such a possibility is discovered, the author goes through the whole journal with a

highlighter, emphasizing the material having to do with the particular theme or story. This strategy really opens up the substance of the material because the reading self perceives it from a perspective quite different from the writing self. And the editing self, looking at the collection of fragments from the journal, sees it in another way again.

A further elaboration of this technique is to invite a friend to read the lines that you have highlighted out loud. Hearing your own material read in another's voice, with different emphasis and varied style, allows hearing in yet another, often fresher, way. Application of this device allows more writing to flow as you begin to synthesize the various elements, or attempt to carry the story forward in another, perhaps novel way. The journal writer writes, reads, listens, and responds. Having worked with one such subject or topic or story, the teacher can make another pass, this time with another color of highlighter, bringing together the already written material having to do with a second aspect of the inquiry.

One of the great strengths of working with a journal is that it leads itself along. It suggests questions, identifies new areas to explore, reveals meaningful absences, and uncovers recurring patterns. As the teacher researcher becomes more and more aware of the rich material contained in the journal, it becomes possible to use the journal itself to answer some of the questions, to gather the clues together, and to follow the paths to see where they may lead. The author of every journal gives the reader all that is needed to move the inquiry ahead. It is in the writing of the journal, of course, and it is also in the *reading*.

By thinking about research as a personal, as well as a professional endeavor, we can engage in classroom inquiry that is meaningful and really relevant in our own lives. We must constantly be reminded that classroom research is not just about children; it is also very much about the teacher. Long after this year's group of students move on to the next grade or the next teacher, you will still be there—learning about teaching and examining your practice. Your research about that process extends far beyond one class in one given year. It is about you and your profession in a much larger sense.

We have discussed two ways in which the personal can be brought to bear on teacher research: (a) calling upon your own autobiography as a means to reflect on your own style, attitudes, prior experience, and knowledge, and (b) using journal writing as a means to describe, reflect, and assess the study of your teaching and learning. Both autobiography and journal writing are tools for your use as you look at what your teaching is like. Both can also be tools for the students in your class to use as they engage in researching with you. What experiences have they had prior to this year that affect them as learners in your class? In what other ways have they encountered what you are teaching them now? What might be their views of effective teaching? Asking students to keep research journals during a study is a wonderful way to help young people learn to think about their own learning—and to become active in the classroom as teachers themselves.

You might ask students to keep journals of "exit slips" that they complete each day at the end of class. Exit slips might be reflections in which students think about what they learned that day, *how* they learned it, and what they anticipate tomorrow. The slips might be a place where they can record the most significant event of the day or the most surprising learning. Journals might be in the form of letters to the teacher, advising, suggesting, and contributing to the planning of learning for the next day or week.

These are tools not just for teacher research, but for learning. Research is meant to be *used* by teachers. Teacher research often begins with the individual but is shared with colleagues in a more public setting, as this book illustrates. When we start with ourselves and our students, however, we start with what is most meaningful and most useful. Then we move on from there.

REFERENCES

Allport, G. (1955). *Becoming.* New Haven: Yale University Press.

Argyris, C. (1982). *Reasoning, learning, and action.* San Francisco: Jossey-Bass.

Apple, M. (1993). *Official knowledge: Democratic education in a conservative age.* New York: Routledge.

Atwell, N. (1993). Foreword. In L. Patterson, C. M. Santa, K. G. Short, & K. Smith (Eds.), *Teachers as researchers: Reflection and action* (pp. VII–X). Newark, DE: International Reading Association.

Ayers, W. (1993). *To teach: The journey of a teacher.* New York: Teachers College Press.

Cantor, N. (1953). *The teaching-learning process.* New York: Dryden Press.

Daniels, H., & Bizar, M. (1998). *Methods that matter.* New York: Stenhouse.

Dewey, J. (1922). *Human nature and conduct.* New York: Holt.

Dewey, J. (1929). *Sources of a science education.* Cleveland, OH: Kappa Delta Pi Society.

Fulwiler, T. (1987a). (Ed.). *The journal book.* Portsmouth, NH: Heinemann.

Fulwiler, T. (1987b). *Teaching with writing.* Portsmouth, NH: Heinemann.

Gardner, H. (1983). *Frames of mind: The theory of multiple intelligences.* New York: Basic Books.

Grant, C., & Zeichner, K. (1984). On becoming a reflective teacher. In C. Grant (Ed.), *Preparing for reflective teaching* (pp. 1–18). Boston: Allyn and Bacon.

Grumet, M. (1978). Curriculum as theatre: Merely players. *Curriculum Inquiry, 8,* 37–62.

Grumet, M. (1987). The politics of personal knowledge. *Curriculum Inquiry, 17*(3), 319–329.

Holly, M. L. (1989). *Writing to grow: Keeping a personal-professional journal.* Portsmouth, NH: Heinemann.

Isaacs, J. A., & Brodine, J. S. (1994). *Journals in the classroom.* Winnipeg, Manitoba, Canada: Pequis Publishers.

Jalongo, M. R. (1992). Teachers' stories: Our ways of knowing. *Educational Leadership, 49*(7), 68–73.

Lewin, K. (1948). *Resolving social conflicts.* New York: Harper.

Lortie, D. (1975). *The schoolteacher.* Chicago: University of Chicago Press.

Lytle, S., & Cochran-Smith, M. (1990). Learning from teacher research: A working typology. *Teachers College Record, 92*(1).

Miller, J. (1992). Exploring power and authority issues in a collaborative research project. *Theory Into Practice, 31*(2), 165–172.

Progoff, I. (1975). *At a journal workshop.* New York: Dialogue House Library.

Rilke, R. M. (1934). *Letters to a young poet: Letter #8* (pp. 64–65). M. D. Herter Norton (Trans.). New York: W. W. Norton and Company, Inc.

Rogers, C. (1961). *On becoming a person.* Boston: Houghton-Mifflin.

Routman, R. (1991). *Invitations.* Portsmouth, NH: Heinemann.

Schon, D. (1983). *The reflective practitioner.* New York: Basic Books.

Schon, D. (1987). *Educating the reflective practitioner.* San Francisco: Jossey-Bass.

Schubert, W. (1992). Personal theorizing about teacher personal theorizing. In E. Ross, J. Cornett, & G. McCutcheon (Eds.), *Teacher personal theorizing* (pp. 257–272). Albany, NY: State University of New York Press.

Schubert, W., & Schubert, A. (1984, April). *Sources of a theory of action research in progressive education.* Paper presented at the annual meeting of the American Educational Research Association, New Orleans, LA.

Shores, E. (1995). Interview with Howard Gardner. *Dimensions of Early Childhood, 23*(4), 5–7.

Zemelman, S., & Daniels, H. (1988). *A community of writers: Teaching writing in the junior and senior high school.* Portsmouth, NH: Heinemann.

2

ACTION RESEARCH RATIONALE AND PLANNING: DEVELOPING A FRAMEWORK FOR TEACHER INQUIRY

Joseph C. Fischer

> *I like to try to find ways into a subject that will catch everybody's interests. . . . I like to see the most productive of questions get born out of laughter, and the most frustrating of brick walls give way to an idea that has been there all along.*
> —Duckworth (1986, p. 481)

This chapter rests on the belief that action research is a natural part of teaching. It holds that effective teaching is informed by personal knowledge, trial and error, reflection on practice, and conversations with colleagues. To be a teacher means to observe students and study classroom interactions, to explore a variety of effective ways of teaching, and to build conceptual frameworks that can guide one's work. Teaching also involves reflecting on the nature of human development, examining the place of schools in society, and developing a personal philosophy of education. All this is a personal as well as a professional quest, a journey toward making sense out of and finding satisfaction in one's teaching. It is the work of teacher researchers.

I have found that when teachers view research as being quite separate from teaching and mainly the purview of specialists, they have difficulty seeing themselves as researchers (or finding time for research). I also have discovered that when teachers are invited to discuss their work in supportive settings, they identify a rich variety of questions, wonderment, concerns, and issues they wish to explore further.

The central work of teacher action research is to identify effective educational practices and to design ways of helping classrooms and schools become democratic communities of quality learning and teaching. Ultimately, the basic reason for teachers doing research is to address the essential educational issues and concerns of the day, including advocating for all learners, working for social justice and human rights, and educating citizens to build a more peaceful and livable society. Finally, teachers engaged in research must find professional satisfaction in pursuing their own questions and ideas about the nature of education and the meaning of human learning and living.

My purpose in this chapter is to examine a variety of paths teachers take as they begin to inquire and reflect upon their work. Specifically, the aims are to: (a) discuss how reflections on teaching constitute a vital foundation for doing research; (b) describe how teachers identify research interests, formulate research questions, and develop frameworks that can orient their inquiry; and (c) provide guidelines for research planning, useful for a variety of settings and purposes.

REFLECTIONS ON TEACHING AS A BASIS FOR RESEARCH

Duckworth (1986) told us that what she enjoys about teaching is knowing "that teachers are as interested as I am in how people learn, so the dialogue is deeply felt. I always learn . . . when I see the endless variations on how they use what they learn in their own teaching." Her teaching was based on the belief that "people must construct their own knowledge and must assimilate new experiences in ways that make sense to them" (p. 481). She viewed her own teaching as a form of research.

Eisner (1985) noted that teachers have a unique and central role to play in creating knowledge about teaching: "One must have a great deal of experience with classroom practice to be able to distinguish what is significant about one set of practices or another." This requires not only a "sensitivity to the emerging qualities of classroom life, but also a set of ideas, theories, or models that enable one to distinguish the significant from the trivial" (pp. 220–223).

In supportive settings among trusting colleagues, teachers are able to express the concerns and issues they face in their work and celebrate the insights realized through self-examination and reflection on teaching practice and student learning. To facilitate such discussions and reflection, and to help frame possible research questions and topics, I have found the following set of questions useful:

- As you think about your teaching, how do you know when something really went well? What do you feel you are good at? How did you get good at it?
- As you think about your work, what stands out? Briefly, how would you describe yourself as a teacher?
- What role do your feelings and intuition play in the way you think about teaching? What intrigues you about teaching, learning, students? What are you working on now?
- What dilemmas and problems are you facing in your work? How might we approach working on solving these?

Gordon Will, a high school biology teacher, described how self-reflection came to play a central role in his teaching. Throughout his career, new questions were always unfolding, and new knowledge was built on previous knowledge—but not without struggle and hard work.

Fifteen years ago I found myself covering the content, and did not find ownership in my teaching. It was a struggle before I began to realize that I did not need to give lectures revealing my wisdom. I learned to be more introspective. Today, I am more consciously aware of what I am doing, of what makes things work. I am beginning my 30th year of teaching and still ask, "What is it that I do?" My classes are my research. The students give me clues for what to do.

Early in my teaching career, I often did activities because I thought that the students would enjoy doing them. They sometimes fit into a particular unit, but often did not. Gradually I gathered them into one unit—a kind of "science methods" or "scientific inquiry" unit that we did during the first weeks of school. I wanted students to experience science, to lay a foundation, to set a tone for the year. I wanted that "first" unit to say something, to illustrate what I thought was important, what I valued. Most importantly, it was meant to get students engaged, excited and curious about science.

Thinking about ways to make geometry more relevant and satisfying for her 10th graders, Jan De Stefano decided to try out discovery and collaborative learning strategies with her class. She hoped to find ways to help students learn geometry through more of an inductive than a deductive approach. Her observations on the first day illustrate how she and her students were learning and researching together.

> I walked between the two rows trying to observe what they were writing. Believe me, it was nothing that made any sense. I then suggested that we discuss the problem. "Let's start with what kind of diagram we have up there. Does anyone know what that's called?" Well, finally we started talking.
>
> We discussed segments, angles, rays, symbols, etc. . . . I never wrote one definition on the board. We never did solve the problem, at least not that day. I was feeling great about the experience. It was new, it was different, but mostly it worked. We conversed in our new language . . .

De Stefano's research project eventually revealed how students discover an underlying mathematical system through class discussions and reflection. After a month of not looking at their texts, she asked students to compare their definitions with those in their books.

> Their facial expressions and responses were enjoyable for me. Apparently their definitions weren't so different from the ones in their book. We discussed the words—their meanings and the book's meanings. I now explained that we were building a mathematical system, composed of definitions and statements that we would use throughout the course of geometry. The words are just the start of that system. The class was able to see different methods of solving the same proof. This is when the class really became interesting for me. This group was solving problems that I would never have used with this class level before. What is even more interesting is that I learned different ways to prove problems than I had ever thought possible.

Significantly, the strategy included student reflections on what was happening in their mathematical thinking. De Stefano was tapping what was making sense to students and what meanings they were finding in their work. Eventually, she found that her research questions contained more elaborate and basic issues:

> After eighteen plus years of teaching mathematics, I am finally zeroing in on the meaning of learning and the meaning of educating my students. Too often, I have seen teachers obsessed with the notion of teaching a particular subject, forgetting that what we are teaching is not as important as to whom we are teaching and for what purpose in mind. Somewhere toward the end of September or the beginning of October, this

group became "my class." I felt a closeness with them, probably because we were really students together. They were learning geometry, and I was learning how to teach geometry in a new way.

We use our intellect as well as our feelings to develop true meaning and real learning. Good teachers, who are good learners, must realize the importance of interacting with their students and generating feelings of warmth and acceptance. Real teaching is not the subject you are teaching, but the people you are teaching.

De Stefano's research demonstrates the power of guiding discussions with students about how they come to learn what they have learned. Such reflections are both effective instructional strategies and valuable methods of collecting rich research data. Typical questions used by teacher researchers to foster such dialogue and reflective thinking include:

- What do we see here? What do you think is happening?
- What did we do in the last month that really worked for you?
- How do you feel about this class?
- What suggestions do you have to make our classroom a place where learning can be more enjoyable for you?
- What makes for a good day in this class?
- How do you like to learn best?
- What have we learned together? How did you go about doing it?
- What worked for you? What didn't? What could we do differently?
- What might be our next step?

BEGINNING WITH OBSERVATIONS AND INTERESTS: FINDING REASONS FOR DOING RESEARCH

I believe that interests are signs and symptoms of growing power. I believe that they represent dawning capacities. Accordingly the constant and careful observation of interests is of the utmost importance for the educator. (John Dewey, *My Pedagogic Creed*, 1897; cited in Dworkin, 1959, p. 29)

That teachers' research interests can be considered "dawning capacities" is a very attractive idea. Ultimately, interests in doing research represent what teachers value in their work, what they are committed to, and what they have learned through observation and self appraisal. The basic reason for doing research rests on each teacher's belief about their work—about how students learn, how to improve schools, and how schools might contribute to a more peaceful, just, and democratic society. Topics for research are varied and generally stem from heartfelt desires for improving teaching and gaining professional satisfaction, success, and fulfillment.

Classroom events, student interactions, unexpected surprises—all that transpires in school—have potential for research about teaching and learning. Varied emotional responses to these events, reflections about teaching experiences, and attitudes about learning illustrate that possibilities for research are multiple and extensive.

How to sort out possible topics is one of the chief struggles for novice teacher researchers. How does one prioritize, make choices, focus on certain observations and interests? One way to begin is to study research interests of other teachers, and their reasons for pursuing a particular topic. We can group research interests and rationales under four general types: (a) interest in knowing how students learn, (b) wanting to innovate in a curriculum area, (c) desire for change in one's teaching, and (d) search for connections and meaning in one's work.

An Interest in Knowing How Students Learn

Curiosity about how students learn, how they think about their learning, and ways they make meaning, are main reasons why teachers engage in research. Observing students is central to teaching and forms an equally critical aspect of teacher research.

A desire to know how students become active learners became a research concern for Sue Hahn. Writing in her research journal, she described how she tried to begin each school day:

> I'm anxious to see the children, listen to whatever they want to tell me, and get them ready for the day, hopefully filled with many new beginnings. A new day of school is a chance to try a new approach. I think teachers are unique in that they don't give up easily and will try over and over again until they succeed in getting through to their children.

Chuck Sentell remembered his third graders asking him, "Mr. Sentell, are we going to get a chance to read?" He had been using a mastery learning skill program during reading with his class:

> The children helped me ease up on my role of complete structure, and of blindly following the district's curriculum mandates with little regard for the student's needs and interests. Good teachers know what kids can do. You can forget what is going on. But the students bring you back. You must continue to try to know their perspective. Over the years I've learned to be good at kid-watching.

Mary Ann Stocking's research study focused on helping her sixth graders develop effective social skills and participate in class discussions about their learning. Beginning her 27th year teaching in Chicago public schools, she wrote in her research journal how her students began to work together.

> We are separate islands yet. We've started our journals and will soon move into groups. The journals have helped me know what they are interested in, and the students tell me what they know about me. As I look at these students, I think about when I was 15 and my Mom felt it was time to visit her aging mother in Poland. Going over on the boat I read *Anna and The King of Siam*. Little did I know that years later I would return to that book to teach the pain and anxiety that people suffer as traditions and customs change.
>
> My sixth grade class and I share stories of poverty. We talk about games and the rules each game is played by. Then, I tell them the story of *Kim*, by Rudyard Kipling and how he learned the game of life. Our conversations in class lead to an openness and a willingness to participate in the game called School.

Interests in Curriculum Innovation

A frequent source of ideas for research stems from a desire to try out something new, to "be updated" in a content area, or to work on some area of curriculum development. Many teachers view action research as an opportunity to construct curriculum with their students, as Georgia Vidmont did with her first graders: "The children have ideas about first grade: 'we're going to learn how to read.' Still, this group is anxious to experiment, afraid to try it out. I try to build the curriculum around them, their likes and interests, who's talkative, who's quiet." Jurate Harris told how she began constructing curriculum with her students early in her career, and how class discussions helped shape and reshape what they did.

> All I had my first year of teaching was a stack of books, the kids and me. No curriculum objectives, no teacher's guide, no resource materials, just an empty room. I was responsible for teaching language arts to junior high school students. My thought was, if I really knew the students well I could teach them. That empty room helped make me an exploring teacher always looking for materials, trying to get to know the students, and creating opportunities for them to inquire and interact. I was always trying to keep in mind the big picture. 'What is this for?' 'Why are we doing this?' I always wanted the students' world and the things we did in school to connect.

A Desire for Change in One's Teaching

For many teachers, the desire for change or even transformation is a main reason behind their interest in doing research. Cynthia Moore, teaching in a Chicago public school, reflected on her teaching and how doing research with colleagues might be useful for her:

> As I look and listen to the various people, it is as if we are all crying out to be heard for the first time. It is as if each of us is looking for support and help. I feel at times I can change everything that is wrong, but then I look for strength to get from one day to the other. If there were more people like us, we would begin to make a difference, we would begin to start that long hard change in the school system.

Sonja Groves wrote frankly about being discouraged in teaching and her hopes for change:

> Each school year I start out with these great plans about all the wonderful things I would like to do with my children. I'm all excited in September and by December everything that I'd thought about doing is just thrown out. There is no time for it. Over the past few years I've become more of a disciplinarian than a teacher. I would be much more satisfied with the children being in control of themselves rather than to only cooperate or behave because of me standing there.

In thinking about her teaching, Lynette Emmons described her students' daily struggle for survival. She wondered how action research might help her understand and face the overwhelming realities of her teaching and her students' living condition:

> Every day I see students who have little or no hope for their future. How to help Tatianna who witnessed her mother's murder? Or Dajuan who fears women since his mother deserted him? Or Freddie who wants to die because his future looks awful? We need to talk about the reality of the children. I come home so stressed out, I want to scream. It is as if no one is listening to me or the children. I have been accused of caring too much. Is that possible? I try to make my classroom atmosphere one of creativity and ease. We validate each other's feelings and all feel like part of a family.

Search for Connections and Meaning

As teachers explore possible topics for research, they often examine beliefs that guide their teaching, as Pamela Flewelling did: "I feel it is so important to constantly reflect on what is happening around you and to allow your students to do the same. What am I doing that is in line with my philosophy? What am I doing that can be changed to meet my beliefs?" Elizabeth Chase felt that examining one's philosophy can suggest topics for research:

> I really believe that a person's philosophy about life very much affects their teaching philosophy. I am very interested in learning more about group dynamics. How can I further develop students' sense of responsibility when working in a small group without me? Even though I strove to play a facilitative role last year, I was still a very central (annoyingly at times) figure.

Chase began to compare the image she had of herself as a teacher with what she felt she was actually doing in class. Her research was being conceived with a vision (framework) she had of herself as a teacher.

Many teachers are inspired for doing research by their reading, as was Mary Ban:

> I really got into (a book by) Carl Rogers and couldn't seem to put it down. Not only did I find it interesting at an academic level, but I also found it to be extremely uplifting mentally. I feel like something amazing is going to happen with the way that I teach this year, and I feel like I am on the brink of discovering things about me that I haven't been pushed to discover yet.

SELECTING A TOPIC AND DEVELOPING RESEARCH QUESTIONS

Discussing research ideas with colleagues has the potential for identifying and clarifying research topics and questions. Tentative ideas and questions can become "working ideas" and "guiding questions" as teachers share their research interests. Through dialogue, you can discover that multiple perspectives enrich your "seeds of ideas" and exploring of topics for inquiry (Whitehead, 1967). Group support and discussions can stimulate the vaguest beginnings of an idea and help make sense out of multifaceted realities that teachers face in their work.

Brainstorming is a useful way for you to help each other "map out" research interests and ideas. The goal is to both generate many ideas and perspectives, and find connections and natural guidelines that help guide the research journey. Brainstorming also serves in helping you feel more comfortable about the seemingly heavy and serious work of research. (See the Samuel and Sheldon teacher story after chap. 7.) Some possible questions that can guide brainstorming include:

- As you think about your students and teaching, what seems to be working well, and what would you like to improve?
- What strategies might you use to help students learn more effectively?
- What ideas may be useful to help students build a classroom climate for learning?
- What would you like to know more about when it comes to teaching your grade level or subject area?
- What intrigues you about your classroom or teaching?

Another way to identify research topics is to formulate "what if" type questions. This process elicits images of what could be, of visions about what teaching and schools could become. Such images often reveal the beliefs and philosophical stances teachers hold of their work. Gathering "what if" sentences can reveal how hopes for teaching correspond to teaching realities and practice. Examples of "what if" questions follow.

- What if students in seventh grade worked once a week as buddies with first graders?

- What if science and art were integrated subjects? Literature and history?
- What if we had no ability groupings for reading/language arts?
- What if high school students spent one day a month in community service and did action research projects?
- What if one day of the week were dedicated to workshops and projects on topics that students organized to enrich curriculum objectives?
- What if one afternoon a week teachers met to design curriculum and share best teaching practices?
- What if grandparents came to school to talk about their childhood, growing up, grandchildren?
- What if primary grades used cross-age learning, (e.g., combining kindergarten and first, second with third)?
- What if primary teachers kept their students for 2 years?

Deciding on a research topic and formulating research questions can become an all-absorbing preoccupation. Most teachers find, however, that once they decide on an idea, the work of research tends to take on a life of its own. This probably happens because the "working idea" itself suggests an inherent structure that can help guide the research project. Moreover, intuitions and feelings about teaching often suggest a potential focus for research. The challenge is to look for patterns and themes as you reflect on these feelings and as you brainstorm ideas. In developing a framework for research, it is prudent to keep possibilities open, to take note that ideas might be interconnected, and that action research is a cyclical process.

As chapter 1 in this text suggests, it is useful to keep a journal, not only as you begin to gather ideas for inquiry but also all during the action research process. Journal writing is an important tool for reflecting on your teaching practices and observing students. Moreover, keeping a research journal will help you in finding patterns and connections, analyzing events, interpreting information, and making tentative conclusions. It is a practical way of getting started on the research journey.

Beginning action research activities does not have to wait until you design a full-fledged plan or proposal. Rather, reflecting on practice can begin during any part of the teaching year. Through journal writing, reflection, and sharing ideas with colleagues, teachers come to discover that research questions evolve and become more elaborate over time. They discover that action research is a recursive process of observing, questioning, planning, trying out strategies, describing, analyzing, interpreting, and sharing insights with colleagues.

TYPES OF RESEARCH QUESTIONS

Although research questions overlap and interconnect, we can identify three types or groups they tend to fall under. The aim of the typology is to illustrate possible areas for research projects and to help you explore ideas and consider possible guiding questions. These are offered to illustrate possible types of research questions, but it should be emphasized that typical research questions encompass elements of each grouping. Moreover, it will be seen that the scope of the questions is quite varied, ranging from large guiding questions to more specific ones.

Settings and Context

Research questions often originate from concerns for improving schools, building positive classroom climates, and creating effective opportunities for learning and teaching in a school. Some examples are:

- What rewards for teaching and learning are present in this school?
- What values about teaching and learning do the faculty hold?
- What makes for an effective school culture for learning and teaching?
- What roles do parents play in the life of this school and in the learning of their children?
- What voice do students and teachers have in setting goals?
- How do students view their life in this school over the years they are here? How do their attitudes change year by year?
- How does this school provide opportunities for students to take charge of their learning?
- Is there a real community of learners here? How could one be created?
- How does this school community deal with conflict, antisocial behavior, abuse, or neglect?

- How does this school community build on the strengths and gifts of all students and faculty members?
- What are some ways to build a climate for learning in my classroom?
- What makes for a good day—for me and for the students?
- How can I help students reflect on their work, assess their learning, and feel good about their accomplishments?
- How can positive relationships, interactions, and communication be fostered in my classroom?
- How might internal discipline and self-discipline replace external and teacher-directed rules?

Teaching Strategies and Content

Research questions of this type deal with instructional strategies, ideas for constructing curriculum, fostering active learning, and guiding student self-evaluation. Some examples are:

- What are some practical ways to help students construct personal and positive learning strategies?
- How do I foster class discussions and help students generate questions to promote active learning?
- How do I create opportunities for inquiry and research in all content areas?
- How do we integrate subjects, use thematic learning, and use technology throughout the curriculum?
- How do we create peer learning across grade levels?
- How do we introduce more hands-on activities in social studies, math and science?
- How do I use writing to help students learn to be critical thinkers and problem solvers?
- How might a literature-based language arts approach improve communication and interpersonal relationships?
- How do we help students reflect on and evaluate their own learning?
- How do we use a variety of assessment measures to foster learning for all students (e.g., writing samples, portfolios, exhibitions, journals, student-generated tests, self-evaluation)?

Visions and Hopes for Teaching

These types of questions include exploring professional development interests, visions for teaching, and hopes of what schools can be. One way of tapping these is to reflect on your teaching career, noting your main learnings, concerns, and questions about your work that emerge. Some examples of such questions are:

- What motivated me to enter teaching, and what keeps me in the teaching field?
- Who were my mentors?
- Who influenced and still influences my learning and teaching?
- As I look back over my career, what stands out? How have I evolved as a teacher? What would I change?
- When do I feel good about my work? When do I feel I have the "touch" in my work?
- Do I have a personal style of teaching?
- What images do I have of my teaching? What image do students have? How do I reconcile my teaching image with public images?

In conducting their research, teachers usually find that initial research questions become more elaborate and often unearth more basic issues and concerns. Over time, teacher researchers come to realize that their central questions ultimately are interpretive ones that address the issues of meaning and value. Pursuing deeply felt questions and ideas helps uncover the narratives and meanings present in classrooms. What attracts teachers to inquiry about their profession is the same impulse that calls scientists and artists to study theirs: curiosity about ideas, the desire to be creative, and hopes of being of service to others.

RESEARCH PLANNING: A DYNAMIC PROCESS

A typical view of teacher research is that it follows a series of linear steps that include: (a) designing a research proposal, (b) doing a review of the literature, (c) trying out some strategy in the classroom, (d) collecting information, (e) analyzing and interpreting data, and (f) writing up the findings. In fact, these are recursive processes, which unfold through action and reflection and become more elaborate over time (see chap. 3). In this perspective, classroom observations, trying out ideas, reflections, and interpretations continue to evolve. Moreover, research planning itself is an ongoing process, which continues to be informed by experience, experimentation, reflection, reading, and dialogue with colleagues. Kemmis and McTaggart (1988) offered that teacher action research develops through a *self-reflective spiral* of planning, acting, observing, reflecting, and then replanning, further implementation, observing, and reflecting. We argue throughout this text that teacher action research is enhanced in group settings through systematic dialogue and critique.

Teacher research is an interactive process, encompassing ever-increasing complexities of planning, action, reflection, evaluation, and dialogue with colleagues. It is a process of constructing knowledge and meaning, and includes the following elements:

1. During early explorations of a topic for inquiry, teachers reflect on experiences, observe students, and consider what is working and what might need change. The purpose is to build on good practices, describe what is happening, identify problems, and try out new ideas.

2. As they reflect upon their practices, teacher researchers look for patterns and connections. This includes noticing ways students approach learning, what was learned, and how instructional strategies evolved and worked. Initial questions become both more elaborate and clear.

3. Gradually, teacher introspection and inquiry include critical examination of beliefs and frames of reference behind one's work. Studying relevant literature and discussion with colleagues further help illuminate the efficacy of instructional strategies, research actions, descriptions, analysis, and tentative interpretations.

4. Descriptions, analysis of data, and interpretations about what is taking place become more elaborate (through building on previous insights, choices, and actions).

5. Research experiences, insights, and tentative conclusions shared with colleagues are ongoing and collaborative experiences. Drafting and reporting on research findings take place at various stages of the research study.

To help you construct research plans, two general guidelines are presented below (see Fig. 2.1). They are fundamentally similar but fo-

Planning Guideline A

1. School Context

Briefly describe the school in terms of students, faculty, curriculum, and mission. Outline central goals that relate to your research topic. How were these established? What problems and special concerns are present in the school that your research project hopes to address?

2. Focus of Research Project

Briefly state what it is that you intend to investigate or implement. What is the main problem and what are the specific questions you hope to address?

3. Rationale

Why is this project important to you and your students? How does doing this research support school or grade level goals and concerns? How does it support your professional development?

4. Expected Impact on Student Learning

Briefly state your vision for the possible impact of this project on student learning. What do you anticipate or hope will happen beneficially as a result of it?

5. Criteria to Determine Effectiveness

What indicators do you think will best reveal the results of your project (e.g., number of books read, increased motivation, better test scores, better communication, positive relationships)? What sources of data will you use to document and evaluate your project, and why (e.g., essays, student portfolios, journals, class work, discussions, test results, interviews, surveys, videos, photos, displays, presentations)?

6. Implementation Plan (Steps and Timeline)

Outline the steps you intend to take in order to implement your project. Although you may later decide to alter your course, or change the order of the steps, it helps to have a plan mapped out ahead of time. Include a timeline that will allow you ample time to experiment, gather and analyze data, write a summary of your learnings and findings, and present your project to colleagues.

7. Information Sources

What books, authors, articles, other teachers, or sources of information (e.g., ERIC, Internet web sites, workshops) do you anticipate consulting in order to find out more about your research topic? List several possibilities.

8. Resources Needed

List any resources you anticipate needing to carry out this project (e.g., instructional materials, supplies, tape recorders, video equipment, cameras, transportation for field trips, after-school salary support).

FIG. 2.1. Research planning guidelines.

Planning Guideline B

1. Focus

Briefly state your research problem and main questions you plan to address. Describe the context of your inquiry, noting the school and classroom communities where it will be conducted. Outline main issues embedded in your research problem. (Keep in mind that questions evolve and will continue to take shape as you try out strategies, read, and discuss your ideas with colleagues.)

2. Rationale

Describe why you want to undertake this project (e.g., what relevance it has for your professional development, how it fits into your teaching experience, and how it may benefit students and schools). Consider how your study may contribute to the education profession's understanding of your topic, and what you hope to learn from it. What challenges do you anticipate in conducting your research project?

3. Preliminary Review of or Response to Literature

Summarize your main learnings from reviewing literature (and interviews you may have conducted with colleagues) about your study. State how these sources provide practical orientation and strategies for your proposed study. Delineate how findings from your readings relate to what you have learned from your own teaching.

4. Instructional and Learning Strategies to be Implemented

Describe instructional and learning strategies you hope to try out. Outline particular aspects that will be the focus of your project. As your study evolves you may find it necessary to modify, eliminate, or add aspects. State how students will help select relevant approaches and strategies, and how they will evaluate their learning.

5. Research Methods

Summarize the type of research methods that are most appropriate for carrying out your study (e.g., descriptive, narrative, interpretive, action research, case study, program evaluation). Describe how you will document what happens in terms of instructional process and learning indicators (e.g., observations, portfolios, student work, interviews, tests, surveys, class discussions, reflection journals, student comments, displays, lesson plans, records, documents, videos, photos).

6. Timeline

Delineate main project activities and approximate timeline when you propose to implement them (e.g., library research, instructional strategies, discussion with colleagues, ongoing documentation and evaluation, analysis and interpretation, writing and editing report, and presentation to colleagues).

7. References

List sources you have consulted and intend to read to help guide your study.

FIG. 2.1. *(Continued)*

cus on somewhat different contexts and purposes, and can be adapted to your needs. The first guideline was originally designed for teachers doing research in schools as part of school reform and professional development programs, which usually emphasize practical applications and performance accountability. Often teachers negotiate their research plans with district offices, and sometimes submit them to outside funding agencies. This format is adapted from Weston's (1998) work with teachers in Chicago public schools (see chap. 9).

The second guideline reflects typical expectations for university course work, where the emphasis tends to place teacher research within a conceptual or theoretical framework and requires a more extensive review of the literature. In some contexts, such a guideline is called a *proposal*. It is important to stress the basic similarity of these research planning guidelines. Plans can be less or more elaborate, depending on your intent, audience, time, and resources. The differences are mainly in the specific purposes of individual teacher researchers, school districts, and university degree programs. Both frameworks are designed to support teachers in ongoing reflections on their teaching practices and collaboratively constructing knowledge about their work.

CONCLUSIONS

> To talk about the personal reality of teachers is to consider their lived lives and their pursuits of meaning in contexts that include a concern for the social dimensions of teaching for the strategic and for the existentially unique. The realities we construct mean what they mean because we have internalized common ways of thinking about them and talking about them. But, at the same time, each of us looks upon the common world from a particular standpoint. (Maxine Greene, in Lieberman & Miller, 1991, p. 4)

Greene (1991) considered teacher inquiry as a way to illuminate teaching realities and effectiveness. She saw inquiry as a language that helps describe and clarify what captures our attention: "We live in continuing transactions with the natural and human world around us. . . . Only as we begin moving into the life of language, thematizing, symbolizing, making sense, do we begin to single out certain profiles, certain aspects of the flux of things to attend to and to name" (in Lieberman & Miller, 1991, p. 4).

Martin Buber's (1947) writings on dialogue and education eloquently remind us that our main work in teaching is in communion with others. Discussions with colleagues about research can help identify what is important and valuable in our work, what visions we hold for education, and what meanings we find in our teaching. Importantly, such dialogue helps us put into words the complex experiences of our professional lives—an essential aspect of the work of teacher action research. Moreover, such discussions help identify best educational practices and the meanings that schooling has for us and our students.

Polanyi (1962) inspired a dramatic shift in our thinking about how we engage in science, undertake research, construct knowledge, and create meaning. He believed that central to this work is what each person brings to it, and called this thought-provoking idea *personal knowledge*. "I have shown that into every act of knowing there enters a passionate contribution of the person knowing what is being known, and that this coefficient is no mere imperfection but a vital component of his knowledge" (p. viii). Within this perspective, teacher action research is our personal narrative of our life's work, our personal and shared vision of what schools can be, and our moral dedication to improving our profession and society.

Behind each teacher's research interests are particular perspectives, belief systems, and visions for teaching. The task is to explore the underlying structures embedded in our questions and wonderments about our work. There are layers of meanings present in classrooms that can be explored through particular kinds of questions that teachers ask. How we see reality is the starting point of the questions we ask about our work. In turn, our questioning is a way of uncovering the narratives and meanings present in our classrooms.

Teacher researchers are finding that as they try out new ideas and reflect on their work, they are able to see themselves as creators of meaning and as theory builders in their own right. They become more aware that they are interpreting their practice through the lens of their unique perspectives, searches for meaning, and conceptual frameworks constructed throughout their career.

Research experiences are illuminated by the meanings we attach to them, *and* by the messages our colleagues find in them. Discussions with other teachers can help identify what stands out in our research, what we are trying to accomplish, and what further meanings we might discover in our inquiry. Importantly, such dialogue helps us put into words the complex experiences of our teaching that we are trying to understand.

As teachers engage in action research, one of the most satisfying aspects of their experience is the personal mark they put on their inquiry—their own voice that emerges in their writings and conversations. From somewhat tentative beginnings, their ideas and research questions evolve in unique and significant ways. And, as they discuss their work with their colleagues, they find pleasure in the meanings they discover in telling their research stories.

REFERENCES

Buber, M. (1947). *Between man and man*. Boston: Beacon Press.

Dewey, J. (1959). My pedagogic creed. In M. S. Dworkin (Ed.), *Dewey on education: Selections* (p. 29). New York: Teachers College Press.

Duckworth, E. (1986). Teaching as research. *Harvard Educational Review, 56*(4), 481–495.

Eisner, E. W. (1985). *The educational imagination: On the design and evaluation of school programs* (4th ed.). New York: Macmillan.

Greene, M. (1991). Teaching: The question of personal reality. In A. Lieberman & L. Miller (Eds.), *Staff development for education in the '90s: New demands, new realities, new perspectives* (pp. 3–14). New York: Teachers College Press.

Kemmis, S., & McTaggart, R. (1988). *The action research planner*. Victoria, Australia: Deakin University Press.

Lieberman, A., & Miller, L. (Eds.). (1991). *Staff development for education in the '90s: New demands, new realities, new perspectives*. New York: Teachers College Press.

Polanyi, M. (1962). *Personal knowledge: Towards a post-critical philosophy*. Chicago: University of Chicago Press.

Weston, N. (1998). Building a learning community through teacher action research: Honoring teacher wisdom in three Chicago public schools. *School Community Journal, 8*(1), 57–71.

Whitehead, A. N. (1967). *The aims of education, and other essays*. New York: Free Press.

3

TEACHERS' WORK: METHODS FOR RESEARCHING TEACHING

Gail Burnaford

It is not enough that teachers' work should be studied; they need to study it themselves.

—Stenhouse (1975)

The Stenhouse quote raises a question: Just what do we mean by "teachers' work"? Is teachers' work teaching? Is it researching? Is it curriculum development? All three? These are essential questions for any teacher who explores research in her classroom. Understanding how these elements weave together and inform each other helps teachers perceive how researching is a way of conceiving of teaching itself (Elliott, 1990). The challenge is to develop research skills that are inherently good for teachers, good for students, and good for the curriculum that unfolds in the classroom. A researcher's primary goal is to understand; a teacher's primary goal is to help students learn; a curriculum developer's role is to plan and design materials for engaging learning (Wong, 1999). None of these three roles can exist without the other two. If they are interdependent, then what is the strand that could connect the three? Is it ideal that the three functions be related in the person of the classroom teacher?

This chapter examines the ways in which the methods of doing research can become an integral part of the teaching experience itself. Some writers have suggested that teacher research is in fact a new genre of research, different from the research methods that others have identified as quantitative or qualitative in nature and different from research that comes exclusively from the university community (Baumann, 1996). We believe that this is in fact true because teacher research has different purposes, different incentives, and a different audience than traditional academic research.

All teachers acknowledge that their first responsibility is to teach. That is their work. We believe that this work can be enhanced by the adoption of research methods in the classroom. James Baumann (1996) described his venture into the world of classroom inquiry and how he managed to balance teaching and research. In the end, he believed that the research methods themselves made him a better teacher. When he became a teacher researcher, he began keeping a journal, taking inventories, creating detailed lesson plans, collecting and analyzing student work, interviewing students and parents, and videotaping his teaching. These are methods researchers use; they are also the stuff of good teaching.

Teachers who are researchers are demonstrating that the process of inquiry is valuable and valued. Teacher researchers who engage in research with their students and with colleagues solve problems and develop curriculum that responds to their immediate needs. Teachers who see themselves as researchers make the routine of teaching, the demands of standardized testing, and the often implicit norms of a school building the focus for questioning and learning. When this happens, schools change, classrooms look different, and curriculum is enriched.

I look at two dimensions of doing research as teaching in this chapter: methods for collecting information, and methods for interpreting information through active reflection. Then I examine how the research process helps teachers design curriculum. I hope to provide a picture of how research, teaching, and planning curriculum can be coherent and compelling for teachers and students.

METHODS FOR COLLECTING INFORMATION IN AND THROUGH TEACHING

Relating to the Research Literature: What Other Teachers are Doing

University researchers have wondered why school practitioners have not always adapted what they do in response to current research results as published in the literature. But now that teacher research, sometimes called "first-order research" (Hollingsworth, 1992), is becoming more and more common in schools across the country, it may well be that there is also an increased demand for the results and recommendations from academic research. Why should this be? Because as teachers develop their own research methods and examine their practice in close proximity to the field, they are also looking beyond their classrooms in order to discern what other researchers are saying and doing. This is not to say that teachers have not been consumers of research in the past. Teachers, as a matter of course, have always been on the lookout for ideas to use in their teaching. They share ideas through conversation, order materials through workshops and teacher centers, and search available journals for the newest methods and materials. Learning about what other teachers are doing in a subject area or research focus is a natural activity for an inquiring teacher. Such an exploration may be viewed as a means of enhancing one's understanding of a theme, topic, or research question to be investigated in the classroom.

But when a teacher also does research, the reading of others' research findings becomes purposeful, engaging, and often critical. Teacher research, in a sense, makes what has been traditionally called a *review* of the literature into more of a *response* to the literature as teachers read, react, and build on what they encounter.

How does one delve into books and journal articles in order to do classroom research? The first step is to return to the central question that is driving the research (see chap. 2). When that question is real, immediate, and of great interest, the literature already published about the topic is a natural place to find ideas about how to proceed. Some would argue that such a venture impedes the work of a teacher who comes to the process with a felt need that is context-specific and real. Reading the literature of a content area or educational topic may deter teachers from devising their own solutions to problems and using their own "educational imagination" to make decisions (Eisner, 1994).

Case in point: One fifth-grade teacher had read none of the literature concerning literature circles, for example, but designed her research around an idea that she and her fifth-grade students invented together called Reading Teams. In effect, she and her class had developed their own curricular strategy, for which there might be parallels in other classrooms, but that is uniquely their own. I would guess that this group of fifth graders assumed much greater ownership of that endeavor than they would have with a similar version of literature circles imported by their teacher. The process gives "the students the chance to be thinkers" (Hyde & Bizar, 1989, p. 3).

And yet, the profession is a community of learners; we cannot ignore the experiences present in the writings of other researchers that can be beneficial to teachers in the process of their own research. Reading with a teacher researcher's eye means trying to understand others' research with special attention to one's own practice. Looking at the writings of teacher authors or other educational researchers does not imply a comparison to one's own practice, but rather suggests that we might learn from a careful response to others' work, based on our own grounded experience. Nixon (1987) described the knowledge gained not as a literature of our findings, but rather as an accumulation of stories, of histories, in order to inform us.

Reading research literature is often a new experience for teacher researchers, one that deserves discussion in a teacher research collaborative setting. It may be useful for teacher research groups to analyze the ways to approach the research literature in journals and books. Figure 3.1 shows a set of questions for response to research that are helpful for discussion and/or journaling (Zeuli, 1992).

Migra (1992) suggested that teachers think about a set of reflective questions while they read the literature about teaching (see Fig. 3.2).

Figure 3.3 shows still another format for responding to an article or videotape that collaborators in a teacher research study group have all read (Miller, 1999).

Figure 3.4 illustrates a format we have used in reading articles and books that connect to teacher research.

Figure 3.5 shows a double-entry journal format that may be useful to teacher researchers. The columns are an effective way to write what seems interesting in the reading in the right column and immediately

---

What is the main thing the author seems to be saying, and how does he or she convince the reader? What does the author do to make you believe the article?
Is there anything in the article you have trouble understanding?
What conclusions, if any, would you draw from the article for your teaching, and why these conclusions?
Did you enjoy any article more than the others did? Why or why not?
In light of how you think research should help teachers, does any article succeed more than any other? Why or why not?
Did the authors use similar kinds of evidence in each article to support their views? Was the evidence any more or less convincing?

FIG. 3.1. Questions for teacher response to research literature (Zeuli, 1992, pp. 7, 8).

What experiences do you bring with you to this activity?

Do these writers or speakers seem to be speaking to you?

Have they sufficiently convinced you that they are in touch with the realities and complexities of the classroom?

Do these ideas inspire, bore, enlighten, anger, educate, or confuse you?

FIG. 3.2. Reflective questions for literature about teaching (Migra, 1992).

This guide is used as a study group begins to learn from external information about how students learn best and about good instructional strategies. When reading articles, it is suggested that members of the study group read and react to the article individually. Then, as a group, collectively look at the implications from the reading.

Title of article or videotape

Author or presenter

What does the author say about content?

What does the author say about instruction?

What does the author say about assessing student learning?

FIG. 3.3. Structured response sheet for articles or videotapes. Adapted from the Center for Educational Leaders, Florida Atlantic University, Christine Miller (1999).

- What are the two or three big ideas in this article or book?
- How does this article/book relate to your research interest or question?
- What did this author learn about the topic during her/his research?
- How will you apply what you have read in your own classroom?
- What questions do you have for this author/teacher researcher?
- What other reading do you feel that you should do now that you have read this article?

FIG. 3.4. Responding to articles and books as teacher researchers (Hobson & Burnaford).

Passage/Quote of Interest to Me	My Response/What It Means for My Research

FIG. 3.5. Double-entry journal.

respond to that passage, describing impressions, connections, and personal related ideas in the left column.

There are subtle dangers in relying solely on the literature, rather than viewing it through the perspectives gained from practical experiences. Hattrup and Bickel (1993) described a teacher research collaboration project involving university researchers and classroom teachers called Thinking Mathematics. The goal of the project was to combine the clinical insights of teachers, the recent research on mathematics, and the National Council of Teachers of Mathematics (NCTM) standards in order to construct a meaningful math curriculum for a school district.

They began the project by asking the teachers to spend time reading other people's research, after which they would gather and discuss that reading with the university participants. What resulted from this approach was that the teachers became increasingly reluctant to share their classroom knowledge with each other or the university researchers. They became quite concerned with what the products of this collaborative effort should look like, including what was required and when. The goal of the research, "to connect to teachers' own practice," was subsumed by a preoccupation with the research literature and procedures, and teachers' own voices became lost. Fortunately, the group soon realized what was occurring, and the teachers' own experiential knowledge became essential to the success of the curriculum project.

The Thinking Mathematics project offers some insight for teacher researchers, whether they are working collaboratively or individually within their own classrooms. It's probably not necessary to be consumers of vast amounts of research in the field; the goal of accessing information is to turn attention to what knowledge can continue to be generated and consciously documented in the classroom. "To be generative, knowledge must become the object of thought and interpretation, called upon over and over again as a way to link, interpret, and explain new information that students encounter" (Resnick & Klopfer, 1989, p. 209). Even as we read about the work that others have done, we can be consciously linking, interpreting, and explaining, using our own voices as teachers.

Some teachers have found it beneficial to refrain from immediate judgment of the applicability of the ideas inherent in a book, article, or workshop presentation. One teacher described the process as responding to what jumps out, then letting it incubate for a while. Likewise, teacher researchers may want to read and listen for a while without trying to determine where or how this material will be used or written about. Kelsay (1991) called this "meandering through the research process" (p. 18), when teachers sample the smorgasbord available without evaluating its immediate usefulness in the classroom. Instead, they seek understanding and a deeper knowledge about what other teachers think and feel. The essence of the question is the opening up, and keeping open, of possibilities (Van Maanen, 1990). Such is the nature of effective exploration of what is out there. If we consider what we do with students as a curriculum of possibilities, we are opening ourselves to learning beyond our own experiences.

Reading the literature also has tremendous implications for curriculum. Often, teachers are unaware of the kinds of ideas being traded in the field and the ways in which other teachers in other school systems throughout the country are teaching and learning. Teachers often feel isolated in their own classrooms. Access to professional organizations related to subject areas they teach may assist teachers as they extend the dialogue beyond their own classrooms or schools. Many teachers are unaware of the journals being published each month that pertain to their teaching grade level, content area specialization, or the profession as a whole. These journals seem readily available to teacher educators, but are not always present in the lives of classroom teachers. Even though many schools provide a professional library for teachers, teachers seldom have enough time or the incentive to delve into its holdings. A teacher research study invites teachers to look at what is available; the project provides real motivation for the search because what is learned applies directly to the classroom.

PLANNING A RESEARCH STUDY

To re-search means to look again; it comes from the French verb *chercher*, to look for, or to seek, and the Latin verb *circare*, which means to go around. Learning to use research tools in the classroom gives a teacher the capacity to "go around" one's practice, that is, to examine it and study it closely. The study is richer if there are multiple means of collecting information that include both observational techniques and nonobservational strategies. In this kind of research, it is very appro-

priate—in fact, necessary—to use the first person and to own the processes as an individual (see chap. 8). Who you are and what your initial
ideas and thoughts are about the topic become important to the success of the study. Teacher researchers do not strive for dispassionate
objectivity; they work toward systematic and detailed data that teach
them something about their professional world.

Research is not static; it evolves as a class changes and as students
learn. Teacher researchers adapt their strategies for doing research as
the landscape changes. Even as we collect information about what is
happening, we are inevitably transforming what is happening in the
classroom. Once a research question is in place and a teacher researcher has informed himself or herself as much as possible about the topic
area or domain, it is time to design a plan for investigation. According to
Bogden and Biklen (1982), data are "the rough materials researchers collect from the world they are studying" (p. 73). Data are both the evidence
and the clues in this adventure; they are what supports the reflections
and the analysis, and they are what is used to make meaning for future
researching in a classroom. There is no single way of doing research in
the classroom, so the real question is, what works?

The aim of data collection in teacher research "is description and interpretation from the inside rather than the strict measurement and
predication of variables using a quantitative approach" (McKernan,
1991, p. 59). Teachers engaging in research use their own personal and
professional lenses of experience. Miller (1999) suggests that before
teacher researchers begin to collect data, they need to consider the
5W's and 1H. *Why* are you collecting this data? *What* exactly are you collecting? *Where* are you going to collect it? *When* are you going to collect
it and for how long? *Who* is going to collect it? *How* will data be analyzed and findings shared? These questions—asked and answered by individual teachers and teacher study groups—will save much time and
energy as the study progresses.

Some preliminary data may also be useful that can be obtained from
sources in the school. There may be a need for demographic or test
score data on students, for example. There may also be a need for data
pertaining to requirements in the curriculum, standards, or general information about the school and community. Whether or not these
pieces of data are important to the study is at the discretion of the
teachers doing the research.

The three key questions that help us think about collecting data and
interpreting it are:

1. What do I see?
2. What do I need to know that I cannot always see?
3. What does it mean?

OBSERVATIONAL DATA COLLECTION METHODS: WHAT DO I SEE?

Field Notes

The philosopher Goethe said that the hardest thing to see is what's in front of your eyes. There is a need for us to learn to look—and to see systematically. Teacher researchers often begin their studies with the basic question, What do I see? They respond to that question through a process known as the collection of field notes. Field notes are "the written account of what the researcher hears, sees, experiences, and thinks" (Bogden & Biklen, 1982, p. 74). Field notes help the researcher reconstruct dialogue using language that is as close as possible to that which is heard in the classroom. They help describe the specifics of setting and interaction.

Collecting field notes in a classroom sometimes means that a teacher "juggles the green roll book in one hand with the tape recorder in the other" (Johnston, 1988, p. 17). For some, a tape recorder is a necessity because the actual scripting of conversations and occurrences while they are happening is impossible during the teacher's day. Many teacher researchers set up a video camera in their classroom on a semipermanent basis, so that students become accustomed to it. Although the camera may not always be turned on, the teacher researcher is ready to capture data in the moment when it seems relevant to a question or topic.

Others find ways to use Post-It notes or labels in a plan book to make brief notations to be expanded on later. One teacher researcher called these notes "word pictures." Many researchers keep research logs or journals in which various kinds of data, including the elaboration of field notes, are stored. Taking observational field notes requires teachers to devise some method that works for them and that helps to highlight the focus that the research study intends. Some use manila folders that are categorized ahead of time, perhaps by students' names, discussion groups, or lab partners. Others use index cards, similarly categorized (Samway, 1994).

When we observe in the classroom, we are necessarily selective; we can't look at everything. The observational field notes must be designed to help the researcher research with intent and direction. Teachers often say that learning to use the tool of field notes can sometimes overwhelm the process. The notes can become so extensive that it's difficult to determine what is going on and what to attend to in a given day. That's why it is important to have a focus, question, or central problem to return to periodically as data collection continues.

At the end of a day or week of accumulating field notes, teacher researchers often return to what they have collected and write about it. Researchers generally suggest that it is best to write about an event or a time period as soon as possible before you discuss it with anyone; verbal language appears to change what has occurred as the speaker shapes the conversation. Individual writing offers a teacher time to process it independently first (see chap. 1). It is sometimes useful to accompany field notes with a floor plan or diagram of the classroom or other learning environment, especially if collaborators are going to help you look at the data. Some teacher researchers also use checklists that are efficient tools to note whether something is absent or present.

By the very fact that we collect specific information, select certain pieces of a discussion, or directly quote a particular student, we attach meanings to those episodes. Collecting field notes systematically and carefully over a substantial amount of time helps us avoid telling anecdotes without sufficient evidence from the data. If we want to be able to point to our work as researchers with personal and professional authority, field notes must point to patterns or themes that can be supported with data.

Observational field notes do not yield definitive answers. They do yield insights for teachers who are looking carefully. After a week of collecting field notes, one teacher researcher exclaimed, "I wish I knew exactly what I was looking for!" Keeping one's eyes open for what may happen, being aware of the central focus or question for the research, and revisiting the field notes both individually and with colleagues all help a researcher to "see." See chapter 4 for more detail on how technology can assist with the process of collecting and interpreting field notes.

Shadow Studies

Another means of collecting observational data is through the shadow study. One of my favorite resources for this approach to research is found in Chris Stevenson's book, *Teaching Ten to Fourteen Year Olds*

(1998), in which he describes how one might "shadow" an adolescent for a full school day and what one might learn from such a venture. Doing a shadow study requires that a researcher have a block of time in order to systematically observe and record events in a participant's day. Usually, the accounts are anecdotal and consist of an accumulation of episodes recorded, kept, for example, every 5–7 min, over a full day, or several weeks of shorter time periods. Sometimes the shadow study is followed by an interview in which the observer/researcher can question the person shadowed more fully about events and anecdotes that occurred during the study.

Stevenson (1998) claimed that no special expertise is necessary to conduct a shadow study. "What is essential is attentiveness," he noted (p. 29). That attentiveness becomes the hallmark of successful teacher research. Doing a shadow study takes the teacher researcher beyond the classroom walls to see what can be learned outside. The decision to conduct a shadow study is dependent on the nature of the inquiry. Would shadowing a person shed new light on the research question or topic under study? There are also ethical issues that need to be confronted; if a student is shadowed, parental permission must be sought and granted, disclosure or means of dissemination agreed on, and administration fully in agreement. What then might be the incentive?

Stevenson suggested that shadow studies are especially helpful for global questions about what students experience in schools. The account by Ted Sizer, *Horace's Compromise* (1984), was a fictional shadow study in which a high school English teacher and a teenage student were shadowed as they moved through a typical high school day in an average U.S. community. The story was striking, and the potential for learning about exactly what students—or teachers—experience is great. Suppose you were interested in students' exposure to group or cooperative learning through the school day. Suppose you were interested in how a teacher might use grouping differently in different class periods during the day. Or perhaps you wanted to note how kindergarten children make transitions between activities. A series of shadow studies would reveal larger patterns and help teacher researchers to understand their own teaching behaviors in their own classrooms.

Shadow studies are especially useful tools for teacher preparation students doing observations in schools. We have learned that focused observation, with a particular methodology in mind, is far more useful than generalized time spent in classrooms as required "observation" prior to student teaching. Shadow studies are less overwhelming than general field notes for beginning researchers; they provide a direction for seeing and they provide access to new insights about schooling.

But this method of observation is also critically important for experienced teachers to consider. Stevenson wrote:

> Regardless of the observer's prior role in schools, doing at least one shadow study of a student is essential to recognizing what schooling is like from the other side of the desk. Using the technique forces the observer to experience school from the perspective of the student and, in so doing, to raise pertinent issues and questions for further study. (p. 42)

Video/Photographs

A visual artist friend, Cynthia Weiss, works in classrooms to integrate the arts. I often tease her because she never seems to go anywhere without her carousel of slides. For her, the world is full of visual images, whereas for me, the world is full of print and text. When she wants to look closely at what children are thinking, feeling, and doing, she looks at photographs of them working. She examines the physical environment of the classroom; she looks at how they interact with each other, frozen in time through a photographic slide. Her visual images are data. They serve as illustration, demonstration, and exhibition. They are sometimes unexpectedly telling, and they underscore the need for multiple ways of knowing what is happening. Sometimes teacher researchers give students disposable cameras to record an event or a classroom lesson. It may be that the camera held by a participant who is unaware of the research agenda of the teacher may be the most informative. Teacher researchers also use disposable cameras to record intentional data of process as well as product.

For my visual artist friend, visual images reveal just as much as written text because the visual is a medium she is familiar with and can access. Observational data present a framework for her that is sometimes not as obvious to me. If we share the data we collect with each other, she teaches me to see images. I, in turn, tell her what I see in written text. Some researchers have asked, how do we study the other without studying ourselves? Most teacher researchers would say we cannot. We study the other to learn about ourselves. Sometimes the methods we choose as part of our research design begin that process of self-revelation.

Teacher research groups also tap into the power of video as a tool for reflecting and re-searching classrooms. Video clubs are a good way to begin the research process and seek out a question or topic to pursue (Sherin, 1998). Sharing clips of video of your classroom with others and asking, "What do you see here?" is both exhilarating and, at times, unnerving.

A teacher research group in California used videoanalysis as the primary tool for their research (Achinstein, Meyer, Phillips, Tichy, & Williamson, 1999). Each time they met, a member of the group shared a video clip of students interacting in a small group. They viewed the discourse that they have as a process of community building, with the video as the focus for conversation. They have articulated a process whereby the presenting teacher describes the context for the video clip before viewing and shares his or her inquiry questions about the segment. After viewing, the other teachers ask clarifying questions, praise, and critique the classroom interaction they have witnessed. They provide the presenting teacher with some response to the inquiry questions posed, and then the group links this viewing experience to the collective inquiry of the group. At the next teacher research group meeting, the presenter gives a brief follow-up. Video analysis has been a factor in teacher preparation for many years; why not utilize it as a tool in teacher research?

Analysis of Artifacts: Protocols for Looking at Student Work

Teachers who focus on student learning and achievement cannot ignore the power of looking closely at what students produce as evidence. Teacher research study groups that I have visited have used a process for looking at writing samples, pieces of art, or completed tests by students in order to learn what they can about how a student processes information, solves problems, and addresses complex topics and issues. By studying artifacts from the portfolio of individual children, teachers can learn much about their teaching and how they might address the needs of all students in their classrooms.

Artifact analysis may take many forms, depending on the nature of the research topic that a teacher chooses. Using our initial observation questions is a good beginning: *What do I see? What does it mean?* The Coalition of Essential Schools journal, *Horace*, presented a series of protocols in detail that help groups of teachers make meaning from classroom artifacts (Cushman, 1996). There are many variations on the process, but basically, it consists of the following steps:

- Teacher presents copies of a selected piece of student work or an artifact to the group without comment.
- Participants discuss the particular characteristics of the student's work. The presenting teacher does not participate. (*What do* you *see?*)
- The participants raise questions about the work and speculate on what the student may be struggling with or working on. (*What does it mean?*)
- The presenting teacher then has a chance to speak and give his or her perspective on the student's work—but only after hearing this previous discussion from colleagues. (*What do* I *see?*)
- The group discusses the wider implications of what they have been analyzing and suggest ways to use what they have learned to improve their teaching. (*What does it mean?*)

NONOBSERVATIONAL DATA COLLECTION METHODS: WHAT DO I NEED TO KNOW THAT I CAN'T ALWAYS SEE?

Interviews

Several years ago, I was introduced to a book by Holstein and Gubrium (1995) called *The Active Interview*. The title intrigued me; what did it mean to make an interview active? I had imagined an interview as a series of questions and answers. I as the interviewer prepared a series of standard questions to ask, and the interviewee answered them one at a time. How was an "active interview" different from this, and what might such an interview contribute to teacher research?

Holstein and Gubrium characterized an active interview as one in which the meaning emerges and is actively constructed within the interview. In other words, the person being interviewed plays a role in that construction of meaning in ways that the researcher may not foresee. In an active interview, questions guide but they do not control; they serve as "more of a conversational agenda than a procedural directive" (p. 76). They are improvisational, yet focused. In such an interview, the respondent might even be asked what kinds of questions he or she thinks should be posed. (As a high school teacher, I often asked my students to provide questions I should have asked on a final exam. They got credit for these questions and their responses to them. This seems similar to the approach Holstein and Gubrium described.)

As I read *The Active Interview*, I kept thinking about teacher researchers and interviewing. Did active interviewing require a specialized kind of expertise that teachers working in classrooms may not have? Was this something that professional researchers could do, but not classroom teachers? I began to explore these questions with preservice teachers as they conducted research in classrooms where they were doing field experiences. Together, we devised some ways in which active interviewing could play a useful role in teacher research.

Active Interviewing Recommendations.

- Use questions in an interview initially to set the focus and establish some history with the respondent.
- Inform the respondent about your research and why this interview is important.
- Share what you believe to be significant data you have or what you have learned thus far in your own personal research.
- Invite and set up the interview as a conversation, not a series of questions and answers. This needs to be done overtly and explicitly, as most people expect interviews to be the latter.
- Think of the interview in teacher research as an opportunity for respondents to tell their stories. Think of it as *storytelling* and use that terminology with the respondent.
- Suggest links or connections with other topics, ideas, or issues as they occur.
- Suggest alternative perspectives and viewpoints. The interviewer is not faceless and without opinions in an active interview. The interviewer is a teacher researcher, set squarely in the midst of his or her work.
- Capture *how* something is said through process notes (either during or after the interview).
- Note signs of confusion, reluctance, ambiguity, or contradiction. A typed transcript often obscures the most important data.
- Be ready to go in directions that you had not anticipated.

Interviews in teacher research can be conducted with parents who may offer another perspective on students' learning. They can also be useful with children who become part of the research to improve their own learning. Interviews can be a means to communicate with and learn from colleagues in your own building and in other contexts who are interested in similar issues and topics. They can be conducted via the Internet and via the telephone. They fill in the gaps that one can't always address through classroom-based observation. They often take teacher research in new directions, especially if they are active and engaging to the participants.

Focus Groups

A focus group is, quite simply, a group interview. Focus groups are often used in business and industry. They are common in marketing, in hospitals, universities, and other contexts in which researchers want to know what matters to people. Focus groups are an excellent way for teacher researchers to create circumstances in which a conversation about their research interests yields more than individual interviews might do.

Focus groups are usually composed of a group of people—usually more than 5 and less than 10—who are familiar with the topic to be discussed. The group members are interested in the topic, and the focus group gives them an opportunity to discuss it with people they might not otherwise encounter for this purpose. Participants share and compare; they tell their stories; they may even develop new ideas about the topic.

A teacher researcher serves as the moderator of the discussion. This person is a participant, but also has the task of keeping the discussion within the realm of the topic. The teacher researcher has convened the group and has prepared specific, yet flexible, guidelines for questions. He or she gives the group a brief outline of why she has called the group together, what the research question or interest is, and how the data collected might be used in the research study. Where appropriate, the teacher researcher may seek informed consent and discuss confidentiality, if needed (Morgan, 1998, pp. 86–87). Sometimes the session is tape-recorded and later transcribed; sometimes the teacher researcher brings along a colleague to take notes.

Teacher researchers may use focus groups for data collection in order to help them define just what it is they want to look more closely at in their own practice. They may be just at the beginning stages of a question or issue and need to hear conversation in order to narrow the focus or decide what to do next.

A preservice teacher researcher, Alyson Boim, designed a focus group with parents from the local elementary school for this purpose.

As a young, single, prospective elementary teacher, she knew that she really didn't understand the perspective of parents too well. She developed a set of guiding questions for this parent focus group in order to find out more about what it was like to be a parent of an elementary school child and to learn what parents might expect from a first-year teacher. This focus group gave her the impetus to design a research study with active parent involvement; it helped her to be less fearful of parent engagement in her classroom as she began her career.

Other teacher researchers have used focus groups to try out their ideas on others interested in the topic. A middle school science teacher was working on inquiry-based science projects to augment a rather traditional textbook-based curriculum in her school. She invited other middle school science teachers in her district for dinner at a local restaurant to share ideas about inquiry-based, problem-centered learning.

Teacher researchers might share the results of their research study with a focus group of interested individuals. Others often have insights as to why certain results were achieved and others were not. Focus group participants who were not involved in the research in the classroom might see things with fresh eyes and offer ideas on next steps to teacher researchers.

Focus groups represent a "friendly, respectful research method," as David Morgan (1998, p. 59) described it. His book, *The Focus Group Handbook*, is an accessible guide to get started with this approach to data collection. A final note: Focus groups are another means to intersect teaching and research. Students who are members of focus groups in their classrooms can learn to utilize the technique for their own research. Seeing group discussion as research invites students to learn about the different purposes for discussing. A discussion cannot be called a focus group if it is not used for research. Talking with students about when and how to use focus groups in the curriculum opens up new possibilities.

Surveys

I am sometimes puzzled by first-time teacher researchers who are beginning to develop their ideas for a classroom study. "I am going to give a survey," is sometimes the first reaction to the charge to collect information. Why? Why is it that surveys or questionnaires come to mind first as "real research"? Teacher researchers need to ask, what do I hope to achieve by administering a survey that I can't accomplish in another way? If we do not ask that question, we often go first to a survey and then realize that such instruments are not as helpful as we thought.

Successful survey users in teacher research have adapted the methodology to their own purposes. They test out their own premises and assumptions with a larger population—beyond their own classroom. They may have already done research—through interviews, focus groups, and literature review—in order to discern what is of importance. They have learned about survey question development and have piloted the survey with participants who have provided valuable feedback about the items on the survey. They have determined how they will probably use the survey results, and how those results might intersect with results from other data sources, such as their own field notes, journal logs, and classroom artifacts pertaining to the topic.

A teacher researcher who used a survey successfully wanted to know what literature was most commonly taught in the ninth grade at urban and suburban schools in metropolitan Chicago. Jane Goldenberg was interested in determining if there was a canon of literature classics that was uniformly taught in ninth grade, and, if so, what books were included. Before administering the survey, she interviewed department chairs, collected book lists as available from high schools, and investigated survey methodology. The survey was then administered to a number of schools and the results were used to empirically present specifics of the literature taught in ninth grade (Goldenberg, 1999). As a preservice teacher, Jane's research helped to acquaint her with the literature that she would most likely be teaching in a high school English class. The survey played a key role in her work. (Incidentally, Jane found that the classic most often used in ninth grade literature classes was *Romeo and Juliet*.)

Arlene Fink (1995) wrote a concise book on the subject of survey research called *The Survey Handbook*. Fink's work can help teacher researchers with the particulars of survey methodology. Key recommendations for the purposes of teacher research include:

- Define all terms for yourself and those who participate in the survey.
- Accompany a survey with a brief introduction as to the purpose and use of the survey.
- Address issues of anonymity or confidentiality as appropriate.
- Decide when a forced choice item is appropriate; forced choice responses can be easily quantified. (Forced choice items include yes/

no questions, Likert-scale questions, and others in which the respondent has the answer options provided.)

- Open-ended items provide different data from forced choice; decide what you will do with unexpected responses to such items.
- Consider using focus group discussions as a basis for designing a follow-up survey with a larger group; focus groups often reveal issues and questions you may not have thought of by yourself.

METHODS FOR INTERPRETING INFORMATION: WHAT DOES IT MEAN?

Teacher researchers tell me that this step in the research process is the most challenging and, at times, can be the most overwhelming. Collecting videotape, audiotape, students' work, and field notes seems to be doable for most teachers. But what do we do with all that information once we've collected it? First, experienced teacher researchers can tell you not to let it mount up over time. Teacher researchers look at the data as they go along; they write about what they are thinking and they pose preliminary ideas for discussion with colleagues long before they are "finished" with their investigation. Ongoing reflection is satisfying and makes the research worthwhile; looking at a mountain of information at the end of a month of collecting data can be a hopeless process.

As the data are collected, when you begin to analyze what it all means and what you have learned through this process, it is appropriate to return to the research question. The moment when you decide it is time to return to the data and see what they reveal might also be the time to rethink why you chose this particular area of inquiry, this topic, this question. This is especially important now as you prepare to interpret the information because the question has inevitably been reshaped by your focused attention to it over time. It is never too late, then, to reframe the question to reveal your new understanding of what you have been studying. Your experience is now different; thus your approach to the interpretation of the data is different now than when you first began to collect data.

Knowledge is the result of human activity, not something removed from the act of teaching. Knowledge about the question you have been considering comes in and through what you and your students and/or colleagues have been examining. The interpretations you reach and the conclusions you arrive at are not for all time; they are not necessarily generalizable, and they are not conclusive conclusions. They are for *this* time in *this* place; they are for your good and for your students' well-being, even though your learning will extend your practice and be useful for others. That said, how do we make meaning from data collected in teacher research?

We have looked at several observational and nonobservational approaches to collecting information. Field notes by themselves may not be sufficient. Field notes coupled with a shadow study and a series of focus groups are more revealing. We began with methods of data collection that responded to the question, *what do I see?* Then we moved on to find data that responded to the question, *what do I need to know that I cannot always see?*

Now we turn to interpreting the data we've collected and asking the question, *what does it mean?* The process of responding to these questions is sometimes known as "crunching." Others call it "squeezing" the data to see what we can get (Calhoun, 1994). There are many more approaches that could be useful, but these are excellent beginnings for both experienced and novice teacher researchers. They can be applied and reapplied; they work for groups and individual researchers. They are the stuff of teacher research.

Some teacher researchers have found it useful to collect all information and then rank order the data collected, in terms of importance and interest. They work with the data that are of most importance first and see what emerges from there, looking at other data in comparison. Others look at all the data sources as they are collected and make preliminary conclusions in progress. Regardless of how the process is constructed, here are three possible ways of coding to make sense of the data collected.

Coding

In order to interpret the data you have collected, it is important to determine the categories that seem to emerge. A category is basically a naming of similar topics under one heading. For example, if your research question centers on how to establish a community in your fourth-grade class, categories might emerge as follows: (a) children's literature that has a community theme, (b) collaborative activities or strategies, (c) parental roles in supporting community, and (d) student interactions with each other. From those categories, the researcher then crunches the data to find patterns across the categories. What can you learn about how community is established in your classroom by looking at the strategies you have tried and the interactions students have had with each other? How do you see the parental support strategies you've implemented intersecting with the literature that students have read? Patterns and categories are the means for interpreting the data. We begin to establish both patterns and categories by coding what we have collected. Results from interviews, focus groups, surveys, shadow studies, and many other forms of data can be coded.

Open coding refers to a process of breaking down, examining, comparing, and categorizing data. It is, for many teacher researchers, the first step in interpreting the data. Teacher researcher Nancy Hubbard was studying the effect of learning about Gardner's (1983) personal intelligences on first-year teachers and how she as a mentor could better support novice teachers, tapping into intrapersonal and interpersonal intelligences. (See her story after chap. 7.) She interviewed the first-year teachers extensively and had mounds of transcripts. She began by looking for specific categories of responses that matched the characteristics of the intrapersonal and interpersonal intelligences. She color-coded those responses using colored dots on chart paper and mounted the excerpts on the wall. The color-coded visual helped her really see what she had found.

Axial coding involves putting the data back together again in new ways after this process of open coding and proceeding to make connections between and across categories. After Nancy made her visual on the wall with categories color-coded, she then was able to see new patterns of behavior and reactions to events and situations that the first-year teachers encountered. Patterns unfolded from categories as Nancy coded the data she had collected, so when she began to reflect on what she had learned, she had a different set of patterns than she did when she began. Axial coding makes way for new patterns that the teacher researcher discovers along the way.

Selective coding is another means of coding and occurs when a teacher researcher selects a core category and then systematically relates it to other categories. This approach is useful when the teacher has a specific focus that is clear and is curious about how other factors affect that focus. One teacher researcher was interested in how students responded to various means of assessing their learning. She was trying to expand her own repertoire of assessment strategies, so her focus for one research period was to initiate self-evaluation for each unit or project her middle school students did. The core category was the self-evaluation component; the other means of evaluation were always connected and/or compared to that category.

Coding is a technique used by qualitative researchers routinely. Adapting the strategy to teacher research provides teachers with a systematic structure and a means of attending to what is important. If we think in terms of categories and patterns, we can sort through data and find the pieces that tell the story we are interested in at the time. Other parts of the videotape or the transcript may be useful for other research topics or questions at a later date. Refer to chapter 4 for information on how software packages can assist with coding the data.

HOW TRUSTWORTHY IS THIS WORK?

How can we trust what we have found and interpreted? Although teacher research is an approach to understanding that does not require generalizability or objectivity in the way that empirical research does, we also recognize the need to validate our work. As Sue Jungck says (see chap. 8), many teachers wonder, at least initially, is this *real* research? Although this discussion is ongoing in teacher research circles, there are a few terms and approaches to consider to help you determine trustworthiness or validity of your study.

- *Triangulation* is a term used for the conscious intersecting of multiple methods for data collection. It is the process of comparing the findings of different techniques (McMillan, 2000). If data are received from more than one lens and then categorized, it is likely to be more valid.
- We encourage researchers to take what they have learned and what they think they have seen in the study back to the participants. As a general rule, I always remind myself, when in doubt, ask the students. If we ask them, "Is this what happened?," "Is this what you experienced?," "Did I get it right?," we will learn more than if we had relied solely on our own interpretation.
- David Hobson, coeditor of this text, often asks teachers, "What's missing? What's not here?"

- Look for what does not fit the categories and patterns you have discerned. In research jargon, this is called *outlier analysis*. There may be more learning there than you realize.

CAN TEACHER RESEARCH BE RELIABLE?

We have found two ways that work for teacher researchers:

- Long-term involvement. Teachers are typically engaged over long periods of time with the questions that inform their work. Data collected over time can affirm or challenge what you believe you are finding. Teachers have the advantage of being there and continuing the research long after visiting researchers may have gone.
- Coding checks. Particularly if you are working with a research study group (see Kelli Visconti's story after chap. 7), or with other collaborators, it's always useful to have other teachers code the data from your study. What do they see that you might have missed? How might their categories shape your thinking? Hobson's chapter 5 in this text describes the ways in which teacher researchers can support each other—and give valuable response to findings and interpretations along the way.

Interpretation is more than just a summary of what has occurred during teacher research. It is really a process of reflection on one's own teaching and learning. It is a means by which a story can be told and new knowledge can be created about being a professional teacher. It is in the acts of interpretation and reflection that the roles of researcher and teacher come together.

CURRICULUM INVENTED IN THE CLASSROOM—WITH STUDENTS

Recently, while discussing teacher research at a faculty meeting in a suburban school, the curriculum director raised her hand and asked a question. "You know, I've been listening to all this stuff about collecting and interpreting data, and I think I understand what it's about. But, I can't help but ask, Isn't this just good curriculum development? I still don't see the difference between teachers doing research and teachers developing good curriculum."

Her question raised more questions and challenged us to think about the ways in which teacher research is really related to "just good curriculum development" and the ways in which it is a distinct process. Teacher research need not always be about classroom curriculum. Sometimes research focuses on personal and intellectual growth for teachers, which may or may not be immediately reflected in classroom events. Sometimes research focuses on interactions among adults that, while they indirectly affect curriculum, may not be the results of most interest. But for many teacher researchers, the reason and motivation for conducting inquiry is the desire to improve teaching and learning in the classroom—and that's all about curriculum. (See Judith Lachance Whitcomb's story after chap. 7.) If we acknowledge that, then we also face the fact that curriculum is changed when teacher researchers step in, collect data, and interpret what they are doing. The resulting action taken, shapes the curriculum.

Often the curricular reality of schooling is invented somewhere other than the classroom. Curriculum mandates, teacher-proof text-books, and systemwide objectives often preclude the task of creating curriculum that is personal, immediate, and in fact alive. Bissex and Bullock (1987) noted that "classroom-based research presents a serious challenge to current and traditional education and to the public's definition of what teachers are and do" (p. xi). A teacher research approach to curriculum not only alters the way we think of teachers and their roles; it also suggests a new way to think about students and the ways in which they learn.

Yet, quite often, the curriculum teachers feel obligated to address attempts to cover vast amounts of information at the expense of deepening thought in selected, integrated subject areas. In a classroom where teacher research is occurring, there are many opportunities to become builders of knowledge. When teachers see themselves as helping to construct knowledge as it is lived daily with children, children may begin to understand that curriculum is developed in and through their own learning as they participate in researching their classroom.

Carol Santa, a curriculum director for a large district, wrote:

> I have chosen not to spend my time in my office, writing fat curriculum guides. In fact, our entire district curriculum fits neatly in one slim folder.

> Teachers found our previous curriculum manuals cumbersome—more useful for pressing flowers than for guiding instruction. (Santa, 1990, p. 65)

Curriculum, for teacher action researchers, is something that is lived; it is what and how we teach and learn in school buildings and playgrounds. It is what children experience.

What happens to life in classrooms when action research is going on? How exactly might the curriculum be "transformed" by this process of collaborative research? As teachers begin to do classroom research, they: (a) see curriculum as a means to integrate knowledge and people, (b) listen to what students think and feel, and (c) engage students actively in the development and analysis of their own learning. These observations about how teacher research impacts curriculum suggest that seeing the classroom as a place for investigation and inquiry makes a statement about what knowledge is of most value and who is the rightful owner of the process of knowing and questioning. These are deep issues of power and authority; they situate teachers and students at the center of teaching and learning.

Integrating Knowledge: Seeing Curriculum as Inquiry

"It's the starting place which is in question. It's different when it begins with *me* and *my students* than when it begins with the content," one teacher researcher explained. The strategies do not drive the inquiry; rather, the inquiry reveals the strategies that the classroom researchers collaboratively design. In this classroom, at this time, with this group of people, a variety of choices and decisions can be made that will enrich each person's learning and allow each to take responsibility for growth.

Fourth-grade teacher Bonnie Anastos explored an approach to integrating her social studies curriculum by working with students' questions and interests focused on Knight's book, *Talking Walls* (1992). Bonnie Anastos explained:

> It is my belief that an integrated curriculum helps students make connections for themselves, is a more interesting, exciting, and motivating way to learn, and is beneficial to students at all levels. But, exactly how would I accomplish such a goal with my students? I needed to generate student interest and allow as much student choice as possible. I chose a day and

time to share *Talking Walls*, the book that served as the foundation of this entire unit and my teacher research. (Anastos, 1996, pp. 9–10)

As we look more closely, we can see the relationships between the processes in teacher action research and those utilized in integrating curriculum (Burnaford, Beane, & Brodhagen, 1994). Teacher action research is drawn from the experiences of all the participants in the classroom context. In teacher action research, one begins with the questions and issues raised in the classroom; that starting place is also ideal when designing integrative curriculum. Teacher action researchers work with students as co-researchers; in an integrative curriculum, students are active participants in shaping and planning curriculum. Bonnie Anastos wrote:

As I gathered the class on the rug, so many different thoughts were racing through my head. I wanted this to go perfectly, and I wanted the students to be as interested and excited about the story as I was. I held up the picture book and asked if anyone had seen the picture on the front before. Hands shot up, but no one answered correctly. Then I opened to the first page. That wall was very familiar and everyone wanted to tell about it. I refrained from reading the text. It left the students with wonder as to what it might say about each wall. As we progressed through the picture book, some walls were very familiar to the students, and they were quick to shout out the names, but others filled them with questions.

When I finished the book, I asked the students if they wanted to learn more about some of the walls and they enthusiastically said yes. I suggested we first list all the walls we could remember from the book because they would probably be the ones we were most interested in. Rather than use hands, I asked the students to just call out the names of the walls. They began: "The Great Wall of China," "the cave paintings in Australia," "the rock walls built by farmers," "Mecca," "The Berlin Wall," "Mandela's prison wall" . . . The children had recalled all eighteen walls featured in the book!

Next I asked the students to tell me what they wanted to find out about the walls. For my own security, in case I needed to prompt the students, I had prepared a card with key questions that I wanted to include in the study. To my disbelief, the class came up with every question and more that I had on my card. (Anastos, p. 14, 15)

Bonnie's students took the challenge and used their own curiosities as the basis for research. Their research was also her research on the shaping of an integrative curriculum. The class ultimately chose four walls to focus on in detail: the Great Wall of China, the Walls of the Pueblo Indians, the Vietnam Veterans' Memorial Wall, and the Berlin Wall. In groups, they began to find out more. The research process led them to think about how to illustrate what they were learning . . . and that led to poetry, art, graphic organizers. They examined the materials walls were made of . . . that led to architecture, geology, and mathematical scale.

When teachers actively examine their classrooms through the lens of action research, their teaching may "borrow" from other subjects, in terms of methods and strategies, as they see the usefulness of these techniques. There is much in the literature that describes the power of integrative curriculum in which children's literature is applied to mathematics and science, fine arts is used as an integral part of a language arts or foreign language curriculum, or mathematical concepts are reinforced through fiction (Beane, 1990; Burnaford et al., 1994; Jacobs, 1989; Stevenson & Carr, 1993; Whitin & Wilde, 1992). This is what happened in Bonnie's classroom. When we invite students to take part, we invite some sharing of the control of what students learn and how they learn it; such input most assuredly changes the research focus and the curriculum when it occurs.

> While in the midst of this project, it was difficult to know exactly what was happening. I kept notes, as a teacher researcher, about what I was seeing, hearing, and thinking, and I collected artifacts. But I did not consider what all my findings would say until the wall murals were taken down, rolled up, and stored in the closet.
>
> For all the wondering happening during our study of walls, there were also problems that I recorded and would need to address in a subsequent teacher research project. My observations showed that those students who are slow learners and the students who have difficulty with behavior control experienced the same roadblocks to their learning while involved in this integrated study as they do at other times. The average and faster learning students had greater success and achievement than they experience with a traditional curriculum.
>
> Each day we would discuss different parts of the project (research, note cards, report, mapping) and students were expected to finish parts, then move on to the next component. But some students needed more direction than that. I needed to step back and adjust. (Anastos, p. 27, 30–31)

As teachers look at the dynamics of their classroom and the nature of the content they are teaching, they often begin to see the connections between what they do and what others are doing. That too is integration.

> Before I began this project, I met with the art teacher. She is the most creative person I have ever worked with and she helped me bring the walls to life. I presented my idea of a wax museum and explained that we would need large murals of each wall. She loved the idea and was thrilled to be included and to integrate the arts in this project. (Anastos, p. 18)

Bonnie Anastos learned something about her students, about the world social studies curriculum, and about herself during this research.

> I was not "teaching" as most of us view teaching, which is giving information that the students take in, retain, and then give back. I was teaching them how to learn and discover, how to teach themselves, and how to work with others. The students had discovered a great deal of information that was new knowledge for me as well. I felt very satisfied that my students were able to take charge of their own learning. In this way. (Anastos, p. 26)

The Affective Curriculum: Teacher Researchers Listen to What Kids Think and Feel

Dewey noted the importance of attention to the affective aspects of learning, that is, how students and teachers feel about what and how they are learning (Dewey, 1902/1990). This affective dimension of learning about a subject often becomes the primary focus of the research for teachers. A project might begin with an attention to a content field; then the teacher research might, through a process of data collection with students, realize the power of having students as co-researchers, tapping into their feelings and ideas for how to make the classroom curriculum stronger and richer.

This is what high school chemistry teacher Craig Hill discovered:

> I had been teaching chemistry for three years at a college preparatory high school where the enrollment is selective. The school claims to have "the best and the brightest" student body. Ninety-nine percent of the graduates go on to college. As a college student, I realized that chemistry had meaning for me. Thinking back, it was when I was in organic chemistry class that I first took responsibility for my own learning. But many of

my students believe that to be good at science, they have to be good at memorization. Many of my students ask, "Why do I need to know this stuff?" The material seems meaningless to them. So this is where my research began; how could I make chemistry meaningful for them—and what made it meaningful for me? (Burnaford, Fischer, & Hobson, 1996)

Craig began his study by reading about the concept of *constructivism* and how it has contributed to science education today (National Center for Improving Science Education, 1991). Constructivist theory suggests that teachers teach science by letting students *use the process of science to learn science.*

A person has to experience the knowledge and let it soak into previous concepts in order for knowledge to either be gained or dismissed. I realized that, if I taught with that process in mind, students could begin to answer the question, "Why do we have to know this stuff?" for themselves. (Burnaford, Fischer, & Hobson, 1996)

In order for Craig to test his understanding of constructivism and how it would affect his curriculum, he needed constant and, at times, exasperating input from students. He needed to know how they were learning and he needed to hear how they were experiencing this very different way of teaching.

I asked my students, who were my co-researchers, for their comments. One stated it beautifully: "Mainly, no one knew how to get started. To design an assignment, you must first understand the material. But no one understood it at first." Another student offered a comment after class one day: "I have an idea. How about you teach and we learn?" This remark smacked me on the side of the head! Yet another student helped me understand: "For some of us, it's very easy to make A's when you write stuff down for later processing. Later, you really think about it. Sometimes, you actually listen to what is said in class, sometimes you just write it down and maybe think about it later. But when you have to both find the material and also think and learn, and you still want an A, it becomes complex." (Burnaford et al., 1996)

Craig Hill sought input from his students at many steps along the way during his research. He asked them to offer their suggestions for how to improve his teaching next time, and he required them to write a self-evaluation to reflect on how and what they had learned as individuals. At times, as their responses suggest, they were often confused, anxious, and even angry about how they were learning chemistry. The class discussed the constructivist process, they modeled it, and they wrote about it. He learned something about the support systems and the guidance necessary from the teacher in order to make a constructivist approach to chemistry practical and accessible. He did so by listening to his students.

> Next year, I will introduce increased autonomy to students much more slowly. From the first day, the students will gain experience setting educational goals and achieving them, but they will have more regular checkpoints in place and other aspects of responsibility will be monitored more throughout a unit of study. Ultimately though, the students will experience chemistry labs in which *their* questions are explored and not someone else's. *Their* ideas and prior experiences will lead to their learning of chemistry. (Burnaford et al., 1996)

Active Engagement in Curriculum Making: A Feature of Teacher Research

A third pattern appears as teachers examine the relationship between the child and the curriculum. When teachers engage in classroom research, they realize as they proceed that they desperately need the active involvement, support, and feedback from their students in this endeavor. Craig Hill wrote:

> I had been an actor on a stage performing and the students were the audience. Each day, four shows in all, I would perform chemistry. Sometimes the audience would love it and at other times, the performance would be a flop. I began to investigate how to alter the "shows," based on the constructivist principle that each student is different. (Burnaford et al., 1996)

Craig Hill realized that engagement is more than just the surveying of a class on the success or failure of a lesson or an approach. Rather, this involvement of students in the research process is a valuable opportunity for the learners to also be the teachers, and for their needs, experiences, and interests to be at the heart of the curriculum decision-making process. Both Craig Hill, at the high school level, and Bonnie Anastos, at the elementary school level, learned that this is an important feature of doing research that transformed their classroom.

As Craig Hill's research suggests, students often ask, "Why are we doing this anyway?" An action research approach to curriculum invites this question—both in the asking and the answering. No one has *the* answer, but the class can come up with many answers as students participate in the decisions about how to learn in their own classrooms.

Stevenson (1986) noted that "when we inquire, we ask others to teach us—to help us close the gap between our understanding of a topic and theirs" (p. 5). If those "others" are our students, the research process becomes collaborative and the curriculum comes alive. It is probably wise to find out what students think early in the process about the focus of the research or the research question, if it involves them immediately and directly. Their early feedback could shape the eventual design and planning. Similarly, the results of the research project can be shared with those who provided that original information, namely, students, parents, community, and teacher colleagues who have shared in the inquiry.

What kinds of curricular decision making can result when the students are active curriculum planners with a teacher? What would happen if we conceived of teacher research as a means of curriculum development with *students as co-researchers and observers in the research process* rather than as subjects of a laboratory experiment? The potential for such study is inherent in teacher research. Van Maanen (1990) reminded us that current educational research tends toward abstraction, thereby losing touch with "the life world of living with children" (p. 135). If we consider the students as co-researchers in classroom study, curriculum planning and the resulting content become incontrovertibly transformed.

These three patterns that we have observed in teacher researchers' classroom transform the lived curriculum. Although they may not occur in all teacher research, we have noticed that teachers who are researchers pay attention to one or more of them at some time during their research. Teacher researchers inevitably look around for connections to other subjects and other ways of knowing when they explore their own content fields. They often look to students for responses, ideas, and even guidance as they try new approaches. And, as they become inquirers, they see the power of inquiry as a way of learning for students as well.

In these ways, teacher researchers' curriculum is shaped by their research. For many, the teacher research becomes part of the curriculum, not separate from it. Viewing action research *as* curriculum, rather than something being done *to* curriculum, is a shift in definition that is transformative.

Teaching, research, and curriculum design can inform and support each other in inquiring classrooms. Carol Avery wrote of finishing a year-long teacher research project in her elementary classroom. As she gathered with her colleagues in their research study group, the facilitator began with, "So, what are you researching next year?" (Avery, 1990). For a moment, she was taken aback. And then she realized it would be difficult *not* to continue the process of being a teacher—who is also a researcher.

WEB SITES

http://trochim.human.cornell.edu/index.html   Site for social research methods.

http://www.socsciresearch.com/   McGraw Hill Ryerson research resources for the social sciences.

http://www.aera.net   American Educational Research Association.

http://www.ascd.org   Association for Supervision and Curriculum Development.

LISTSERVS FOR EDUCATIONAL RESEARCHERS

Listserv@unmvma.unm.edu   QUALSRED (qualitative research in education).

Listserv@qucdn.queensu.ca   SMKCC-L (subject matter knowledge and conceptual change).

REFERENCES

Achinstein, B., Meyer, T., Phillips, M., Tichy, S., & Williamson, P. (1999, April). *Learning through talk and talking to learn*. Paper presented at the Annual Meeting of the American Educational Research Association, Montreal, Canada.

Anastos, B. (1996). *Talking Walls*: A teacher-researcher plans with students. *KASCD Journal, 14*(1), 7–34.

Avery, C. S. (1990). Learning to research/researching to learn. In M. W. Olson (Ed.), *Opening the door to classroom research* (pp. 32–44). Newark, DE: International Reading Association.

Baumann, J. F. (1996). Conflict or compatibility in classroom inquiry? One teacher's struggle to balance teaching and research. *Educational Researcher, 25*(7), 29–36.

Beane, J. A. (1990). *A middle school curriculum: From rhetoric to reality*. Columbus, OH: National Middle School Association.

Bissex, G. L., & Bullock, R. H. (1987). *Seeing for ourselves: Case-study research by teachers of writing*. Portsmouth, NH: Heinemann.

Bogden, R. C., & Biklen, S. K. (1982). *Seeing for ourselves: Case-study research by teachers of writing*. Boston: Allyn and Bacon.

Burnaford, G., Beane, J., & Brodhagen, B. (1994). Teacher action research: Inside an integrative curriculum. *Middle School Journal, 25*(3), 5–13.

Burnaford, G., Fischer, J., & Hobson, D. (1996). *Teachers doing research: Practical possibilities*. Mahwah, NJ: Lawrence Erlbaum Associates.

Calhoun, E. (1994). *How to use action research in the self-renewing school*. Alexandria, VA: Association for Supervision and Curriculum Development.

Cushman, K. (1996). Looking collaboratively at student work: An essential toolkit. *Horace, Journal of the Coalition of Essential Schools, 13*(2), 1–12.

Dewey, J. (1990). *The child and the curriculum*. Chicago: University of Chicago Press. (Original work published 1902)

Eisner, E. W. (1994). *The educational imagination* (3rd ed.). New York: Macmillan.

Elliott, J. (1990). Teachers as researchers: Implications for supervision and for teacher education. *Teaching and Teacher Education, 6*(1), 1–26.

Fink, A. (1995). *The survey handbook*. Thousand Oaks, CA: Sage.

Gardner, H. (1983). *Frames of mind*. New York: Basic Books.

Goldenberg, J. (1999, September). Writers' bloc. *Chicago Magazine*, pp. 73–80.

Hattrup, R. A., & Bickel, W. E. (1993). Teacher–researcher collaborations: Resolving the tensions. *Educational Leadership, 50*(6), 38–40.

Hollingsworth, S. (1992). *Teachers as researchers: A review of the literature*. Occasional Paper No. ERIC 142. ED351315.

Holstein, J. A., & Gubrium, J. F. (1995). *The active interview*. Thousand Oaks, CA: Sage.

Hyde, A. A., & Bizar, M. (1989). *Thinking in context: Teaching cognitive processes across the elementary school curriculum*. New York: Longman.

Jacobs, H. H. (1989). *Interdisciplinary curriculum: Design and implementation*. Alexandria, VA: Association for Supervision and Curriculum Development.

Johnston, P. (November 1988). *Looking from the inside: A teacher-researcher's view of theory and practice*. Paper presented at the Ethnography Forum, Philadelphia, PA.

Kelsay, K. L. (1991). When experience is the best teacher: The teacher as researcher. *Action in Teacher Education, 13*(1), 14–21.

Knight, M. B. (1992). *Talking walls*. Gardiner, ME: Tilbury House.

McKernan, J. (1991). *Curriculum action research: A handbook of methods and resources for the reflective practitioner*. New York: St. Martin's Press.

McMillan, J. H. (2000). *Educational research: Fundamentals for the consumer* (3rd ed.). New York: Longman.

Migra, E. (1992). *Teachers' classroom inquiry*. Unpublished paper, National-Louis University, Evanston, IL.

Miller, C. (1999). *Schoolwide action research process.* The Educational Leadership Center, Florida Atlantic University, Boca Raton, FL.

Morgan, D. L. (1998). *The focus group guidebook.* Thousand Oaks, CA: Sage.

National Center for Improving Science Education. (1991). *The high stakes of high school science.* Andover, MA: The Network.

Nixon, J. (1987, Winter). Contradictions and continuities. *Peabody Journal of Education,* pp. 20–32.

Resnick, L. B., & Klopfer, L. E. (1989). *Toward the thinking curriculum: Current cognitive research.* Alexandria, VA: Association for Supervision and Curriculum Development.

Samway, K. D. (1994, Autumn). But it's hard to keep fieldnotes while also teaching. *TESOL Journal,* pp. 47–48.

Santa, C. M. (1990). Teaching as research. In M. W. Olson (Ed.), *Opening the door to classroom research.* Newark, DE: International Reading Association.

Sherin, M. G. (1998). Developing teachers' ability to identify student conceptions during instruction. In S. B. Berenson, K. R. Dawkins, M. Blanton, W. N. Coulombe, K. Norwood, & L. Stiff (Eds.), *Proceedings of the Twentieth Annual Meeting of the North American Chapter of the International Group for the Psychology of Mathematics Education* (pp. 761–767). Columbus, OH: ERIC Clearinghouse for Science, Mathematics, and Environmental Education.

Sizer, T. R. (1984). *Horace's compromise: The dilemma of the American high school.* Boston: Houghton Mifflin.

Stenhouse, L. (1975). *An introduction to curriculum research and development.* London: Heinemann.

Stevenson, C. (1986). *Teachers as inquirers: Strategies for learning with and about early adolescents.* Columbus, OH: National Middle School Association.

Stevenson, C. (1998). *Teaching ten to fourteen year olds* (2nd ed.). New York: Longman.

Stevenson, C., & Carr, J. F. (1993). *Integrated studies in the middle grades: Dancing through walls.* New York: Teachers College Press.

Van Maanen, M. (1990). *Researching lived experience: Human science for an action sensitive pedagogy.* Albany: State University of New York Press.

Whitin, D. J., & Wilde, G. (1992). *Living and learning mathematics: Stories and strategies for supporting mathematical literacy.* Portsmouth, NH: Heinemann.

Wong, E. D. (1999). Challenges confronting the researcher/teacher: Conflicts of purpose and conduct. *Educational Researcher, 24*(3), 22–28.

Zeuli, J. S. (1992). *How do teachers understand research when they read it?* East Lansing, MI: National Center for Research on Teacher Learning.

4

TEACHER RESEARCHERS
GO ONLINE

David Hobson

Louanne Smolin
University of Illinois at Chicago

THIS BOOK GOES ONLINE

Our web page is http://www.teachersdoingresearch.com.

- Want to correspond with the 20 authors? Send an e-mail via the web page to any of the 20 writers represented in these pages.
- Want to interact with other teacher researchers? Ongoing discussion forums can be accessed through the web page about both the processes and products of teacher research.
- Want to access Internet resources, many of which are mentioned in the book? Go to the web site for instruction.
- Want to pose a query of other teacher researchers? Go to the web site to find out how.

One of the ways computer technology is impacting education is how it is transforming the traditional textbook. No longer must teachers and students wait 10 years for the next edition of a popular text. The first edition of this text was in some important ways out of date in just a year or two, but the book was in hard copy print so there was nothing we could do. In a few short years, that has changed. Now, when a book is published, the means are available to keep it up to date via the Internet.

In addition, the nature of textual materials is changing because of, in part, the application of technology to distance education. Moore and Kearsley (1996) distinguished three types of interactions that are practiced in successful distance education programs delivered by some form of technology: learner–content interaction, learner–instructor interaction, and learner–learner interaction. Thinking of an electronic journal, Dillner (1999) expanded these categories to describe four types of interactions that can now take place: reader–content, reader–author, reader–reader, and author–content.

In short, we are on our way to an electronic book format, which will likely act as a supplement to, but not a substitute for, for the traditional hard copy text. This new form may be structured more in layers arranged like a pyramid. A new book of this kind would elicit a new kind of reading (Darnton, 1999).

TEACHERS AND TECHNOLOGY: GAPS IN PERSONAL AND PROFESSIONAL USE

Children are going online in droves, more so than their teachers. Fewer than 2 of 10 teachers in the United States are serious users of the new information technologies. Some technology experts delight in this information and call for more and better teacher "training" and for the purchase of more and more equipment. Teachers are often perceived as the problem, obviously; they need to be brought up to speed (Cuban, 1999). Cuban pointed out a puzzling additional fact, however: 7 of 10 teachers have computers at home and use them extensively.

So the problem becomes more understandable: Why do teachers not use computer technology more *at school*? Asked in this more specific way, the question isn't so difficult to answer: Teachers are slow to use technology at school because policymakers ignore teachers' voices about the specifics of what they need. The enduring workplace conditions within which teachers teach leave little time or space for fooling with computers; many inherent flaws are still present in the technologies; teachers have neither the time nor the energy to struggle with crashes and breakdowns; and the advice from the experts is ever-changing. Until some of these conditions change in the real world of schools, the lag is very likely to remain (Cuban, 1999). This is not a new problem. Teachers are frequently the targets for criticism when there are problems with schooling, but they are very infrequently asked for solutions. The problem with this familiar scenario, as every teacher knows, is that in the final analysis it is the teacher who decides what's going to happen in the classroom. Teachers are the gateway to change (Cuban, 1986).

THE DIGITAL DIVIDE: TECHNOLOGY ACCESS FOR SOME?

What is the digital divide (1999)? It is unequal access to technology by various groups. This divide plays itself out on many levels, including the local school. Think about technology in your school. Do some teachers seem to hold the technology "power"? Do some seem to have access to more technology than others? Does their ease of access go beyond interest? How is technology distributed within your school setting? Are there clear policies for the equitable distribution of newly acquired technology as well as for technology staff development?

Sometimes the digital divide occurs because of limited opportunities for education. Some teachers may find it difficult to implement technology, and formalized opportunities to learn how to do so are difficult to provide or do not exist. This only serves to solidify the divide between the "haves" and the "have nots."

If a lack of clarity exists concerning how technology is acquired and distributed in your school, if you see differential levels of technology access, and if it is tacitly known by school community members that certain teachers "own" the school's technology, you are experiencing the "digital divide" on a local level. This digital divide is created by a difference: Some have access to technology and some do not. When this difference is ignored, when it is accepted as a natural course of events, and when no formal policies and procedures exist to establish equity, a digital divide can occur.

The digital divide gets played on grander scales. Of great concern to many teachers is the inequality of opportunity for computer access to specific groups. The children who arrive in teachers' classrooms are not equally experienced with computers and the Internet.

The introduction of technology into schools should definitely not be seen as a panacea. It seems highly unlikely that such problems as the intractable high rates of poverty, the continuing disintegration of families, and the pervasive unequal educational opportunities for rich and poor are likely to be fundamentally changed by information technology (Postman, 1995). Perhaps technology may even exacerbate a problem.

The racial divide remains stark, with African American and Hispanic families less than half as likely as Whites to explore the Internet from home, work, or school. The divide was even greater when the Census Bureau looked at a comparison of home use of the Internet among Whites and African American/Hispanic families, about three to one. Women are less likely to purchase and use computers than men. Children in two-parent households are nearly four times as likely to have access to the Internet as children in single-parent households (Clausing, 1999).

Most of the discrepancies in computer use correlate with income levels and education. Sixty-one percent of Whites and 54% of Blacks in households earning more than $75,000 per year used the Internet regularly, but the figures drop to 17% of Whites and 8% of Blacks when families are earning $15,000 to $35,000 per year (Jerald & Orlofsky, 1999).

These statistics are sobering to teachers. We need to be especially sensitive to how these inequalities play out in our schools and among our students. The rapid infusion of technology in our schools may be serving to further exacerbate the gulf between Black and White, rich and poor, and the children of two- and one-parent families. Rather than serving to reduce educational inequalities, these technologies may create and solidify inequalities as never before (Bruce, 1999). As Seymour Papert, the inventor of Logo, remarked, if teachers want to teach a classroom full of children to write, and only bring eight pencils into the school, they will likely be disappointed with the results (Cox, 1987). The current trends in the differential infusion of technology are most disturbing. It is unclear exactly what individual teachers can do to redress these differences in educational opportunity among their students, but certainly we need to resist the forces that continue to link technological literacy with patterns of racism and poverty. We need to insist on and support more equitable distributions of technology.

Implications of the Digital Divide for Teacher Research

The digital divide can have a ripple effect as it specifically relates to teacher research. As is further discussed in this chapter, through electronic communication, many teacher researchers are creating collaborative research communities and are sharing their work. Minority districts or impoverished districts with limited access to technology will also have limited access to these communities of learners and teacher researchers outside of their districts. These professionals may also become isolated from the contributions of universities and from the possibilities of developing partnerships with other schools, community organizations, and universities.

If certain groups of teachers do not have access to technology, then these examples of technology-rich teacher research will not happen there. We will lack their rich contributions, and our professional understandings will be based on partial knowledge.

USING TECHNOLOGY FOR TEACHER RESEARCH

Embracing technology involves a considerable learning curve; it just doesn't happen overnight. The tea-bag approach known as the inservice workshop doesn't do it. A course in this software package or that hardware configuration just gets one started. It takes time, patience, experimentation, getting help along the way, and plenty of trial and error. The one resource in shortest supply at school is time.

The many teacher researchers who have written in this book understand this. We understand that the processes of teacher research must be made time efficient. That is why we have organized this chapter in the way we have. It is "hands-on." It is frankly "how-to." We have tried to present each strategy for using technology in teacher research step by step. Our whole effort here is to save time, energy, false starts, and dead ends.

Teachers do use computers in their lives. In a recent survey, the number of teachers saying they have computers at home or at school reached 97% (James, 1999). Most have computers at home. They go online. They locate information. They purchase products. They have some favorite web sites for finding creative lesson plans, innovative curriculum, and a variety of teaching resources. When it comes to conducting practitioner research, especially, there are numerous ways in which the computer can be put to use. Just in the last few years, computer technologies have been sufficiently refined to help teachers explore a variety of resources and processes for doing teacher research.

The purpose of this chapter is to describe each of these dimensions and to provide specific resources for and examples of their use in teacher research. Although many readers may already be familiar with the venues we are about to describe, this chapter can hopefully challenge you to apply diverse technology to your teacher research. We display step-by-step applications throughout these pages that are designed to be of practical help.

Throughout this chapter, we demonstrate the variety of ways in which teachers have used technology while conducting research. We encourage you to explore, reflect, and discover the unique and personal ways that you can use technology within your research process.

BEGINNING WITH THE SELF: JOURNAL KEEPING GOES ONLINE

In chapter 1 of this text, many ideas and practices were recommended for journal keeping as a means for doing teacher research. Computer technology has made possible new applications for journal keepers. It's a lot easier nowadays to keep a journal on the computer. The leather-bound three-ring notebook that David has been using for 20 years can remain in use, but instead of consisting exclusively of handwriting and lots of Scotch-taped artifacts, it now consists mostly of typewritten material printed out from the computer, punched with three holes, and inserted into the notebook.

An early casualty of the frequent use of computers, it has been widely reported, was high-quality handwriting. Suddenly, this trend is changing; handwriting is enjoying an upward spiral with the advent of scanners and optical recognition software (optical character recognition, OCR). A note can now be written with a ballpoint pen in a pocket journal; this writing, provided it is legible, can be scanned at home and then treated with OCR software.

Alternatively, one of the hand-held pocket computers can export handwritten or typewritten copy directly into a home or school computer. And, if one is far from home, or writing from a classroom computer, the entry can be sent by e-mail to the electronic journal. No longer is the electronic journal a trade-off of benefits when compared to a handwritten journal. Today, technology has mirrored many of the characteristics of the old-fashioned journal and, as we show later, added a few interesting improvements as well. One can still add notes written by hand with a ballpoint pen on paper, or draw a doodle, or Scotch-tape a cartoon in the pages of the journal.

Teacher research topics typically come from a variety of venues. Some come from school-wide curriculum initiatives, some are sparked by school reform efforts, others come from teacher researcher collaboratives that decide to focus their effort in particular ways, and still others are born from an interest in studying the efficacy of curricular or instructional experiments. Probably the most powerful approach to teacher research comes from the actual ground of an individual teacher's own practice. This emphasis on the individual teacher in the individual classroom does not obviate any of the more collective venues from which the impetus for teacher research may spring. Whatever the genesis of the research idea, it is in the actual practice of the teacher that it really occurs and is studied. As has often been said, if you want to learn about your teaching, try to change it: then watch carefully what happens.

The *personal journal* or the *teacher journal* that describes classroom life, can be a great place in which to discover one's most dynamic research ideas. Sit down and read over a month's worth of daily entries and discover in the pages what the ongoing topics are, what issues are most problematic, which children "get the ink," which themes are most recurring. What are the low points? Where are the points of aliveness, of joy? This journal writing is data and can be subjected to computer analysis. See the later section on data collection and analysis for some specific and practical suggestions for how to do this. Transforming personal or classroom or research writing into an electronic journal can open a variety of doors to multiple possibilities (see chap. 1).

The *double-entry journal* is easy to accomplish on the computer. Simply use the Table icon and choose two columns to record a piece of data on the left and your response/commentary on the right (see chap. 3).

The *daily log* is facilitated by the computer too. Why not write it on the classroom computer during a lunch break or prep period, or after school, and take it home on a disk or e-mail it? The daily log can be directly imported into an electronic journal.

The *steppingstones* activity and the *clustering* strategy for organizing conceptual thinking are both easily done on the computer using software called Inspiration. (See the Resources section at the end of this chapter.)

Dialogue with a person is facilitated by the computer. Write an entry. Send it to a correspondent via e-mail. When the message is received, your friend can click on "Reply" and enter his or her comments right into the original message, like electronic Post-Its, and return it. The same message may go back and forth several times as you each add and respond to each other's comments. Or this response journal may become more serial in nature as each simply adds on to the journal in turn, thereby creating a response journal with successive chapters accumulating over what could be a considerable period of time. The whole of the correspondence is available at your fingertips at each writing, and it can be analyzed by software in a variety of ways as well.

Underlinings from a text are easily added to the electronic journal. Just select the fragments to be included, scan them into the computer, and import them into the appropriate place in the journal. Taking handwritten notes on multicolored note cards is fast becoming a thing of the past; the same thing can now be accomplished more quickly and easily by using technology.

Writing a *journal of the journals* is much facilitated by computer technology. Open the electronic journal file, then open the "journal of the journals" file you are writing. Click on the Window icon and click on split screen. Now, both the journal material you are reading and the journal you are writing are displayed on the screen. If you want to use text already in one file in the other file, it's as easy as copying and pasting.

Response journaling in a group is easily accomplished online by using a class web page, such as the one made available by Nicenet (http://www.nicenet.org). A teacher can set up a free web page limited to participation by members of a class (each has a password) in about 10 minutes. The directions are easy to follow. A class member can write an entry and, by clicking on a list of the persons in the class, can send it to everyone or to individual classmates selected. The recipients of the message can reply only to the author or to the group as a whole. In a classroom setting, with children or adults, this can really bring response journaling alive; the audience is real and the frequency of messaging mushrooms quickly.

David recently used this technology as a data collection device with good results. He asked students to write entrance and exit slips and to post them on the web page after class. Other students were able to respond to the writings of classmates, thus adding a dialogue feature. David was able to download all of these writings, both the original entries and the threaded conversations, for later analysis, a process made much simpler by the availability of the data in digital form.

A *group journal* is easily facilitated by computer technology. Want to create a history of the class? Have one historian write a report about each class and post it on your class web page. Each member of the class can access this accumulating history from his or her own computer at any time, maybe adding a response. If someone misses a class, a record is there. Parents can receive passwords, allowing access to the class history as well. Perhaps the group journal is focused on some aspect of the teacher research underway and can provide data for that endeavor. An electronic group journal greatly increases the immediacy, the accessibility, and the interactivity of the participants corresponding with each other, as well as providing a record of that interaction for the teacher researcher.

Thus far we have addressed various electronic applications of journal keeping parallel to the organization of chapter 1 in an effort to give some practical hands-on help for bridging the gap between the handwritten journal and the electronic journal. There is still more to this electronic evolution than may readily meet the eye, especially when it comes to collaboration.

LEARNING WITH EACH OTHER: COLLABORATION ONLINE

Our profession still is not well organized to facilitate collegial interaction and collaboration. The school day unfolds period by period; the subjects are still largely considered discipline by discipline in high schools, with students moving from class to class. For all the efforts at reorganization associated with the school reform of recent years, many teachers remain for the most part separated and isolated from one another even in their own buildings. The systemic nature of schools is comprised of a complicated web of microsystemic influence including grade levels, academic departments, general education, special education, English as a second language (ESL), and Chapter I. Each of these is governed by its own set of rules, regulations, and procedures stemming from macrosystems outside the school building (Welch, 1998, p. 30). Professionals within schools have limited opportunities to interact and solve problems. School schedules and physical layout perpetuate isolation of individuals and resources that minimizes direct communication between professionals (Ware, 1994). Schools have been described as "segmented, egg-crate institutions" in which teachers are isolated (McLaughlin & Yee, 1988, p. 40). It is relatively rare that teachers have regular exposure to best practice, say, in a 50-mile radius of where they work.

New communication technology holds out the promise of reducing the isolation of the teaching profession. No longer does the individual teacher need to feel that he or she is laboring alone in the classroom. Given the Internet, like-minded professional teachers are only a "click" away. Here are a few ways to use technology to communicate with others and access resources for teacher research.

Defining and Enriching Literature Searches

What are some specific examples of how teacher researchers have actually used technology within their research? How might we use technology to find researchers who have used technology in their action research? In what ways has technology helped them?

Technology can become a partner as you gather information related to questions that you may have. To discover resources related to research questions, we used two services within an Internet-based service called the Educational Resources Information Center (ERIC). ERIC is a federally funded national information system that provides a variety of information services related to a broad range of education-related issues.

Let's begin with a keyword search using ASK ERIC:

A. Think about some keywords that you can combine in order to focus your query so that you will get a manageable number of resources. We combined the terms: *technology in education, action research,* and *research methods.*

B. Open up your Internet software and type in the following URL: http://ericir.syr.edu/Eric/. See Fig. 4.3 later in this chapter for a template of this web page.

C. Type your terms into the spaces provided: Term 1, Term 2, Term 3. You focus your search by choosing AND between terms. You can expand your search by choosing OR between terms. For example, in the search we conducted, we labeled my terms "technology in Education" AND "Action research" OR "qualitative research methods". Doing this, we received a list of all articles combining technology in education with the broader category of action research and qualitative research methods.

D. Click Submit. You will be advanced to a page in which you can check to make sure that ERIC has received your terms correctly. If correct, click Submit again. If incorrect, click your Back button to return to the previous page, and retype your terms.

E. ERIC will provide you with a list of resources. You can read the abstracts of each resource by clicking on its corresponding link.

Another way to gather resources is to use an ERIC service that invites you to actually submit a questionnaire. A research specialist will take that questionnaire, devise a search strategy, and send you the results of the search to you via e-mail.

A. Using your Internet connection, go to the following web page: http://www.askeric.org/Qa/
Complete the form by indicating your name and e-mail address. Type in a question that you would like answered. Louanne asked a research specialist the following: "I am looking for information and resource materials for teachers wishing to begin the process of action research. In particular, I would like to find resources where they can connect with other people—i.e. discussion forums related to teacher action research. Thank you!"

B. Continue to complete the form. For example, one question asks: "Would you like our response to address any specific educational level(s)? Check any that apply." You then indicate any areas between early childhood through adult education.

C. When complete, you may submit your query by clicking the Submit button. Within 2 business days you will receive a list of print and electronic resources. Louanne's query resulted in a listing of 33 resources!

Teacher researchers can also extend and enrich their literature searches by finding bibliographic references cited in educational papers published on the web. Rick Parkeny, an educational researcher, wrote: "There are many articles, either published originally or as WEB-docs or as reprinted from traditional venues, that have wonderful reference lists—use these to supplement traditional lit-searches" (personal communication, August 2, 1999).

Conducting Interviews and Focus Groups

Louanne began using technology as a way to conduct interviews with individuals across geographic boundaries (Smolin, 1998). Through a colleague, she posted a message on a computer science professionals' listserv asking female computer scientists to discuss their high school computing experiences. Five women participated in this project. Because these interviews occurred through e-mail, they were ongoing. Therefore, rather than scheduling one or two interviews with each women, Louanne was able to establish and maintain an ongoing dialogue with each woman over a 5-month period of time. Data analysis did not require any transcription of audiotapes. Through her e-mail program, all communication could be stored on Louanne's hard drive. (See chap. 3 for more on doing interviews for teacher research.)

Although these interviews were rich and informative, they were one-way. Louanne could interact with each participant, and each partici-pant could interact with one another if e-mail addresses were shared. However, they could not all communicate as a group. Since that time, Louanne has become more and more familiar with other electronic ways to communicate. These ways can go beyond one-on-one dia-logues. Louanne's ERIC Q and A search led her to not only print re-sources, but to electronic resources such as discussion forums, listservs, and chats.

Discussion forums, listservs, and chat rooms build upon the capabil-ity of e-mail to connect individuals who may or may not be separated by time and place. They each have unique features that distinguish them from e-mail and from each other. Discussion forums, listservs, and chat rooms are different from e-mail, because, rather than private person-to-person communication, they are person-to-group and group-to-group communication. Although they are restricted to only those in-dividuals who subscribe, they are nonetheless public because many people can subscribe to these services.

Discussion forums and listservs differ from one another. The best way to describe this difference is through a metaphor of a bulletin board and how an individual interacts with a bulletin board. We see bulletin boards all over the place . . . in our schools, in grocery stores, and at the professional conferences that we attend. Generally, bulletin boards are organized around themes or topics. A school bulletin board might list upcoming events. A classroom bulletin board might be de-voted to current events. Although these bulletin boards are ever-present, we only use them when we want or need to use them.

When using a listserv, all messages posted on the listserv are sent to the subscriber, even if he or she has not requested that specific infor-mation. In contrast, a discussion forum subscriber "goes to" a bulletin board that is posted somewhere—usually on the World Wide Web. Mes-sages do not come through that subscriber's e-mail, and the subscriber can decide when he or she wants to read messages by accessing the fo-rum's particular World Wide Web site.

Figures 4.1 and 4.2 show examples of a listserv and a discussion fo-rum and how each is accessed. In Fig. 4.1, notice that listserv messages are accessed through an individual's e-mail program, in this case Louanne's. What you can see are the results of Louanne's query to the

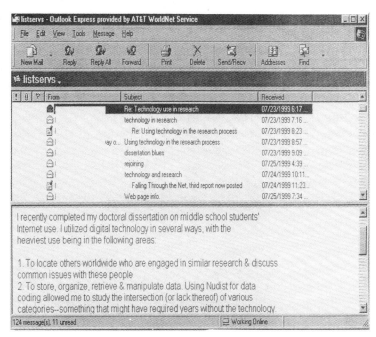

FIG. 4.1. E-mail program showing listserv messages.

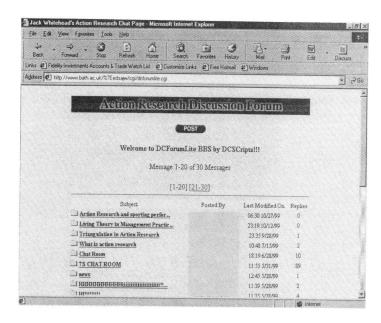

FIG. 4.2. Jack Whitehead's action research web site.

listserv requesting subscribers to discuss their use of technology in research. Out of nine messages that are displayed, five relate to her query and the remaining four do not. Yet she receives all of the messages, even those she may not be interested in reading.

Discussion Forums. Discussion forums and listservs are electronic bulletin boards. They differ from one another in the way that we interact with them. Similar to the way we interact with actual bulletin boards, we go to a discussion forum. It is a public space in which anyone who subscribes may enter. Once we have entered a forum, we can read messages that members send. Messages are topically organized, so when one person sends a message about a particular topic and another person responds or adds to it, a "thread" is formed.

A discussion forum is accessed through a World Wide Web address or by using specialized "newsreader" software. Figure 4.2 shows an example of an action research discussion forum that is accessed via a web page.

To read a message, one can click on the message of interest. In Fig. 4.3, Louanne chose to read messages related to feminism and action re-

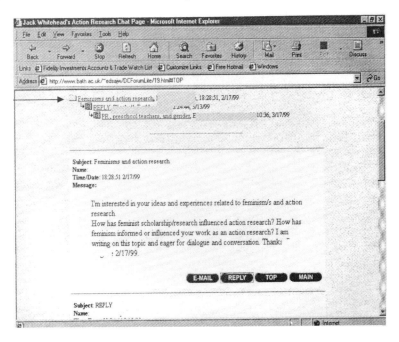

FIG. 4.3. A discussion "thread."

search. This topic is called a *thread*, because in addition to the original message, there are two replies. Notice the communication and navigation "buttons" located on the bottom right-hand side of the message form. The *communication* buttons allow a reader to interact within the message thread. For example, if Louanne wanted to add her thoughts to this particular feminism and action research thread, she could either e-mail a private comment that would only be received by the author of the message, or post a new message to the thread by selecting Reply. In so doing, anyone who reads this discussion thread would have access to Louanne's reply. *Navigation* buttons enable a reader to move more easily within a discussion forum. In the feminism and action research thread, if Louanne wanted to return to the beginning of the thread, she would choose Top. To return to the main menu of the forum (as pictured in Fig. 4.2), she would choose Main.

Discussion forums differ in the ways that an individual subscribes to them. Usually, one must fill out a form posted on the web site by the managers of the forum; the form includes e-mail addresses and asks the new subscriber to choose a password. The new subscriber then sends off the form via the web page and will generally get confirmation through e-mail that he or she has become a member. Instructions for login and logout are then provided.

There are many discussion forums related to content areas. These forums may be helpful to you at different stages in your research process. For example, you may join a subject matter discussion forum to learn how others are working in an area similar to the one in which you are interested. If you do so, think about:

- What are other researchers saying about your topic?
- How are the experiences that led them to question a phenomena similar to your own? How are they different?
- How is an ongoing conversation with practitioner researchers going to affect you and your research?

It is possible that new avenues of thought will open up for you. You may find that by communicating with others, your insights into your questions are growing. Perhaps they will help you to refine and focus your questions.

Here is a listing of some content area discussion forums:

http://forum.swarthmore.edu/join.forum.html The Math Forum is an online community related to math education. This forum is committed to providing discussion between all individuals interested in math. After entering this site, choose Public Discussions at the Math Forum for a listing of discussion forums related to math education.

http://www.ncte.org/chat/ The National Council of Teachers of English sponsors a number of "talk" opportunities. After arriving at this web site, click on Web Forums to get a list of current online discussion threads.

http://www.ncss.org/wwwboard1/ When you arrive at the National Council for The Social Studies home page, click on Discussion Board. Then you may enter the Discussion Area. Next, you can either join an existing threaded discussion or post a new message. To post a new message, click on "To post a new message, click here," and fill in the form that has been provided. To check any replies, return to this web site, find your message query, and see whether any replies have been posted.

http://www.nsta.org/messages/ The National Science Teachers Association sponsors a discussion board. You can respond to messages by clicking on "Search the messages for a word or pattern." In this way you can quickly find any messages regarding your topic. You can also post new messages by choosing "Post a new message" and completing the form. To check any replies, return to this web site, find your message query, and see whether any replies have been posted.

Listservs. When we interact on a listserv, the bulletin board comes to us through our e-mail. Messages are not organized by topic. Whenever someone sends a message to a listserv, each subscriber to that listserv receives that message through his or her private e-mail. It is up to the subscriber to organize the messages by topic or theme. Sometimes listservs have many members and are very lively. Subscribers can receive hundreds of e-mail messages on a daily basis!

To join a listserv, you must send a message to that listserv using your e-mail. Generally, most listservs ask that you type the words "SUBSCRIBE Your Name" in the body of the message.

Louanne subscribed to three listservs. She had technical difficulties subscribing to one of them and experienced difficulty getting technical support. This was an indicator of a lack of stability in the service. This helped her to make a decision that this would not be a good listserv to join. To subscribe to the remaining two listservs she sent the following message (through e-mail) to each:

From: Louanne Smolin

To: XTAR

Subject: Using Technology in Teacher Research

I am currently collaborating on a chapter for a book entitled "Teachers Doing Research" edited by Burnaford, Hobson, and Fischer. I am specifically exploring how a researcher might integrate web-based resources within his/her research process. I am of course drawing on my experiences as a researcher, but am also talking to other researchers to develop a wider perspective. Using technology has helped me to generate a dialogue with others of similar interests. Technology has also helped me to organize data, helping me in my process of uncovering patterns and themes. In this way, technology tools have helped me to establish a very close relationship with my data . . . it has afforded me deeper access into that data.

For those of you involved in research, I would greatly appreciate any comments you have about your experiences using web-based technologies within your research process, and any insights about the connections between the internet and the research process. Of course, all will be cited. Thank you so much for your time!

Louanne Smolin, Assistant Professor, University of Illinois, Chicago

Louanne receives dozens of messages through her listserv subscriptions on a daily basis! Of course, because a subscriber to a listserv receives all messages sent to that listserv, only a percentage of the messages she received pertained to her questions.

There are a number of listservs related to teacher research. Following is a list of web sites for some of these. As you access their web site, you will be instructed how to subscribe.

XTAR http://listproc.appstate.edu:8000/guest/register Xstar is a listserv "intended to enable Teacher Researchers to share their inquiries, their questions and their findings, their insights, problems and suggestions with colleagues in schools and universities all over the world."

http://tile.net/lists/actionresearch.html This listserv is related to action research. To subscribe, click on the e-mail address and you will be provided with a message form to mail. Follow the directions to fill in the message.

http://tile.net/lists/trgroup.html This listserv is intended for teacher researchers. As for the preceding one, to subscribe, click on the e-

mail address and you will be provided with a message form to mail
and follow the directions indicating what to type in the body of the
message.

Chat. Chat rooms invite collaboration in real time. Chats differ from
discussion forums and listservs in that they are synchronous, rather
than asynchronous. When you participate in a chat, other collaborators
are doing so at the same time as you. The metaphor that describes a
chat is a room in which people gather together at specified times.

Create Your Own! Not finding what you need? Create your own! The
following three web sites offer individuals the ability to start their own
discussion forums and chats.

http://www.egroups.com/ Egroups offers individuals the ability to
start their own threaded discussion group. Once created, you can invite individuals to join your group by sending them an e-mail message. This service also provides the opportunity to engage in
"livetime" chats and to share web-site links with members of your
group. The service is free, but includes advertising.

http://www.nicenet.org Nicenet uses the Internet Classroom Assistant (ICA), an integrated web-page structure or template that teachers
can use to create a web presence. The ICA provides an individual with
the ability to create a home page, to organize conferences (i.e., discussion forums), to send and receive personal messages to all members
of the web site, and to share web-site links. To create a class with all of
these features, click on "Create a class." A form will guide you through
the development process. Once registered, you will receive a class
key that can be given to individuals interested in joining your website.

http://yahoo.com Yahoo offers many topically related newsgroups
and online chats, including those related to education. You can also
create your own chat room or club. To create a chat room, click on
Chat and follow the registration instructions. Once you are registered
you will have the ability to create a "club." In addition to livetime chat-
ting, once a club is formed, members can create discussion forums
and can share web links. For example, members in your club can discuss teacher research related to language arts and can share web
links that might be useful for teachers engaged in action projects related to language arts.

It remains to be seen how research will be affected by these new forms of communication. How is what we learn shaped by conversations with people we never meet in person? How is that form of inquiry different from seeking out individuals in our schools and communities, conducting interviews, and forming focus groups to explore a research interest? Can a research project employ both face-to-face research methods and technology-assisted methods with similar results or satisfaction? We continue to explore the answers to these questions.

Developing Conversations Between Creators and Consumers of Research

Through her listserv discussions, Louanne learned how some researchers use technology as a tool for their research. Many of these researchers shared that they use typical web search engines to find e-mail or web-page addresses of researchers that they have read. Researcher Anne Hird uses web-based university catalogs to locate educators that teach courses related to her research topic. She can then e-mail these individuals. Dr. Hird wrote: "As a medium for communication, email allows me to introduce myself and my research and state concisely my reason for contacting the person. In turn, the other person can respond at his/her convenience and to the extent to which he/she desires (in contrast to telephone in which a conversation can wander)" (personal communication, August 2, 1999).

http://www.csd.org/arc.html offers an online database. Individuals can use this database to look up others' work and contact them. Teachers can also use the database search on a grade level and content area. You are given a list of researchers, their abstracts, and their contact information, along with a link to the full text document.

These services provide a number of different ways for creators and readers of research to communicate. What are potential benefits of doing so? The Online Action Research Project (Strunk & Fowler-Frey, 1996) explored this question. The Online Action Research Project (OAR) was developed in 1992 to conduct action research related to English as a second language (ESL) and adult basic education (ABE) classroom practices. In addition to goals related to literacy, technology was infused throughout the project. Through the OAR project, "computer supported collaboration assisted teachers to develop and refine their research projects by providing the opportunity for ongoing dialog with research partners from different sites" (p. 1). An online database (1992) of project participants was also created to facilitate communication and collaboration between classroom researchers of like interests, to document research findings related to literacy, and to provide a forum for other teachers and educators interested in conducting action research.

OAR researchers communicated regularly with a participant partner and joined in a virtual meeting online once a month. Teacher researchers recorded their reflections about various aspects of engaging in action research as well as how communicating online with a partner influenced their attitudes toward working with computers. Although most of the reflections related to researchers' growing confidence and use of computers, some of their comments noted interesting connections between technology and action research. For example, one researcher, John Caliguiri, reported, "[Using the online network] gave me another purpose, one more directly related to my classroom experience. Setting a goal of communicating with my partner made me want to have something interesting to communicate" (cited in Strunk & Fowler-Frey, 1996, p. 203). It appears that for this researcher, a sense of audience and collaboration helped him to keep his research in focus, to reflect on it so that he would, in fact, have something to share.

Using technology also facilitated a strong focus on the local contexts of teacher researchers' classrooms. One participant noted that the online collaboration between participants and the technology support team created an aspect of peer coaching "by an entire team of dedicated, knowledgeable colleagues. I would not even compare this experience to an ordinary inservice. It was indeed more like participating in an electronic symposium centered on my classroom situation" (p. 5).

As we begin to think about research as a collaborative process, electronic network provide opportunities for us to expand our collegial networks if we so desire. In doing so, we can keep our research in focus, but have the potential to broaden our ideas about it. As we communicate with an expanding network of practitioner researchers, we are exposed to multiple perspectives that can serve to widen our understandings and deepen our insights into research.

RESEARCH SHAPING TECHNOLOGY: ONE RESEARCHER'S EXPERIENCE

Through Louanne's research into gender and technology, she learned that technology is more than a neutral tool. Rather, its use is situated within a culture. Researchers who have studied the cultural aspects of computing have noted that those involved in using computers actively interpret their interactions with them and use these interpretations to shape their technology use (Kerr, 1990; Schofield, 1995; Sheingold, Hawkins, & Char, 1984; Turkle, 1995). Just as our understanding of the world is shaped by our underlying assumptions and beliefs, so too are our interactions with computers. It is because of this that the computer becomes more than a neutral tool.

Turkle and Papert (1990, 1992) used a cultural lens to study females' interactions with computers. Their participants did not create computer programs using the dominant approach—a hierarchical, rule-driven, problem-solving method. They used alternative styles. These participants did not create their programs from an objective, distanced stance. Their interactions with their machines were characterized by negotiating behaviors, indicating that they were developing a relationship with the object. They each exemplified unique, personal styles. So, rather than seeing a dominant approach to programming, Turkle and Papert (1990, 1992) began to see a multiplicity of personal styles.

Louanne wanted to learn more about these styles and how an individual develops her programming style. Although Turkle and Papert (1990, 1992) discovered a multiplicity of programming styles, their discoveries occurred within the context of computing. Louanne was interested in looking both in and outside the computer classroom. As a way to understand how young women's experiences both in and outside the computer classroom relate to their engagement with technology, she interviewed a high school sophomore about her experiences with technology. She learned much about technology and about using technology in the research process through her literature study and her interactions with Kelly, her research participant.

How did what Louanne learned "about" technology from her research relate to "how" she and others can use technology within their research? Turkle and Papert (1990, 1992) discovered that many students of computing did not approach programming in the "normative" way that is characterized through an objective, distanced stance. Like Turkle's and Papert's discoveries, rather than distancing herself from her research, technology helped Louanne to keep her research close at hand. Technology helped her to bridge the gap between what she was seeing and what she was beginning to learn and to know. It helped her to delve deeply into her question and systematically analyze the data that facilitated her understanding of what she was seeing. It helped her to uncover insights about what she was learning.

Turkle and Papert (1990, 1992) saw that their participants developed unique programming styles that were very personalized and individualistic. Kelly helped Louanne to understand that these unique and personalized styles develop through relationships established with people and objects both in and outside of the computing environment. As Louanne learned about how others have used technology for their research, she saw that some researchers made similar meanings about using technology for research and this helped them in ways similar to the ways in which it helped her. Others made different meanings and therefore the ways in which they used technology within their research were different from her ways. Louanne realized that there is a multitude of unique and personal ways to use technology within research and that these ways are based on each researcher's unique personal experiences and relationships.

Here are some of the specific ways that researchers have used technology to explore their research data.

Conceiving and Organizing Data

Like many research questions, Louanne's inquiry encompassed a few major themes such as the history of technology, feminist studies, gender, and the sciences. A huge body of theoretical and research literature corresponding to these themes was readily available. Yet literature related to her specific question "how do young women interact with technology?" was slim. How could Louanne develop greater insight into her question by connecting these vast amounts of literature to her particular question? By connecting literature to her particular research, that question would grow. How could she let that happen without losing sight of her focus? How could she reframe her question so that she could make sense of it and again refine a focus?

Louanne began by organizing her word processed research journals and literature notes into themed "folders" stored on the hard drive of her computer. This was a start, but it was cumbersome because there was a limit to how many documents she could peruse at once. She used a tool called Inspiration, a computerized graphic organizer software program. As stated in the manual, Inspiration "is a powerful visual learning tool that inspires and enables students and adults to gather and construct ideas, organize thinking and share information." Inspiration helped Louanne generate ideas, expand her thoughts, discover connec-

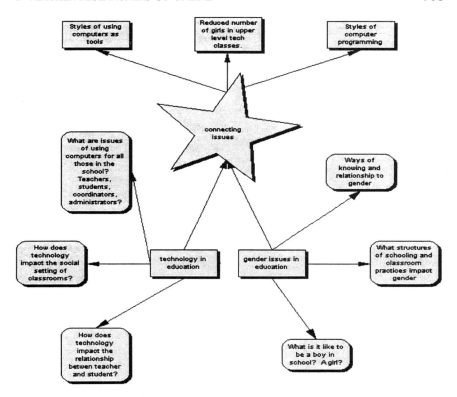

FIG. 4.4. Organizing thoughts about gender and technology using Inspiration software.

As you read this, think about your action research project or one that you think you would like to pursue. We invite you to download a demo version of Inspiration and experiment. Go to http://www.engagingminds.com/inspiration/descript.html and click on Download a demo version. Follow the steps to download.

You will receive a fully functioning program that you may explore for 30 days.

tions, and generate new ideas. Figure 4.4 shows an example of one of her early attempts to organize her thoughts about gender and technology.

The Inspiration software helped Louanne in many phases of her research. She was able to efficiently organize themes from the literature that would help her with a literature review. Following readings of literature, she used Inspiration to organize themes that emerged. As she began to collect data, she used this tool to connect what she was learning with her personal and professional experiences.

Analyzing and Interpreting Data

For her research, Louanne and Kelly engaged in weekly conversations over the course of approximately 6 months. Each interview generated between 40 and 70 pages of text. Needless to say, the thought of organizing and making sense out of these 300 pages of raw data was overwhelming.

Louanne used a qualitative data analysis (QDA) software program designed to organize raw observational and interview data. One example of a QDA software program is Nud*ist (Scolari/Sage Publications, www.scolari.com). With her computer and her QDA software, Louanne could transfer all of her "raw" text, or the exact words that were spoken during the interviews into a document, read from either printouts or her computer screen, and then use the QDA software to group this raw data into categories based on the patterns and themes that emerged as she read through the data. What would have taken her days and weeks took hours. She organized the data into patterns and themes, printed out pages and pages of this categorized data, and stepped back and read this product. In her mind, a troubling question kept surfacing: "So what?" What do all of these themes and patterns mean?

Two years later, after exploring QDA software, one of Louanne's students said to her, "I don't see the point of this . . . I would rather do this manually, with markers and scissors." So what? Although she used the technology, Louanne didn't spend much time thinking about how it actually helped her. How *do* the features of qualitative data analysis software impact the research process?

Knafl and Webster (as cited in Este, Sieppert, & Barsky, 1998) argued that "we can distinguish between data management, a *mechanical* process, and analytic activities, which are *conceptual* processes. Data management is a reductionistic activity in that data is converted to smaller, manageable units that can be manipulated and retrieved. Analytic activities are constructionist because they focus on processing these data pieces into new, conceptually based entities" (pp. 140–141). This is an important distinction. As teacher researchers, we can keep track of the data and keep it organized so that we can find what we are looking for by devising a *means of data management* using the computer. But to actually *analyze* the data requires a human being, the researcher, to actually think about and conceptualize the ideas and insights collected.

The qualitative data analysis software that Louanne used was "designed specifically as a tool for qualitative research that goes beyond the generic cut and paste features word processors in order to simplify the task of assigning codes to chunks of data, assembling the chunks that go together and thus reduce the volume of words into smaller and more *analyzable* units" (Handler & Turner, 1992, p. vii). By making the mechanical aspects more efficient, data became more analyzable.

How specifically did this happen? Although the software helped with the "mechanical tasks," it didn't do the thinking or lay out an analysis for Louanne. As Burnaford describes in chapter 3, the researcher still needs to identify categories through some kind of coding process. Teacher researcher Nancy Brankis wrote about the research process that she and her second graders engaged in. During this project, while her second graders kept journals, Brankis also kept a research journal. Reflecting on her journal, she wrote:

> I realize that even when not writing, my mind mentally writes as a researcher. I capture details, look for patterns, and am much more intimately involved in the process of learning than in its product. It was not the integration of journals in the classroom that has made such a profound impact on learning with my students. It was my personal discovery that I am more comfortable orchestrating learning than controlling it. (See Brankis teacher story after this chapter.)

There is a connection between this passage and technology. For Brankis, journal writing was a technology that she and her students used. Yet, as she wrote, it wasn't the "technology" itself that had the impact on her learning, it was her personal discovery. The process of using technology to "crunch data" helps a researcher get closer to the data.

Technology helped researcher Anne Hird posed questions that emerged through the process of her analysis. In her discussion of the virtues of speed and efficiency that data analysis software provided her, she stated, "Yes, I could have completed some of the same data analysis tasks without Nud*ist, but my questions and data would have been 'stale' by then. The depth of my research is in part due to my asking questions in the analysis that I might not have asked given a manual coding system" (personal communication, August 2, 1999).

As a way to explore the relationship between technology and learning, students in St. Pierre-Hirtle's language arts class used electronic portfolios. In one journal, a student wrote that technology helped to "bring my ideas to the screen. Technology gives me an alternative way of communicating my ideas instead of just writing on paper" (St. Pierre-Hirtle, 1996, p. 87). Through her observations and reflections on their writings, St. Pierre-Hirtle realized that

> technology can serve multiple purposes in the classroom. In addition to its support of organizational and procedural issues, it enhanced students' abilities to compose, revise, and edit. My language arts students felt that, as long as their work was saved on a disk, they were never done, and they wanted to continue making changes. (p. 87)

Rather than focusing on an end product, what became important to St. Pierre-Hirtle's students was the process of editing and revising. Using technology helped her students to continually dig deeper and "tinker," moving back and forth between what was in their minds and what was on the screen.

As these researchers discovered, Dreyfus (1992) noted that "software will not build theories for researchers, but it can support the researchers' efforts by helping organize data into coherent forms" (p. 141). Yet, although qualitative research software can facilitate a researcher's process, some note concerns. For example, if a teacher researcher assumes that the mechanical and analytic processing of data are one and the same, then he or she may assume that it is the software that does the analysis, and not the researcher. This assumption may lead a researcher to become distanced from the research. "There is a danger that the technology could assume precedence over the art of qualitative research, as the technology-based processes dictate the nature and path of inquiry on the part of researchers," rather than the researcher directing the inquiry (Hesse-Biber, as cited in Este et al., 1998, p. 141).

PUBLISHING TEACHER RESEARCH IN HARD COPY OR ONLINE

A continuing problem in public schooling is the relative lack of classroom teacher influence on teacher education programs in colleges and universities as well as on the profession at large. The educational research establishment has pretty much ignored teachers' knowledge of their craft. In a recent edition of the *Handbook of Research on Teaching*, published by the American Educational Research Association, there are 35 chapters and a thousand pages, yet not one chapter was written by a classroom teacher. There are, in fact, few references to anything a teacher has written (Zeichner, 1994, pp. 71–72).

Stenhouse (1975) emphasized the importance of teachers making public their research so that other teachers can benefit from what they learned, and so that teacher educators, university researchers, and policymakers can incorporate the knowledge generated by teacher researchers into courses for preservice or practicing teachers.

One of the odd and telling truisms about the subject of educational research is how comparatively few studies there are of university teaching. It also appears that university teachers are not known for using in their own teaching the practices they urge on teachers in elementary and secondary schools (Cuban, 1984). Perhaps a more practical inquiry would provide a welcome antidote to a current educational practice that separates knowledge about teaching and learning from the practice of teaching and learning (Ayers, 1990).

Elementary teacher Lynne Yermanock Strieb offered:

> When people hear I'm a first grade teacher their eyes glaze over; when they hear that I write about my teaching, they are much more interested. That doesn't make me happy. It is my teaching that I want valued more than the writing and publishing. At the same time, I believe it is partly through the sharing of stories about classrooms, in our own words, that teaching and teachers will come to be valued by the public at large. (Threatt et al., 1994, p. 227)

It appears that the voice of the classroom-based teacher researcher is increasingly finding venues in which to be read. There are an increasing number of professional journals, both print and electronic, that publish the work of practitioners, including several that make a point of showcasing the research of classroom teachers.

Teaching and Change provides an open forum for reporting the experiences of classroom teachers. It is a journal in which teachers from every level can discuss and debate the change process with Americans committed to helping students learn. The journal is devoted to helping teachers as they work to strengthen their learning communities.

Networks: An Electronic Journal of Teacher Research is the first online journal dedicated to teacher research. The articles published cover teacher research, as well as research based on collaborative inquiry; they also cover issues related to teacher inquiry, such as methodology, ethics, book reviews, work-in-progress reports, responses to published articles, and discussions on current issues. The current issue is available at the web site for browsing (http://www.oise.utoronto.ca/~ctd/networks/); an index is also provided by topic and author. Also featured is a discussion forum for interaction with the authors and readers.

The Alliance for Achievement is an Annenberg Foundation-sponsored project, working in Chicago schools, that publishes teacher action research projects on a web page. Teachers in these schools visit each other's classrooms based on what they have shared and read there (http://www.adi@adi.org).

INFUSING TECHNOLOGY IN TEACHER RESEARCH

The influx of new technology seems like attempting to board a train while it is traveling at a very high speed (Rice, 1984). The train seems unlikely to derail, it carries a very large number of passengers, and it has picked up much momentum. And most surprising of all, it seems always to be ahead of schedule, traveling at ever faster speeds. The teacher's quandary seems to be how to get on the train without being run over (McMahen & Dawson, 1995). Or alternatively, perhaps a more appropriate image is that of cybersurfing, of trying to catch the technological wave (Dixon, 1999).

One of the most interesting research studies into the infusion of technology into schools is that sponsored by Apple Computer, called the ACOT (Apple Classroom of Tomorrow) research, in which researchers discovered that teachers passed through five stages: entry, adoption, adaptation, appropriation, and invention.

In the *entry* stage, teachers continued teaching as they had been, their most familiar tools continued to be blackboards, workbooks, textbooks, and ditto sheets, and they used these materials to support the familiar three activities of lecturing, student recitation, and seatwork. They "demonstrated little inclination to significantly change their instruction" (Sandholtz, Ringstaff, & Dwyer, 1997, p. 171). As the computers were introduced in their classrooms, they worried about these problems: discipline, resource management, and personal frustration.

In the *adoption* phase, their struggles seemed to abate as teachers learned to use technology to support familiar activities such as traditional textbook-based drill-and-practice instruction. Students still received lectures, performed recitations, and did individualized seatwork. Although technology was now present in the classroom, the instructional activity remained much the same, albeit with additional tools.

During *adaptation*, the technology began to be integrated into traditional classroom practice. The familiar forms of lecture, recitation, and seatwork were still the dominant formats for student work, but now these were assisted 30–40% of the time with word processors, databases, graphic programs, and computer-assisted instruction (CAI) packages. Now teachers were reporting that students produced more, faster. Teachers also noted that students were becoming more engaged in classroom tasks.

What happened in the *appropriation* phase, which generally occurred in the second year of the project, depended on each teacher's degree of individual mastery of the technology. As teachers reached this stage, their roles began to shift quite obviously and some new and different instructional patterns began to emerge:

> Team teaching, interdisciplinary project-based instruction and individually paced instruction became more and more common. . . . To accommodate more ambitions class projects, teachers even altered the foundation of the traditional school day: the master schedule. At both elementary and secondary schools, this type of teamed, project-based learning activity opened up opportunities to step back and observe the results of their own pedagogic shifts. What they saw was their students' highly evolved skill with technology, ability to learn on their own, and movement away from competitive work patterns toward collaborative ones. (Dwyer, Ringstaff, & Sandholtz, 1991, pp. 48–49)

The last stage of the ACOT model of instructional evolution, the *invention* phase, was intended to include the new learning environments that teachers will create. The changes reported by these researchers are very dramatic. Teachers moved from using the new technological resources simply for replicating traditional instructional strategies,

> to view learning as an active, creative, and socially interactive process then they were when they entered the program. Knowledge is now held more as something children must construct and less like something that can be transferred intact. The nature of these teachers' classrooms, the permissions they grant their students, and their own instructional behaviors demonstrate this shift in action. . . . The direction of their change was toward child-centered rather than curriculum-centered instruction, toward collaborative tasks rather than individual tasks, toward active rather than passive learning. (Dwyer et al., 1991, p. 50)

These are rather dramatic shifts. It's hard to know precisely to what to attribute them. Was it simply having the technology in the classrooms? Was it the fact that each and every teacher got a personal laptop to take and use at home, in addition to the desktops in the classroom? Was it that the project was being intensely studied and perhaps teachers were given opportunities and were actively encouraged to reflect on their own attitudes, assumptions, and beliefs about learning and instruction? Were teachers talking more with each other about what they were doing? Were they confronting their actions and reflecting critically on the results of their choices? The ACOT researchers assert that "Teachers beliefs may be best modified while they are in the thick of change, taking risks and facing uncertainty" (Sandholtz et al., 1997, p. 52).

How did ACOT teachers evolve through the stages? One of the ways was a support process called *unit of practice* (UOP). With this process, "teachers select a teaching episode that has been particularly successful in the past and then think about how they might enhance or extend it using technology"(Sandholtz et al., 1997, p. 123).

The unit of practice process could help you link your teacher action research with your classroom curriculum. As you use the techniques outlined in this book, how might you use them with your students in a curriculum piece in which you and your students have successfully engaged? For example, if your students are engaged in an inquiry project related to a specific topic, how might they use the software program Inspiration to brainstorm inquiry questions related to their topic? How might they use desktop publishing software to record information they are gathering and their reflections about this information in a double-entry journal? How might they join a discussion forum in order to dialogue with experts working in areas related to their topic of inquiry? If you are interested in such inquiry, please join the related discussion forum on the teachersdoingresearch.com web site.

TEACHERS CONNECTING TECHNOLOGY, TEACHING, AND RESEARCH

There is much to learn about how the use of computer technology for supporting the conduct of teacher research will impact on curriculum, instruction, and students in classrooms. As Cuban wrote, although teachers are using technology personally, this use doesn't always flow into classroom curriculum: a disjuncture exists. In one study, Hird

(1999) found that middle school students use the Internet differently at school than at home. At home the eighth graders are engaged in a variety of communications functions (including e-mail, chat rooms, and "instant messaging") that were not used in school even though the school's Internet use policy made provisions for use of e-mail and did not ban other communications functions. While at school the only Internet function they used was the Web, because teachers had the expectation that information on the Internet should be gathered in the same way that an encyclopedia or library book might be used.

Teenagers in school set aside the strategies they use at home for using the Internet. Hird believed that students are honoring what they perceive to be their teachers' understanding of the Internet, even though the students believe they know more than their teachers do about it. "Preserving the teacher–student relationship to which they are accustomed," Hird asserted, "takes precedence over maximizing the use of the Internet" (p. 8).

Having discovered that students did their most constructive online learning outside of school, Hird suggested that teachers may experience more freedom as online learners if they, too, learn to use the Internet for their own learning needs outside of school. She raised the thought-provoking idea that investing professional development resources exclusively in in-school applications may be a mistake. If teachers are fluent Internet users themselves before they take on the task of integrating technology into their teaching, perhaps they will be better able to envision new ways of infusing technology into their teaching.

This idea squares with our own personal experiences; we each began to explore the new technologies ourselves for our own learning and then later introduced various of the practices we discovered into our teaching. The frontier for experimentation with computer technology for many teachers may be found at home, as well as at school, and it may be as much in the search for personal learning as in strictly school applications. Professional development is not an exclusively in-school phenomenon.

Perhaps using technology within the teacher research process can serve as a license for experimentation, providing an effective bridge between teachers' personal use of computers and integrating them within classrooms. We learned that, as we used some of the techniques described in this chapter in conducting teacher research, our role underwent a fundamental change from teacher to learner. In this role of learner, we discovered that all of the things we were doing, our students could also be doing in their work as learners. We assume that you may be experiencing a similar process as you read these pages; you are likely thinking about how to use some of the technology in your classroom. You may already be embarking on a learning curve bridging your personal use of computers to your classroom instruction, and to teacher research.

INTERNET RESOURCES SUPPORTING TEACHER RESEARCH

Abstracts and Articles

Action Research Collaborative of Greater St. Louis offers abstracts of teacher research projects which can be accessed by grade level and/ or key categories. Contact information is also provided: http://www. csd.org/arc.html

Action Research in England: The Center for Action Research in Professional Practice at Bath University, U.K. sponsors this web page from which one can download abstracts and articles: http://www.bath.ac. uk/~edsajw

Alliance for Achievement Teacher Action Research Project Abstracts sponsored by the Annenberg Foundation are published on this site: http://www.adi@adi.org

Educational Action Research is an international journal concerned with exploring the unity between educational research and practice: http:// www.triangle.co.uk/ear/index.htm

Networks: An OnLine Journal for Teacher Research: Organized by Gordon Wells at the University of Toronto publishes the work of teacher researchers and book reviews online and offers access to the XTAR listserv: http://www.oise.utoronto.ca/~ctd/networks

Ontario Action Researcher: The *Ontario Action Researcher* is a refereed electronic journal intended for elementary, secondary, and university teachers. The primary aim is to serve the needs of teachers in Ontario, however, readership and writing from elsewhere in Canada and the world are welcomed. The *Ontario Action Researcher* promotes the development of educational knowledge through action research by elementary, secondary, and university teachers. Within this context, the journal strives to support personal and professional growth. http://www.unipissing.ca/oar/

Reading Online is an electronic journal of classroom literacy practice and research for K–12 educators, especially as it supports the integration of digital and networked technologies in classrooms through forums: http://www.readingonline.org

ERIC Database Resources

Search the ERIC Database, the world's largest source of education information, with more than 1 million abstracts of documents and journal articles on education and practice: http://ericir.syr.edu/Eric/

Ask ERIC: Use an on-line form to ask the ERIC staff for assistance in identifying resources on your research topic: http://askeric.org/

Discussion Boards From the Subject Areas

Math Forum: This is the math education community center on the Internet: http://forum.swarthmore.edu/join.forum.html

National Council for the Social Studies (NCSS) sponsors a discussion board that is accessed by going to the home page and then clicking on Discussion board: http://www.ncss.org/

National Council of Teachers of English (NCTE) "Conversations" entry page will be found here: http://www.ncte.org/chat

National Science Teachers Association (NSTA) sponsors a discussion board: http://www.nsta.org/messages/

The National Writing Project (NWP) Virtual Institute: This site will connect you with numerous resources for teacher researchers into writing and show you how to join the "Netheads"—an NWP networking special interest group—as well as lead to the home pages of the various NWP sites and upcoming MOO resources: http://www-gse.berkeley.edu/Research/NWP/VirtInst/index.html

LDOnLine offers a variety of resources including audio clips, bulletin boards, chats, an Internet calendar, a newsletter, as well as a search function that can be accessed by either issues or authors: http://www.ldonline.org

Listservs

Action Research Listserv can be accessed: http://tile.net/lists/actionresearch.html

RTEACHER: The mailing list (listserv) for *The Reading Teacher* on which you can participate in online discussions about issues of literacy, technology and teacher research: http://web.syr.edu/~djleu/RTEACHER/directions.html

XTAR: This listserv is sponsored by Appalachian State University for teacher researchers to communicate with each other: http://listproc.appstate.edu:8000/quest/register

Other Resources

Blackboard.com: This is a free online course web site that supports the creation of a virtual class featuring threaded discussions and real-time chat capabilities with 5 MB of space. http://www.Blackboard.com

Egroups.com offers individuals the ability to start their own threaded discussion group. This site is supported by imbedded advertising: http://www.egroups.com

Nicenet.org web pages for teachers: Make your own class web page by using the online template provided. Class members register for this free service by using a special class "key": http://www.nicenet.org

Yahoo.com offers news groups and online chats and allows you to create your own chat room: http://yahoo.com

Recent books on action research are available on a page from the Southern Cross University site: http://www.scu.edu.au/schools/sawd/arr/books.html#a-9

Action Research Laboratory for High School Teachers: A model of professional development for teachers at Highland Park High School in Illinois: http://mypage.goplay.com/Action_Research_Laborator/home.html

Education World: A listing of over 110,000 education web links by a commercial provider: http://www.education-world.com/

REFERENCES

Ayers, W. (1990). Rethinking the profession of teaching: A progressive option. *Action in Teacher Education, 1*(12), 1–5.

Bruce, B. (1999). Challenges for the evaluation of new information and communication technologies. *Journal of Adolescent and Adult Literacy, 42*(6), 450–455.

Clausing, J. (1999, December 10). A push to narrow disparities in training and access to the web. *New York Times*, p. A25.

Cox, C. (1987). An interview with Seymour Papert. *Curriculum Review, 26*(3), 14–18.

Cuban, L. (1984). *How teachers taught: Constancy and change in American classrooms 1890–1980.* New York: Longman.

Cuban, L. (1986). *Teachers and machines: The classroom use of technology since 1920.* New York: Teachers College Press.

Cuban, L. (1999, August 4). The technology puzzle: Why is greater access not translating into better classroom use? *Education Week,* pp. 68–47.

Darnton, R. (1999, March 18). The new age of the book. *New York Review of Books,* pp. 5–7.

Digital Divide. (1999, July 9). *New York Times,* p. A12. National Telecommunications and Information Administration. Available at web site: http://www.ntia.coc-gov.

Dillner, M. (1999, April). *Interactivity as a model for electronic publication and peer review.* Paper presented at the annual meeting of the American Educational Research Association, Montreal, Canada.

Dixon, J. (1999). Cybersurfing: A new professor catches the wave. In C. Falba, N. Studler, T. Bean, J. Dixon, P. Markos, M. McKiney, & S. Zehm (Eds.), Choreographing change one step at a time. *Action in Teacher Education, 21*(1), 61–75.

Dreyfus, H. (1992). *What computers still can't do: A critique of artificial reason.* Cambridge: MIT Press.

Dwyer, D., Ringstaff, C., & Sandholtz, J. (1991). Changes in teachers' beliefs and practices in technology-rich classrooms. *Educational Leadership, 48*(8), 45–52.

Este, D., Sieppert, J., & Barsky, A. (1998). Teaching and learning qualitative research with and without qualitative data analysis software. *Journal of Research on Computing in Education, 31*(2), 138–154.

Handler, M., & Turner, S. (1992). *Data Collector.* Intellimation Library for the Macintosh, Santa Barbara, CA.

Hird, A. (1999). *Middle school students' classroom Internet use: An ethnographic study of technology use and constructivist learning.* Unpublished dissertation, University of Rhode Island–Rhode Island College.

James, F. (1999, September 24). Computers flunking in schools, poll finds. *New York Times,* p. 17.

Jerald, C., & Orlofsky, G. (1999, September 23). Raising the bar on school technology. *Education Week,* p. 59.

Kerr, S. T. (1990). Technology: Education: Justice: Care or thoughts on reading Carol Gilligan. *Educational Technology, 30*(11), 7–12.

McLaughlin, M., & Yee, S. M. (1988). School as a place to have a career. In A. Lieberman (Ed.), *Building a professional culture in schools* (pp. 23–44). New York: Teachers College Press.

McMahen, C., & Dawson, A. J. (1995). The design and implementation of environmental computer-mediated communication (CMC) projects. *Journal of Research on Computing in Education, 27*(3), 318–335.

Moore, M., & Kearsley, G. (1996). *Distance education: A systems view.* Boston: Wadsworth.

Online Action Research Database. (1992). Washington, DC: National Institute for Literacy. (ERIC Document Reproduction Service No. ED 372 302)

Postman, N. (1995). *The end of education: Redefining the value of school.* New York: Knopf.

Rice, R. E. (1984). Evaluating new media systems. In J. Johnston (Ed.), *Evaluating the new information technologies* (pp. 53–71). San Francisco: Jossey-Bass.

Sandholtz, C., Ringstaff, C., & Dwyer, D. (1997). *Teaching with technology: Creating student centered classrooms.* New York: Teachers College Press.

Schofield, J. W. (1995). *Computers and classroom culture.* Cambridge: Cambridge University Press.

Smolin, L. (1998). *The story behind the keys: A phenomenological exploration of a female student and her relationship with technology.* Unpublished dissertation, National-Louis University, Evanston, IL.

Sheingold, K., Hawkins, J., & Char, C. (1984). I'm the thinkist, you're the typist: The interaction of technology and the social life of classrooms. *Journal of Social Studies, 40*(3), 49–61.

St. Pierre-Hirtle, J. (1996). Technology and reflection: Knowing our world and our work. In Z. Donoahue, M. Van Tassel, & L. Patterson (Ed.), *Research in the classroom: Talk, texts, and inquiry* (pp. 81–90). Newark: International Reading Association.

Stenhouse, L. (1975). *An introduction to curriculum research and development.* London: Heinemann.

Strunk, S. J., & Fowler-Frey, J. (1996). *ESL online action research.* Final report. Lancaster, PA: Lancaster-Lebanon Intermediate Unit 13. (ERIC Document Reproduction Service No. ED 406 861)

Threatt, S., Buchanan, J., Morgan, B., Strieb, L., Sugarman, J., Swenson, J., Teel, K., & Tomlinson, J. (1994). Teachers' voices in the conversation about teacher research. In S. Hollingsworth & H. Sockett (Eds.), *Ninety-third yearbook of the National Society for the Study of Education* (pp. 222–244). Chicago: University of Chicago Press.

Turkle, S. (1995). *Life on the screen: Identity in the age of the internet.* New York: Simon and Schuster.

Turkle, S., & Papert, S. (1990). Epistemological pluralism: Styles and voices within the computer culture. *Signs: Journal of Women in Culture and Society, 16*(1), 128–157.

Turkle, S., & Papert, S. (1992). Epistemological pluralism and the reevaluation of the concrete. *Journal of Mathematical Behavior, 11*(1), 3–33.

Ware, L. P. (1994). Contextual barriers to collaboration. *Journal of Educational and Psychological Consultation, 5,* 339–357.

Welch, M. (1998). Collaboration: Staying on the bandwagon. *Journal of Teacher Education, 49*(1), 26–37.

Zeichner, K. (1994). Personal renewal and social construction through teacher research. In S. Hollingsworth & H. Sockett (Eds.), *Teacher research and educational reform: Ninety-third yearbook of the National Society for the Study of Education* (pp. 66–84). Chicago: University of Chicago Press.

In Practice—Part I

1. Using one of the guidelines in chapter 2 or the series of questions that follow, devise a plan to present to your district for funding to support your teacher action research project. Decide who the plan should be introduced to and when.

   District Funding Proposal questions might include:

   - What do you want to study?
   - Why is this study important to you?
   - What will be the scope of your inquiry?
   - What kind of information do you think you will need to conduct your research?
   - Are you interested in collaborating on this project?
   - If so, with whom?
   - What materials do you think you will need?

   Estimate costs for your research. Provide a tentative timeline.

2. Once you have developed a working plan or proposal for your research, construct a preliminary picture. What do you know already about your issue or topic? What currently exists? What has occurred previously in your own experience or in your building?

3. Choose one article that describes some aspect of your research topic or interest. Write to the author of that article, explaining how your current research will contribute to that author's understanding of the topic.

4. Visit three web sites noted in chapter 4 that pertain to teacher research. Report the major points of interest and discussion on those web sites. Critique each one for its communicative ability, interest level, and timely focus.

5. Visit three web sites related to your research topic or focus. Report what each might contribute to your work. Critique each one for its communicative ability, interest level, and timely focus.

6. Even though your research is based in your own classroom and/or school context, find at least one research partner/informant on line to converse or share data with. How does long-distance, non-face-to-face collaboration affect your research?

7. Write a letter or send an e-mail to one of the teacher researchers in this book. What are you interested in asking that teacher? What common experiences do you have to discuss?

8. Begin to keep a teacher research journal in which you maintain a "written record of practice." After writing daily for a week or two, try writing a "journal of the journals" as Hobson describes in chapter 1. What themes or recurring patterns occur, if any? How does the journal inform you about what is happening in your classroom?

DISCOVERING THE REAL LEARNER WITHIN: JOURNAL KEEPING WITH SECOND-GRADE CHILDREN

Nancy Brankis
Lincolnshire-Prairie View Schools

In my practice as a second-grade teacher, "burn-out" hadn't yet arrived, but the idea of returning each day to the same classroom with the prescribed curriculum had lost its luster. Certainly, I explored through staff-development sessions and educational texts the ideals of integrated curriculum, thematic approaches, process writing, whole language philosophy, and all the other up-to-date suggested practices. Yet the comfortable, real implementation of these approaches to learning was not truly finding its way into my classroom in any cohesive form.

In the midst of trying desperately to actualize my teaching practice, I entered a graduate program and began the life of an adult student. Parallels existed between my adult classroom learning situation and the environment of my second-grade students. Both groups were in self-contained situations, both had curricula and certain texts with requirements, and all of us shared the trepidations of school life.

Part of the requirement in my graduate program was to keep a daily journal of my own thoughts, questions, experiences, and practices as an educator. The idea of having to maintain a response journal on a daily basis without boundaries was foreign and unsettling to me. I really didn't understand its purpose or reward. Busywork did not appeal to me, yet I had the expectation that all children should be motivated to accomplish my prescribed tasks, so why shouldn't that same expectation apply to me as a student? I decided to give it my best shot and started writing. After a time, I found a pattern emerging in my journal entries. My teaching seemed to be a series of wonderfully crafted units, themes, and projects, yet they were all defined by *me*. I felt glory in the products that resulted. Yet I began to question, "Where is the child?" in the scheme of the learning.

Through the process of keeping a journal, I recognized how I had gone through my teaching life seeing it as a series of lesson plans; I had not been highly reflective, and seemed to move from one year to the next without really looking at why I was doing things. Sullivan (1989) referred to a journal as the "Lost and Found" of the self. I began to take notice of my own revitalized desire to learn and wondered about the power of response journaling and its implications for use in my own second-grade setting.

No journaling experiences existed for my students and I began to envision its potential impact. Journal writing, I imagined, could be a means of providing wholeness to a curriculum. I felt it could be used as a timeline of student growth and an eventual table of contents. It could be a place where one's life and learning had a place to authentically unfold.

RESEARCHING AND IMPLEMENTING JOURNALS IN CLASSROOMS

Research begins when one starts to question, wonder, and seek answers. Journal writing is quite a personal method of learning and one that I theorized could accommodate any student at any level of functioning. I had questions that needed answers. In what ways would students' critical thinking skills evolve? How would students use journal writing as a place to capture thought, organize and clarify thinking, reflect, and grow as learners? In what ways can journaling stimulate questioning and self-learning? How does journal writing provide connections, coherence, and a framework for learning? Are students becoming more empowered in their learning as a result of personal journals? I certainly had an agenda in tackling the topic of journal writing across the curriculum. I wanted to capture with my own group of students the impact that journaling was having on changing myself from a passive learner to a very active, passionate participant.

I had developed a focus for researching journal writing, but it was time to move from speculation to the actual collection of data. I shared my intent to research journal writing with my graduate peers and principal, as well as with other teachers in my school. There were several of us who had similar interests and we formed an informal research "buddy group." As a group of researchers, we linked up and developed a network of sharing data. My topic seemed infectious! Teachers fed me helpful articles and wanted to know how to implement journals in their classrooms, as soon as I figured it all out. My principal anxiously awaited a future time when I could share what I was doing with the staff. Re-familiarizing myself with the university library was accomplished and many searches for materials were completed. At last with a roomful of books, journal articles, people to interview, my own personal research journal, and the computer turned on, I was ready to begin.

> Research Plan Entry: Finally, I'm starting my project. I've assembled numerous books and articles and don't know where to begin. What is it that I'm really trying to do? How many articles will be needed? How to assemble all this knowledge by "experts" into some pattern. Am I excited? Hmmm. I'm starting with *Active Voice* by James Moffett. I like some of his chapter headings.

> (Four days later) Sitting at dining room table trying to figure out where to begin. Find out what experts in the field have found to be true for them. Now how to figure out exactly how to put all info together. I think I'll read, jot down ideas and see if groups of knowledge emerge.

> (Twenty days later) I am struggling. I have no motivation to begin this project. I guess I don't have a plan and it's disturbing me. I don't know how to fit this together. In bed the other night, some ideas did come to me.

Good journals, according to Fulwiler (1987), have common features regardless of subject and age level. The journal is written in the first person. It focuses on the "I" and demonstrates what the writer thinks as opposed to what others think. Journals are ongoing debates with the writer and his or her several selves. Language is natural and experimentation with style is a feature. Journalers have more questions than they have answers. They speculate and wonder aloud on paper about meaning, events, issues, facts, readings, and find it a free place to experiment without fear of condemnation.

"The importance of a responsive audience is confirmed by research showing that children invent more interest and energy in journal writing when their teacher writes back to them" (Calkins, 1986, p. 101). Students are able to communicate freely at a more complex level. Inventive spelling is encouraged and language mechanics are determined by the student's own level of written language functioning. By responding directly to students' journals, the teacher is able to model conventional spelling, syntax, and mechanics, and elaborate on the students' earlier entries. An indirect editing process takes place.

D'Arcy (1987) explored the student–writer situation. She felt that teachers of writing look at the words on a page rather than through the words to the meaning. Teachers who concern themselves more with grammar, spelling, and mechanics tend to view writing as a code. She found that students come to form an impression of themselves as successful writers if they are able to encode. Students who struggle with this ability see themselves as failed writers. As a result of D'Arcy using journals in her classroom, she felt her students were freed to catch thoughts as they came, their own voices were heard, and they were given space for rehearsal and reflection in their journals. The students demonstrated their knowledge and gained confidence as learner–writers.

At first I felt compelled to read everything that even remotely related to the topic of using journals in a classroom. However, after some experience, I became more selfish and discriminating. I was drawn to those pieces of research that were done by teachers. There was such a personal element to their writings. Their investment in searching to make a difference for their students was so clear and inspiring. I found a camaraderie with those authors. These researchers all seemed to have a story to tell. Their motivation to change their teaching and involve students intimately in the learning process was evident. My research began with the reading and writing educators and later expanded to include math, science, and political science areas as well.

I chose the beginning of a new school year to begin my study. My new group came noisily flooding into the room with supplies bursting from their backpacks. I wanted us to capture this first day and so I pulled out a large stack of blank books. I started out by introducing the book as their own "Feelings Journal." Their very own book was a place in which they had the freedom to write about anything. The children had pencils, crayons, markers, and were busily creating their covers. As I watched, I noticed that different colors and themes reflected different children. Monsters, frogs, turtles, and rainbows all adorned their covers (see Fig. 1.1).

FIG. 1.1. Children's journal covers.

Research Journal Entry: I'm sure I'll quickly get to know their books, not by name but by cover. I just overheard, "You know, school isn't so bad."

Use of the "Feelings Journal" continued. There seemed to be an immediate acceptance and I wondered if the children had experienced using them before. Wonderful conversations were shared with many children desiring to know as much about me as I wished to know about them (see Fig. 1.2 for samples of these conversations).

Feeling such success, I decided to introduce the "Learning Journal." I explained that this was the journal that would have topics given to them in which they would be asked to respond in their own way about ideas learned in class. With the first topic given, questions were numer-

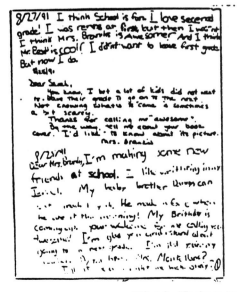
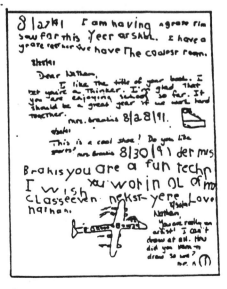

FIG. 1.2. "Feelings journal" conversations.

ous. "Can we make a list?" "How much do I have to write?" Some children immediately made excuses to go to the bathroom and others needed to sharpen their pencils. I answered as best I could, but really with no experience to support my replies.

> Research Journal Entry: Struggle. They aren't turned on by this. Only the third entry—maybe it will grow on them . . . like mold.

"Ahhhh" (yawn), says Matt. "Matt, I don't see anything in your journal." "I can't think of anything," he replies (see Fig. 1.3).

> Research Journal Entry: Alison continues to sharpen pencil. Four more pencil sharpenings. Ah, the quest to avoid journaling spreads. Many are not on task. They write one thing and say they're done. The extensions of thought, the build-up of critical thinking is not showing itself. Humming, whispering. It's started to rain; this distracts them. Oh great, now thunder!

We continued forward using our journals and started sharing our responses. I noticed that as they sat listening to others' ideas, they became quite passive. I realized the richness of conversations that were present, and needed a way for children to capture this exchange of ideas. I suggested that when they hear an idea that appealed to them, they should write that down in their journal. "Isn't that cheating?" asked one. It became apparent that the ethic of worksheets is to do one's own work. Therefore, the idea of cheating had already been instilled in them. It would be a hard task to challenge that idea in these very young, literal minds. "Oh, no!" I replied. "Sharing ideas and learning from each other is the way scientists have made great discoveries. As a matter of fact, I think that every time you would like to accept

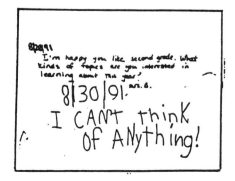
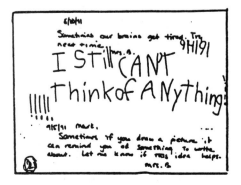

FIG. 1.3. "I can't think of anything."

someone else's idea, you should put a star next to it. That will show me that you are a star learner, a person able to learn from others."

> Research Journal Entry: I enjoy keeping my research journal and already find that I'm far more intimate with my class at this point in time as a result of these journals.

I found that as I continued to work with the journals the handling of them seemed to fall in place. I experimented and fine-tuned the process as we moved along. The beauty of the journal was that it allowed each child the decision to shape his or her learning. So many times in the past I had dictated what was to be learned. We shape children's learning through our questions and answers. This avenue for the collection of thought gave each child the freedom to outline, expand, and react to thoughts.

> Research Journal Entry: I'm letting the journals just be a part of their daily lives. The children know I don't collect them all the time, I don't edit or grade or really challenge them. It's funny—they don't seem to be writing less, trying to get out of work or appear unmotivated—they keep getting better and I'm doing less!
>
> Yes! I'm doing less. This might be the *key*. The ideas, thoughts, expressions come from them—not me—No control—No absolute answers. They own their journals. Maybe they *feel* because it is their journal, *truly theirs*—not mine that it is a free, honest, safe place to learn. No public arena to be embarrassed, wrong, just a SAFE place to think.

I had realized that the journals allowed each child to be heard in his or her own voice. Each child was unique and expressive. Prior to discussing my journaling research with fellow staff members, I asked each student to write a letter in his or her journal about their likes and dislikes of its use. I felt if they had an audience other than myself, they might be inspired to write and share their perceptions honestly.

Figure 1.4 shows one child's comment to teachers about journaling.

Through the use of my own detailed research journal and my current journal, I realize that even when not writing, my mind mentally writes as a researcher. I capture details, look for patterns, and am much more intimately involved in the process of learning than in its product. I believe that research is valid and vital if change is to occur. It was not the integration of journals in the classroom that has made such a profound impact on learning with my students. It was my personal discovery that I am more com-

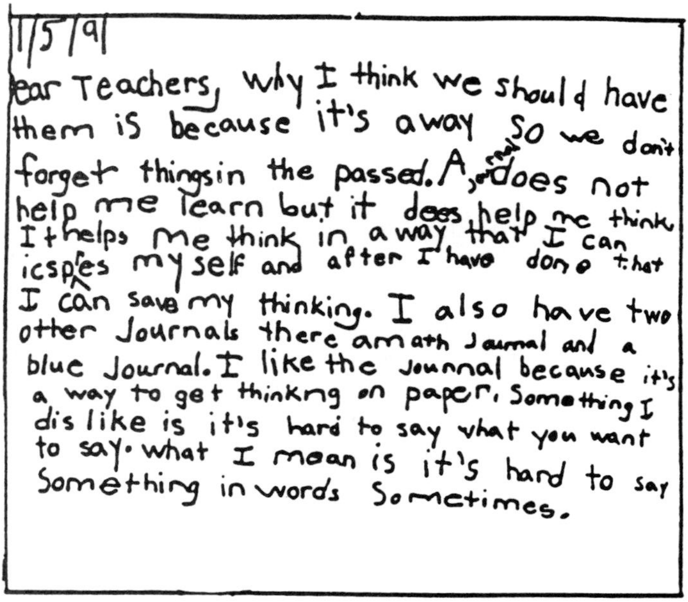

> 1/5/9|
>
> ear Teachers, why I think we should have them is because it's a way so we don't forget things in the passed. A does not help me learn but it does help me think, I helps me think in a way that I can icspies myself and after I have done that I can save my thinking. I also have two other Journals there am a math Journal and a blue Journal. I like the Journal because it's a way to get thinking on paper. Something I dis like is it's hard to say what you want to say. what I mean is it's hard to say Something in words Sometimes.

FIG. 1.4.   A child's view of journal writing.

fortable orchestrating learning than controlling it. Authentic teaching is a misnomer. It is the process of authentic learning that is powerful and life-long. I am no longer the teacher in the classroom, but rather the learner. I share in the process with my students and adult peers. We take responsibility in our learning and the creation of our own text. We reflect on our thoughts and self-evaluate. Research is discovery, but what I really discovered was myself.

REFERENCES

Calkins, L. (1986). *The art of teaching writing.* Portsmouth: Heinemann Educational Books.
D'Arcy, P. (1987). Writing to learn. In T. Fulwiler (Ed.), *The Journal Book* (pp. 41–46). Portsmouth: Boynton/Cook.
Fulwiler, T. (1987). *The Journal Book.* Portsmouth: Boynton/Cook.
Sullivan, A. (1989). Liberating the urge to write: From classroom journals to lifelong writing. *English Journal, 78,* 55–61.

Overcoming Paradigm Paralysis: A High School Teacher Revisits Foreign Language Education

Emmerich Koller
Glenbrook South High School

Whatever you can do or dream, you can begin.
Boldness has genius, power and magic in it.
Begin it now.

—Goethe, 1804

A NEW BEGINNING

At age 50, after 27 years of teaching, I have found something that has made teaching very exciting again. I am quite aware of the fact that by expressing such enthusiasm, especially among some of my more tired colleagues, I run the risk of being trivialized as an idealist, or someone who by some miracle escaped the disappointments that often come with many years in the trenches and therefore not qualified to address true veterans in the field. The fact is that I have not escaped most of the tribulations of public school teaching and I am well acquainted with that burned-out feeling. That, more than anything else, gives me legitimacy and a right to tell my story.

It is my hope to embolden my colleagues out there who might also be willing to dream as I did, regardless of age or specialty, and to encourage them as Goethe does: to begin it now. What follows is an account of how I managed to move from *paradigm paralysis* to a fundamentally new approach to my teaching.

There were several arguments against embarking on such an adventure. Two years ago, I would have argued against expending too much effort for an uncertain outcome. The daily demands of teaching and the extra, often unnecessary burdens placed on teachers by their administrators are often so demanding that any serious consideration of making a radical shift is usually dismissed outright. The other deterring element was the perception that something that works well enough shouldn't be fixed. I am a German teacher at a suburban high school north of Chicago and I have received national recognition for my work. My students have accumulated a record number of awards for their outstanding achievements in German. Obviously things were going well enough. Why change anything?

My reasons for change were, first, that I had been experiencing some dissatisfaction with the way my slower students fared in my classes. Second, I was determined not to allow myself to fade yet; I still wanted to learn and grow. Third, I've managed to maintain the basic belief that most students' potential is much greater than what we educators manage to elicit.

It has always been my professional goal to help my students realize their full potential and never to be content to settle for the average. I think most of my students have sensed my sincerity and faith in them and that, more than anything else, explains their success in the past. But there were others who did not succeed, whom I could not reach. In this I found the frustration and the dissonance in my professional life—the problem that I wanted to tackle and hopefully solve. And so I made it the task of my research project to find a way that would transform both the atmosphere and the learning process in my classroom, to such an extent that it would make learning truly joyful and, consequently, more effective. I decided to seek my solution where I had not looked before, in the exciting new findings of brain research. Isn't it curious that as professionals dealing with the mind, we teachers in general show little interest in the functioning of the brain? Even a cursory glance at brain research and its implications for education made me realize that the task I was about to undertake was not going to be a mere intellectual exercise. For so many years I have successfully used traditional concrete-sequential teaching methods that called for a lot of memorization on the part of my students. I felt safe and secure with that approach. It brought me respect within my profession and my students occasionally feared me as a *macho* teacher, dubbing me "Killer Koller." As I became aware of the unusual methods that brain-based teaching called for and the fundamental changes I would have to undergo, I came to know the real meaning of *paradigm paralysis*. It stands for a real monster that makes any significant change difficult, if not impossible.

A MONSTER WITHIN US

Confronting my paralysis often reminded me of a story by Dick Gackenbach (1977) called *Harry and the Terrible Whatzit* that I used to read to my little daughter. There was this little boy, Harry, who was deathly afraid of the terrible "Whatzit" down in his basement. One day Harry simply could not avoid going down there because his mom had gone there earlier to get a jar of pickles and had not returned yet. He had to go and help her. Unbeknownst to him, she had gone to the garden by way of another door. Once in the basement, Harry had to confront this double-headed, three-clawed, six-toed, long-horned "Whatzit" who predictably jumped out from behind the furnace, his hiding place. Having no choice in the matter, little Harry confronted the terrible "Whatzit," displaying his courage with a broom stick. To the emboldened boy's great surprise the "Whatzit" turned out to be a cowardly monster who grew smaller and smaller with each threat and swat. Before vanishing completely, Harry magnanimously sent the whimpering, now miniscule monster to Sheldon Parker, who lived next door. Making a significant change, a *paradigm shift*, means confronting a monster within us and it takes some courage and perseverance.

I began with a thorough examination of my perceptions and paradigms. I asked myself, if perhaps I was so blinded by the old methods of foreign language instruction, and even by my past success, that I did not see the new opportunities that could perhaps revolutionize my teaching in such a way that all my students could profit equally well.

THE OLD APPROACH

There have always been some students who sat there in front of me, whose faces and body language exhibited utter boredom and disinterest. There were some who tried sincerely to learn the language, but after 3 or 4 years have barely mastered the fundamental skills. And there were those who came into my class unable to pay attention due to the emotional pain and stress they were carrying with them. How could I reach such students? Clearly the old approach didn't reach them.

When I first began teaching as a young man, fresh out of college, I was not hampered by any foreign language methods. No one had told me how to conduct a language class before I actually stood in front of my first group of students. For that reason my teaching was unique, unorthodox perhaps, yet effective. Then I had to become certified and I had to take methods courses. To fit into a new school I had to teach German the way languages were traditionally taught in that particular school. To be tenured I had to go along with the latest fad, which was followed by several more "perfect solutions" to language teaching. Paradigm was forced upon paradigm. All along I was able to maintain a reasonable amount of individuality, and when it produced remarkable results, I also regained autonomy in my classroom and some freedom to explore and search for an approach that would add a new dimension to my work. My hope was to blend old and new, to retain those aspects of my teaching that had brought me success and give them new meaning and relevance within the framework of a new approach.

"ACCELERATED LEARNING": THE NEW APPROACH

As I explored foreign language brain-based approaches, I encountered terms such as suggestopedia, whole-brain learning, optimalearning, the natural approach, total physical response, and superlearning, all of which rest on basically the same assumptions that I discuss shortly. Here in America these approaches all gather under one umbrella, The Society for Accelerated Learning and Teaching (SALT). Accelerated learning stands for brain-based learning, that is, natural learning and therefore accelerated (Rose, 1985; Schuster & Gritton, 1986). Accelerated learning takes into account what we have learned from psychology and the recent findings of brain research. The various methods are still evolving and changing with the increasing understanding of how our brain works. Those who implement these methods are motivated by the fact that even though we are just beginning to understand how our brain functions, we already know enough to see the error of our old ways, and with some courage and imagination we could make drastic changes in our teaching that would bring about dramatic changes in learning as well.

A PARADIGM PIONEER

Dr. Georgi Lozanov, a renowned psychiatrist, physician, and educational researcher in Bulgaria, was the first to combine the results of psychology, yoga and brain research with education. In 1979, Lozanov coined the term "suggestopedia" to refer to the application of suggestion to the improvement of education and learning (Lozanov, 1979). He has applied his findings to language teaching to prove his theory and he achieved incredible results (Lozanov & Gateva, 1988). His methods have been adopted and used by many schools first in Eastern Europe and Russia, and in the last two decades, throughout the world.

Suggestopedia is a brain-based learning method that is designed to tap our brain's vast, unused capacity. It is estimated that we use only about 5% of our brain's capacity. From psychology, Lozanov incorporates the use of suggestive factors in teaching. We all know, for example, that a teacher's tone of voice, dress, attitude, even facial expression can trigger interest or rejection in students. From yoga, Lozanov took the ideas of mind and body rhythms, as well as techniques for relaxation and concentration. From neurology and biology comes the knowledge of hemisphericity and its importance in education. The left brain hemisphere takes care of verbal–intellectual-sequential functions, whereas the right brain hemisphere takes care of intuitive–spacial-associative ones. Unfortunately, in traditional teaching the left hemisphere is addressed much more and the right hemisphere is often ignored. Lozanov does not advocate that learning become right-hemisphere-dominant, but that both hemispheres be engaged equally, because that makes learning most effective.

In summary, Lozanov's suggestopedia rests on the following tenets:

1. We have a great innate potential that needs to be tapped.
2. Suggestion is the means by which we tap our reserve capacities.
3. We always operate with conscious and subconscious levels simultaneously. These must be carefully orchestrated for best effect.
4. The negative norms in us must be desuggested.
5. Every stimulus is associated, coded, symbolized, and generalized.
6. The teacher's authority and trustworthiness is essential for learning.

7. A child-like and playful state is an effective way to tap reserve capacities.
8. Pseudopassivity is a highly receptive state that is necessary for absorbing information. Appropriate music helps us to attain this state.
9. In communication several levels are operating simultaneously. Those below the level of consciousness such as tone of voice, facial expression, and posture, can be very significant.
10. Peripheral stimuli can be orchestrated to suggest a desired outcome. One must never underestimate the significance of peripheral perceptions.
11. Suggestopedic teaching and learning is always joyful and pleasant. Without this the reserves will not be reached.
12. Music and role-playing are important features of suggestopedia.

I had no difficulty accepting most of the basic principles of brain-based learning as formulated by Lozanov and other pioneers. They made sense to me and often I felt like saying: "Why didn't I think of that?" But it was quite another matter putting these principles into practice. One doesn't need courage to read about and even accept brain-based teaching theories, but one does need a fair amount of courage to set aside old teaching habits, prepare an accelerated learning lesson, and then walk into a classroom and teach it with conviction!

Initially, I could not envision myself implementing these approaches in my classroom. Classical music to read dialogues to? "Surfing" with the music? Warm-up and breathing exercises? Visualizations and mind calming? Dimmed lights? Mind maps? Changing seats all the time? Self-corrected quizzes? No threat, no pressure? I considered all these practices as truly "far-out" and initially I couldn't see myself implementing them in my classes.

PUTTING THEORY INTO PRACTICE

One of the German classes that I faced each day during my earliest stage of transition was my Academy 3 class, a group of talented students in their third year of German that was just finishing chapter one of Franz Kafka's (1971) *Verwandlung* (*Metamorphosis*). I came up with a number of different activities that the students could choose from.

These activities included preparing mind maps, acting out parts of the story, and writing poems, songs, and lists of various grammar structures.

Such assignments were quite new to this group and so I was anxious to see what would develop. To my surprise, their reaction was very positive and the activities truly enjoyable. Brian, for example, decided to simultaneously act out and describe the predicament of Gregor Samsa, the hero of the story, who after a night of restless dreams wakes up to discover that he has turned into an ugly bug. Lying there on his back on top of my desk, his limbs flailing helplessly in imitation of the bug's many legs, and recounting Gregor's inner confusion in the language of the author was a scene not soon to be forgotten by his classmates. Jonathan and Emily wrote and presented creative poems. Andy wrote and composed a song about Gregor. For his performance we had to go to a room with a piano because he accompanied himself as he sang his song. All of this was, of course, done in German.

One would not consider these activities as too different or unique to the accelerated learning approach. No doubt, one could find such activities in other foreign language classes. But they were different for this class, and for me it was the easiest possible entry into accelerated learning. Many of the students chose to do a mind map. Such an exercise helps one to organize the main ideas of a theme in a manner that corresponds much more to the way our brain functions. This type of outline is not linear and systematic in the traditional sense. A mind map is an expanding and creative development of a central theme, with major elements branching off from the center in all directions and seeking out, as it were, related and interconnected aspects as they move further from the center (see Fig. 7.1).

I began my first-year German class with some relaxation exercises. A typical accelerated learning session usually begins with a short physical warm-up to get the blood flowing, some breathing exercises to get oxygen into the brain, and a short mind-calming session to make both mind and body relaxed, and thus more receptive to learning. Threat and stress are two of the most serious obstacles to learning. My classes are no exception. Because this was a totally new procedure for my students and a difficult step for me, I first explained the underlying theory behind all these activities. The students' reaction was mixed. None of them reacted negatively, but they did wonder what was happening to me. With a grin on their faces, they asked me if I was all right. The boys seemed to be a little embarrassed, perhaps for me. I did not use music

FIG. 7.1. Mind map of Kafka's *Metamorphosis*.

at first. I was sure they would reject it outright. In the end the use of classical music was the most popular feature of this new approach.

Other changes that I made for this class at this early stage were: the introduction of frequent self-corrected quizzes; grouping the chapter's vocabulary according to some meaningful pattern; seating students in a semi-circle; doing mind maps with text and drawings on the board; and assigning mind maps as homework. I encouraged the students to be as artistic as they could be. Once the students were fully aware of what I was looking for, these mind maps became works of art. All of them ended up on the classroom's bulletin board. For most of these students it was the first time they had their work displayed in my classroom. The reason behind this assigment is obvious. Students will remember drawings much better than plain words in a vocabulary list, especially if they themselves did the drawing and writing. It is a right-brain activity. If they also get a positive emotional feedback, such information becomes firmly anchored in their long-term memory. As my confidence grew, I tried other strategies that I thought would be practical and useful and I implemented them in all of my classes.

It soon became clear that my students really liked this new approach. Eric and Danielle, for example, flourished particularly well. The transformation that took place in these two students corresponded perfectly to the predictions of accelerated learning experts. Both of these students had great difficulties in my classes and I often wondered why they even bothered to go on. Suddenly they were receiving As and turning in unexpectedly creative projects. Eric used to hide in class; now he spoke up and wanted to read the text to the accompaniment of the music. I was pleasantly surprised by his good delivery. He and his partner, Dan, were involved in radio and television broadcasting and they made use of their expertise to do projects for their German class. They presented their projects with much humor and enthusiasm to everyone's enjoyment in class.

Danielle, who had received only low grades since her first year, was now in her third year suddenly getting As. She kept saying that what we were doing now was "simply awesome." I have never seen her as excited and happy in my class. On one occasion she did a video with Lisa and she included her entire family who all played parts. After one of the classes, she asked me to see her last four grades in my grade book. They were all As. The moment was as gratifying to me as it was to her. She wished that all her classes could be taught this way. For Danielle, an artistic, creative, and imaginative person, this was the perfect approach because it gave her the opportunity to receive and process information that suited her learning style. Her homework revealed all her talents. I assured her that she was never less smart than her classmates; she just had not been taught in the way she learned best.

In my concluding notations in my journal I noted that accelerated learning works indeed, and that the students liked it and asked for more. A return to the old approach would have caused a rebellion. They were cooperative, enthusiastic, and also creative. Often they suggested original ways to cover the material. They especially enjoyed the Baroque music. They spoke German more freely, their grades were higher than normal and they had smiles on their faces. On the negative side, I found the physical environment not conducive to this approach. The lack of windows, patched linoleum floors, bright fluorescent lights that could not be dimmed, uncomfortable chairs, a less-than-adequate sound system, insufficient bulletin board space, and yellow walls produced a classroom that lacked warmth and friendliness.

SCHNUPF DIE SCHNECKE

Toward the end of the first semester I introduced a truly mind-blowing teaching aid, a puppet. The purpose was to ease the fear of students who are sometimes timid when they are required to speak in class. It is so much easier to have a conversation with a cute puppet than one's teacher. The puppet is a snail named Schnupf die Schnecke (Sniffles the Snail). I introduced Schnupf as a refugee snail from Strasbourg. Bilingual since birth, he now speaks only German. He escaped from France after his entire family was wiped out by escargot-eaters. Schnupf is now a resident of the Black Forest and currently at my school on a cultural exchange. After an initial expression of disbelief by some of my students, Schnupf was soon accepted in class. Once he was actually kidnapped and held hostage an entire weekend by one of the students and threatened to be taken to a French restaurant unless I promised not to give an upcoming test. Another student borrowed him for a weekend and now insists on personally carrying him back to my office after each appearance in class. Furthermore, if Schnupf is not brought to class on a regular basis students begin to clamor for him. Clearly, Schnupf has added a dimension to my class that far exceeds my expectation. I believe Schnupf has allowed some students to escape to a secure world where there is no fear of making mistakes.

CONCLUSION

After 10 weeks I administered a survey for two reasons. I needed my students' honest reaction to accelerated learning and I also needed their feedback that might support me in my request for more financial assistance down the road. A quick glance at this survey shows that all my students found the accelerated learning approach to be more fun than the traditional approach. Most said that it is less difficult and more interesting. Most of them also felt that they were learning more vocabulary and useful expressions and that they were more comfortable, relaxed, and motivated. Only one student would have preferred the traditional approach. The majority wanted more music, more mind calming, and self-corrected quizzes. They especially liked acting out roles and thought the amount of homework for the course was appropriate.

Because my initial experimentation with accelerated learning proved to be quite successful, I subsequently adopted this approach for all of my classes to the point of writing my own text and producing sound and videotapes to accompany the text.

It has been a most interesting journey that started with a puzzlement caused by seemingly unmotivated and low-achieving students in my classes. Even though a practical solution to the problem was hoped for, it was not anticipated. The journey itself with its discoveries along the way would have been sufficient reward. However, because I have actually found a solution, I consider myself fortunate indeed.

The puzzlement that led me on my journey came from observing some of my students attending but not learning much in my classroom in spite of my best efforts. Juxtaposed to such observations was a basic belief of mine that anyone who learned his native language can also learn a second language if the right conditions for learning can be found.

My own experience with language learning and our poor rate of success in foreign languages convinced me that the methods used in most schools are fundamentally flawed. When I arrived in this country at the age of 19 with no prior knowledge of English, I was not put into a class where I was made to memorize vocabulary words and grammar rules, and I never filled out a worksheet. My progress in such a class would have been slow at best. Instead, I was placed into freshman college classes along with all my new American classmates. The input was massive and it came from all directions. The information was not systematic and no one established an artificial plan of studies for me. No expert educator made me learn the conjugation of verbs first and perhaps the relative clauses last. I was exposed to the simplest and most complicated structures of the language all at once. This type of input was truly abstract–random and my own brain found the language patterns all by itself because our brain is the best pattern-finding machine there is.

We in education have traditionally ignored the capacities of our brain. For centuries we have organized all information, packaged it as we saw fit, then doled it out piecemeal. Because such a process is unnatural, it induces stress in the learner, causing the learner to downshift. The poor performance that follows causes further stress and ultimately failure. With our well-intentioned but ill-guided actions, we educators can actually choke off the brain's natural and almost limitless potential to absorb and synthesize information.

My acquisition of English was not accomplished in the classroom alone; indeed, most of it took place outside the classroom, where learning was truly natural and joyful because it was supported by a universe of stimuli that enabled my whole brain to be engaged. I will never forget my first truly American breakfast. My first contact with a box of American cereal was not just a word on a list, but it was encountered with all my senses. The cornflakes had a taste and smell unlike anything else I had eaten before; it came in a neat, colorful box within which there was a bag, the significance of which escaped me at the time. The crunching sound of the flakes was also unique and in the process of eating them, I also learned the words for milk and sugar, spoon and bowl, sweet and good, and probably many others. And because I actually managed to convey to my breakfast companions that corn is eaten only by farm animals where I came from, I also learned the words for horse, pig, and duck, and some basic cultural differences. I walked away from that first American breakfast table with scores of new words and concepts that I was never going to forget again. Hundreds of such experiences through each day and many thousands in the following weeks and months went into my language acquisition experience.

How can we expect our students to learn a language with little mini-dialogs at the beginning of each chapter, a list of vocabulary at the end, and some grammar drills in-between? I know my experience cannot be duplicated in a high school classroom, but much can be done to make learning more brain compatible.

We know now that a relaxed mind is more receptive to information, that music helps to establish that relaxed state, that the mind absorbs knowledge also subconsciously, that the brain has a vast potential that we are not tapping, that it can deal with much more knowledge than we allow it to receive and that it assimilates knowledge in many more ways than just the linear, logical sequence so common in our schools. All these aspects can be orchestrated in a classroom in such a way that the learner is actually unaware of the intent of these techniques or of the near automatic learning that is taking place. The learner is immersed in an experience that is joyful because learning that is natural is always joyful. Once this condition is established in a learning environment, learning becomes limitless.

Putting into action that which my mind found to be right was very challenging—it meant overcoming paradigm paralysis. As I struggled to put theory into practice I found the challenges formidable but not insurmountable. My transformation was a gradual, sometimes painful, sometimes exhilarating process that continues today and may never be completed. Therein lies not only the challenge but also the reward for

141

daring to do something new, because success lies in the journey, not in the destination.

REFERENCES

Gackenbach, D. (1977). *Harry and the terrible whatzit.* New York: Houghton Mifflin.
Goethe, J. W. (1804). *Goethe on Shakespeare: Selections from Carlyle's translation of Wilhelm Meisters.* London: De La More Press.
Kafka, F. (1971). *The complete stories of Franz Kafka.* New York: Schocken Books.
Lozanov, G. (1979). *Suggestology and Suggestopedy.* The Lozanov Report to the UNESCO.
Lozanov, G., & Gateva, G. (1988). *The foreign language teacher's suggestopedic manual.* New York: Gordon and Breach Science Publishers.
Rose, C. (1985). *Accelerated learning.* England: Clays Ltd.
Schuster, D. H., & Gritton, C. E. (1986). *Suggestive accelerative learning techniques.* New York: Gordon and Breach.

RELATED READINGS

Caine, R. N., & Caine, G. (1991). *Making connections: Teaching and the human brain.* Alexandria, VA: Banta Company.
Christensen, R., Neal, B. W., & Christensen, J. (filmmakers). (1989). *Paradigms* (a video film). Infinity Limited and Charthouse Learning Corporation.
Connolly, C. (1992, April). *SALT Basics.* Workshop given at the International Society for Accelerated Learning and Teaching Conference, Minneapolis, MN.
Covey, S. R. (1989). *The habits of highly effective people.* New York: Simon and Schuster.
Dewey, J. (1938). *Experience and education.* New York: Macmillan Publishing Co.
Dhority, L. (1984). *Acquisition through creative teaching.* Sharon, MA: Center for Continuing Development.
Eggers, P. (1984, Dec. 4) Suggestopedia: An innovation in language learning. *Media & Methods,* 17–19.
Ellison, L. (1992, April). *Educator's guide to the brain.* Paper presented at the International SALT Conference, Minneapolis, MN.
Ellison, L. (1990, Fall). What does the brain have to do with learning. *Holistic Education Review,* 41–46.
Ellison, L. (1990). Whole brain strategies do accelerate learning. *Consortium for Whole Brain Learning, 9*(3), 1–2.
Gold, L. (1992, April). *A day unlike all other days.* Workshop given at the International SALT Conference, Minneapolis, MN.
Hart, L. (1983). *Human brain, human learning.* New York: Longman.
Krashen, S. D., & Terrell, T. D. (1983). *The natural approach.* Hayward, CA: The Alemany Press.
Krashen, S. D. (1982). *Principles and practice in second language acquisition.* Exeter, England: A. Wheaton & Co. Ltd.

Rand, P., & Gompartz, R. (1992, April). *Optima learning*. Paper presented at the International SALT Conference, Minneapolis.

Schaefer, D. A. (1980). My experience with the Lozanov Methods. *Foreign Language Annals, 15*(5), 273–283.

Schmidt, C. (1992). *The Lozanov method*. Letter distributed at the International SALT Conference 1992, Minneapolis, MN.

Sternberg, R. J. (1992, April). *The Nature of intelligence*. Paper presented at the International Society for Accelerated Learning and Teaching Conference, Minneapolis, MN.

RACING TO RESEARCH: INQUIRY IN MIDDLE SCHOOL INDUSTRIAL ARTS

Wallace Shilkus
Elm Place Middle School

INDUSTRIAL ARTS AND TEACHER RESEARCH

I am an industrial education teacher at Elm Place Middle School in Highland Park, IL. Seventh- and eighth-grade students at Elm Place can elect to enroll in either woodworking, drafting, architecture, or transportation classes, open to all students. In this writing, I attempt to show how I, my students, and my adult classmates grew together during my action research project.

In the past I've found myself constantly defending my program, and, at times, even myself. I now believe this type of thinking delayed my return to higher education, having a 17-year hiatus from attending any professional courses past my bachelor's degree. As I returned to school for my master's degree, I found myself curious about the ways in which the industrial arts were relevant to middle school students. First, I wanted to explore methods to activate my students' multiple intelligences (Gardner, 1983). I wondered whether my methods of instruction reached all the students in my classes. I was inquisitive about finding alternative methods to activate my students' intelligences. I wanted to explore different ways to reach all my students.

Although classes such as industrial arts that involve hands-on activities are extremely popular with the students, many districts are eliminating industrial arts in favor of computer stations and modular labs. A student who elects to take my classes learns more than tools and how to use them in class. There are many benefits of hands-on learning that students experience in industrial arts on a consistent, daily basis. How could my action research help me document my teaching methods and the benefits my students gain?

Learning by doing is a theme that many educators have stressed since Dewey's argument that children should be active learners. This sort of learning is different from traditional education; in industrial arts classes, teachers put students in action first and then ask them to reflect on their experiences. In traditional classes, teachers set the knowledge before their students and hope they will apply the knowledge in some sort of action. In my classes, I set the action first and almost always see knowledge coming from that action. Including the students in discovering new procedures and ideas happens on a fairly consistent basis in many of my classes. Lessons and demonstrations demand active participation on the students' parts. Individual projects pose diverse problems, demand relatively distinct ways of working, and employ processes requiring different types of learning.

I feel that industrial arts activities are valuable because they are experienced by the students as real, not bound between the covers of a book. Feedback is immediate, students are called on to direct their own activities, and they take their own next steps. Students need the opportunity to participate in experiences that go beyond the mere accumulation of information. In these ways, industrial education can be an important contribution to students' development, especially in the middle school.

Little did I know that enrolling in a master's of education course would fuel my passion toward the subject that I teach. Given the freedom to choose my action research project was frightening at first but became clear after the first few months of research. I saw this opportunity as a way to let others become aware of the importance of this endangered subject. I also saw this as a chance to demonstrate what happens in the shop, involving my teacher colleagues, my students, and my classroom. I would use both cross- and peer-tutoring approaches with a reversal of sorts: My students would teach the adults who were in my graduate class.

RACE CARS AND THE MULTIPLE INTELLIGENCES

I had a program currently in place where the seventh and eighth graders who elected my car racing class teamed with one or two fourth graders from a selected class in our school. The veterans would meet once or twice a week and assist the rookies in the design and construction of a CO_2-powered race car during the nine week class.

Due to the wide range of abilities needed in my transportation technology classes to produce a successful CO_2-powered race car, I found multiple intelligences theories made sense for me to investigate during this project. Howard Gardner (1983) proposed seven intelligences that rarely operate independently and often complement each other. Although examples of logical-mathematical, linguistic, spatial, bodily-kinesthetic, and interpersonal and intrapersonal intelligences were evident in most activities, I had no true link to the musical intelligence other than music played during lab time. I found myself examining my style to see if I could possibly engage more of the intelligences in my teaching.

I saw that completing a successful race car utilized almost all of the intelligences. A student needs to understand at least some concepts of measuring skills (logical-mathematical) in order to have the car activated in the starting gate. More important is the students' ability to realize why the measurements are important, and how they affect the performance. During the early stages of this class the students need to visualize both aerodynamic principles and design ideas (spatial). These two factors in the students' cars are usually the most crucial. The actual construction—the shaping, sanding, and filing (bodily-kinesthetic)—are directly related to the students' progress during the design stage. There was very little chance for written work (linguistic), and I saw a need to improve this in my classes. The class atmosphere and size restrictions lend themselves to developing one's feelings toward classmates (interpersonal skills), as evidenced in the peer tutoring. I felt that this might be the most important lesson I could give to my students.

During the class, I had the students put their thoughts in a journal (linguistic/intrapersonal) responding to my writing prompts. Student journal keeping assisted me during this action research project in identifying students' strengths and weaknesses. I also planned pre and post surveys from tutors and tutees, along with adult responses from my graduate class (linguistic/ interpersonal). I took the classes on walking field trips during the design stage, in order for students to see actual examples of aerodynamics and how they pertained to their projects (spatial, kinesthetic). Students recorded material losses during three stages of the construction and followed close specifications in constructing a successful race car (logical-mathematical). The students needed to develop a sense of what aerodynamic principles are and how to apply them to their individual design. Sketching and drawing (spatial) were crucial areas of this project; they allowed the students to relate what they knew through a method other than actual demonstration. The students' favorite part of the class was definitely the actual construction (kinesthetic) of the cars.

TUTORING: VETERANS AND ROOKIES IN RACING

We started the buddy project and, initially, the veterans (middle school students) wanted nothing to do with the rookies (fourth graders), and the rookies wanted nothing to do with design; they wanted to work immediately. The fourth-grade teacher had taught many of the veterans and guided me to possible positive pairings, and we began the project. After pairing, the tutors and tutees immediately sat down and began to draw.

I journaled with both groups and saw that all students had their own way to explain; the methods were interesting. Many students elected to draw their definitions of aerodynamics, with drawings ranging from bullets to bicycle helmets to even professional basketball players. Drawing of the positive airflow made the concept easier for many students to understand. A positive sign was the detailed drawing from some of the veterans, who used skills obtained in other industrial arts classes in their work. I also saw the deficiencies that needed to be addressed. This made individual instruction easier for me and my students.

The seventh- and eighth-grade tutors were warming up to the fourth-grade rookies, who seemed to parallel and sometimes exceed their tutors' classroom talents during the sessions. In many cases, I saw a marked improvement in class participation and behavior. Students were forming a tutoring system in the classroom too, not just with their tutees. I observed many students who asked for additional work; they wanted and enjoyed helping someone else. I was witnessing a form of community being born.

Even though we eventually had a class car race, I truly don't believe that the order of finish mattered to many of the participants. One student even deliberately constructed his car to lose, stating that he didn't care to win; he just wanted to learn and have fun! I saw this as a result of the noncompetitive atmosphere this class developed along the way. In addition, I viewed this as a message that the construction of the car was a very rewarding experience for the students; the product was their own.

ADULT STUDENTS AS ROOKIE RACERS

I had told my middle school class of my plans to bring the group of experienced teachers from my graduate class to the shop to build and race a CO_2 race car just like they were doing. Suddenly I had a vision of my students reversing roles with me on a different level. They would critique the adults' designs and offer suggestions for a successful race car. I felt that the students would find this experience memorable and fun. I could measure the students' progress by the suggestions they offered, the comments they gave, and the checking of the cars' specifications.

We decided on a night for the adults to construct their cars. The tutors were chosen, and each was given three adult students. The adult students were responsible for the filing, shaping, and construction of wheels and axles. I asked the tutors what they expected through a preactivity survey. There were no rules as to how they taught their tutees, but I did remind them that they were chosen for this research because of their abilities and attitudes.

The adults were asked to describe the classroom atmosphere in a journal entry. We proceeded to view an actual race in the hallway so the adults had some sort of idea of how fast the cars could go and how to influence their method and choice of material removal. We adjourned for dinner and then proceeded to engage in a 2-hour lab, videotaped with two cameras.

I helped only when necessary. Many times I wanted to lead, but I held back and observed the tutors eventually achieving the desired outcome. I felt that interrupting would misplace the trust I placed in the tutors and rob the adults of a rewarding experience. The atmosphere in the lab was very similar to a typical day in the shop. I felt that this contributed to the overall success and comfort of the activity.

During my observation I noticed that the amount of work that the adults expected was different then the actual work taking place. They commented on how physically difficult the filing and shaping of the wood was. I felt that even though the adults understood the importance of programs like mine, they didn't truly understand until they performed the task at hand. The adults were being transformed into middle school students again. Many adults had nothing but praise for their tutors.

We culminated this activity a few weeks later with a single elimination race held at the school where the master's class met. We videotaped the event and all had fun, even though one car broke during the race. There was a sense of healthy competition, a sense that we all were winners. This activity was a smashing success! Some members of my middle school class commented that the fourth-grade sketches were better than the adult sketches. I saw that many of my students were able to offer suggestions that had validity; their suggestions showed me that they had grasped the concepts that I wanted them to achieve. Since my research, I have added a critique unit in all car racing classes. I saw that the students appreciate seeing the finished product before they design and construct their own.

A postactivity survey gave me more data about the experience. As expected, most participants preferred making the car, rather than designing of the car. This is a small problem in exploratories; everyone wants to work. I saw that the design unit of this course is vital to constructing a successful race car. I need to make this aspect even more interesting for my students. Activities such as car critique and revision exercises are important in this class. Several adults commented on how seeing a finished car helped them in designing their car. They also responded to the atmosphere of the industrial arts classroom. "I felt free to walk around and learn from my classmates." "I was proud of the fact that I did all the work myself!" "Are there seating charts? I bet not."

One question was directed toward competition between classmates. When asked if they looked at other classmates' cars, many of the graduate class reported that they did, just as students in my middle school classes had reported. Both adults and middle school students want and need some type of feedback as they progress. It was motivating for both groups to see others work.

One comment had special significance to me. It was from a home economics teacher. I was interested in her response because of the similarities in the kind of teaching we do in the middle school. She wrote:

> This activity was good for me on a number of levels—it parallels what I do. I know now (after breaking my car) some of the frustrations my kids must feel in my sewing class, i.e., feeling unsure about how to proceed, waiting for a turn at a machine, time constraints. This response made me think

about what I can do to eliminate these feelings in my classroom. How can I boost one's self-esteem and encourage creativity? As much as I like to think I can see things through a student's eyes, it's refreshing to be proved wrong on this point!

Having my graduate school classmates taught by my students was a highlight of this action research project. I saw a group of people who not only were having a good time, but were learning about themselves at the same time. At times I almost felt like an outsider, although I knew I could very well be swamped with requests for help at any time. Still, I put my trust in my students; this is the premise of a class like mine. I hope that some of my fellow classmates put themselves in the students' shoes that night and felt what it was like to be the student again.

I've noticed changes in myself and my students as a result of this project. Presenting information in different manners has made it possible to reach more students, not just the students who excel in traditional classes. I see that taking different approaches, based on the multiple intelligences, has helped me reach more of the-hard-to-motivate students. Using student journal prompts allowed me to see what the kids had learned in their own words.

One characteristic of the middle school philosophy is to ensure success for all students. Industrial education does this; it is one of the few classes that promotes student socialization skills on a continuous basis, explores the full variety of multiple intelligences, and appeals to several learning styles. Unlike many traditional, subject-centered classrooms, all different types of learning happen each day in my shop. I can only hope my students learn as much as I did during this project.

WEB SITE

http:///www.ewacars.com/ Racing cars

REFERENCE

Gardner, H. (1983). *Frames of mind*. New York: Basic Books.

THE PERSONAL AND THE PROFESSIONAL: LEARNING ABOUT GENDER IN MIDDLE SCHOOL PHYSICAL EDUCATION

Rick Moon
Fremont Middle School

THE REASONS FOR MY RESEARCH

I am a K–8 physical education teacher and coach at Fremont School in Mundelein, IL. My wife and I are parents of two girls, Amy, age 10, and Kelsey, age 8. In this chapter, I will try to relate what happened in my life as a teacher, coach, and father during my two-year research project that focused on gender stereotypes.

I believe that my interest in this topic, particularly as it relates to athletics and physical education (PE), can be directly traced to the birth of my daughters. Prior to that point in my life, I concentrated solely on male athletics. I coached all the boys sports programs at Fremont since 1979 and, though I helped score or officiate some of the girls' athletic competitions, I realize now that I did not have much respect for them. Regretfully, I was among those who felt "it's just a girl's game."

At the time of my research I had learned most of what I knew about teaching from experience, and most of that experience came from teaching physical education to boys. Looking back, I see that my undergraduate physical education teachers were almost all males who had very firm beliefs about gender roles. The following is an excerpt from a notebook I turned in to one of those college PE teachers in 1976:

> Our society is being taken over by women who won't allow their children to play any rough sports and condemn any fighting. By doing this, the

young boys of our society are becoming sissies. It is our job as PE teachers to teach combativeness, roughness, and physical contact to students, without causing serious injury, in order to prevent women and sissies from taking over our society. My teacher responded to this with the words: "And don't ever forget it!"

The fact that my first-born child was a daughter was clearly the impetus to change this perspective. I immediately became more observant of the girls in my physical education classes and I helped out at the girls' basketball games more during that first year after Amy was born than I ever had before. In fact, it was then that I decided to coach a girls' basketball team. During my research, I have listened to girls and boys, regardless of age, saying that boys are all stronger, faster and more highly skilled than girls, and that teams are unfair if one has more boys than the other. I have observed highly skilled girls hold back and not perform up to their capabilities for fear of what others might think or say about them because they are not "supposed" to be good. I have seen less skilled boys find ways not to play so they could avoid the negative comments from others for not performing at a "boys level" of play. Through my research, I sought to explore these attitudes and experiment with methods in physical education that could challenge them to rethink these gender stereotypes.

My teacher action research project was also my way of examining my own perceptions and beliefs about girls and athletics. In addition though, it was a way to experiment with different methods and approaches to teaching physical education. I decided to focus on the elements of competition and cooperation, as they relate to gender in physical education. Ultimately, I discovered that the more attentive I was to my own attitudes about gender in my classes, the more responsive the students were. Also, I learned that a physical education curriculum that is balanced between competition and cooperation is one that allows for the active participation of everyone, not just the athletically talented.

When young children ranked a list of desirable school behaviors, girls identified "to be nice" and "to be smart" as the most important, whereas boys identified "to be a leader" and "to be good in sports" (Caplan & Kinsbourne, 1974). Children tend to define sports as more masculine than feminine (Stein, 1971). Boys learn very quickly that demonstrations of athletic skill earn the praise and attention of adults, especially from fathers who show more emotion and enthusiasm for sports than anything else (Lever, 1978).

From a sixth-grade girl, during a flag football skill drill: "Do we have to play football? Can't we play tea party or something?"

"Have we conveniently allowed lesser skilled females to congregate in the game room and flee the playing fields?" (Greendorfer, 1980). Much research indicates that females often exhibit less self-confidence in achievement situations than males (Sadker & Sadker, 1986; Feather & Simon, 1973; Maccoby & Jacklin, 1980). Because competition is an achievement situation, women may demonstrate some lack of self-confidence when they face competitive sports activities. Lower self-confidence in turn affects their performance and success in physical education classes, which are highly competitive in focus.

"If our goal in physical education is physical development and not development in becoming competitive, it would appear that a physical education program that emphasizes sports, rather than other forms of physical activities, discriminates against women" (Nicholson, 1983, p. 280). It is often true that poor execution of sports skills by some females can be attributed to incomplete learning and not enough practice rather than a consequence of lack of ability. Positive reinforcement from others and positive personal expectations are important ingredients in the sports socialization process. I intended to investigate how to instill both of these factors more consistently in all students in my physical education classes during my research.

TAKING ACTION

My classes were practicing throwing and catching when the head of maintenance came into the gym. I told him I was trying to eliminate the bad habit some kids have of throwing off the wrong foot. He said, "Oh, you mean they throw like girls?"

Throughout my 1st 13 years of teaching, I shared the gym with a female physical education teacher. Typically, she was the "girls' gym teacher" and I was the "boys' gym teacher." I shudder to think about it now, but what we had was a female teaching girls to "play like girls" and a male teaching boys to "play like boys." Is it any wonder that the competitions we had, pitting the boys against the girls, were often rather unpleasant situations? I remember a basketball unit when the girls' teacher did not allow the girls to steal the ball or block shots. She thought the games would get too sloppy and rough. She believed that she was providing the appropriate playing environment in which the girls could develop their basketball skills without becoming overly pre-occupied with winning. I, however, was busy in the next gym teaching the boys to play an aggressive, winner-takes-all basketball game!

Greendorfer (1980) pointed out that boys and girls define appropri-ateness and importance of activities differently. Girls tend to empha-size effort whereas boys tend to emphasize ability in their play. Boys stress winning, play more competitive games, and highly value sports activities. Girls tend not to be rewarded for participating in physical ac-tivity and do not highly value competition or master of skill in sport; rather, girls play less goal-oriented games that involve less complex rules and fewer number of players or participants (Lever, 1978; Greendorfer, 1980).

The first change I made through my action research was to bring the boys and girls back together again for coeducational classes in grades 1–5. (The middle school program was already coeducational.) The change eventually met with great success. Our students were learning skills in a cooperative atmosphere where active participation by all stu-dents was stressed. In past years, I would readily allow girls to "slack off" during activities, believing I was doing them a favor. I soon came to the realization that allowing them to do so was a great disservice. The year I began my research project, I did not tolerate lack of effort from any students. I started the school year with constant encouragement towards active participation in activities where skills were being learned and improved. This directly and positively carried over into competitive activities. Once the students had developed and practiced skills, they were much more eager to display them in a competitive ac-tivity.

> From one eighth-grade girl who chose not to play in a coed game one day:
> "We must make a great play every time or we get ridiculed by the boys."

I also tried to make sure that the competitions were fair. I have had absolutely no boys versus girls competitions. Insisting on active partic-ipation from everyone also resulted in fewer complaints from the boys about having too many girls on their teams or in their groups. I believe that those kinds of complaints were more about the lack of effort, ac-tual or perceived, than because their teammates were boys or girls.

Another change I made in my curriculum was to change from the Presidential Physical Fitness Test to the American Association of Health, Physical Education, Recreation, and Dance Fitness Program (AAHPERD). After analyzing both, I became aware that the Presidential test used different standards for girls and boys on all five of the tests through all ages, 6 through 17. Girls were, in other words, required to do less to achieve the same awards as the boys. More important, students got the idea that what was considered physically fit for girls was far less demanding than for boys. The AAHPERD program based the students' fitness levels on five tests. Before the age of nine, the standards were exactly the same for boys and girls on four of the five tests.

FURTHER REFLECTIONS

As I was collecting data during my observations of physical education classes, which were coeducational and noncompetitive along gender lines, I occasionally noted an interesting phenomenon. Consider this story from my research journal:

> I play a game with fourth graders called "Elimination." The game involves throwing and catching skills as players try to eliminate other players by either throwing the ball and hitting them with it or catching the ball when they throw it at you. The first time we played, the game was very individualized. Everyone had opportunities to throw, catch, run, and dodge.
>
> Soon however, an interesting change occurred. Two of the higher skilled boys teamed up to try to eliminate everyone else. The next "level" of boys then teamed up to try to survive and would occasionally win too. The girls never tried to form their own teams but did eventually try to team up with the two boys' teams. They would usually stay in the game until the other team was eliminated and the boys with whom they had joined turned on them. The girls would then scatter and be systematically eliminated by the rather sophisticated teamwork of the boys. Another group of girls simply ran from the action, choosing to escape being hit by the ball over the chance to throw it.

All the students were very active, yet the observations I collected from this game, as well as from others during my research, offer some interesting reflections into gender differences in physical education. It seems that the boys in my classes were more comfortable with organizing themselves into teams that then allowed them a greater opportunity to win. The girls did not display that willingness to organize themselves quickly and efficiently into teams nearly as often. Is it because more boys had experiences outside of school with team sports and were thus accustomed to this approach? Is it because parents trained their boys to play as team members even in casual outdoor play at home? As I continue being a teacher-researcher, this is a subject I would like to explore in greater detail.

FINAL THOUGHTS

My research on competition, cooperation, and gender role stereotypes changed my role as a teacher by helping me to become more observant than ever before in my classes. Instead of just teaching my students, I became much more aware of my *learning from them*. Things had begun to get fairly routine and there were some things I felt were in need of change. My research gave me a reason to make a few of these changes.

Note: All throughout her last pregnancy, my wife claimed she was going to have a boy. "Only a boy would cause this much trouble" were her exact words. Perhaps Kelsey Lynn was getting a head start on shattering gender stereotypes. Anyway, she looked great in the *blue* sweater her Grandma knit for her!

REFERENCES

Caplan, P. J., & Kinsbourne, M. (1974). Sex differences in response to school failure. *Journal of Learning Disabilities, 7*(4), 232–235.

Feather, N., & Simon, J. (1973). Causal attributions for success and failure at university examinations. *Journal of Educational Psychology, 64*(1), 46–56.

Greendorfer, S. (1980). Gender differences in physical activity. *Motor Skills: Theory Into Practice, 4*(2), 83–90.

Lever, J. (1978). Sex differences in the complexity of children's play. *American Sociological Review, 43*, 471–483.

Maccoby, E., & Jacklin, C. (1980). Sex differences in aggression: A rejoinder and reprise. *Child Development, 51*(4), 964–980.

Nicholson, L. (1983). The ethics of gender discrimination. In B. Postow (Ed.), *Women, Philosophy, and Sport*. Trenton, NJ: The Scarecrow Press.

Sadker, M., & Sadker, D. (1986). Sexism in the classroom: From grade school to graduate school. *Phi Delta Kappan, 67*(7), 512–515.

Stein, A. (1971). The influence of masculine, feminine, and neutral tasks on children's achievement behavior, expectancies of success, and attainment values. *Child Development, 42*(1), 195–207.

LAPTOPS: LANGUAGE ARTS FOR STUDENTS WITH LEARNING DISABILITIES: AN ACTION RESEARCH CURRICULUM DEVELOPMENT PROJECT

Martha C. Stephens
Clarke Middle School

More than 6 years ago I "went back to the classroom." I took four important things with me: a new PhD in learning disabilities, 25 years of kindergarten through college teaching, experience, a silvery-gray head full of notions about teaching students with learning problems, and lots of energy. My assignment was to teach in a middle school resource classroom for mainstreamed sixth graders with learning disabilities. Although returning to the classroom was personally demanding, it could not compare with the relentless emotional, social, and academic demands placed on my students. Increasingly, I became impressed by how faithfully they arrived at school each day to face another daunting 8 hours of almost certain academic frustration.

Still fresh is the mental picture of students entering the classroom, dragged down by a load of books the majority of which they couldn't read. Ironically, the school bags actually did contain the things of which literacy was made: notebooks, pencils, textbooks, and library books. But in reality the bags were props to hide what, for most students, had become a very shameful secret of illiteracy.

Throughout that first year, I thought a great deal about this bookbag phenomenon. I even developed a theory: that the weight of the book bag was inversely proportional to its owner's ability to read. But why would my students expend so much energy hiding the fact that they could not read? Were they fervently carrying dreams that, some day, some way, they might actually become readers, even writers? It occurred to me that if the energy used to hide their "disabilities" could somehow be redirected, its force would empower my students to stay the difficult course toward literacy. Eventually I was led to ask: How can I reorganize my instruction to more effectively help these students with learning difficulties become better readers and writers?

It took 6 years to answer this question. It also produced a curriculum, LAPTOPS: a Language Arts Program for Thinking, Organizing, and Practicing for Success. I was its primary creator, a teacher of middle school youngsters diagnosed with severe reading and writing problems. My classroom was located in an inner-city middle school in a district near a major city in the southeastern United States.

In this chapter, as I explore its evolution, I discuss eight critical factors that shaped LAPTOPS. Then I share some of the outcomes of my research, as well as the implications of my findings for future projects.

CURRICULUM PERSPECTIVES
AND THEORETICAL FRAMEWORK

A major influence on this action research project came from the last three decades of curriculum investigations related to the birth of the learning disabilities field. One of the earliest sources of research data originated from the Child Service Demonstration Centers that were funded nationwide by the Bureau of Education for the Handicapped between 1975 and 1977. Among other topics, researchers studied various curriculum approaches with regard to how they might provide optimum learning experiences that might be beneficial for students with learning disabilities. These students were, by definition, of average or above average intelligence, but were experiencing information-processing problems caused by a disorder in either understanding or using written or spoken language (Smith, 1994).

Zigmond and Miller (1992) summarized several important curriculum themes from the early 1970s. They reported that the designers of the Kansas model looked at the effectiveness of a learning strategies approach (i.e., teaching techniques, principles, and rules that enable the student to learn independently and to solve problems successfully). The originators of the Oklahoma model examined the instructional impact of combining academic skill remediation with compensatory strategies (i.e., combining the direct instruction of basic reading and writing skills with strategies such as using books on tape and peer note taking that circumvents deficit skill areas). The Texas group investigated a social-behavioral program designed to build positive self-concepts, develop communication skills, and foster self-responsibility that accompanied a remedial reading/problem-solving emphasis. And the Pittsburgh group researched the effect of a curriculum that integrated remedial math and reading into a nonacademic strand (i.e., self-management, social skills, organizational considerations, and study skills). LAPTOPS incorporates elements from this era by adapting components from the 1970s such as direct reading instruction procedures, highly structured note-taking activities, behavior management tools, the use of techniques such as books on tape, and the use of small, incremental learning steps that provide learners with high rates of success.

In the 1980s and 1990s, investigators studied transition issues, that is, how the curriculum content could enable students with learning disabilities to become contributing adults in the nonschool community (Brolen, 1978). Bruck (1985) looked at unemployment and postsecondary-education demographics; Johnson (1986), as well as Mosberg and Johns (1994), examined the reading characteristics of adults with learning disabilities; Bireley and Manley (1980) investigated motivational indicators that may predict future-life success among young adults with learning disabilities. LAPTOPS incorporates the last two decades of this research by its survival-skill-oriented subject matter. Its reading program teaches students how to read for the information they will need in future family and work settings.

In the 1990s, I began to embrace many elements from another important curriculum focus, Vygotskian social constructivism. I applied constructivist ideology to classroom practices because its pedagogy was effective especially when applied to the instruction of at-risk readers and writers. Particularly influential to the LAPTOPS development were the best-practices notions from the work of Dixon-Krauss (1996) and Powell (1993), such as effective learning within a socially meaningful activity, internal versus external knowledge, natural versus cultural mental behaviors, self-regulation, the zone of proximal development, and scaffolding.

METHODS OF INQUIRY

During 3 years in a resource classroom, and for the subsequent 3 years in a self-contained setting, I collected data from the following sources:

student journals, reading comprehension exercises, sight-word drills, teacher-made books-on-tape programs, homework, student assessments, progress reports, notes from parents, excerpts from individual educational plans (IEPs), student quotes, and lesson plans. According to Leedy (1997), I had many elements of an action research project. Here is its story.

FACTORS SHAPING THE CURRICULUM DEVELOPMENT PROJECT

Eight factors emerged to critically affect the LAPTOPS project. They were: my choice of a theoretical framework, the classroom's characteristics, various language arts methodologies, the conceptualization of the LAPTOPS acronym, my choice of management tools, journal writing, course content areas, and participant reactions, which included test data, anecdotal notes, end-of-the-year documentation on individual educational plans (IEPs), and feedback from parents, students, and other teachers.

The LAPTOPS Acronym

In the first year, my special education resource class was next to the gifted classroom. In many ways the two programs were similar. Like its sister next door, the gifted program was a "pull-out" model. In other words, both programs pulled out small groups of students from regular education classes to participate in special learning activities. Both classes received academic enrichment. Both sets of students had been chosen for placement according to state and federal guidelines. And both sets of students were intensely aware that they had been awarded a special label.

The acronym for the gifted program was TAPS, which stood for Teaching Advanced Placement Students. I observed how readily the students who attended classes in the TAPS program used this title to indicate a fierce pride in belonging to such an elite group. The acronym seemed to enliven the program with positive vibes by setting it apart, by giving it importance. Perhaps, I thought, I could also endow my students with a similar sense of importance toward their program if I invented a name for it as well. My students, too, were a special group with remarkable abilities. Many drew exceptionally well, had astounding memories for movie sequences, could build intricate structures with Erector sets, and dictated very imaginative fiction works such as "How I Taught Einstein Everything He Knew in Middle School." Because I wanted the acronym to be upbeat, indicate the importance of problem-solving skills, stress the need for organizational skills, and emphasize the importance of repeated practice, I settled on TOPS: Thinking, Organizing, and Practicing for Success, added to the focus of the curriculum, Language Arts Program (LAP).

I believe this simple act of giving my program a name was a very influential factor in the entire curriculum development process. This act alone gave both momentum and focus to the entire LAPTOPS phenomenon. Somehow, the name assignment endowed me and my students with the instructional rights and privileges equal to those of the "gifted" program participants. Both developing and promoting the acronym gave my endeavors a respectability factor at least as high as I envisioned being attributed to the gifted program in the eyes of students, teachers, and parents. Historically, the naming process marked the formal beginning of the development of a program with substance and form and content and purpose, providing a forward movement to my work.

Theoretical Framework

A major influence on the LAPTOPS curriculum was its social constructivism (Vygotsky, 1962). I tried to benchmark LAPTOPS with its pedagogy by consciously applying zone-of-proximal-development strategies, putting learning in a socially meaningful context, transforming lower order thinking into higher order thinking through social interaction, and developing self-regulatory materials. Social constructivism is also prominent in the importance I placed on language development and thinking skills. I also employed aspects of mechanistic behaviorism (Heshusius, 1989), because I incorporated a structured classroom management system, objective assessment procedures, delineated teaching protocols, sequential instructional components, and repetitive drills.

Classroom Characteristics

Over the 6-year period, LAPTOPS naturally changed due to three factors: its delivery model, classroom demographics, and diagnostic categories. During the first 3 years, I taught in a sixth-grade resource classroom. This delivery model allowed "the student to leave the regular classroom for at least one period a day to receive instruction individually or in small groups from a specially trained teacher" (Smith, 1994, p. 530). Approximately 30 students diagnosed according to state and federal guidelines as either students with mild intellectual disorders (MID), behavior disorders (BD), and/or learning disabilities (LD) attended for up to three periods of daily instruction in basic reading, reading comprehension, written expression, math reasoning, and/or math calculation.

For the last 3 years, I taught a group of 8 to 14 middle school youngsters in a self-contained classroom for students diagnosed with moderate to severe learning disabilities (LD). I also taught several "other health impaired" (OHI) students, a student with a dual diagnosis of learning disabilities/visual impairment (LD/VI), and a student with a dual diagnosis of behavior disorders/learning disorders (BD/LD). The students attended most reading, writing, math, social studies, and science classes in the self-contained LD classroom, while attending homeroom, lunch, selected academic classes, and exploratories (i.e., physical education, art, computer, and outdoor education classes) with chronological age peers.

The range of characteristics both within and among the students in the self-contained setting was remarkably diverse. For instance, one sixth grader diagnosed other health impaired (OHI) could word call on an eighth-grade level, comprehend a written text on a third-grade level, complete math operations on a first-grade level, and surf the Internet with the proficiency of an adult. Another sixth grader, who demonstrated the expressive language skills of a preschooler, installed and connected a printer by following the graphic directions, although he read at a beginning second-grade level. Collectively, the students in the classroom had four shunts in their heads, and many took an assortment of medicine for hyperactivity, seizures, aggression, and depression.

Language Arts Methodologies

The curriculum changed over each of the six yearly intervals as my repertoire of methodologies expanded. Each new method learned over the years found its way into the reading, spelling, and math review programs I wrote. In the first 4 years, I drew on the following approaches:

the Fernald visual–auditory–kinesthetic–tactile method (Fernald, 1943), the Bloomfield–Barnhardt linguistic approach (Bloomfield & Barnhart, 1961), the neurological impress method, the Distar reading program (Smith, 1994, p. 432), certain recommended visual perceptual strategies, (Smith, 1994, p. 392), the whole-language approach (Goodman, 1986), the learning-strategies approaches (Alley & Deshler, 1979), and the adapted techniques of Lehtinen such as color coding, highlighting, and hands-on learning (Lehtinen, 1955).

During the fifth and sixth years of the study, I received inservice training in two phonemic awareness programs: the Herman method for reversing reading failure (Herman, 1976) and the Lindamood phoneme sequencing program for reading, spelling, and speech (Lindamood & Lindamood, 1998). Both programs use a tightly prescribed set of methods and materials to teach phonetic awareness; both programs incorporate the writing of the basic sounds to practice and reinforce reading skills. Both are especially effective methodologies when used with one to four students for 20 to 30 minutes per session.

Management Tools

The management tools greatly facilitated the student LAPTOPS curriculum because they promoted on-task behavior. They included point sheets, a reward system, work folders with practice sheets, small-group instruction, and learning centers. Daily, I filled each student's work folder with review activities that reinforced earlier direct-instructed reading, spelling, math, and writing. The point sheet, a centerpiece of the behavior management system, offered students the opportunity to earn or lose points based on their performances. Valued behaviors were getting to work, staying on task, and following directions. Students could trade points for either prizes or privileges. In addition, they could share point sheets with others, a procedure that encouraged group interaction toward a common goal.

In the third year, one of the activities was the actual production by the students of the TOPS reading program for sale. We copied word labels, made color-coded word cards, made black-letter word cards, and collated and stapled the packets. We also wrote mailing labels, stamped the packages, and took our packets to the post office for mailing. My students, who assembled the programs, served as their own on-the-job supervisors. They monitored each other's production of each reading packet by using checklists for each work phase. We figured out the cost of each packet and set the price so as to earn about $20 per packet. The money was used to buy supplementary reading materials.

Journal Writing

Journal writing was very important to the life of this curriculum project. During the first year in the resource phase, students wrote in their journals for 20 minutes, once or twice a day. Sometimes they wrote spontaneously about whatever was on their minds; at other times, they used writing prompts. At first, word production was minimal for a number of students. I encouraged the most reluctant writers by offering a point payoff, for every letter; then, for every word; and, finally, for every 10 words. This motivational system seemed very effective in getting the act of writing under way. During the second and third years of the resource phase, writing productivity increased to a much higher level compared to the earlier years. In fact, students began entering school essay contests, as well as writing chapter books. At one graduate seminar in which my students demonstrated the TOPS reading program, we concluded with a question–answer session. A teacher in the audience asked of one student, "When did you first realize you were a writer?" He replied without hesitation, "When I discovered I had at least one good book in me."

In the self-contained years, journaling evolved into an all-purpose think pad in which students wrote daily to parents about TOPS classroom activities, recorded homework assignments, entered phone numbers of friends, took classroom notes, and "doodled" to relieve tension. Daily, parents signed each journal entry to signify that they had read it. The parents and I also wrote notes and messages back and forth to one another. We exchanged photographs, which, in turn, provided future writing prompts. Thus, the journal became a history of our thoughts and actions over the 10 months of instruction.

In fact, using the journal as a source for home–school communication inspired me to create *The TOPS News*, a weekly publication. During the entire fifth year, I incorporated the reading skills being taught by reviewing in-class topics such as careers, social studies, science, and current events within the text of the news. Topics ranged from Antarctica to Africa, earthquakes to bomb threats. I increased the type size from 12-point to 18-point on behalf of a student diagnosed with both a visual impairment and a learning disability. Happily, 18-point type proved beneficial to all students, so I have used it ever since.

Content

During the resource years, the LAPTOPS reading program provided my students with accessibility to the mainstreamed textual information in the content areas: science, social studies, language arts, health, and physical education. Most students were unable to "word call" above a third-grade level, much less comprehend the information. Consequently, unless someone read the text to them, their textbooks were of very little informational value, except, perhaps, for the pictures and maps.

I developed a two-step method that I hoped would scaffold the information in the regular education texts over into my students' brains. First, I put the texts on tape. Second, I rewrote key parts of each assignment into a comparatively lower reading level such that it would render the texts both readable and as accurate. The trick in lowering the reading level was to make the text simple enough for the student to read it easily, while at the same time, complex enough to transmit the inherent message.

I believe that the taped texts along with the rewritten excerpts helped a large number of my students become more literate than they would have been without these modifications. These resources provided a degree of confidence about the information presented in the regular education setting. For example, a science teacher approached me after her class had finished a unit on biomes: "Cal used to hide behind his book whenever I asked for classroom volunteers to read. During the last few weeks I've noticed a change. He's come out from behind his book. He even raises his hand to read."

Participant Reactions

Teachers commented positively about LAPTOPS during the 3 resource years, because I had rewritten subject-area books and handouts into simpler formats. Colleagues reported that the mainstreamed students from my classes demonstrated changes in oral reading confidence. Some teachers asked me for copies of the simplified texts, worksheets, and books-on-tape excerpts to use with non-special-education students.

Six years of data indicate good student progress in both reading and writing skills. Many students who used the LAPTOPS materials experienced both test score and grade improvements, both in my classes and in the mainstreamed settings. Students provided with interventions such as rewritten textual information and recorded selections on audio tape demonstrated a yearly growth from 1 to 3 years in reading comprehension, basic reading skills, and written expression skills on both formal and informal assessments. For instance, an eighth-grade student who was failing during the first semester had raised his grade to a B average by June. As a result of the progress, he remarked, "This is the first year in my whole school career that I really deserve to be promoted." The feeling of entitlement to good grades was a powerful motivator, especially for this student who long had thought his ordeals with the printed word were his fault.

Parents of TOPS students cited improvements in both reading accuracy and spontaneity. For instance, they would say, "He's reading more road signs," or "When we go out to eat, she's actually reading *us* the menu!" One parent reported that his son, unassisted, looked up insurance information for the family business in the Yellow Pages. Dad was thrilled because not only did his son find the information, but, for good measure, he proceeded to regale the family with a reading of the entire insurance section.

STEPHEN'S STORY

Near the end of this study, a particularly poignant classroom memory was made. It illustrates the powerful impact of a reading breakthrough on a youngster, especially one who has been struggling to read for many years.

This story is about Stephen and my cellular phone. I have found the phone to be a useful tool whenever a remarkable learning moment occurs. "Oh my goodness," I would say immediately after a particularly stunning accomplishment, "We've just had another breakthrough. Get the phone!" Then, the spotlighted learner would phone the designated V.I.P. in life to celebrate.

Months earlier, Stephen had arrived in class. His reading ability consisted of recognizing 12 sight words—one for every year of his life . . . or two sight words for every painful year in public school. At first, whenever a word came at him on a word card he actually ducked his head as though a toxic object had been shot his way. Although he had made slow forward progress, he spoke all words as though he were a robot. He worked laboriously and dutifully until released from the bondage of the reading lesson.

I wished fervently that he could find some level of delight in reading, and I longed for him to value his own progress. I wanted him to acknowledge that, against great odds, he was in fact learning to read after years of failure. I wanted him to assume the self-identity: Reader.

In January, Stephen's mother, a single parent, was diagnosed with a serious medical problem. The illness had been discovered during routine surgery, and, of course, it had a traumatic effect in almost every aspect of Stephen's life. We made frequent phone calls from the classroom to her hospital room, a feeble attempt on our parts to help. Even though school routines seemed absurdly incongruous in the face of his mom's life-threatening condition, we continued our work in the Herman reading program, the journaling, and the LAPTOPS reading lessons.

And then it happened. Around 10:00 a.m. on a February morning in a messy Georgia classroom, Stephen became A Reader. We had just completed an exercise from the Herman reading program in which he had aced a list of nonsense words (fam, sik, mep, buv, roc). He walked over to the study table, picked up a newspaper, and began reading the headlines out loud—slowly, carefully, ever so passionately, ever so accurately. I was thrilled. He was thrilled. The entire classroom was thrilled. We called his mom immediately so she could be thrilled. Luckily she was available, and most likely very surprised, when her son said, "Hi, mom, I have a little surprise for you," and then proceeded to read.

Some time later, as the two of us were walking to the lunchroom, I commented, "You seem so happy, today. Any special reason?" "Because," he replied without hesitation, "this is the day I *really* began to read."

CONCLUSIONS

At the beginning of my story, I described how students carried heavy book bags filled with unreadable textbooks to my classroom. Then, I described how I was led to try to ameliorate the "book-bag phenomenon" by action researching my way into a curriculum process, a process that has now become the central framework for all my classroom work. When I began, I had very little insight about what I was doing. Initially, I thought I was writing reading programs to enable students to access information otherwise not attainable due to their reading difficulties. Then as the reading, spelling, and math review programs began accumulating, I thought I was creating an entire language arts curriculum, the contents of which addressed specific students' reading and writing differences. Now, in retrospect, I know, my most important work actually was the development of a process. True enough, I had ended up with an impressive stash of instructional products, but more influential was the ongoing process that kept LAPTOPS viable.

I wrote part of this paper on the computer in my classroom. While writing, I would stop to share parts of it with students. "I am writing the story of our classroom," I said. "Would you like to hear some of it?" As I read certain excerpts, the classroom grew stunningly quiet. "That's Shawna! That's Elton!" they would call out. They seemed delighted that their learning story was receiving such a place of importance.

From time to time, students would come up to the computer to stand quietly beside me while I worked. One child stood beside me for a long time, studying my text unfolding on the screen. Then I realized with a thrill that his lips were moving. He was reading along with my writing! I stopped what I was doing and smiled at him. "Do you realize that when you came to my classroom, you were reading words like 'top,' 'fit,' and 'pat'? Now you're able to read all these hard words in my paper!" He was a very contemplative person, saying very little during most conversations, so I was not surprised that he made no reply. I too remained quiet for a while. Then I asked, "Do you think that you have become a better reader since you came into this class?" He nodded. We both remained unhurried, reflective. Then I asked, "Do you think that you will continue to become a better reader as long as you are in this class?" He nodded. More silence. And then I asked, "Do you think that some day, you will go on and on reading, even when you're not in this class?" "Well," he replied finally after much thought, "I'm still so very new at this."

The book-bag phenomenon continues; however, my outlook about it has changed as a result of my research. I have come to understand that I cannot completely solve the illiteracy problem among my students with learning disabilities, but I can work toward resolving it by referring to an organized plan, a mental model, a curriculum process. I have also come to understand that it is the process that drives the product, not the other way around. My process, that is, the interaction of eight curricular elements, operates to resolve the tough illiteracy issues facing students with learning disabilities. Furthermore, the process elements (or factors) interacting as a whole are more influential on student outcomes than any one individual factor operating alone.

Six years later my effort to teach students with learning disabilities continues, but now, as a result of my action research, the effort is grounded in the curriculum process that I originated during the development of LAPTOPS: a Language Arts Program for Thinking, Organizing, and Practicing for Success. Throughout the years, the interaction of the eight LAPTOPS factors was reshaped continuously as I tried to adjust a behavior-management strategy here, apply a different reading approach there, according to the day-to-day assessed needs of my students.

Whenever I start up a new school year, I experience a sense of panic. However, since the LAPTOPS study, I have a clearer notion of how I will proceed. Yet, beginning is still scary because . . . I'm always so very new at this.

WEB SITES

http://teachervision.com Resources for special education

http://www.ldanatl.org/ Learning Disabilities Association of America (LDA)

http://www.ldonline.org/ LD OnLine

http://www.ldresources.com/ LD Resources

REFERENCES

Alley, G., & Deshler, D. (1979). *Teaching the learning disabled adolescent: Strategies and methods*. Denver, CO: London.

Birely, M., & Manley, E. (1980). The learning disabled student in a college environment: A report of Wright State's program. *Journal of Learning Disabilities, 13*, 7–10.

Bloomfield, L., & Barnhart, C. L. (1961). *Let's read: A linguistic approach*. Detroit, MI: Wayne State University Press.

Brolen, D. E. (1978). *Life centered career education: A competency based approach*. Reston, VA: Council for Exceptional Children.

Bruck, M. (1985). The adult functioning of children with specific learning disabilities: A follow-up study. In I. E. Siegel (Ed.), *Advances in applied developmental psychology*. Norwood, NJ: Ablex.

Dixon-Krauss, L. (1996). *Vygotsky in the classroom: Mediated literacy instruction and assessment*. White Plains, NY: Longman.

Elements of literature: Introductory course. (1997). Annotated teacher's edition. Austin, TX: Holt, Rinehart and Winston.

Fernald, G. M. (1943). *Remedial techniques in basic school subjects*. New York: McGraw-Hill.

Goodman, K. S. (1986). *What's whole in whole language?* Portsmouth, NH: Heinemann.

Herman, R. (1976). *The Herman method for reversing reading failure*. Sherman Oaks, CA: Herman Method Institute.

Heshusius, L. (1989). The Newtonian mechanistic paradigm, special education, and contours of alternatives: An overview. *Journal of Learning Disabilities, 22*(7), 403–415.

Johnson, D. J. (1986). Remediation for dyslexic adults. In G. T. Pavlidis & D. F. Fisher (Eds.), *Dyslexia: Its neuropsychology and treatment*. New York: John Wiley & Sons.

Leedy, P. D. (1997). *Practical research: Planning and design* (6th ed.). Columbus, OH: Merrill.

Lehtinen, L. (1955). Appendix. In A. A. Strauss & N. C. Kephart (Eds.), *Psychopathology and education of the brain-injured child. Vol. 2: Progress in theory and clinic*. New York: Grune & Stratton.

Lindamood, P., & Lindamood, P. (1998). *The Lindamood phoneme sequencing program for reading, spelling, and speech: The LiPS program* (3rd ed.). Austin, TX: Pro-ed.

Mosberg, L., & Johns, D. (1994). Reading and listening comprehension in college students with developmental dyslexia. *Learning Disabilities Research & Practice, 9*, 130–135.

Powell, W. R. (1993). *Classroom literacy instruction and assessment from the Vygotskian perspective*. Paper presented at the 38th annual convention of the International Reading Association, San Antonio, TX.

Smith, C. R. (1994). *Learning disabilities: The interaction of learner, task, and setting*. Boston: Allyn and Bacon.

Vygotsky, L. S. (1962). *Thought and language* (E. Hanfmann & G. Vakar, Eds. and Trans.). Cambridge, MA: MIT Press.

Zigmond, N., & Miller, S. (1992). Improving high school programs for students with learning disabilities: A matter of substance as well as form. In F. R. Rusch, L. Destefano, J. Chadsey-Rusch, L. A. Phelps, & E. Sxymanski (Eds.), *Transition from school to adult life*. Sycamore, IL: Sycamore.

II

SCHOOL AND PROFESSIONAL CONTEXTS

5

LEARNING WITH EACH OTHER: COLLABORATION IN TEACHER RESEARCH

David Hobson

A triangular prism hangs from a thin filigree thread in my study windows. I look through it into the yard outside whenever I notice the refracted colors slowly moving around the room as the day progresses. Peering through the prism, I watch just-budding forsythia blur into golden clumps of color, separated now from the distinct arching of branches and framed in a new version of spring. Later, as the sun sets, the forsythia reappear as golden, violet, blue and orange dots across the table where I sit writing. Both points of seeing present shifting versions of the environment surrounding me; these versions depend not only on the slight motion of the hanging crystal itself but also on the angles from which I look through and around the prism.
—Miller (1990b, p. 86)

Miller uses the image of the prism when she teaches and thinks about curriculum. It seems to me that this metaphor works wonderfully when applied to teacher research, particularly to collaborative efforts made by teacher researchers. As with a prism, they look from various angles at the phenomenon they are studying and try to think of their own active roles in creating those vantage points. The colors of the prism are refracted, just as a teacher's research is a reflection of a particular situation, itself in continuing motion, yet caught momentarily as a temporary rendering of reality. The moving dots of color in Miller's description remind us that no one construction necessarily signals completion of the inquiry or represents a definitive view. Teacher research is very much a prismatic study, particularly when you add in all of the additional vantage points and ways of seeing that are brought by the members of the teacher research group.

TEACHING: AN ISOLATING PROFESSION

> We must pay attention to the adults who open the doors, ring the bells, hand out the books and the homework assignments. And we need to pay attention not only to teachers' relations to the children, but to their relations to one another as well. What do they know of one another's work? When and how do they work together—if they work together? (Grumet, 1989, p. 21)

Teachers often remark on the fact that they have very rare opportunities to converse with colleagues. This idea comes as a surprise to many people, particularly to those entering the profession. The image of being isolated doesn't easily fit with the picture many of us have of teachers. But Huberman (1993) reminded us that many teachers derive their most important professional satisfactions from interactions with students instead of with peers. It is not from students that teachers are so isolated; it is from other adults. To many teacher researchers, finding ways to overcome the customary isolation from their peers becomes an integral part of their research.

The isolation in schools begins when the new teacher starts out, and learns that entry to the teacher's world of work is done "person by person, each working largely in isolation from others" (Lortie, 1975, p. 74). This situation becomes the permanent state of affairs for their teaching, "the base of their occupational culture" (Hargreaves, 1993, p. 72). The teacher can hardly escape the architecture of schools that organizes classrooms into cellular patterns separating each one from the others. A teacher's whole day may be spent in one just one room. An elementary teacher put it this way:

> I live in my own little world in my classroom. Sometimes I think that my children and I share a secret life that is off limits to anyone else. We just go about our business, like so many peas in a pod. (Lieberman & Miller, 1984, p. 6)

The high school teacher may also be confined to a single classroom all day; it's the students who move from one place to another around the building. Meanwhile, teachers can find it extremely difficult to steal a few minutes to converse with a colleague and may even choose to spend their lunch breaks in their rooms catching up on paperwork. Teaching can be a lonely profession even when the isolation is somewhat self-imposed.

Being private is thought by some to be a rule of thumb of the teaching profession:

> What does it mean to be private? It means not sharing experiences about teaching, about classes, about students, about perceptions. (Lieberman & Miller, 1984, p. 8)

Or, in the words of one teacher, "You seal off the room and you deal with the students. It is safer to be private. There is some safety in the tradition, even though it keeps you lonely" (p. 9).

The classroom tends to be a territory staked out by the individual teacher and its boundary is not to be violated lightly. Schools are simply not organized to facilitate interaction among teachers. Choosing a degree of isolation is a way to fend off the disruptions and distractions that so often come from being too caught up in an overwhelming system. Flinders (1988) saw this response "as protecting the time and energy required to meet immediate instructional demands," noticing that "it is not uncommon to respond to increased job demands by closing the office door, handling luncheon appointments, and 'hiding out' in whatever ways we can" (p. 25). There is little or no time allocated for teachers to get together and the schedule is often so tight and complicated that even if there was some time, few teachers would have the luxury of having it at the same time or day or place. Teachers are typically divided from each other by grade level and subject area differences. They rarely set foot in each other's schools or visit their colleague's classrooms. Moreover, few teachers have experienced teacher education or staff development programs that acquainted them with how to work with colleagues as well as with children. All of these factors combine to separate teachers from each other. "The very act of teaching is invisible to one's peers" (Lieberman & Miller, 1984, p. 9).

TEACHERS WANT TO COLLABORATE

Teachers are very interested in sharing practice, even eager to do so, given the necessary time and resources, but some are unaccustomed to this practice and somewhat afraid of exposing themselves to potential criticism from their peers. In schools, there is often little time and less reward for teacher talk. We perceive teacher talk as a means of diagnosis, a time to think out loud, to explore, analyze, and to problem solve. Teacher talk involves time to listen, to share, and to interact. Given a safe place to air their uncertainties, teachers love to talk together, to share practice, and to wonder out loud about what to do with many of the real issues they face in their everyday teaching lives. They can give each other a kind of feedback available from no other source that reduces their anxiety about being effective teachers. Rather than the more usual "listening to experts" approach that seems to characterize so much of formal teacher development, teachers seem most open to the teachings and wonderings of their colleagues. They listen closely to the stories that seem to come from an experience base that all can recognize. Teachers can give each other a hearing and can offer each other empathy, understanding, and practical help.

Teacher research offers classroom practitioners an opportunity for availing themselves of the resources of colleagues on the issues and concerns that have practical importance to them. Teacher research does not consist of a set of tasks imposed from above by school authorities. It need not be characterized by the sort of "contrived collegiality" described by Hargreaves and Dawe (1990), which occurs on those occasions when teachers are "invited." Kelli Visconti describes her own research in which she established a teacher support and collaboration group in her elementary school (see Visconti's teacher research in this volume after chap. 7). Establishing teacher research community groups enables teachers to celebrate their successes with each other, create and re-create ways of helping groups of children learn more effectively, and strengthen the connections teachers have with each other. She discusses the role of a group facilitator who shares in the construction of such a climate where problem solving, sharing, and affirmation can take place.

There are many interactive contexts in which teacher research happens. Two teachers may embark on a project together as occurred when a high school English teacher and a kindergarten teacher put their students together in a reading and tutoring program and studied what happened. Large groups of teachers may also embark on a project together. The context of a teacher researcher study group of six is a powerful one, as evidenced by the work of Miller (1990a, 1992) who chronicled nearly 3 years of meetings of such a small group as they worked on "extending the concept of teacher-as-researcher into reciprocal and interactive forms" (p. ix). I found that a teacher education course of 15 provided an excellent context for conducting a collaborative interview project with retired teachers (Hobson, 2000) and then again with aspiring teachers (Hobson, in Joseph and Burnaford, 2000). The student–teacher seminar comprised of preservice teachers along with their cooperating teachers and university supervisors provides yet another context for conducting classroom inquiries.

Whatever the context, participants enjoin the process of conducting some classroom-based teacher research. The group is meant to be a place where teachers can get some help with that process.

GROUP BUILDING: LEARNING TO WORK TOGETHER

Teacher researchers often form groups in order to gather additional perspectives on their classroom inquiry. Occasionally, teachers may have worked in the same building for 20 years, eaten lunch in the same room, and endured faculty meetings together, but these shared experiences do not necessarily make it easier for these teachers to become a cohesive group. In any case, every group that has a new purpose, or a new configuration of members, is in some fundamental ways a new group.

Probably the two most pressing questions present in such a first gathering are these: Who are these people? and do I feel that I belong here? Learning how to work well together is an important initial task. One way to address these concerns is to spend some time talking with one another and to surface some of the content of the conversations with the whole group. There are many wonderful sources for group-building activities that you may want to consult. Many researchers have investigated the subject and written about it, including the following: Brandes and Ginnis (1986); Cohen (1994); Hanson (1981); Lippitt, Hooyman, Sashkin, and Kaplan (1980); Pfeiffer and Jones (1969); Schmuck and Schmuck (1997); and Watson (1974). Often, working with just one other teacher researcher for a while is an effective way to begin building community in a research group. Two strategies for building group cohesion that are particularly useful for groups of teachers about to embark on teacher researching are called *paired interviewing* and *pairing and sharing*. Both help to lay the groundwork for collaboration in classroom inquiry.

Paired Interviewing. Each teacher chooses a person with whom to pair up, each interviewing the other for a set period of time. A few prompts may help the process get rolling:

- Why are you here?
- How did you decide to join? Was it really an option?
- What are you concerned about in your classroom?
- Are there common things that we want to work on as a group?
- Do two or three of us have a similar research interest?
- What works for you?
- What can you share that was a huge flop?
- What are your expectations for this group?

Responses are recorded by the interviewer using magic markers on a large piece of newsprint, which is posted on the wall for sharing with the entire group. In the debriefing that follows, each participant introduces the teacher interviewed to the others. Polaroid photographs can be taken and attached to the newsprint.

This is an effective first meeting start-up activity because it allows teachers to arrive at different times without being disruptive, it minimizes the directiveness of the facilitator, it provides an orientation to the content and process of what is to come, and it encourages teachers to make a transition from the world of schooling to this community of adult learners. It maximizes interaction, it allows the participants to learn a lot about each other in a short period of time, and it serves to dissolve anxiety associated with any new social situation.

It is important for teachers to become comfortable with each other as rapidly as possible. Both facilitating a high degree of interaction between group members and helping a lot of information to surface quickly contribute to a climate in which teachers can feel an increasing sense of belonging.

Often teachers who are beginning to think about developing some teacher research initiatives have a variety of concerns and worries that may be nagging at them. Many teachers have rather narrow notions of how research is defined, much of this learned in their own university experiences that may have become quite dated during the intervening years. Getting these issues expressed and responded to by members of the group often contributes to developing a more comfortable atmosphere for all present.

Pairing and Sharing. Members of the group are asked to write in an effort to identify and briefly describe the issues and concerns uppermost in their minds about joining this teacher research group. Here are some possible prompts:

- Why did you join us for this teacher research discussion?
- Is there an aspect of teacher research that concerns or interests you?
- What obstacles do you need to overcome in order to do research in your classroom?
- What do you have going for you?
- What are your hopes for this group of teacher researchers?
- What are your fears concerning this venture?

The teachers write in their journals for perhaps 10 or 15 minutes about the beginnings of the teacher research group, perhaps using one of the prompts as a jumping off point. After 15 minutes, the writings are exchanged with another teacher in the group and read. Each teacher offers a response to the writing of one colleague, starting at the point on the page where the author left off, perhaps complimenting or expressing appreciation for points raised, asking a question or two, sharing corollary thoughts or experiences, or maybe expressing additional ideas. The notebooks are exchanged again, read and responded to. There may be several rounds of exchanges, but it is important to finish with the original journal writer bringing the entire dialogue to a close.

Often, after a period of written pairing and sharing, there will be a need in the group for some verbal interaction. Particularly in this circumstance where one purpose of the activity is group-building, time should be taken to bring some of the content of the exchanges into the whole group. Each pair may be asked to briefly describe the substance of their exchange and to prepare to report on their findings to the group. Similar ideas are often developed in several dyads and a lively discussion will ensue. Some of the concerns will pertain to various elements of the research process and so can be used to begin to define and clarify the research initiatives that are already taking shape. Many of the topics, especially at the beginning, will be focused on individual and social concerns involving participation in the group. It often comes as a great relief to hear various members give words to the feelings of stagefright, uncertainty, confusion, and general anxiety that often accompany participation in new social situations that may call for a degree of risk taking. Sharing these concerns is one effective way that a group can begin the process of building its own identity.

LISTENING AND RESPONDING
TO OTHER TEACHER RESEARCHERS

Teachers are quite familiar with this process as it is applied to students. A child is invited to sit for 15 minutes in the author's chair, for example, in the expectation that others will listen and respond. Just as we put children in the author's chair in classrooms, a teacher research group can allow its own members to avail themselves of the resources of the group. It may be difficult for the kindergarten and the fifth-grade teacher to listen to each other because their worlds seem so far apart. However, just as we encourage students to learn to listen to each other in the author's chair, and see what they can contribute and learn for themselves, so each teacher can take the experience he or she is hearing about, respond as a colleague, and see how this teacher research can be applied to his or her own situation. Every time you listen to someone else, you gain something.

Ron Lippitt, an early proponent of working with groups to gain knowledge, described a support group in Ann Arbor that he belonged to that encouraged any member to use the time of the group in a particular way—for example, for brainstorming, for responding to draft writing, for role playing, or problem solving. One member of the group acted as secretary, and members scheduled increments of the group's time on a first come-first serve basis. I have found this is a practice that lends itself well to a group of teacher researchers because it permits exploration of various subjects from many different vantage points.

> When I have been listened to and when I have been heard, I am able to reperceive my world in a new way and to go on . . . It is astonishing how elements which seem insoluble become soluble when someone hears; how confusions which seem irremediable turn into relatively clear flowing streams when one is understood. I have deeply appreciated the times that I have experienced this sensitive, empathic, concentrated listening. (Rogers, 1969, pp. 225–226)

Early in the process of teacher research collaboration, teachers might ask, How do we want to give and receive feedback regarding what we're trying in the classroom? What kinds of feedback and response would be most useful and helpful? Giving helpful feedback is a skill; learning to do it is unlikely to be accomplished from reading guidelines like these, but through practice. In a group of teacher researchers, where the giving and getting of feedback is such an important element, it is important to provide frequent opportunities for such practice. In one particular collaborating session, for example, one teacher gave several specific suggestions for ways to help students in another researcher's classroom solve word problems. The next time the group met, the first order of business was to see whether the feedback was helpful, whether the strategies suggested were used and if so, with what measure of success. Giving "feedback on the feedback" in this way helped all of these teacher researchers develop additional insight on how better to elicit helpful responses next time.

Receiving Feedback

Elbow (1973) offered excellent advice regarding listening to feedback that is perfectly applicable to teacher researchers receiving response to their work in progress. He suggested that you might need to bite your tongue because if you can't help talking, you will keep your responders from sharing their reactions with you. Try not to make apologies or give explanations or ask questions until you are sure that the responders have finished telling you how they perceived the experience of your work. It is very tempting to try to shape the kind of response you are getting, but try to resist this temptation. In short, according to Elbow:

> Be quiet and listen. (Elbow, 1973, p. 101)

Tape recording sessions will help teacher researchers remember the feedback they receive from colleagues. Sometimes it's helpful, at the end of a feedback session, to take a few minutes in which everyone can write exit slips describing the substance of what occurred.

Brainstorming

Every teacher has experimented with brainstorming as a way of working with kids, of generating a large number of ideas quickly, of encouraging creativity and lateral thinking, and of bringing everyone in a group to the common task. The key is to keep the ideas flowing from the group as fast as possible, just writing everything down on the blackboard (or, even better, on newsprint so you can take it away with you), and not stopping to comment on anyone else's ideas. The scribe writes everything in no particular order and makes no attempt to rank or organize the responses in any way so that the suggestions quickly become anonymous. It's important to write down as much of what the brainstormer says as possible. The scribe must take particular pains not to influence the content by inadvertently using the power of the chalk. It is very important for the facilitator to model the behaviors of not commenting, not shaping, not interpreting, not censoring, not rescuing the group from a momentary silence, but instead respecting each and every one of the contributions that naturally flow.

After the brainstorm is completed, there are several ways to proceed. If the work in question is a group production (for example, if the group is developing options for some action it may want to take), the group may organize the ideas into categories, or put them into order of importance, or arrange them in order of some developmental priority. If the purpose of the brainstorm is to generate ideas in response to the request of a group member, then it may be best to leave the categorization to the individual teacher researcher. If the purpose is to generate different ways of looking at this collection of ideas, then it might help to make copies of the list of ideas for everyone in the group, scissor them apart, and ask each person to organize the resulting puzzle pieces into some schema. These conceptions might then be handed over to the individual teacher researcher for further work, or can be reported out in the group and discussed further.

Being Interviewed

Hunt (1987) offered this very practical technique. First, the teacher describes the research topic in 10 words or less. Next, the teacher prepares a rough interview guide on the topic chosen. This consists of four questions drawn from Kolb's (1984) experiential cycle:

1. What has your experience with this topic been?
2. From your own experience, what do you think are its most important features?
3. In terms of your own experience with this topic, what are your hunches about how it works (i.e., how do you make sense of it)?
4. Based on your understanding of this topic, what is the first step to take in investigating it?

Finally, the teacher researcher asks another group member to conduct the actual tape-recorded interview. In this way, the teacher becomes the first participant in his or her own research. This is a reversal of roles, but a reversal defined such that the teacher researcher's own ideas can be brought out. Hunt (1987) called this "the Golden Rule in developing research methods" (p. 118). He continued, "becoming a participant in your own research project is a very valuable source of feedback for tuning into whatever methods are used."

Teacher researchers are often amazed when they listen to the tape-recorded interviews and discover how much they already knew about the subject. Bringing tacit knowledge to explicit awareness in this way comes as a wonderful surprise and can form the basis for many other techniques for accomplishing similar discoveries.

Periodic Conferencing

The periodic conference is a way to use oral discourse as a means for discovering the progress one is making. I have found that a monthly conference arranged between two teacher researchers works very well. An oral report on progress to date on the research project is given, concluding with an identification of apparent next steps. The interviewer reflects, asks clarifiying questions, draws out, and tries to develop a clear understanding of what the teacher researcher is reporting. The interviewee keeps the tape.

One month later, the process is repeated, again with a tape recorder, but starting at the place on the tape where the conferees left off at their last meeting. The main purpose served by this technique is a clarifying one. Speaking is much like writing; one can do it to learn. Recording the conversation on tape opens up the possibility of giving the oral discourse a rehearing. The accumulating record of several conversations over a period of time provides a sense of continuity and developmental process. It is very difficult, when one is fully invested in a conversation, trying to find the right words, stopping and starting, working through the various confusions, to leave the interpersonal interaction with a clear understanding of just what transpired. Having the tape recording for later listening allows one to recapture the conversation and perhaps to extend it further.

Interactive Journal Writing

Miller (1990a) and the five classroom teachers she collaborated with over several years attempted to develop collaborative reflections on the contexts and assumptions that influenced and framed their practice. They tried to invent forms of inquiry both in their classrooms and in their teacher research group that would "extend the concept of teacher-as-researcher into reciprocal and interactive forms" (p. ix). Miller describes the "formation and constant reformation of their collaborative processes" and their recognition "that 'finding voices' is not a definitive event but rather a continuous process" (p. xi). One of the principle processes they explored was interactive dialogue journal writing:

> I proposed that we keep journals as yet another space for dialogue to take place. The teachers agreed that they would engage in dialogue journal writing with me; that is, we would write back and forth to one another about whatever issues emerged in our individual and collective inquiries. . . . The goal of dialogue journal writing is to carry on a discussion about some important topic over several days, within a classroom context, or over several weeks or months, within a collaborative context such as our research group. (p. 26)

Response feeds the interactive journal writing process. Infrequent response generally causes the process to atrophy and fall into disuse. What kinds of journal responses might one teacher make to another as they both conduct their own teacher research projects? What forms of written feedback from a colleague would be useful? Here are some possible sentence completions which can be used as prompts:

> I'd love to hear more about . . .
> This part confuses me, I'm not sure what happened . . .
> How did you feel about this?
> When you described _____, it made me think of . . .
> I was wondering about the part where . . .

Networking With Other Practitioners

The group of teacher researchers is, of course, itself a small network. In the collaborative research project I conducted (Hobson, 1994) with a group of teacher researchers involving the interviewing of 34 retired teachers, we found all of our interviewees from among our personal network of colleagues, friends, and acquaintances. The power inherent in activating even a small human network is enormous. It is hard to imagine any practical inquiry into behavior in a classroom that would not in some way parallel activities that other teachers are already conducting somewhere. It may be a relatively easy task to identify these human resources by calling upon those networks already in place. Computer technology and the Internet have greatly expanded the possibilities for networking with colleagues. In chapter 4, many of these opportunities are described.

Gathering Information Outside the Classroom With Other Teachers' Help

A teacher-research group can also provide support in identifying relevant information for each other. When a group of colleagues is directly connected with the work you are doing, it's incredible how much related information they stumble on in their travels that finds its way quickly to you.

Collecting Data With the Help of Colleagues

There are many ways that teacher researcher colleagues can support each other in gathering data. Do you need to try out a paper-and-pencil instrument to see how it works? A teacher researcher might do a trial run in her class. Do you need additional pairs of eyes, ears, and hands to make observations in your classroom? How about trading such a task with a teacher researcher in your group? Maybe you need a set of student writings in response to a particular topic or issue? The teachers in your group could produce student responses that may help you to proceed. Collecting data need not be a solitary task. Get help! *Collaborative Analysis: Finding Meaning Together*, by Van Maanen (1990), described the structure of a collaborative conversation as resembling what Socrates called the situation of "talking together like friends":

> Friends do not try to make the other weak; in contrast, friends aim to bring out strength . . . They do this by trying to formulate the underlying themes or meanings that inhere in the text or that still inhere in the phenomenon, thus allowing the author to see the limits of his or her present vision and to transcend those limits. (pp. 100–101)

Teacher researchers may select sections of tape-recorded conversations that seem especially salient and play them for a group of teacher researchers. The group could write responses to the taped selections and then discuss their perspectives. Many new insights develop through this procedure. It is also useful to do with videotaped incidents and events. Bringing the combined perspectives of a group of people to the task of making meaning can open up many new ways of thinking about the data one has in hand.

Although the classroom may often serve to isolate the teacher from other teachers, it is a place where teachers are in almost constant interaction with *students*. It is from a teacher's relationship with his or her students that many of the deepest satisfactions of teaching spring. Therefore, it seems to make sense that we consider the role of students in classroom research. *Every single one of the teacher research strategies we've described in this text can be used by and with students at all levels.*

> Whenever people decide to learn, they undertake research. If teachers wish deliberately to learn about their teaching, they must research. If children wish to learn about electricity, they must research. . . . All teachers should be experts in "action research" so that they can show all students how to be "action researchers." (Boomer, 1987, p. 8)

The teacher research group is one place where the pleasures of teaching and learning are to be found. A student research group is another. One teacher thought she might try to bridge the gap between these two contexts:

> Last year the light dawned! I had been learning about the importance of personal and group reflection, a significant life and learning skill. I had discovered that learning comes from thinking for yourself and listening to input from others. Suddenly, I became excited. How could I teach my 21 third graders what I had so painlessly learned. . . . What had been the process? How could I duplicate this experience in my classroom? (Nalle, 1993, p. 45)

COLLABORATION IN THE CLASSROOM: CO-RESEARCHING WITH STUDENTS

In their study, Lieberman and Miller (1984) found that elementary teachers believed that the only significant rewards of the teaching profession lay in the students' "words, behaviors, expressions and suggestions" (p. 2). Although we would like to think there are numerous other rewards inherent in teaching, interaction with students and success with their learning seem to be of major significance to teachers who continue to return to the classroom year after year.

If the students are the reason that many teachers continue to teach, how might their role affect the process of being a teacher researcher? Paley (1986) discussed the role of young children in that process. She wrote about when she began teaching kindergarten—full of curriculum guide activities, scheduled reading time, nap time, calendar time, play time and, at first, unaware that the "distractions might be the sounds of children thinking" (p. 122). She continued:

> Suddenly, I was truly curious about my role in the classroom, but there were no researchers ready to set up an incriminating study to show me when—and perhaps why—I consistently veered away from the child's agenda. Then I discovered the tape-recorder and knew, after transcribing the first tape, that I could become my own best witness. (p. 123)

She learned then that the act of teaching can become a "daily search for the child's point of view" (p. 124).

Similarly, Sitton (1980) saw the child as the informant of the teacher, which certainly represents something of a shift in roles. Sitton maintained that good teachers, and teachers who survive, have always done this. In order to view students as the ones who have information to share with us in the adult world, we must first find out what *they* know (p. 544). Then teaching becomes informed and can be adjusted—to a child's world and to what the child brings to the classroom. This process is what Jervis (1986) referred to as "a teacher's quest for a child's questions" (pp. 132–133) and it can be the beginning of a teacher's own inquiry.

Such a process of co-researching doesn't just happen with high school students. Nancy Hubbard, a second-grade teacher, explains: "Throughout the project, I found that I was not the one who would always have to plan the lessons. During my research, the children's questions and interests guided the direction of the curriculum. They posed the questions, stated the problems, and we solved them together" (see Nancy Hubbard's teacher research after chap. 7).

A special education teacher researcher was very interested in the role of special needs children in the regular education classroom. As she read more about special education, she noticed that mainstreaming and inclusion were always presented from the viewpoint of adults. Parents, teachers, legislators, lobbyists, and administrators were well represented. "Where is the voice of the children?" she commented. Her research focused on those voices; she asked them what they thought about being included in regular education classrooms. She encouraged them to write about it, talk about it, reflect on it. She was the observer, the inquirer, the learner.

Similarly, a fifth-grade teacher was exploring the ways to make reading more enjoyable for her class. She tried several different methods, tapping into the very latest ideas from the literature, and having some success, though not at all what she had envisioned when she began her research. She realized that she would have to keep searching. Finally, after thinking about it for awhile, she decided to ask her students for their solutions. That was just what she needed. The *children* had a few ideas which moved them forward, one of which was what they called "Reading Teams." Reading Teams became the central element of reading literature in her class for the rest of the year. It was *the children* who had devised the method; the teacher observed, questioned, and learned.

These stories illustrate a legitimate kind of partnership between teacher and student that reflects a mutual respect between parties who are seeking to increase learning in a classroom or school. There are a variety of ways in which students can play an essential role in teacher action research. One way is to teach students research methodologies in order to engage them in the data collection within a school. The Stay in School Partnership Program in the city of New York did that with urban youth who were in danger of dropping out. In order to find out what programming might be useful, they needed to know what the lives of the students were like and how school fit into those lives (Farrell, Peguero, Lindsey, & White, 1988). Students were selected to interview other students, tape conversations with their peers, and then participate in the analysis of the data and contribute to the formulation of research questions based on their research. The students found that the words "interesting" and "boring" came up often when they talked with their peers about school. With that information, researchers together sought to discover exactly what those words meant, with students offering a variety of examples in both categories!

At Aloha High School in Portland, Oregon, students conducted interviews on school climate issues (Johnson & Henstrand, 1993). They believed that this method would yield more honest responses from students as they attempted to find out what the climate for education was like at Aloha. They asked questions such as, "What makes you want to come to Aloha each day?," "How do you get along with people at

Aloha?," and "What helps you really learn in classes at Aloha?" This data, analyzed and interpreted by teachers and students together, served as a starting place for an ongoing research project on meaningful education at the high school.

Students who participate in action research as data collectors as well as data analyzers have the opportunity to offer constructive questions that adults may not think of, which may yield useful responses from their peers. They may also offer some interesting interpretations of results that present a youthful perspective on the issues at hand. This method of involving students can take place at the classroom level as well as the school level.

Perhaps historically, we have underestimated the role students can play in making constructive educational decisions. Teachers who have asked the students have consistently been surprised and pleased at the power of the suggestions and ideas the young learners have offered. Such a means of researching what is meaningful calls for a shift in thinking and a shift in control in some respects. It also yields a measure of ownership and investment in the outcomes of teacher research projects to the students. A teacher asked recently, "Do you think I should *tell* my fourth graders that I will be doing research on methods of teaching science with manipulatives this year?" The response from her colleagues: "*Tell* them! How about *asking them to be researchers too!*"

"In a community of learners, adults and children learn simultaneously and in the same place to think critically and analytically and to solve problems that are important to them. In a community of learners, learning is endemic and mutually visible" (Barth, 1990, p. 43). Teacher researchers we know are very reluctant to view their students as the "subjects" of their research. Students can be catalysts for change; they can offer a fresh perspective with sometimes jarring honesty. Students are not pawns in the research process; they are collaborators and participants in what Barth terms "the community of learners."

> Through dialogue, the teacher-of-the-students and the students-of-the-teacher cease to exist and a new term emerges; teacher–student with students–teachers. The teacher is no longer merely the one-who-teaches, but one who is himself taught in dialogue with the students, who in turn, while being taught, also teach. (Freire, 1972, p. 67)

Teaching, after all, is a process of engaging learners in trying to make meaning, to make sense of our world. Designing environments and facilitating processes that foster inquiry is the primary task of teachers. Great teachers visibly enact the process of inquiry with their students. They are constantly wondering, looking, gathering information, studying it to reveal meaning, and thinking again. Teachers and students reinforce this process in each other, celebrate each other's developmental reachings, and lead each other along.

REFERENCES

Barth, R. S. (1990). *Improving schools from within*. San Francisco: Jossey-Bass.

Boomer, G. (1987). Addressing the problem of elsewhereness: A case for action research in schools. In D. Goswami & P. Stillman (Eds.), *Reclaiming the classroom: Teacher research as an agency for change* (pp. 4–12). Portsmouth, NH: Boynton/Cook Heinemann.

Brandes, D., & Ginnis, P. (1986). *A Guide to student-centred learning*. Oxford: Basil Blackwell.

Cohen, E. (1994). *Designing groupwork: Strategies for the heterogeneous classroom* (2nd ed.). New York: Teachers College Press.

Elbow, P. (1973). *Writing without teachers*. London: Oxford University Press.

Farrell, E., Peguero, G., Lindsey, R., & White, R. (1988). Giving voice to high school students: Pressure and boredom, ya know what I'm sayin'? *American Educational Research Journal, 25*(4), 489–502.

Flinders, K. (1988). Teacher isolation and the new reform. *Journal of Curriculum and Supervision, 4*, 17–29.

Freire, P. (1972). *Pedagogy of the oppressed*. New York: Herder and Herder.

Grumet, M. R. (1989). Dinner at Abigail's: Nurturing collaboration. *National Education Association, January*, 20–25.

Hanson, P. (1981). *Learning through groups: A trainer's guide*. San Diego: University Associates.

Hargreaves, A. (1993). Individualism and individuality: reinterpreting the teacher culture. In J. Little & M. McLaughlin (Eds.), *Teachers' work: Individuals, colleagues, and contexts* (pp. 51–76). New York: Teachers College Press.

Hargreaves, A., & Dawe, R. (1990). Paths of professional development: Contrived collegiality, collaborative culture, and the case of peer coaching. *Teaching and Teacher Education, 6*, 227–241.

Hobson, D. (2000). Across the generations: Conversations with retired teachers. In P. Joseph & G. Burnaford (Eds.), *Images of schoolteachers in twentieth-century America* (2nd ed., pp.). Mahwah, NJ: Lawrence Erlbaum Associates. (First edition St. Martin's Press, New York, 1994)

Huberman, M. (1993). The model of the independent artisan in teachers' professional relations. In J. Little & M. McLaughlin (Eds.), *Teachers' work: Individuals, colleagues, and contexts* (pp. 11–50). New York: Teachers College Press.

Hunt, D. (1987). *Beginning with ourselves*. Cambridge, MA: Brookline.

Jervis, K. (1986). A teacher's quest for a child's questions. *Harvard Educational Review, 56*(2), 132–150.

Johnson, D. G., & Henstrand, J. (1993). Action research: Using student interviewers to link research and practice. *Teaching and Change, 1*(1), 29–44.

Kolb, D. (1984). *Experiential learning.* Englewood Cliffs, NJ: Prentice-Hall.

Lieberman, A., & Miller, L. (1984). *Teachers, their world and their work: Implications for school improvement.* Arlington, VA: Association for Supervision and Curriculum Development.

Lippitt, R., Hooyman, G., Sashkin, M., & Kaplan, J. (Eds.). (1980). *Resourcebook for planned change.* Ann Arbor: Human Resource Development Associates.

Lortie, D. (1975). *The schoolteacher: A sociological study.* Chicago: University of Chicago Press.

Miller, J. (1990a). *Creating spaces and finding voices: Teachers collaborating for empowerment.* Albany: State University of New York Press.

Miller, J. (1990b). Teachers as curriculum creators. In J. Sears & J. Marshall (Eds.), *Teaching and thinking about curriculum* (pp. 83–96). New York: Teachers College Press.

Miller, J. (1992). Shifting the boundaries: Teachers challenge contemporary curriculum thought. *Theory Into Practice, 31*(3), 245–251.

Nalle, K. (1993). Democratic processing of children's classroom concerns. *Teaching and Change, 1*(1), 45–54.

Paley, V. G. (1986). On listening to what the children say. *Harvard Educational Review, 56*(2), 122–131.

Pfeiffer, W., & Jones, J. (1969). *A handbook for structured experiences for human relations training* (Vols. 1–4). San Diego, CA: University Associates.

Rogers, C. (1969). *Freedom to learn.* Columbus, OH: Charles Merrill.

Schmuck, R., & Schmuck, P. (1997). *Group processes in the classroom* (2nd ed.). Dubuque, IA: Wm. Brown.

Sitton, T. (1980). The child as informant: The teacher as ethnographer. *Language Arts, 57*(5), 540–545.

Van Maanen, M. (1990). *Researching lived experience.* Albany: State University of New York Press.

Watson, G. (1974). *Verbal and non-verbal methods for working with groups* (Vols. I and II). New York: Harper.

6

SCHOOL AND UNIVERSITY TEACHER ACTION RESEARCH: MAINTAINING THE PERSONAL IN THE PUBLIC CONTEXT

Gail Burnaford

THE PERSONAL IN THE PUBLIC CONTEXT: IS PERSONAL CHANGE ENOUGH?

Since we published the first edition of this book, I have watched as the literature in the field of teacher action research has expanded. I have been involved with projects that have stretched my own conceptualization of teacher research, its uses, and its tremendous challenges in the public arena.

I began as an instructor in a field-based master's program, in which teacher research has been a cornerstone of practice for more than 20 years (Burnaford & Hobson, 1995). I accepted the general paradigm of teacher research in that context as a medium for individual reflection, action in one's own professional life, and the building of effective practice one classroom at a time. At the same time, I began research on my own practice at the university level, collecting data about my work as a teacher educator who also facilitates teacher research in schools (Burnaford, 1997). Then I began assisting school districts interested in experimenting with teacher action research as a conscious mechanism for promoting school reform. My work with teacher researchers focused more on establishing connections between them through the sharing of practice in forums such as research roundtables and online teacher research conversations.

For the past 2 years, I have been working to integrate teacher action research as a part of preservice teacher education at Northwestern University. Northwestern is known as a research institution; its faculty members in the School of Education and Social Policy are acknowledged for their high-quality research in which teachers, university professors, and graduate students design curriculum and learning environments to enhance student learning. I had to ask myself how universities and school systems relate to my own definition of teacher action research.

Ken Zeichner, who has also worked with both preservice and experienced teachers in doing research, recently challenged us: "We need to take teacher research much more seriously and take a hard look at the purposes toward which it is directed" (Zeichner, 1994, p. 67). While working with prospective teachers, I have been challenged in my thinking. They have asked me repeatedly, "Is this research?" "How can my single research project make any difference in a large high school?" "What will my principal think about me being a researcher when I'm supposed to be teaching?" "How does this kind of research connect to university research?"

I have come to the conclusion that the personal transformations that occur through teacher research are situated in a context, and that context must be acknowledged in the work. When teacher researcher Vida Schaffel explored how her second-grade children learn to read and write, she enjoyed the collaborative response of her master's project study group and became excited about the possibilities for future research in her classroom. But once her research group dissolved and her master's degree was acquired, she found herself back in a school that did not understand or support teacher research. She became frustrated and discontented; she needed the support of others who were inquiring about their practice and had a forum for discussing what they were learning: she did not find that in her own school. (See Schaffel's teacher story after chap. 7.)

Kelli Visconti had a similar experience; she followed up her own initial work as a teacher researcher by attending the International Conference on Teacher Research in 1995. There she met others who have managed to sustain teacher research in their schools. She returned to her fifth-grade classroom, determined to begin a study group. (See Visconti's story after chap. 7.) She has struggled to maintain the group and highlight its importance for some doubters, and the group continues to meet. Both Schaffel's and Visconti's experiences illustrate how important support is for continuing this work. Teachers do not work in vacuums, and a single positive teacher research study may not be sufficient as an end in itself. "We cannot be neutral," Zeichner (1994, p. 68) maintained. We must face the challenges of doing teacher research in public and with others.

We use the terms *teacher research* and *teacher action research* interchangeably in this book so far. When schools adopt this approach to reform and/or professional development, however, often the word *teacher* is dropped, and the approach is referred to as simply *action research*. This may give us some idea of the larger scope of the research when it is more than an individual project or study by a single teacher in a classroom. It also conveys a specific message about ownership and investment in results. Both words belong—*teacher* and *action*—when this research is enacted in a school community.

In order for school-wide teacher action research to work, the school culture must be one of a learning, social system, regardless of the exact approach to reform (Berlin, 1996; Holly, 1987). In such a system, collaborative teacher learning is as much a function of the school as student learning (Holly, p. 96). In fact, the two—teacher learning and student learning—are seen as two sides of the same coin. Such schools are generally democratic and participative; they strive to achieve community—for adults and for students. In my experience, it is the building of that culture that is essential before and during action research initiatives and that ensures its success on a more-than-individual-classroom level. Lieberman and Miller (1994) noted the importance of teacher action research as a part of something larger and not an add-on entity in a school: "As a solitary innovation, teacher research has a poor chance for survival" (p. 204).

If doing teacher research is contextualized, and if we see collaboration for change as an essential piece of the work, then we need to examine how the public arenas shape and refine the inquiry. Although personal change may be enough to satisfy an individual teacher for the short term, it is not enough to generate and sustain the support systems and structures to make teacher research a part of the profession that will not go away with the next reform initiative. If teacher research is here to stay, regardless of the other movements, networks, consortia, and grant projects that appear, then the personal and the public need to arrive at some understandings of each other. We have to ask, what is the institutional impact of teacher action research? We cannot be content with the individualized impact of classroom learning, although such personal growth cannot be overestimated in a professional teacher's life. Our emphasis for this book continues to be how to do classroom-based research, but such inquiry must be grounded in and supported by an organizational foundation. Otherwise, teachers will do just one project, as per the Ontario initiative, described next, and then it will be over.

Holly (1987) used the image of cul-de-sac rather than a turnpike for meaningful improvement. If an approach is a cul-de-sac, it doesn't go anywhere. If we envision the turnpike, there are plenty of destinations along the way. That is the dilemma we face as teacher research begins to take on new importance in school communities. That is the focus of this chapter.

SCHOOL-BASED MODELS FOR TEACHER ACTION RESEARCH: POTENTIAL AND PURPOSE MADE PUBLIC

A 3-year school-wide project in Ontario, Canada, had teacher research as the primary means of reform as a basic premise (Harris & Drake, 1997). The project was firmly supported by the principal of the school, who described the approach as "teacher-driven professional development" (p. 22). Participation in the initiative was mandatory. To begin the project, the teachers were asked to name the issues that they felt were of concern. Faculty members were then grouped on teams to study and address these issues.

At the end of the 3 years, the action research efforts were over and the project did not continue. The principal moved to another position; teachers were asked to comment on the project. The majority of the teachers saw the effort as successful, even though it did not continue. What were the obstacles to continuing what was perceived as a positive program, both for individual teachers and for the school as a whole?

The experiences at this Ontario school underscore several basic components that need time and attention if larger applications of teacher research methods are to be successful. The three components that were most problematic at the structural level in the Ontario project were required participation, uncertainty relative to goals and focus, and mandated collaboration. For these Ontario teachers, the personal and the public contexts did not cross sufficiently to maintain teacher action research beyond the life of the mandated initiative. Looking more closely at how individual teachers can relate to school action research projects may provide insight on models that accomplish that connection.

Table 6.1 shows several models for school-based action research. These models characterize possible sequences schools may opt for when undertaking teacher action research. I have defined these models for discussion purposes; they are not mutually exclusive, and none of them exist in a pure form. Each model has a slightly different goal; incentives and rewards also may be slightly altered in order to achieve the intended goals. The audience for the work is not always the same, and the processes for data collection and interpretation are dependent on the model's design and structure. Finally, the source of leadership for teacher action research in each of these models may be different.

Some school systems have opted for teacher action research as one approach to school reform among many. In order to sign on to do action research, faculty members ascribe to the general, school-wide goal stated at the beginning of the initiative (see Model 1). Focus on one particular goal sharpens the actual work of research geared to increasing achievement and enhancing teaching effectiveness. In this approach to action research, teachers work on the three I's—initiation, implementation, and institutionalization—a process lasting as long as 5 years on a general goal. Within the school goal, teachers still choose more subject- or grade-level-specific questions to examine within their own practice.

Some school-based action research plans include the adoption of study groups, with peer coaching as a key component of the process (see Model 2). At Highland Park High School (HPHS), action research lab teams are optional and voluntary. The issues they decided to study were chosen by the participants and the outcomes were clear; even the process was/is always one of experimentation. (See Joe Senese's story after chap. 7.) Unlike the school in Ontario, HPHS began with small numbers and "grew" a teacher action research base for change. And while the first teams were learning about how to do action research, the school as a whole was working on this collaborative, community-oriented base that Holly (1987) and Lieberman and Miller (1994) described. If action research is to be more than an idiosyncratic trend—unique in a school's routine—it must be "grown" from a culture that does more than action research to build a democratic, participative culture for learning.

TABLE 6.1
School-Based Models for Teacher Action Research

	Model 1: Whole-School Action Research	Model 2: Teacher Action Research Lab Teams	Model 3: University Courses as Basis for Teacher Action Research	Model 4: Teacher Study Groups Doing Action Research
Goals	General school improvement/increased student achievement	Collaborative professional development/improving teaching	Independent professional development/critical mass of teachers involved over time	Independent professional development/improving teaching
Impetus/source of initiative	School administration	School administration—choice of professional development approaches	University outreach/teachers seeking degrees	Groups of interested teachers
Incentives/rewards for participation	Stipends / Time allotment during inservice days	Choice / Time allotment during inservice days	Graduate degree/undergraduate degree	Sharing, collaboration (not necessarily any time or stipends provided)
Data collection and interpretation processes	Study groups based on interest, grade level, or assigned topics	Lab teams/teacher-developed questions/shared results	Graduate class/individual teacher	In study group
Outcome(s)	Write-up	Write-ups, either individual or lab team/publishing/presenting	Assigned project	None, necessarily
Audience(s)	Whole school and administration	Variable	Variable—may be no outside audience	Study-group members or other faculty
Leadership	School administrators/hired consultants	Lab team leaders	Individual teacher/university professor	Study-group members

A teacher action research initiative can be school based, even if it is initiated at a university and supported by teachers who are engaged in the process as part of a degree program (see Model 3). Although the task is a challenge, if the process is planned well, there is potential for genuine interaction between the goals of a university degree program, with teacher action research at the center, and a school district's desire to build a design featuring reflective professional development. There is always the danger of the institutionalizing of the model, however, in which the needs and interests of the teacher researchers are even farther removed from the goals. Still, teachers often first learn of action research in a preservice or graduate university program; building deliberately on that experience would benefit school-based initiatives.

Model 4 reflects a teacher-initiated, teacher-sustained study group formate for teacher inquiry. (See Kelli Visconti's teacher story after chap. 7.) Although study groups may be part of a school's professional development/inservice program, they may also be a means for teachers to examine specific, individual goals in a collaborative context without administrative direction. Study groups may operate as book discussion clubs or forums to examine children's work. They may be teacher writing forums as well. Sustaining study groups is often a challenge; rewards are often connected to building friendships and relationships with colleagues, rather than external or monetary benefits for performance-based change.

Examining elements of teacher action research across these four models provides a basis for discussion in a school regarding what is possible and beneficial. Understanding elements of scope, ownership, leadership, and incentives will contribute to a useful, context-specific design for school-based teacher action research.

SUSTAINING AND SUPPORTING TEACHER ACTION RESEARCH IN SCHOOLS

Teacher action research is not effective in a system in which teachers are not given some autonomy to make decisions related to curriculum and teaching practices, do not have time for collegial interaction, and do not have opportunities to serve as teacher leaders with their colleagues. In Chicago, we are struggling once again with the norms of how and what teachers teach in schools. There are more and more scripted curriculum units and less perceived opportunity for teachers to collaboratively plan how they teach the standards-driven curriculum.

Some principals provide 10-week standardized content tests across classrooms, and results are disseminated among the staff. Other schools have reduced or eliminated planning time and inservice days, or such times have been precluded by administrative tasks. In this climate, it is only honest and fair to express concern for the healthy future of teacher action research. If teachers are pitted against each other for the highest test scores for the quarter, how can they listen to each other, provide feedback to each other as they try new strategies, or sustain support for each other when students are struggling?

Some schools have managed to positively link teacher learning with student learning. They have done that by thinking creatively about the support mechanisms necessary and have sometimes gone outside the school to make such supports happen. Creative principals have opened the door to possibilities for research by sponsoring retreats, dinner meetings at restaurants for collegial, unplanned discussion about school issues, grant-supported planning, and affiliation with other schools through networks, consortia, and partnerships. For example, in Chicago, urban teachers have participated in collaboratives such as the Best Practice Network, the Chicago Students at the Center Network, and the Chicago Arts Partnerships in Education, all of which have supported teachers across sites in planning and implementing meaningful curriculum and teaching. Other principals who are working for meaningful reform support cadres of teachers working on projects that are problem based, rather than paying for multisession preplanned workshops with well-known speakers. They are learning that teachers need times to work and talk with each other; these approaches are the seeds for teacher action research, even if that term is not used.

Such positive steps by educational leaders introduces another aspect of teacher research that needs consideration if school-wide efforts are to be successful and individual teachers are to feel that their time has been well-spent. That is the question of audience. What are our expectations of how, when, and whether teacher research should be shared? Zeichner (1994) claimed, "Sometimes teacher research seems too self-serving" (p. 70). If research by practitioners is to serve someone other than the one who has done the research, how can this happen? Teacher action research for whom or what?

When individual teachers develop a research question and begin with a plan or proposal for doing the study, it is becoming increasingly compelling for them to also consider what the possible implications of their study might be—for their teammates, grade level, department, school, and the profession. A response to the literature on the research topic that they choose becomes more of a dialogue, in which teachers converse—if not with the authors of the text, then with each other.

Teachers in southern Florida who are working with the Center for Educational Leaders on Action Research initiatives find ways to share preliminary results of their work with colleagues at regular faculty meetings. They are also encouraged to publish and present at larger venues. Teachers at Highland Park High School who are members of the action research lab teams present a final write-up each year of what they have done and what they have learned. There are often professional development monies available for them to present at conferences and workshops, locally and nationally. (See Senese after chap. 7.)

Beyond audience, if teachers consider the implications of their study for the whole school or for the profession in general, they begin to understand the larger dimensions of education in a democratic society. Who controls knowledge and who owns change? How does change happen? If teachers have informed themselves and investigated best practices, they become part of the process. They have entered into the conversation about how to improve what we offer our students.

A graduate preservice student at Northwestern University conducted an action research project on how schools could be safe environments for gay and lesbian teenagers. He explored local school programs and clubs for gay and lesbian students; he interviewed teacher leaders who have pioneered these efforts in schools; he examined the literature about gay and lesbian adolescent issues; he determined how he could play a role as a teacher in making schools safe for all students. I think that what amazed him most was that there was indeed a community of educators out there who were as concerned as he was about that issue. Through his research, he found members of that community, and he witnessed the constructive action that had been taking place. His research gave him a sense of legitimacy and mission as he began his career. Action research for whom? For this prospective teacher and for his future students. For what? For social and political equity.

LEADERSHIP FOR TEACHER ACTION RESEARCH IN SCHOOLS

Sagor (1992) stated that there are several factors that lead to the abandonment or the continuation of action research efforts in schools. These factors include the significance of the project focus, the amount of support received, the nature of colleagueship, and the performance and encouragement of leadership. The first three dimensions have been discussed here and in other chapters in this volume. The fourth element, leaders and their role in teacher action research, deserves continued study and action research in and of itself.

The literature on action research geared for school administrators recently began to flourish (Glanz, 1999). School principals are beginning to realize the potential for professional development linked to school reform inherent in this movement. However, there is also real potential for mistakes in this endeavor. Teacher action research potentially alters the concept of "failure" (King & Lonnquist, 1993). Teachers who try something in their own classrooms, reflect on outcomes, and retry based on the data gathered cannot be perceived by their administrators as failing. Teachers need to feel that their school encourages a climate for risk-taking in order to undertake this approach to teaching as research. Of course, this doesn't mean that their experimentation is ungrounded and has no basis in what we know about how students learn. Well-designed teacher research is planned on the basis of research and theory, as well as the experiences of other expert teachers. Still, principals of teacher researchers must acknowledge that teachers need a safe working environment in which to explore how best to meet the needs of individual students. If teachers fear failure, they will not risk trying.

In 1999, Governor Jeb Bush instituted a system of grading individual schools as A, B, C, D, or F in Florida schools. His intent was to encourage school principals to be competitive and thereby increase the level of student achievement in their buildings. But in thinking about teacher action research, I have difficulty envisioning an "A" school taking the risk to try something different; I have even more difficulty thinking about how a principal could encourage members of an "F" school to work together to overcome the tremendous odds they are facing by thinking of their teaching as a place for inquiry, imagination, and designing curriculum. My guess is that the "F" school would be much more inclined to teach systematically and directly to the test that gave them that grade in the first place.

School leaders have the responsibility to help make it possible for teachers to work together on research endeavors. Promoting collegial exchanges, affirming the sharing of research results, providing avenues for publishing, and presenting research in faculty circles contribute to a climate of inquiry and collaboration in a school building. "The educational administrators of the future must be much more comfortable about working in a world marked by collegial relationships with teachers and other educators" (Daresh, 1992, p. 233). Many of the South Florida Center for Educational Leaders action research initiatives in schools require that principals participate directly in action research with their faculty. They must attend meetings and share in the conversation about action research; they must collect data and share it with their faculty colleagues. There are implications here for how we prepare people to become administrators; leadership becomes facilitative in a building in which teachers and principals are working together on action research lab teams.

In Little's (1993) analysis of professional development, she placed teachers at the center. Other realities, such as the politics of the school board, the pressures of state mandates, the demands of parents and communities, and the directives from the front office were secondary to the needs and concerns of the teacher and students. Placing teachers at the center of action research initiatives in schools also makes sense; in order to do that, more explicit leadership from teachers in the endeavor is crucial.

We are just beginning to understand how to prepare *teacher* leaders to facilitate action research in their own schools. Because teachers can teach and do action research does not mean that they can help others to do it. Once again, the support of school administrators and other experienced teachers is useful. Recently, I saw an inservice overview from a school district that outlined what participants could "count" for inservice credit. Two items that were *not* eligible were "serving as an Inservice Facilitator" and "breakfast, lunch, dinner, or banquet without a speaker." If we are to encourage teacher leadership and teacher collaboration, why are these activities discounted? Finding ways for more teacher leaders to be involved in the process is not only important to the process of doing research; it is also important to the procedures for linking the research to future policy and curriculum decisions at the school and/or district level.

School districts have discovered that professional development is far more effective if it is organized, implemented, and evaluated by teachers. The Winnetka Teachers Institute does just that in Winnetka, Illinois. Each year, the faculty is polled for what strands they would like to see in their professional development program. Many are continuous over multiple years; some seek outside facilitators and some are teacher led. There is also a teacher action research strand—so termed—

although many of the other strands feature genuine inquiry on specific topics in the strand. All of the planning is done by teachers who encourage, praise, and demonstrate curiosity and interest in what their colleagues are doing. Principals can work toward such a goal by seeing the nurturing of teacher leaders as a mission within their schools (Troen & Boles, 1993). Teachers, in turn, can learn how to be accepting of leadership emerging from their own ranks.

PARTNERING WITH THE UNIVERSITY: TEACHER RESEARCHERS JOIN THE DIALOGUE

> Despite the isolated examples of instances where teacher research and academic research have crossed the borders that divide them, they have essentially been irrelevant to each other. For the most part, educational researchers ignore teachers and teachers ignore them right back. (Evans et al., 1987, in Zeichner, 1995, p. 154)

Not long ago, I had a conversation with Joe Senese, assistant principal at Highland Park High School in suburban Chicago and one of the contributors to this text. (See Senese story after chap. 7.) We discussed the potential for a partnership between the university where I teach and HPHS, with the latter possessing a burgeoning history of action research. Senese was honest in his hesitation: "I have had conversations at conferences about forming a partnership with a university, and, generally, others tell me, 'Don't do it.' Universities make it their project, their agenda, and that's not what we're about here." Since then, I have been exploring exactly what Joe meant, and what can be done about it.

Most of this text has been focused on how teachers conduct classroom research individually or in collaboration with other teachers. This chapter has widened the arena to include school-based initiatives that also involve principals and other administrators. That effort has often been called *action research*. There is another form of research that is termed *collaborative action research* (Oja & Pine, 1987) or *collaborative inquiry* (Catelli, 1995), which takes place between university and school-based researchers. Collaborative action research occurs when: (a) researchers from both the university and the school are involved in defining the question(s), (b) the questions are focused on school-based issues, (c) findings are jointly reported and are used to solve mutually defined problems, (d) school faculty develop research skills and university faculty develop field-based methods, and (e) faculty from both cultures are professionally renewed (Oja & Pine, 1987, p. 97).

Doing collaborative action research, however, presents unique challenges to the notion of "teachers doing research," the title of this book. Therefore, although collaborative action research is not the focus of this book (for a comprehensive look at the literature about collaborative action research, see Mary Rearick's "Action Research: The School University Connection," 1998), it is important to discuss as we deliberate on the larger context within which teachers find themselves when they embark on research with others. Those "others" may, in some cases, be university professors. What then are the hurdles? What are the benefits?

Burbules and Rice, two university researchers, called this approach "dialogue across differences" (1991, p. 393). They asserted that although the aim is meaningful collaboration, there is also the danger that such attempts at dialogue can actually lead to maintaining differences rather than trying to eliminate them (p. 409). There are some definite barriers that need to be addressed if university researchers and teacher researchers are to work together. Here are a few:

1. University researchers consider their expertise to be research; teacher researchers consider their expertise to be teaching.

2. University researchers typically work in three traditional paradigms. There are the positivists, the interpretivists, and the critical theorists (Glesne, 1999). Teacher researchers don't exactly fit under any of those labels; they are, in essence, creating a new paradigm—or worldview—of research.

3. University researchers have generally working principles, within their paradigms for research, for validity and reliability of their methods and results. In other words, they have standards for rigor that are generally understood and accepted in the academic field. Teacher researchers are establishing different standards for success that pertain to practical results and direct application.

4. University researchers perceive that teacher researchers have a general lack of experience with research methodology; teacher researchers have a general perception that university researchers lack classroom experience.

5. Reward systems differ for these two kinds of researchers. David Coulter (1999) said, "University researchers are rewarded for their contributions to scholarly dialogue, not practical discourse" (p. 11). In other

words, they present at conferences, get published, and receive tenure and promotion on the basis of the research knowledge they produce. Teacher researchers are rewarded in their classrooms—by increased expertise as teachers, by increased student learning and engagement, and by meaningful conversation with colleagues.

6. Language and terminology are different for teacher researchers and university researchers. Teachers often tell stories, call on their experiences with specific children, and look to past resources and practices for ideas and insights. Their audience for teacher research is usually other teachers and themselves. University researchers speak and write in scholarly terms with academic audiences in mind.

7. Time and space for dialogue across differences is a challenge. Schedules are often rigid in schools, and teachers often have difficulty coming to university campuses regularly. University researchers are sometimes not as accustomed to working directly in schools and attending to school calendars and schedules.

8. Schools are often limited in terms of technology and other requirements useful for collection design and interpretation of data. University researchers utilize more in terms of technology; teacher researchers often rely on what is available in the school site for their data collection and interpretation of results.

9. Collaboration must be practiced and learned over time; thus, group process needs to be studied and time allotted to it, before, during, and after the actual research process. Neither university researchers nor teacher researchers are accustomed to taking the time to actively learn about how to collaborate, even though both see the need to teach students to do so.

10. University researchers see teacher research as a means of professional development, but not necessarily as a means of knowledge production. Teacher researchers see university research as a means of professional conversation, but not necessarily as a means to directly improve learning and teaching in schools.

If there are so many obstacles to university and teacher researchers who want to collaborate, then why do some still persist? What are the benefits? Judith Lachance Whitcomb's teacher story in this volume attests to the tremendous benefits when this process works well. Table 6.2 reveals some of the benefits and some of the requirements from each of these collaborators.

TABLE 6.2
University Researchers and Teacher Researchers:
What They Give and What They Get From Collaborative Research

University Researchers: What They Give	School/Teacher Researchers: What They Give	University Researchers: What They Get	School/Teacher Researchers: What They Get
Research methods expertise	Access to real students in real classrooms	Access to students and teachers in real-world context	Support to address real issues grounded in classrooms
An outsider's perspective	Expertise in child development, curriculum, teaching	Experience in collaborating with practitioners	Support to look at "the big picture" *and* individual classroom issues
Support for teachers to present and publish their work	Experience in school routines, policies and procedures for getting the work done	Funding for projects linked to student achievement	Data to undergird practice (backup for "why we do what we do," as one teacher said)
Course offerings regarding research and subject-specific topics	Assistance and expertise in classroom management to make research possible	Opportunity to see the connection between knowledge production and application	Guidance in research geared to their own interests
Access to teachers in other schools		Chance to see results of research actually applied	New ideas for their teaching
Access to research done by others			A chance to experience different roles as teachers
			Opportunities to attend and present at conferences and workshops

"Although educational research has produced new understandings and knowledge that, if applied by practitioners, could improve school effectiveness, much of it has remained unused. Consequently, research has had very little impact on school effectiveness" (Huling, Richardson, & Hord, 1983, p. 54).

Both university and teacher researchers have teaching in common (Clandinin & Connelly, 1994, p. 93). They have the chance to learn to work in a common language to improve schooling for children. If they negotiate the purpose and the focus of the research, teachers and university researchers can improve the likelihood that the results of the research will actually be used in the future. School-based work can make university teaching more relevant and grounded. University teachers have much to learn from their K–12 counterparts who know something about how to engage students. Collaborative action research brings both communities together to address the political dimensions of school change and the uses of research. The possibilities are powerful.

David Coulter (1999) called for "dialogic research" across these two communities of researchers. What would such a thing look like? If teachers and professors embraced this notion, we would see many more research conferences and workshops that were attended by both communities of learners. We would see teachers presenting their work in college classrooms and university professors working in teachers' classrooms on research projects with students. We would see more partnership projects, such as Northwestern University's Urban/Suburban Consortium or Chicago Arts Partnerships in Education, in which university professors and teachers/administrators work on projects from the beginning—each with something to learn, each charting a new territory in collaboration, on neutral turf. We would see research highlighted at teacher retreats, faculty meetings, and teacher-led workshops. Research in schools would have to legitimately show that it benefits those schools, teachers, and students; there would be many more parallel research studies in university classrooms in which teacher researchers and university researchers would form action research lab teams on their practice.

Teachers College Press has initiated a Practitioner Inquiry Series that focuses on the work of teacher researchers (see Appendix A). This type of effort demonstrates the value of university/school collaboration. Marilyn Cochran-Smith and Susan L. Lytle, series editors, are both university professors who have supported the work of teacher researchers for many years. Their efforts, and the cooperation of the publisher, have begun an important large-scale move to place teacher research in the domain of "real research" that is legitimate beyond the individual classroom. The teacher researchers featured in the series have become part of the national debate on the issues they have been studying.

One volume in the Practitioner Inquiry Series demonstrated a creative collaboration between university and teacher researchers. The text, *Inside City Schools: Investigating Literacy in the Multicultural Class-*

room (Freedman, Simons, Kalnin, Casareno, & the M-Class Teams, 1999), is a compendium of teacher research studies in New Orleans, Chicago, Boston, and San Francisco on literacy in diverse contexts. At the same time that the teacher researchers were conducting their studies, a University of California Berkeley research team was also studying the process of teacher research occurring in these four sites. Each section of *Inside City Schools* reported teacher research in two ways—the findings of the teacher researchers and the observations of the Berkeley team. Readers learn about the substance of the work that these teachers did; they also learn more about the process of doing teacher research collaboratively in four different urban contexts. This approach serves to further legitimize teacher research in the academic community; as researchers understand more about how teacher research occurs, the findings of that research will find a place in the dialogue.

> Action is not only about doing, but understanding; that is, action can be, as Hannah Arendt (1958) describes, a public dialogue about what is important, good, and just. Action, in this sense, is about creating the possibility for communities to publicly debate what it is that makes them a community. For this dialogue to be an informed dialogue; research must contribute. (Coulter, 1999, p. 12)

Teacher research, university research, action research, and collaborative action research are all under the umbrella of educational research. Beginning the dialogue across contexts will strengthen the work in the larger arena of education.

PRESERVICE TEACHERS DOING TEACHER RESEARCH

Many schools of education are currently puzzled about what to do with teacher research. It is sometimes the basis for a course in the research department, and it is sometimes a course in teacher education. More often than not, if a course actually exists, it is probably not a requirement for a degree and it may be an extension course offered to schools as staff development. Teacher education students are caught in the middle of the debate about what to do with this brand of learning (Anderson & Herr, 1999). This is particularly true when we are talking about preservice teachers, who are learning what it means to be a teacher and experimenting with being researchers at the same time.

Some who have explored the changing curriculum of teacher education in the past 10 years have called for a more realistic kind of teacher preparation "in which the emphasis shifts toward inquiry-oriented activities, interaction amongst learners and the development of reflective skills" (Korthagen & Kessels, 1999, p. 7; Brown, 1992). There is a logical link in these elements to teacher research. Still, actually finding the most meaningful ways to integrate teacher research into preservice teacher education remains a challenge.

Preservice programs that have incorporated an action research component are growing in number in the United States (Gore & Zeichner, 1991; Poetter, Badiali, & Hammond, 1999; Ross, 1987). Teacher educators view action research as a tool for reflection that moves beyond keeping a journal—long a practice for student teachers—into the realm of impacting practice through systematic data collection and interpretation procedures. Research suggests that as preservice teachers become more engaged in their field work during a teacher preparation program, they become more and more focused on "what works" in the immediate situation and less critically reflective in the particular ways that their university coursework encourages (Goodman, 1986; Zeichner & Tabachnick, 1981). The immediate "need to know" results in the beginning teachers adopting the attitudes and methods of their cooperating/mentor teachers without genuine analysis and assessment. An action research approach provides beginning teachers with the tools to systematically rethink their teaching *while* they are teaching. They can then base curricular decisions on real data rather than on the lore of teaching they encounter when they enter schools as student teachers.

It is by no means an easy task, however, to really do research, as a beginning teacher *and* teacher researcher. Student teacher Jan Swenson noted:

> Being a student teacher in someone else's classroom, and in the company of a very experienced teachers, how much could I admit and ask about substance and style when I was so unsure of myself? How can we genuinely ask and answer our own questions given the politics and notion of expertise involved in schools? (Threatt et al., 1994, p. 239)

I have been interested in examining just that issue as I support preservice teachers in being researchers. I have also, in the tradition of being a teacher researcher, looked for models for how others have done things. What I have discovered is that the question of ownership lies at the heart of successful teacher action research at the preservice level. The three designs that follow offer different perspectives on integrating teacher action research into preservice education.

TEACHER ACTION RESEARCH MODELS FOR PRESERVICE TEACHERS

University-Generated Teacher Action Research

Some current teacher research involving preservice teachers stems from a university-generated project assignment for students that requires the willingness, if not the active participation, of experienced teachers in schools (Burbank, 1999; Poetter et al., 1999). Preservice candidates enter the field site with a project idea in mind and try to work within the confines of the school world to complete their projects and satisfy course requirements of the university, hopefully with the support of mentor teachers at the site. Ownership, in this case, is clearly in the hands of the university—and the preservice teacher who selects a topic or question for research. But such research, generated by preservice teachers who are only temporarily at a school site, does not appear to appreciably affect the work of faculty at those sites, nor is collaboration with site faculty a necessary part of the process (Burnaford, 1999).

School Site-Generated Teacher Action Research

Another model recognizes the all-school focus and goals that a school district has as the framework for preservice teacher research that occurs at schools in that district. Presumably, teachers will already be working toward that focus, and preservice teachers could learn immeasurably from collaborating with those grounded in the reality of real research. At Evanston Township High School (ETHS) in Evanston, Illinois, we are currently experimenting with this approach. The school has been focusing on minority achievement in all academic areas. I, as a university liaison, have met with the department chairs at the high school and introduced them to the parameters of the teacher research project that our master's preservice candidates must complete. It is our intention to encourage our preservice teachers to find research questions that connect in some general way to the ETHS goal of enhancing minority achievement. They will receive support from both the school and the university for these endeavors.

The teachers at ETHS do not necessarily think of themselves as "teacher researchers," nor have many of them actually studied the methods of data collection and interpretation in any coursework. A danger is that the preservice candidate will be largely responsible for the "research," and collaboration may be limited because of time. We are working to find ways to make the collaboration more genuine, with opportunities for both faculty at the high school and the university students to help us shape the model. Ownership here is with the high school, in terms of the overarching goal, but resides in the preservice teacher candidate's capacity to do the research as an individual who generates a personally relevant research question. One preservice teacher commented on such a successful collaboration at her field site:

> I think the teachers who have been so welcoming are themselves really interested in the students being successful. Whatever that means. . . . They're interested in change, if necessary. They're all reflective teachers themselves, and they welcome others who want to be reflective and inquiring.

Bates College and the Auburn Public Schools in Auburn, Maine, have tried a partnership in which the teacher in the school develops the question and undergraduate teacher education students do "much of the technical, often repetitive work involved in data collection and analysis" (Wortham, Nigro, & Burns, 1997, p. 4). It is a continuing question whether this structure is optimal for the preservice partners. Wortham et al. further described what happened in this experience when one undergraduate, as the research transpired, began to develop her own research question "and the professor had to direct her back to the original issue" (p. 6). For me, the challenge is to examine how a partnership can work with more than one related question—accommodating both preservice and inservice teachers' interests—and how to develop a genuine process where each can learn from what the other is addressing.

Collaboratively Generated Teacher Action Research

In the third model, both preservice and inservice teachers have studied how to do action research through coursework or workshops. The experienced teachers are already organized into supportive action lab teams who are doing teacher research, and student teachers are invited into this arena. They may be part of a graduate program in which action research is a component, just as it is in the preservice program. Cohorts or pairs of preservice teachers who enter into such a process provide the support for each other as they engage in this process. Inviting preservice teachers to the table during team sessions may open new options (Cochran-Smith, Garfield, & Greenberger, 1992). Preservice teachers often bring a strong sense of the research process, because they are learning about it in their university classes. But they lack the real context for applying methods that their experienced counterparts can provide.

In this model, the experienced teachers can more readily suggest the areas for investigation. They have been in the classroom longer and can identify needs that preservice teachers often struggle to name. The experienced teachers are looking for solutions to problems they have encountered firsthand. The questions that emerge are real; they have not been designed for an external audience or for a course requirement. As apprentice teachers engage in action research, they develop an increased awareness of the decisions they will be making as teachers, as they watch their more experienced colleagues do so through the research.

Ownership in this third model clearly has the potential to be joint; both preservice and inservice teachers are receiving support and incentive to do the research. Both are focused on completing a product for sharing—either with course colleagues, school faculty, or both. Although the expectations may be different for novice and experienced teachers (Radencich, 1998), the idea that both are consciously engaged in the process of research, are learning methods and approaches as they work, and are accountable to an audience of their peers helps both parties to work together for meaningful results.

PRESENTING AND PUBLISHING AS PRESERVICE TEACHERS: VALUING WHAT NOVICE TEACHERS KNOW

In my preservice teacher research course, students prepare poster sessions for each other on the projects we have been investigating in the field (see Fig. 6.1). I encourage them to do a similar kind of visual dis-

Feedback sheet: Specific Poster
As I viewed/discussed this poster, I:
  Thought about . . .
  Would like to know more about . . .
  Am confused by . . .
  Learned that . . .

Feedback sheet: General Comments About These Projects and Action Research
As I viewed the poster exhibits of students' action research, I:

FIG. 6.1. Poster session: Data display and interpretation.

play to share with their field sites; a poster might be the most efficient means of communicating what the preservice candidate has been learning and thinking about. Students have told me that these sessions have helped them see the power of research as a means to help people collaborate. "I also gained a sense of how my peers could help me in my practice," one student commented, as she looked at the action research posters of her classmates. This event may be the precursor to the future when this student feels confident enough to join the professional dialogue, attend conferences, and present her research for others to see. If this prospective teacher sees this potential in her classmates, she will also see it in her faculty peers. One student wrote, "Each poster represented a theory, but also reflected a personal side."

Finding ways to include and value the teacher action research done by novices is a challenge for university educators; it is also a task for field sites where preservice teachers do their work. In some schools, preservice teachers find a venue—in a faculty meeting, a lunch session, or a more social event—to share what their research has been. Making the written products available to teachers at a field site is also beneficial, as is the sharing of preliminary findings or visual displays, such as posters, for feedback from experienced faculty. Bringing the two communities together not only strengthens the work of novice teachers; it enables experienced teachers to share what they know with each other and with the new professionals in the field.

We have looked at three models that might be useful learning tools for thinking about preservice teacher education and teacher research. There is much more to be explored about this topic, and some of the references noted in this section might be helpful to readers who want to focus more on this topic. In order to view teacher research as an integrated part of preservice teacher preparation, research, methods, and field experiences must be connected more coherently. This means thinking about ownership of such experiences and making that ownership explicit. It means communicating across boundaries and being mindful of students' rights and the responsibility for ethical decisions as teachers, student teachers, and teacher educators.

PERSONAL TEACHER RESEARCH IN THE PUBLIC CONTEXT

Teacher research is an individual and, at times, intensely personal endeavor. But, as we have seen, it often takes place in a very public arena among peer educators, university-driven agendas, and school-based policy and reform initiatives. Judy Buchanan wrote: "I am struck by how hard it is to talk about teacher research apart from the students we teach" (Threatt et al., 1994, p. 237). Teacher researchers affect their students, and their students affect them—as teachers and as researchers. The acknowledgment and questioning of just how our research affects other constituencies should be an ongoing part of our reflection. We might ask ourselves questions about teacher action research in the public context. Questions about teacher action research help us discover how the public and the personal connect:

- How does what I am researching affect how and what my students learn?
- How does my involvement with other researchers impact on my teaching and the students in my classroom?
- How are parents affected by what I am doing as a researcher and what I think is important to study?
- And finally, in whose interest is this research?

There is much that we do not know about how to bring the two worlds of school-based action research and individual teacher action research together. We are learning that the purpose, focus, and use for research results must be clear and collectively accepted. We also know that participation and collaboration cannot be mandated or assumed. Both come from a culture of schooling that is larger than the single initiative of "doing action research" in a building. Researchers need to study just how this works in a building where teacher action research is sustained over time and supported by school leaders.

Researchers could examine more closely how teachers learn to collaborate with colleagues who teach with them and how they learn to encourage even those they do not work with directly. Finally, researchers could explore the intersection of mandated goals for school reform and individual teachers' needs, interests, and challenges. How these two are translated into meaningful teacher action research is the challenge of the next generation of teacher researchers.

WEB SITES

http://madison.k12.wi.us/sod/car/abstract.html   Madison, Wisconsin, action research site.

http://elmo.scu.edu.au/schools/sawd/ari/ar.html   Action Research Resources.

http://www.parnet.org/home.cfmPARnet   Participatory Action Research Network (Cornell University).

http://www.uea.ac.uk/care/carn/   Community Action Research Network.

REFERENCES

Anderson, G. L., & Herr, K. (1999). The new paradigm wars: Is there room for rigorous practitioner knowledge in schools and universities? *Educational Researcher, 28*(5), 12–21, 40.

Berlin, D. F. (1996, April). *Teacher action research: The impact of inquiry on curriculum improvement and professional development.* Paper presented at the annual meeting of the American Educational Research Association, New York.

Brown, M. J. M. (1992, April). *Teaching as an interpretive inquiry process.* Paper presented at the annual meeting of the Educational Development Center on Action Research and the Reform of Mathematics and Science Education, Cape Cod, MA.

Burbank, M. D. (1999, February). *Empowering urban teacher research communities.* Paper presented at the annual conference of the Association of Teacher Educators, Chicago.

Burbules, N. C., & Rice, S. (1991). Dialogue across differences: Continuing the conversation. *Harvard Educational Review, 61*(4), 393–416.

Burnaford, G. (1997, April). *Collaborative self-study: A new venue for curriculum theorizing.* Paper presented at the annual meeting of the American Educational Research Association, New York.

Burnaford, G. (1999, April). *School wide inquiry: A self-study of an "outside" teacher researcher.* Paper presented at the annual meeting of the American Educational Research Association, Montreal, Canada.

Burnaford, G., & Hobson, D. (1995). Beginning with the group: Collaboration as the cornerstone of graduate teacher education. *Action in Teacher Education, 17*(3), 67–75.

Catelli, L. A. (1995). Action research and collaborative inquiry in a school–university partnership. *Action in Teacher Education, 16*(4), 25–38.

Clandinin, J., & Connelly, M. (1994). The promise of collaborative research in the political context. In S. Hollingsworth & H. Sockett (Eds.), *Teacher research and educational reform: Ninety-third yearbook of the National Society for the Study of Education* (pp. 86–102). Chicago: University of Chicago Press.

Cochran-Smith, M., Garfield, E., & Greenberger, R. (1992). Student teachers and their teacher: Talking our way into new understandings. In N. A. Branscombe, D. Goswami, & J. Schwartz (Eds.), *Student teaching, teachers learning* (pp. 274–292). Portsmouth, NH: Boynton Cook/Heinemann.

Coulter, D. (1999). The epic and the novel: Dialogism and teacher research. *Educational Researcher, 28*(3), 4–13.

Daresh, J. C. (1992). Reflections on practice: Implications for administrator preparation. In E. W. Ross, J. W. Cornett, & G. McCutcheon (Eds.), *Teacher Personal theorizing: connecting curriculum practice, theory, and research* (pp. 219–235). Albany: State University of New York Press.

Freedman, S. W., Simons, E. R., Kalnin, J. S., Casareno, A., & the M-Class Teams. (1999). *Inside city schools: Investigating literacy in multicultural classrooms.* New York: Teachers College Press.

Glanz, J. (1999). *Action research: An educational leader's guide to school improvement.* Norwood, MA: Christopher Gordon.

Glesne, C. (1999). *Becoming qualitative researchers: An introduction* (2nd ed.). New York: Longman.

Goodman, J. (1986). Making early field experience meaningful: A critical approach. *Journal of Education for Teaching, 12*(2), 109–125.

Gore, J., & Zeichner, K. (1991). Action research and reflective teaching in preservice teacher education: A case study from the United States. *Teaching and Teacher Education, 7*(2), 119–136.

Harris, B., & Drake, S. M. (1997). Implementing high school reform through school-wide action research teams: A three year case study. *Action in Teacher Education, 19*(3), 15–31.

Holly, P. (1987). Action research: Cul-de-sac or turnpike? *Peabody Journal of Education, 64*(3), 71–99.

Huling, L. L., Richardson, J. A., & Hord, S. M. (1983). Three projects show how university/school partnerships can improve effectiveness. *NASSP Bulletin, 67*(465), 54–59.

King, J. A., & Lonnquist, M. P. (1993, April). *Lessons learned from the history of collaborative action research in schools.* Paper presented at the annual meeting of the American Educational Research Association, Atlanta, GA.

Korthagen, F. A. J., & Kessels, J. P. A. M. (1999). Linking theory and practice: Changing the pedagogy of teacher education. *Educational Researcher, 29*(4), 4–17.

Lieberman, A., & Miller, L. (1994). Problems and possibilities of institutionalizing teacher research. In S. Hollingsworth & H. Sockett (Eds.), *Teacher research and educational reform: Ninety-third yearbook of the National Society for for the Study of Education* (pp. 204–220). Chicago: University of Chicago Press.

Little, J. W. (1993). Teachers' professional development in a climate of educational reform. *Educational Evaluation and Policy Analysis, 15*(2), 129–152.

Oja, S. N., & Pine, G. J. (1987). Collaborative action research: Teachers' stages of development in school contexts. *Peabody Journal of Education, 64*(2), 96–115.

Poetter, T., Badiali, B., & Hammond, D. J. (1999, February). *Teacher inquiry in a partner school.* Paper presented at the Association of Teacher Educators annual meeting, Chicago.

Radencich, M. C. (1998). Planning a teacher research course: Challenges and quandaries. *Educational Forum, 62*(3), 265–272.

Rearick, M. L. (1998, April). *Action research: The school university connection.* Paper presented at the annual meeting of the American Educational Research Association, San Diego, CA.

Ross, D. D. (1987). Action research for preservice teachers: A description of why and how. *Peabody Journal of Education, 64*(3), 131–150.

Sagor, R. D. (1992, April). *Collaborative action research: A cultural mechanism for school development and professional restructuring.* Paper presented at the annual meeting of the American Educational Research Association. San Francisco, CA.

Threatt, S., Buchanan, J., Morgan, B., Sugarman, J., Swenson, J., Teel, K., Streib, L., & Tomlinson, J. (1994). Teachers' voices in the conversation about teacher research. In S. Hollingsworth & H. Sockett (Eds.), *Ninety-third yearbook of the National Society for the Study of Education* (pp. 222–244). Chicago: University of Chicago Press.

Troen, V., & Boles, K. (1993, November 3). Teacher leadership: How to make it more than a catch phrase. *Education Week*, pp. 27, 29.

Wortham, S., Nigro, G., & Burns, C. (1997, March). *Facilitating teacher research through school–university partnerships.* Paper presented at the annual meeting of the American Educational Research Association, Chicago.

Zeichner, K. M. (1994). Personal renewal and social construction through teacher research. In S. Hollingsworth & H. Sockett (Eds.), *Teacher research and educational reform: Ninety-third yearbook of the National Society for the Study of Education* (pp. 66–84). Chicago: University of Chicago Press.

Zeichner, K. M. (1995). Beyond the divide of teacher research and academic research. *Teachers and Teaching: Theory and Practice, 1*(2), 153–172.

Zeichner, K. M., & Tabachnick, B. R. (1981). Are the effects of university teacher education "washed out" by school experience? *Journal of Teacher Education, 32*(2), 7–11.

APPENDIX A: THE PRACTITIONER INQUIRY SERIES (MARILYN COCHRAN-SMITH AND SUSAN L. LYTLE, SERIES EDITORS)

Inside City Schools: Investigating Literacy in the Multicultural Classroom, by Sarah Warshauer Freedman, Elizabeth Radin Simons, Julie Shalhope Kalnin, Alex Casareno, and the M-Class teams.

Class Actions: Teaching for Social Justice in Elementary and Middle School, edited by JoBeth Allen.

Teacher/Mentor: A Dialogue for Collaborative Learning, edited by Peg Graham, Sally Hudson-Ross, Chandra Adkins, Patti McWhorter, and Jennifer McDuffie Stewart.

Teaching Other People's Children: Literacy and Learning in a Bilingual Classroom, by Cynthia Ballenger.

Teaching, Multimedia, and Mathematics: Investigations of Real Practice, by Magdalene Lampert and Deborah Loewenberg Ball.

Tensions of Teaching: Beyond Tips to Critical Reflection, by Judith M. Newman.

John Dewey and the Challenge of Classroom Practice, by Stephen M. Fishman and Lucille Practice.

"Sometimes I Can Be Anything": Power, Gender, and Identity in a Primary Classroom, by Karen Gallas.

Learning in Small Moments: Life in an Urban Classroom, by Daniel R. Meier.

Interpeting Teacher Practice: Two Continuing Stories, by Renate Schulz.

Creating Democratic Classrooms: The Struggle to Integrate Theory and Practice, edited by Landon E. Beyer.

7

TEACHER ACTION RESEARCH AND PROFESSIONAL DEVELOPMENT: FOUNDATIONS FOR EDUCATIONAL RENEWAL

Linda S. Tafel
National College of Education

Joseph C. Fischer

> Schools will improve slowly, if at all, if reforms are thrust upon them. Rather, the approach having most promise, in my judgment, is one that will seek to cultivate the capacity of schools to deal with their own problems, to become largely self-renewing. (Goodlad, 1987, p. 134)

Visions for better schools inform teachers' decisions and shape the kinds of inquiry interests they explore during their professional lives. Teacher action research is guided by personal values and beliefs and is enriched and illuminated through dialogue with colleagues and students. Schools become communities of learning, caring, and inquiry, when students and teachers begin to envision what kind of places they want to create, how they want to live, and what brings meaning in their lives. Importantly, schools must find ways to cultivate trusting relationships and help teachers feel valued as colleagues and educational leaders. Such valuing is evident in the opportunities and recognition teachers receive for making key curriculum decisions, authoring school improvement plans, taking ownership of professional development activities, doing research, and assuming leadership in the educational community. Our premise is that to create better schools, teachers must be viewed in dramatically new ways: as leaders, researchers, and authors of their professional development.

In this chapter, we use the term *educational renewal* as a composite concept encompassing both professional development and school improvement. Hence, we see educational renewal as both a personal quest of teachers and a goal for schools as they try to build communities of quality teaching and learning. Our main purpose is to explore how action research can support educational renewal by helping teachers try out new strategies, which, in turn, can provide a more solid foundation for school-wide improvement. We examine how teacher action research can be an effective method of identifying central goals for school improvement. We also note how teacher action research can serve to document the progress and effectiveness of school improvement programs. Finally, we point out how teacher action research involves telling stories that can help frame school improvement agendas and professional development programs.

We believe that teachers doing action research can help us understand the "lived worlds" of teachers and thus serve an important function for educational renewal. We see educational renewal in the larger context of building caring communities and envisioning what school can be (Greene, 1991). Greene felt coming together in community for dialogue makes it possible for teachers not only to consider the realities of their work, but also helps them transcend to higher levels of thinking and living. She held that this happens when teachers begin to think about what it really means to be educators, what it means to be human. Educational renewal is about what is possible for schools and teachers to become, and thus ultimately about something transcendent.

> I am suggesting that a concern for personal reality cannot be divorced from a concern for cooperative action within some sort of community. It is when teachers are together as persons, according to norms and principles they have freely chosen, that interest becomes intensified and commitments are made.... Coming together to determine what is possible, teachers may discover a determination to transcend. (Greene, 1991, p. 13)
>
> It is important to move back in inner time and attempt to recapture the ways in which the meanings of teaching (and schooling) were sedimented over the years. It should not be impossible for individual teachers to reflect back upon the ways in which they have constituted what they take to be the realities of their lived worlds. To look back, to remember is to bind the incidents of past experience, to create patterns in the stream of consciousness. We identify ourselves by means of memory; and, at once, we compose the stories of our lives. (Greene, 1991, p. 11)

We first present a framework for schools to consider as they plan for school improvement and strive to create communities of learning and inquiry. The second part describes a case study of one teacher, Ann Watson-Cohn, illustrating how her professional life of inquiry unfolded, and thus provides lessons for setting school improvement and professional development agendas. In the last part, we discuss how teachers' visions for professional development can provide guidelines for educational renewal.

BUILDING SCHOOLS OF INQUIRY: A CENTRAL FOCUS OF EDUCATIONAL RENEWAL

Currently, visions about how we might best live together in schools are often clouded and sometimes contradictory. Lieberman and Miller (1991) and others have painted pictures of what a "professional" school culture might look like. Although Yee and McLaughlin (in Lieberman & Miller, 1991) described school as a place to have a career, other models for professional or staff development continue to perpetuate the "working on" framework. Tafel and Bertani (1992) argued for an alternative view of "working with" teachers as key to meaningful professional development agendas. The old inservice model, with its many deficit or deficient assumptions about teachers, dies hard.

Schaefer (1967) provided one of the first visions of the school as the center of teacher inquiry. "What could be more engaging than inquiring into the myriad mysteries of the child's world or learning more about ways of fostering the individual student's search for meaning?" (p. 59). But Schaefer also lamented that "teachers have not been freed to study their craft. . . . Instead, they have had to bear a heavy burden of guilt for being unable to resolve difficulties" (p. 59). In outlining what it would take to move from a "blame the teachers" stance toward a school that inquires, Schaefer called for those innovations that to this day have remained unimplemented in most schools—true colleagueship among teaching peers, reduction of bureaucratic control of the teaching profession, and a culture of collaboration.

In working toward visions of what might be, we and our teacher colleagues remain hopeful (as Schaefer was) of remaking a profession, promoting educational change, and improving schools. Through our work together, we have come to recognize the chicken–egg relation-ship between all that takes place with a school culture. Teachers can-not inquire without becoming researchers. Inquiry and research agen-das can provide and have provided the context for professional growth and school change. They help build a framework for "having a career" and for discovering meanings through reflection and inquiry on one's teaching. As we have worked together, we have been intrigued by and embraced Roland Barth's vision of the ideal school:

> A place where teachers and principals talk with one another about prac-tice, observe one another engaged in their work, share their craft knowl-edge with each other, and actively help each other become better. In a col-legial school, adults and students are constantly learning because everyone is a staff developer for everyone else. (Barth, 1990, p. 163)

What do school communities that value learning and inquiry look like? First, we believe they begin with a value base that establishes a commitment to build and sustain a community for inquiry among teachers, among students, and between and among teachers and stu-dents. Teacher Nelda Hobbs loved to tell the story of a big difference between "doing school" and "being a community." So many of our teacher colleagues lamented the lack of excitement, the focus on meet-ing state-mandated objectives, the humdrum of the school experience for both students and teachers. In a community that values learning and inquiry, ideas, activity, questions, and unsolved mysteries are all exciting, perplexing, and challenging. There is energy, enthusiasm, and wonder.

There is, fundamentally, a culture of care. In describing such a cul-ture, Nel Noddings (1984) stated, "We must recognize our longing for relatedness and accept it, and we must commit ourselves to the open-ness that permits us to receive the other" (p. 104). She described the relatedness between teacher and student: "The special gift of the teacher, then, is to receive the student. . . . Her commitment is to him, the cared-for, and he is—through that commitment—set free" (p. 177). We believe teachers can and must create such a culture of care for and with each other. One must meet the other in caring. The teacher's spe-cial gift, then, is to receive not only the student, but also her teacher colleagues, to be committed to them as both teachers and learners, and to extend together their individual and collective inquiry.

In working for educational renewal, we need to understand the fac-tors that influence both the ethical decisions teachers make and the kinds of moral issues that intrigue them. Reflecting on practice should help teachers become more aware of the values operating in their instructional choices and reveal why certain questions and dilemmas about teaching intrigue them. Ultimately, knowing and caring about students and learning is the common ground of teacher research, professional development, and school improvement.

Building communities of caring, learning, and inquiry is basically a moral task. Martin Buber (1947) viewed this ethical dimension of educational renewal as one of entering into communion with others, and considered educating as fundamentally a dialogue, within a caring community:

> The child, in putting things together, learns much that he can learn in no other way. In making something, he gets to know its possibility, its origin and structure and connections, in a way he cannot learn by observation. But there is something else that is not learned in this way, and that is the viaticum of life. The being of the world as an object is learned from within, but not its being as a subject, its saying of I and Thou. What teachers us the saying of Thou is not the originative instinct but the instinct for communion. (pp. 87–88)
>
> This fragile life between birth and death can nevertheless be a fulfillment—if it is a dialogue. In our life and experience we are addressed by thought and speech and action, by producing and by influencing we are able to answer. (p. 92)

REFLECTION AND RENEWAL: ONE TEACHER RESEARCHER'S INQUIRY

To learn about their work, it is only natural that teachers observe, ask questions, consult with colleagues, try out different teaching strategies, and interpret what has taken place—all elements of teacher action research. In our work with teachers, we have found, as Schon (1983) did in his research, that teacher research involves "a continuing process of self-education," and that as teachers become researchers-in-practice, "the practice itself is a source of renewal" (p. 299). In studying the role of reflection in teacher development and learning, Richert believed that

> good teaching does not rest on a set of static, prescribed rules and technical strategies. Rather, shifting circumstances suggest teachers be reflective in their approach to classroom practice. Reflective teachers ap-

proach teaching as problem solving; they see teaching circumstances and conditions as problematic rather than given, and they approach each situation with an openness to both the known and the unknown. (quoted in Lieberman & Miller, 1991, p. 114)

To illustrate the interplay between teacher research, reflection, and educational renewal, we turn to our work over the past several years with Ann Watson-Cohn, who reflected on her professional development through a series of dialogue journals and discussions with us. Ann taught at the Baker Demonstration School of National-Louis University. As did other teachers cited in this text, she found that reflecting on her teaching was essential to her professional growth and satisfaction and that there was a close affinity between her inquiry, intellectual curiosity, and development as a teacher. In an early journal, Ann described her professional growth as a journey of unfolding questions.

One of the most important influences on my teaching during that first year or two was my belief that my colleagues knew a great deal more about teaching reading, or math, or science or social studies, than I did. Lunchtime conversations often centered on instructional problems my peers had. Words, terms, and phrases unknown to me popped up with tantalizing and embarrassingly frequent regularity. Sometimes an instructional activity would be described that was unlike anything I had heard of. I remember to this day someone excitedly describing a successful reading/writing activity involving predictable books. I had never heard of using repetitive stories to generate children's own stories! What a good idea. How did one do this? When could I try it? I immediately started experimenting with this notion in my classroom while looking for additional information about it. And so it went. I heard colleagues talk about things unfamiliar to me, scavenged for information on it, and experimented with everything in my classroom. There was no formal plan to learning, but I certainly had plenty of new questions to answer each week. I didn't like not knowing.

As I reflect on my first years at Baker, they were clearly a time of knowledge building. My questions were guided by what I heard around me. Further, ... I was free to explore within my own classroom. Lots of mistakes were made by me in those days, but I watched, reflected and improved with each successive try. Freedom to experiment with new ideas, latitude within a curriculum to do so and an environment that encouraged and supported creativity in teaching certainly helped my growth as a teacher during those first critical years here.

Ann began to see her personal reality as a teacher as one of exploring ideas and meaning making (Greene, 1991). She talked about how her world of teaching began to expand "beyond the walls of her classroom." She looked more deeply at what her questions revealed about her teaching and learning. Her questions were becoming more focused and often found their source in her observations of her students.

Like most classroom teachers I first viewed the walls of the classroom and the space between them as the only legitimate area of concern for me. Gradually I extended this view to include school-wide issues. I also began to alter the kinds of questions I asked about teaching. Prior to teaching the reading methods course at the end of my second year at Baker, I asked questions about subjects I felt I ought to know about. They were motivated by fear of being found inadequate (by my administrator, my peers, and by myself). In hindsight, I realize this fear had slowly been diminishing each time I worked with a college student in my classroom or spoke to visiting teachers about the kinds of things we did in the room.

Three important outcomes resulted from these experiences. First, my teaching in reading shifted from a skills-based approach to a process-oriented one as a result of the reading and research I did for that course. This in turn influenced instruction in all areas of the curriculum because I now was much more comfortable with the notion of being guided by the children's needs. I planned and altered instruction much more often based on observations of my students. Secondly, I began to believe that classroom teachers could contribute to the field of education in places outside those four classroom walls.

The third outcome was a change in the type of questions I asked. Instead of a scattered and random approach to gathering information about teaching dependent upon what I heard or didn't hear, I became more deliberate in my choice of question. I began by updating my knowledge of math. My need was to find out how to make my practice in this subject area more developmentally appropriate, effective, interesting and challenging for my students. Two well taught courses provided me with an excellent background which in turn led to a further change in the type of questions I asked.

Up until this point I was curious to find out the pieces of information I felt I lacked, but this gradually began to alter. As I attended to the cues the students gave me each day and taught accordingly, questions began to emerge based on these observations. This latest batch of questions tended to be about the ways in which children come to learn, rather than about a broad subject area. I wanted to know things such as: How do children come to understand addition? How do they make the connection between problem-solving strategies and the symbols that represent the operations?

How do I help children use all the cuing systems in order to read fluently? or even, What are some ways we can integrate reading, literature, mathematics? The shift in questions was from a reactive to a proactive stance, and more importantly the source of my questions moved from other adults to the children themselves.

Other questions in the Baker/National environment also affected my teaching in subtle ways. The opportunity to do presentations at state, regional and national conventions gave me a chance to share some of my classroom "experiments." The positive feedback I received on each of these occasions reassured me that I was asking worthy questions and making practical discoveries. It also convinced me further of the need for teachers to share their work with other teachers in public ways.

The final factor to affect my teaching was the role of the teachers at Baker in the school decision-making process. The opportunities to raise, address, and resolve issues affecting us gave me an important sense of not only ownership, but also responsibility. This carried over into a sense of responsibility for my own professional learning. If I didn't know how to teach math well, then it was my job, not someone else's, to improve that knowledge. Faculty decision-making, opportunities to discuss ideas, public ways in which to share them even before they're completely polished and refined (I know that's a radical idea!), freedom to experiment in one's own classroom AND most importantly the chance to do this on your own schedule, guided by your own interests all have the potential to transform teaching practice for teachers.

From her tentative time of anxiety entering a new school, Ann Watson-Cohn gradually found a sense of confidence in herself as a teacher, recognition from colleagues, and ownership of her teaching. Eventually, she began to see herself as wanting to make a contribution to her profession. She emerged from the "four walls of her classroom," and became interested in school-wide issues and later profession-wide ones. Her questions unfolded from ones concerned with how to be a competent teacher of content, to ones of how students learn, and what is behind their learning. She started focusing on "why-type" and "connecting-type" questions. Her inquiry journey began with concerns of her worthiness as a member of a faculty. It did not take long before her observations of students and reflections on her personal interests became the foundations of her inquiry. Eventually, Ann felt a leadership responsibility to work with colleagues on school-wide concerns to build a community of caring, learning, and inquiry at Baker School. She portrayed the kind of commitment to other teachers that Greene (1991) believed can lead to "richer ways of being human" (p. 13).

TEACHERS' VISIONS OF PROFESSIONAL DEVELOPMENT AND TEACHER RESEARCH

When teachers are asked for suggestions about effective and meaningful professional development activities, their most frequent response is that they want more opportunity to reflect on their work and to discuss their teaching and learning with colleagues. This is significant to note, for if schools are to benefit from teacher knowledge and learning, a culture for inquiry, reflection, and dialogue must be created. Our discussions with teachers about professional development reveal a continued quest to learn about teaching, and portray the kinds of school climates that foster or hinder such learning. In this section, we examine the kind of visions for professional development that teachers hold. Such visions provide an essential foundation for creating better schools and, ultimately, more caring, just, and democratic societies.

In thinking about her teaching career, Penny Silvers wrote:

> My professional growth and development has been a "work in progress" filled with many drafts, revisions, conferences with significant others, and attempts at making sense out of my chosen career. It has been a messy and not always predictable learning process. But along the way, there have been opportunities to take learning risks, support from other professionals, and reflective moments that have guided me toward the shaping and developing of my personal vision of what school could be.

Silvers asked a group of colleagues what they found meaningful in any staff development they experienced. In her journal describing their conversation, she wrote:

> The main theme that emerged was that the staff development that was planned by the teachers and which gave them an opportunity to talk together, share ideas, and work toward a common goal—that came from within—meant the most to them.

This idea of interacting with colleagues was echoed by Astrid Martindale, who noted:

> I have found through trial runs at different schools, that teachers don't want to listen to me or anyone as a "how-giver." They prefer to be interactive. The staff meeting in which I proposed that next year's format for

inservices be changed to reflect examining our school culture, looking at our "we-ness," our values etc. was eagerly accepted. I was, am, overjoyed.

A persistent theme of our dialogue with teachers is that episodic inservice events had little impact on their development and learning, and, generally, that the school culture itself did little to encourage teacher learning and development. Penny Silvers wrote:

> I did not gain a strong sense of myself as a professional educator from school itself. Operating from a traditional perspective, the schools where I taught, treated teachers as workers, complete with in-service training, summative supervision, and accountability for student performance on standard measures. I had to find support for my own professional growth outside of school, from colleagues with similar interests, professors who were willing to engage in teacher research with me, and my own reading and reflection.

Bruce Ahlborn found that his best professional development experiences were with colleagues who encouraged him to try out new strategies in his teaching.

> Up until three years ago, I had never experienced a sustained constructivist approach to inservice or staff development. The topics . . . did not provide any sort of activating event that would translate into my classroom and have a beneficial effect on my students. But I do recall events staffed by certain local high school teachers who demonstrated things that they were doing with their students and these presentations were useful and different because I tried their techniques on my students. My students liked these new techniques so I kept doing them and modifying them as I went along.

In formulating her vision for professional development, Carol Porter suggested that:

> Teachers might invite other teachers into their classrooms to observe the application of new strategies or create a video to share with others. By providing an audience for learners, we are providing a reason for them to be reflective practitioners who stand back from the learning and seek to understand it. Through this type of analysis, teachers can begin to construct interpretations that will begin a new cycle of inquiry.

In this vein, Ahlborn believed that teacher development should be people-oriented and as such will consider the culture of the setting as well as the state of the individual in regard to professional and intellectual growth. . . . We need to think of ourselves with the same high regard that Dewey advocated for children.

In thinking about what influenced their learning about teaching and their professional development, many teachers cited a colleague or mentor who both affirmed their learnings and nudged them toward other inquiry and self-discovery paths. They paused to reflect on the images they held of themselves as teachers, what this meant in their development and how they felt about it. Their visions for professional development are grounded in people who are examples of these images. This was the case for Janell Cleland, who remembered the impact her English department chairperson had on her life. They frequently went to the library together pursuing research interests. In her journal to us, Cleland wrote:

For the first time I wasn't looking for activities that would work in class the next day. I wanted to know why some things worked in class and why others did not. Was there a pattern to successes? I explored the writing process with students, telling them we were in this together. We read sections of *Beat Not the Poor Desk* in senior English class and decided together how we could adapt and apply it to ourselves. We created a learning community and took risks. We collaborated and learned together. We revised and improved; it was an exciting two years for me.

Teachers want schools to become intellectual environments in which to teach and learn with their students. This has been a persistent theme in our ongoing conversations with them. Bruce Ahlborn found a personal affinity with Robert Shaefer's book *The School as the Center of Inquiry* (1967) and, in thinking about his students, offered: "When students respond enthusiastically to a particular approach or when a class is alive with the wonder of a new insight or buoyant in the mastery of a new skill, the teacher attains a high pitch of contained excitement and pleasure." He hoped that schools can be a place for like excitement, wonderment, inquiry and discovery for teachers as well.

A major theme in these teacher reflections and visions is that when schools recognize and affirm their learnings and experiences, teachers continue to inquire about their work, share their learnings with their colleagues, and grow professionally. This becomes possible when schools are committed to building a culture of caring and respect for teachers and for students. Several other themes stand out in the teacher stories and visions for professional development presented here.

Teachers told us that their most meaningful professional development entails observing their students, trying out hunches, testing out various practices, reflecting on their work, and being intellectually curious about teaching, learning, and the world of schools. For them, to grow professionally means to live with ambiguity and uncertainty, to take risks, and to learn that mistakes are a natural part of trying out something new. They believe that professional development must be a continuous journey of inquiry, of evaluating and valuing their learning, and of constructing meanings through reflecting on teaching. In their visions for themselves as teachers, they view teaching and learning as inseparable, and believe it is a life's work.

Teachers believe that relating and caring relationships must be central to teaching. To grow professionally involves enhanced communication and empathic understanding between teachers and students, and among teachers. This implies that teachers learn professionally within a school community that honors learning—among students, colleagues, and mentors who share common goals and values, and who trust and respect each other. They have come to realize that caring relationships are required to facilitate learning and inquiry concerns of teachers and students.

Embedded in visions of meaningful professional development are beliefs about what it means to *practice* the teaching profession. This entails exploring teaching ideas with colleagues, finding ways to help students relate to each other, experimenting with new strategies, and finding new awareness of self and profession. This lifetime of practice is greatly enhanced by sharing with colleagues our questions, wonderments, perplexities, and insights.

That teaching must be considered an intellectual rather than a routine task (Dewey, 1933) has been a frequent response in our research with teachers concerning the efficacy of professional development programs they have experienced. Similarly, there is a growing consensus among teachers that professional development plans should be based on a holistic view of learning, provide opportunity for sharing and dialogue among colleagues, affirm and make use of what teachers have learned through experience and reflection, and be an integral and continuous part of the life and culture of the school.

FROM STORIES TO RESEARCH: EDUCATIONAL RENEWAL THROUGH PROFESSIONAL DEVELOPMENT

We have sown the seeds of a view of teacher research and educational renewal that moves us away from the old inservice model. Within a culture of care, teacher research begins with tales of classroom life—stories of children, of lessons, of activity, of good days and bad, of laughter, engagement, and joy of learning. As teachers share those stories openly and with commitment to each other, they grow in their understanding of their professional role, their craft, their art, and helping children grow as learners. Through the sharing of stories about school and classroom life emerge questions that can guide our shared inquiry about how to do what we do better. Through our inquiry comes insight, the ability to deepen our understanding, to recognize both our strengths and our need for growth, renewal and continued inquiry.

With our teacher colleagues, we will continue to construct our theory about how best to build and sustain the relationship between teacher inquiry professional development, and school improvement. We see recurring themes in our research and ongoing dialogue with teachers:

1. Caring relationships and dialogue with colleagues are essential for supporting teachers' questions and pursuing their research. A professional life of inquiry and renewal is possible when schools value collegiality and encourage sharing ideas and learnings among teachers and students. This means telling others about the insights, struggles, and reflections we experience in our teaching. It requires building a school culture in which teachers feel safe in trying out new ideas and exploring ways to improve their teaching. It requires a community of learning, caring, and inquiry. All these are ingredients for educational renewal both at the personal, professional level and at the school level.

2. For educational renewal, teachers need to feel that they have ownership of their teaching, that their decisions are elicited and valued, and that they are responsible for building curriculum and creating communities of learning and inquiry. Teacher authorship must be an essential feature of teacher research, of school improvement, and of professional development initiatives. In studying the field of teacher action research,

Susan Jungck points out that teachers have a central and unique role to play: "the researcher's personal involvement is so integral to the process and outcomes, that the researcher (versus the methods) becomes the key instrument" (see chap. 8). Happily, this is a growing realization and position among the educational research community. Teachers, finally, are being recognized as uniquely able to provide the greatest insights and understanding about teaching practice and student learning. As school people more fully embrace this recognition, teacher research and educational renewal initiatives will be encouraged, supported, and appreciated.

3. Constructing knowledge through reflections on practice is a main goal of teacher research and educational renewal. This entails both a personal responsibility for pursuing one's inquiry, and being encouraged to ask questions, reflect on teaching practice, and share learnings with colleagues. It means there are internal and external dimensions involved in teacher research and teacher development. Again, we find Jungck's discussion of interpretive/constructivist research in this text especially insightful and helpful. She writes about the processes of teacher research that involve "inner reflection and meaning construction, outer observation and activity." Similarly, we have pointed out in this chapter that teacher development is an inner journey of inquiry and reflection within a context of observing students and dialogue with colleagues.

4. As teachers work with their colleagues, they can invite each other to the possibility of creating a caring culture in which wonderment, discovery, relating, and inquiry become the central work of schools. Hopefully, they will continue to cherish this as their vision for schools and as their legacy to the teachers who follow them. In our dialogues with teachers, we are inspired by the many who have begun their journey toward building communities of caring, learning, and inquiry. They have made this their life's work. Influenced by the philosophy of Jean-Paul Sartre, Maxine Greene saw this quest of relating to and caring for others as our life's project.

As we grow older along with others and experienced diverse teachers and teaching situations, we build up a structure of meanings. Many of these meanings derived from the ways in which our choices and purposes were supported or frustrated by other people's choices and purposes in the shifting social worlds of the classrooms we came to know. . . . We may be moved to choose our project because of certain lacks in a social situation in which we are involved. We may want to repair those lacks and make that situation what it might be, rather than what it is. Or our choice of project may be connected with our notion of what we want to make of ourselves, of the kinds of identity we want to create. (Greene, 1991, p. 506)

REFERENCES

Barth, R. S. (1990). *Improving schools from within: Teachers, parents, and principals can make the difference.* San Francisco: Jossey-Bass.

Buber, M. (1947). *Between man and man.* Boston: Beacon Press.

Dewey, J. (1933). *How we think: A restatement of the relation of reflective thinking to the educative process.* Chicago: Henry Regnery.

Goodlad, J. (Ed.). (1987). *The ecology of school renewal: Eighty-sixth yearbook of the national society for the study of education.* Chicago: University of Chicago Press.

Greene, M. (1991). Teaching, the question of personal reality. In A. Lieberman & L. Miller (Eds.), *Staff development for education in the '90s: New demands, new realities, new perspectives* (pp. 3–14). New York: Teachers College Press.

Lieberman, A., & Miller, L. (Eds.). (1991). *Staff development for education in the '90s: New demands, new realities, new perspectives.* New York: Teachers College Press.

Noddings, N. (1984). *Caring: A feminine approach to ethics and moral education.* Berkeley: University of California Press.

Schaefer, R. J. (1967). *The school as a center of inquiry.* New York: Harper & Row.

Schon, D. A. (1983). *The reflective practitioner.* New York: Basic Books.

Tafel, L. S., & Bertani, A. A. (1992). Reconceptualizing staff development for systemic change. *Journal of Staff Development, 13*(4), 42–45.

In Practice—Part II

1. Conduct a social mapping activity, in which you list all the direct and indirect "stakeholders," or people who might be influenced by your teacher action research study. These stakeholders might include groups of people (races, classes, genders), specific constituents, professional associates, or specific people you know in the field.

2. Taking the list from the social mapping activity, brainstorm who would be appropriate collaborators for your study. Who would be willing or able to be full participants? How do you see possible decision making shared with those participants? How do you envision sharing results with appropriate stakeholders?

3. If you are an experienced teacher, contact a local university or college and initiate a communication with a preservice program or teacher. Discuss ways in which teacher action research could be a collaborative venture with preservice teachers in your experience.

4. If you are a preservice teacher candidate, discuss how your field observation journal notes inform potential research questions you have about your own practice. Discuss with colleagues how a meaningful collaboration among mentor teachers and preservice candidates might work.

5. Conduct a discussion with a small group of students about a specific area of the curriculum or classroom procedure that you are curious about. Then design a plan in which the students could be co-researchers to explore the topic further in the classroom. What contributions do the students make that you could not make?

6. Find one other faculty colleague who would be willing to work with you on a collaborative research project for a brief period of time. Meet frequently to discuss what you are finding, then prepare to share your work with a larger group of teachers.

7. Describe the procedures currently in place for professional development in a school system you are familiar with. Then design a model that includes teacher action research. How would such a model be different from the current system? (If your school system already has a teacher action research component, how would you strengthen it?)

8. Construct and distribute a survey of faculty in your building to assess professional development needs and interests. How could the data from this survey be utilized to plan professional development for the next 3 years? What did you, as a teacher researcher, learn from this survey process?

9. Research available grants for teacher research in your state, city, country, and professional associations. Compile a list and distribute it in your building. Write a grant proposal and submit an application for funding.

WHEN THE MOUNTAIN AND MOHAMMED MEET: TEACHERS AND UNIVERSITY PROJECTS— A MODEL FOR EFFECTIVE RESEARCH COLLABORATION

Judith Lachance Whitcomb
Sauganash Elementary School
Chicago Public Schools

WHAT WAS

In the urban schools where I taught, I witnessed too many failures: bright children who were not meeting the "norm" as defined by the curricula, materials, assessments, and methodologies provided by the system. From my perspective, I wondered what the *norm* meant. The majority of these kids were simply not reaching their full potential. Was that ab*norm*al? My undergraduate preservice education had given me a wonderful liberal arts background, but the professional preparation courses had done little or nothing to prepare me to work through this perplexity.

Of course, I had met Plato, Dewey, and Whitehead through theoretical readings and discussions. However, someone neglected to mention that I was going to exercise the wisdom of their combined philosophies in class sizes that frequently went beyond 40 students, with text materials that were some 20 years older than the students themselves. In addition to that, as an upper grade teacher, I was expected to raise the reading scores an average of 2 years so the students would "pass" the local system's standardized norm test. All of this was to be done while meeting the needs of a myriad of behaviors and emotions that live within the confines of a classroom. In response, I began to try to find alternative resources that would tap their potential. And it is probably at this point that I discovered that not all educational researchers were dead. I had, after all, never met a real one.

My efforts were a patchwork quilt reflecting ideas gleaned from the occasional professional literature I was able to read in a schedule filled with developing and finding appropriate instructional materials. (Through the years, class size had lessened and materials had been updated. The materials were, however, still inappropriate.) Most research literature came in summarized form through articles in professional periodicals (i.e., *Instructor*, *Grade Teacher*, NSTA publications). When reading a book that embodied someone's research work, I often felt less than adequate when a book was prefaced with remarks that stated schools were in the Dark Ages when it came to the teaching-learning process. Then they would inform me that their work was going to assist me in learning to discover the inadequacies of my teaching. I knew my students followed different pathways to learning. I was eager to get to the practical suggestions. But the practical approaches that were developed through research initiatives frequently left me wondering, in what schools had the research taken place? Or was it that I was just too inept to implement these ideas?

Through the years, I began to pay more attention to what I saw going on in my classes. New approaches were tried out on a "this didn't work, but this did" basis. When I became a science teacher, I found that I was better able to accurately assess multiple facets of individual student learning through "hands-on" activities that became the backbone of my instructional program. My students and I set up camp and stopped moving toward the mountain of research that was out there somewhere. The time devoted to trying to seek it out and apply the tenets of that body of research to our environment seemed to me to be better spent in my own little research test bed.

In the meantime, over on the mountain, work was being done. Howard Gardner's work brought attention to the fact that we had too narrowly defined the way we looked at "intelligence," in his book *Frames of Mind* (Gardner, 1983). He put a framework around and gave sustenance to that which I had observed in my students and had been perplexed about 13 years earlier when I began my career. Goodlad's work led him to wonder if part of the brain, that part that requires novelty, is asleep during the 12 years of education (Goodlad, 1984). That reflected a feeling that I frequently had when using the traditional tools available to me. Eventually, I would hear about some of this work and would apply concepts to my developing inquiry approach to teaching.

For the most part, research remained distant from our daily life in the classroom. I did not feel as if I were a researcher, and researchers did not walk in my shoes. Occasionally, the principals would pass out some questionnaire from a university research project. We would fill it out and return it. This type of relationship with research initiatives was very linear, and, from my perspective, did not involve productive outcomes. On occasion, we would be asked to have observers in our classroom from a research project. This also had little application to our work in the school. It meant someone would be in the corner, copiously taking notes. It would cause a momentary disruption in our class as we all wondered what, who, why? Shortly, however, we would begin to ignore the observer's presence as we did other noninteractive entities. Rarely would the results of the research be shared with us. When it did, it came in a tome filled with "researchese" that I will have time to read when I retire. The disconnect from my classroom life and that of the researchers was strong.

As time went by, my observations led me to a level of frustration. Although inquiry and hands on activities were predominant in my curricula, I still encountered the "sleeping minds" problems. How to engage children in "minds-on" learning became my challenge. In 1993, I transferred to a new school on the northeast corner of the city. It was a new building that had been wired for computer technology and we had the promise of "at least one computer in every classroom." The computer instructor and myself were fully cognizant of the fact that a computer in every classroom does not provide answers to our concerns about developing "minds-on" curricula, however. We began to search out programs or models that would help us know how to build solid student learning with these new tools.

At a conference, we heard about a program funded by the National Science Foundation and the State of Illinois at Northwestern University. This program, optimistically titled Collaborative Visualization or CoVis, intrigued me as I heard about it in the plenary session. I then attended a break-out session to learn more about it. I was focused on my quest to develop a "minds-on" curriculum infused with technology to promote inquiry. Initially, the overwhelming thought of my trial-and-error approach to curriculum development prevented me from realizing that what we were looking at in CoVis was a research project. Little did I know that Mohammed and the Mountain were about to meet. It was the beginning of what has been for me an excellent professional partnership. It is a partnership that has taught me to value my own professional expertise, to stretch my knowledge and techniques, and, most importantly, it brought a fuller, more challenging curriculum to my students.

WHAT HAPPENED

During the break-out session, I saw researchers talking with teachers. This in itself might not have been enough for me to break camp and begin a trek toward a research project. What was different was the way they were talking with us. Not one of them held a questionnaire in his or her hands, nor were they so busy writing notes that we rarely made eye contact. They were not just listening, either. What I encountered was significant dialogue based on real concerns, although varied, that each practitioner brought to the session.

This was not, however, a quick sell for me on research for practice. I noticed that there was a definite propensity on the part of the researchers to talk with the high school people that were there. Although they referred to K–12 science education in the presentations, their research was focused in two high schools on the Chicago area's North Shore. The bias toward researchers that I had was nurtured as I began to think, "They only want to see what they want to see." I frequently tease one of the researchers by reminding him that at that first meeting, he turned his back on me, a lowly middle/junior high school teacher, in order to talk with urban high school teachers. He vehemently denies it, but it is to me very significant. CoVis had a research agenda, and that agenda had not initially included middle schools. The transformation and the flexibility of this project that I have observed during our work together make up the first step in understanding how the goals of both the researcher and practitioner can be met.

We decided to pursue our investigation of what this project had to offer because it still seemed to be a possibility for getting us where we wanted to be. (Okay, so practitioners have their agendas, too.) During a one-day meeting and subsequent attendance at a Summer Conference in 1995, we began to understand the goals that drove the project. Dr. Eileen Lento, then the Teacher Development Specialist, described the goals of the project on the first day of the summer conference:

Traditionally, K–12 science education has consisted of the teaching of well-established facts. This approach bears little or no resemblance to the question-centered, collaborative practice of real science. Collaborative Visualization refers to development of scientific understanding, which is mediated by scientific visualization tools in a collaborative context.

Your CoVis students will have access to a range of innovative collaboration and communication tools to study atmospheric and environmental science through inquiry-based activities. Specifically, these include: desk top teleconferencing, shared software environments for remote real time collaboration, access to Internet resources, a multimedia scientist's notebook, and scientific visualization software.

(These issues became national concerns in the next few years through works such as the National Science Standards and the Third International Math and Science Study.)

Obviously, my interest was piqued. Certainly the development and utilization of technological software tools and techniques were a major focus of the project. But there was something more; the researchers alluded to problems that I was confronting: How do I get my students beyond "hands-on" to the kind of "minds-on" work that goes on in the real world of science inquiry? Were we actually talking the same language? Did they have a practitioner's sense of what I was dealing with in my classes?

On a daily basis during the conference, I met with members of the CoVis research team. They seemed to be eager to talk with me (as well as other classroom teachers). It was, again, a dialogue. They did not seem to have all of the answers; they did seem to think that, through collaboration, we could find some of the answers.

This research project felt different. Plus, the researchers had a better vision of how technology could enhance my program than in anything else I had investigated. They were concerned with getting kids deeper into a problem through project pedagogies. Wasn't this also my concern? I wanted my students to delve more deeply into the scientific relationships that underlie the typical labs. I wanted students to experience the collaborative and iterative cycle of inquiry the way real-world scientists did. They needed opportunities to ask questions and seek solutions. I wasn't sure about this project pedagogy, but what I heard was sufficiently earth-moving to prompt me to engage in the project's work.

In the fall of 1995, my students and I began a CoVis curriculum, Global Warming. At the time, the curriculum was very loosely structured and definitely geared to a high school audience. In no time at all, we felt like we were in over our heads. The curriculum was enhanced by huge data sets of temperature and CO_2 levels as well as a visualization software tool, Climate Watcher.

We weren't sure of what to do with the data sets. When one of the young researchers contacted me about observing in my classroom as we enacted the curriculum, I reluctantly agreed. We were partners, but I hated opening myself up to observations on my inability to help my students make sense out the material and the software. I needn't have been concerned. There was authentic support in this partnership.

From the first day he came in, Dan, one of the university's research partners, interacted with students. He was at the computers with students as I was working through the technical problems and complex data. He heard the frustrations directly from the students; he rejoiced with them when a problem had been resolved. He offered practical suggestions and was keenly interested in hearing reactions from the children as well as myself as to whether a suggestion was reasonable or not. I felt he was actually seeing the situation from our perspective. And although the researcher notebook had been replaced with a laptop computer, he never was sitting in a corner pecking away at the keys. Rather, whatever notes he felt were necessary were taken after the real work of the classroom had taken place.

When we began to investigate the software, Dan felt there was another researcher who would have a much better perspective on how to introduce this tool to students who had little or no experience with computers, visualizations, or educational software that required thinking. Although I should have been getting the picture at this point that *collaboration* was a key word in this project (on multiple levels), I was concerned. This researcher had worked closely on the development of the software. I thought, "Here comes a computer geek who is a researcher. There will be no communication possible." Once again, I was in a position that would require me to eat my words. When Doug came, he didn't talk computers; he didn't even use them. He engaged the class in a paper-and-pencil activity that paved the way to comfortable use of the software. He taught them, talked with them, and played with them. He was actively teaching the students, learning from them, and modeling a way of working with technology in the class for me.

Something else happened when Doug came into our class. I was struggling with the students to work through to an understanding of what looking at a hundred years of temperature data can do in our arguments for or against the acceleration of global warming. I had students graph small segments of that temperature data on large sheets of craft paper. By having all groups draw the same grid scale on their paper, we were able to connect the subsegments to make a large graph that traveled about our room when posted and aligned. Then we had a noticeable artifact from which I could direct students to look for trends over long periods. Doug was very excited about this technique. He pulled out his camera and took many pictures. That activity remains, in a modified form, in the current (and much improved) Global Warming curriculum. This kind of validation leads to true teacher empowerment.

Teacher empowerment is a much maligned concept. A lot of groups talk about it; few know how to make it real. We as teachers know we want it, but we're not sure of how to define it. Administrators think they are giving it to us when they assign us yet another committee to chair. Researchers think they contribute to it when they place our names into their documents as coauthors (when did I write something?), or in the grateful acknowledgment of our help (how could that small survey response or that noninteractive observation been so crucial?). But here it was, handed to me on a silver platter of genuine interest and excitement. All of those years I had spent seeking alternative ways to help kids construct ideas were being valued. The researcher was recording my class's work to share with others. Empowerment comes from recognizing within yourself the significance of work you have done and then having that validated in a larger community. All teachers have learned to seek that validity within their classrooms from their children, and that creates a sense of worth. The empowerment comes when others seek out and value the expertise you have developed.

This single event did not suddenly empower me. That revelation came to me slowly over a number of years working with the university project. Full understanding of how I was empowered came when I was able to speak within many groups—teachers, administrators, business people, professors, researchers, and government agencies—with confidence about my area of expertise, student learning and curriculum development. When I reflected on how I grew to this, the realization came that it was through my partnership in a research project. It was an honest partnership where my classroom work was an integral and interactive part of the body of knowledge produced. Doug's reaction to my work was the beginning.

Another reason for the success of the collaboration was that the university knew that a single teacher and the ideas from that teacher would thrive within a professional peer network. The university utilized the concept of annual summer conferences and ongoing list servs to connect teachers in classrooms. We shared each other's ideas. The CoVis Community was thriving on the various combined teacher/researcher expertise.

My students and I survived and grew from our Global Warming experience. I was so thrilled to finally be enabled to engage learners in more in-depth activities that I did another of the project's curricula. This time I was much more confident and easily changed the pieces that didn't work for us. About this time, one of the researchers that I had met at the summer conference contacted me. He reminded me about a conversation we had had in which I explained much of my frustration with many facets of science education, two key issues of which were my frustration at my content knowledge limitations and the lack of experts and impartial audiences available to my students. Kevin was working with the concept of telementoring, mentoring over a distance (O'Neill, in press).

In our early conversations, he explained that he wanted to work with educators in classrooms to "design and test practical ways for volunteer scientists to become routinely involved with the daily work of students, using the Internet services newly available to schools" (O'Neill, 1997). How could I not try this one out? Could it be possible that experts would be available to my students during the course of a project? Kevin came into my classroom and brought me to the next level of professional development, that of a teacher researcher. And who would have ever thought that I could put those two descriptors together to describe myself?

Through my work with Kevin, I was encouraged to take what I had learned from my experiences with the two CoVis curricula enacted in my classroom and build a project that would fit the needs my students. It was a huge undertaking toward the end of the school year, when we are usually slowing down. The interactions with the research community in the way that they had evolved that year had energized me and primed my creativity. (Ah, could this be part of the "empowerment" concept?) So it began. It grew into the Community in Balance project, which placed students into a scenario in which they, as environmental engineers, had to explore the potential environmental impact of building a paper mill in an economically stressed community.

Kevin brought the telementoring experiences of one of the suburban high school instructors to the design table (O'Neill, Wagner, & Gomez, 1996). I worked through the components until I was comfortable with the process beginning in my class. Kevin was available for ideas, current research concepts, and support. The project allowed my students to communicate with six mentors across the country. Through my work with Kevin, I learned how to objectively look at my innovations and strategies in the classroom (O'Neill & Gomez, 1998). We would engage in focus sessions that Kevin needed for his work, but they also modeled for me how to avoid the kind of hit-and-miss approach I had in utilizing alternative tools and approaches. I learned how to look critically at an element and analyze the effectiveness of the process, tool, or innovation.

Kevin, like Dan and Doug before him, was a partner in the class. His observations were done within interactions with students and myself and the realities of life in a classroom. He worked with me to survive the technological problems. Most importantly, he brought solid research into my class and helped me learn how to craft it into my curriculum to benefit my students. He did not "assist me" in finding the flaws in my approaches by presenting something that as a researcher he knew would work. He worked with me to see how and if the approaches could be used to meet the needs of our situation. The key was mutual respect. I never felt that I was getting any more than I was giving. The researcher needed the teacher as much as the teacher needed the researcher.

The work with the project continued through the next 2 years. During this time, I was invited to conferences and events, not as a symbol of teacher involvement, but as an equal—someone who had valuable ideas and equal footing with the university researchers. The funding life of CoVis was nearing an end. But when Greg Schrader, another researcher, called me and asked me to do a CoVis curriculum, L.U.M.P., I should have known that the Learning Sciences researchers had a vision in mind to build on what we had learned during the course of CoVis. And indeed they did.

During the fall of the following year, I worked closely with Greg and another researcher. We enacted L.U.M.P. and had weekly grueling focus sessions to examine what worked and what didn't and why I took a particular action. His process for getting information he needed for his research refined my ability to "do research." The work we did together to benefit each of our individual goals became part of one curriculum seed for the Center for Learning Technologies in Urban Schools (LeTUS).

The center, a partnership between the Chicago Public School, Northwestern University, the Detroit Public Schools, and the University of Michigan, focused on infusing technology into curriculum. This project would use the combined expertise of teachers and researchers to develop curricula that would effectively use technologies to promote inquiry based projects. The combined work of the universities within classrooms gave birth to the center's concept of *work circles*. These were formalized groups of teachers and researchers who would use a curriculum seed to build open-ended projects that were structured for use in classrooms. I worked with Greg and others in a work circle that created the ReNUE project (Shrader, Whitcomb, et al., 1999). L.U.M.P. was our seed. We were able to bring both pitfalls and successes from my enactment to the work circle. From that experience and the experiences of the other teachers, we created a project that was teacher-friendly and utilized a software tool, Model It, to bring students to a higher level of scientific literacy.

WAS THE COLLABORATION SUCCESSFUL?

The students who were in my first CoVis group came back from high school frequently to talk about how they felt their participation (even with our pitfalls) had helped them at the high school level. They felt that their thinking, inquiry, paper-writing skills, and even math skills had been enhanced by the project work. They felt that they had entered high school on a more even footing with peers from more affluent sending schools. In the 4 years that my students were involved with the CoVis project, the percent of students meeting or exceeding the state norm on the state assessment tests went from 23% to 76%. I am at a new school now. After 1 year of Center for Learning Technologies-related project work, 94% of the students met or exceeded the state norms. Students talk about science in a way that is more focused on interactions and relationships. They are becoming aware of their role within the physical world, and their ability to talk about that relationship is more sophisticated.

Although reluctant to begin and slightly taken aback by the nontraditional look of the science program, all of my classes have come to value the program of instruction that has evolved through my work with Northwestern. They have come to realize that, rather than the "easy" look of project-based pedagogy, course work is far more rigorous than many of their more traditional classes. They have also demonstrated individual as well as group accountability for learning. There is a story from my last year at my previous school that gives evidence of this. One of my coworkers stated this at a meeting:

I had heard Judy talk about CoVis at several meetings and I thought, "Yeah, yeah, yeah. . . ." Then I went into her eighth grade science classroom a week or so before graduation. Students were working in groups preparing presentations, checking data, and building models. And I thought, "Hmmm. . . ." I went into the classroom again two days before graduation and I saw students presenting. Following the presentations, I saw their peers asking thoughtful, in depth questions. These questions held the presenters accountable for information and providing evidence for what they were saying. The science class wasn't Judy's, it was theirs. Then I thought, "Yeah!"

WHAT MADE IT WORK?

When I look back at the work I have done with Northwestern University researchers, there are key issues that made the collaboration a success.

1. *Flexibility.* The researchers believed that work at the high school level would allow them to develop software tools that could be used to infuse curriculum with technology in order to promote inquiry. They expanded this concept to include middle schools. They also realized through their interactions with students and teachers that excellent software tools without a viable curriculum were not going to change the way science was taught. Their flexibility in changing their research agenda based on their work with teachers and classrooms without changing their ultimate goal was significant.

2. *Collaboration.* This was a partnership. I remember once sitting at a meeting with several researchers. The topic of curriculum came up. On of the members of their team said, "We know how to do curriculum, we don't have to think about that." All of the teachers in the group rolled their eyes and mentally disengaged from the group. We knew about those curricula. They were so belabored with rationale and other troves of information for the lowly teacher that they were totally unusable in our classrooms where we needed specific and simply formated materials that would serve our cramped schedules. In the CoVis and LeTUS Projects, teachers were and are valued as experts in how the curriculum should look and take shape, the child pedagogies that would make a curriculum usable, and their knowledge of developmental appropriateness. Collaboration is built on mutual and authentic respect.

3. *Teacher empowerment.* Working on a two-way street, one that meets the goals of the researcher but also authentically values and uses

the expertise of the teacher, leads to true empowerment. Complementing that with sharing of techniques, such as focus sessions, with practitioners, research communities have the ability to empower teachers as researchers.

4. *Networking.* Capacities within systems and schools to support teacher research and instructional innovations are seldom available. Once our work with the research community is over or we are between researcher interactions, it is difficult to sustain our work as teacher researchers and curriculum developers. By setting up opportunities to build a teacher network, the projects gave teachers a support system for professional development through peer networking. Many of us who sustain our own communication system beyond the life of a project, listserv, or conference come from many communities throughout the United States. New technologies, such as e-mail and teleconferencing, allow us to nurture that network in a efficient manner. That network gives us a support system to continue our work.

5. *Mutual respect.* As I worked with the researchers, I developed an enormous respect for what they do. I began to truly value how their work could enhance my work. I didn't feel that way prior to my involvement within these projects. Researchers were smart people who just didn't get it. And many researchers look at us as opportunities to build their theories by providing test beds into which they could pour knowledge. But not the group I have been privileged to work with. They view us as partners in seeking out the answers to perplexing problems. I'm even surprised at how "researchese" is invading my vocabulary. I find my self *enacting* curricula rather than just *doing it*, and I even caught myself wondering what the *driving question* of my next project was going to be.

From all of my experience of the past 6 years I can make one statement that is absolutely true: When Mohammed and the Mountain meet, student learning peaks.

WEB SITES

http://www.letus.nwu.edu/ Center for Learning Technologies in Urban Schools; Northwestern University Science Project described in Judy Whitcomb's story.

http://csile.oise.utoronto.ca/TM-KB/Pages/abstract.html Kevin's dissertation as described in Judy Whitcomb's story.

http://science-education.org/index.html The Science Center.
metrochicago@nwu.edu Northwestern University Learning Sciences/
CoVis program.

REFERENCES

Gardner, H. (1983). *Frames of mind: The theory of multiple intelligences.* New York: Basic Books.

Goodlad, J. I. (1984). *A place called school: Prospects for the future.* New York: McGraw-Hill.

O'Neill, D. K. (1997). *Engaging science practice through science practitioners: Design experiments in K–12 telementoring.* Unpublished dissertation, Northwestern University, Evanston, IL.

O'Neill, D. K. (in press). Enabling constructivist teaching through telementoring. *Special Services in the Schools, 17*(1/2). (Binghamton, NY: Haworth Press)

O'Neill, D. K., & Gomez, L. M. (1998). Sustaining mentoring relationships on-line. In S. Greenberg & C. Neuwirth (Eds.), *Proceedings of CSCW 98: ACM conference on computer-supported cooperative work*, pp. . New York: Association for Computing Machinery.

O'Neill, D. K., Wagner, R., & Gomez, L. M. (1996). On-line mentors: Experimenting in science class. *Educational Leadership, 54*(3). (Alexandria, VA: Association for Supervision and Curriculum Development)

Shrader, G. W., Lachance Whitcomb, J. A., Finn, L., Williams, K., Walker, L. J., & Gomez, L. (1999, March). *Work in the "Work Circle": A Description of collaborative design to improve teaching practice.* Paper presented at Spencer Foundation Conference, New Orleans, LA.

SHIFTING GEARS: AN URBAN TEACHER RETHINKS HER PRACTICE

Vida Schaffel
Falconer Elementary School
Chicago Public Schools

I began teaching in Chicago in the 1960s, took time out to raise a family, and then returned some 15 years later. In my K–1 classroom, I had a couple of students who were pulled out for English as a second language (ESL). This area was new to me. I found it most intriguing because I, too, learned ESL. A position opened up in ESL and because I had the certification, I was given the job. I worked with students from the kindergarten to the eighth-grade level. I liked working with mixed ethnic groups; I enjoyed their diversity. After a few years, my school became more populated with Hispanic and Polish students and more bilingual classes were created. The demographics were such that there were fewer students in the category of "other," so there was no longer a need for two ESL teachers and I began teaching reading in a pull-out program.

After my 15-year hiatus, I found it hard to believe that so little had changed. The basal was still there, the vocabulary was still contrived, and the stories were not very interesting. There was, however, a new twist in that the new series of basals did reflect an ethnic mix of society, at least in the pictures.

The school was bursting; there were students everywhere. Every classroom and every closet was occupied. A place had to be found where my students in the pull-out program could meet. It was finally decided that the best available space was a vestibule off the back entrance of the balcony of the assembly hall. No one went back there and we wouldn't be disturbed by anyone. If the noise from the music class got too loud, we could just close the door and try to ignore it. The space there was able to accommodate a table, some chairs, a few posters on the wall, a chalkboard, and a teacher's desk. What could be bad? What could be wrong with a place like this, away from everything and everybody, a place where no one could bother you because no one could find you? Most people were unaware of the existence of such a place. My students and I were truly isolated from the rest of the building.

In this new pull-out reading program, I was once again faced with the teacher's guide that told me what to do and how to do it, along with the basal text of mostly uninteresting stories and the accompanying skill-based workbook. I found the basal reading program stifling and the teacher's guide an insult to my intelligence. The stories I liked best in the basal were the folk tales and the fables. Those were the stories the students liked too.

According to Bettelheim and Zelan (1982), the children who teach themselves to read before coming to school read from texts that are of interest to them. So why not read stories in school that are also of interest to the students? I began reading aloud to my students every day. This was a new experience for me. In the past, I read to my students but it was never on a regular basis. The books we shared were predictable stories, patterned stories, and stories rich in language and story content. The students drew pictures about the stories, read words from the stories, and made up their own stories following the pattern set from the book. There was excitement and enthusiasm, and the students looked forward to our time together.

One day, one of the groups came upon what the text referred to as "a book." This was a page that contained pictures with some dialogue that the students were to cut out and staple together to replicate a book. Michelle was first to have her book in order, so I asked her to read it. She began reading her book. She knew all the words. The entire book had a vocabulary of six words. She finished reading the book, looked up at me and said, "This is a book?" How can this possibly be compared to the interesting story content and rich language of the stories she had been exposed to? Is this what reading is all about? More and more I became convinced that to instill a love for reading one must go beyond the basal.

As I began to read the research that had been done in the field, I was surprised to find that I was not alone in my thinking and that there were many educators who also questioned the old basal skill and drill methodology that still prevails in the schools. When teachers complain that it is getting harder and harder to teach reading and the methods that worked years ago are not working now, we have to look to see what we can do to change the tide to achieve better results.

I felt I had to change the way I approached the area of literacy, specifically the teaching of reading. In my research, I was surprised to find that there was a natural connection between the reading and the writing process. I never really connected the two areas before, but now this idea made so much sense to me. Of course the two are connected. I became excited with the prospect of trying out this new approach. Connecting reading and writing in a meaningful, real-life way became the focus of some action research. How does one go about changing one's way of teaching? Can I be a pioneer and try to work it out for myself?

When the requests for the next year's assignments came out, I requested to be put back into a classroom. The pull-out reading program that I was involved in was both fragmented and isolated from the rest of the school program. There was no connection, no continuity with the rest of the day. Something was awry. Reading should be the whole day's program and not a separate piece of it, and writing should be the other component part. It is writing that gives expression to the knowledge that children possess and it is writing that leaves evidence of what they don't know or do not understand (Graves & Stuart, 1985). Writing gives children a vehicle through which to explore the meaning of their past experiences (Cramer, 1978). Goodman and Goodman (1983) affirmed that "people not only learn to read by reading and write by writing, but they also learn to read by writing and write by reading" (p. 592). It would seem that the reading and writing combination is quite strong and would reinforce each other in literacy development.

I was given a second- and third-grade split class. I like the idea of multiage grouping where there can be a helpful give-and-take in the classroom. I saw this as a positive with definite benefits for both groups of students. Because I intended to individualize the reading program, it really did not matter what grade the students were in, for they would all read on their own level and at their own pace. I might add that my colleagues could not understand why I did not object to this split. A split is not looked upon as a favorable placement. My only objection was that there were 36 students in the class. The large number of children is what made the job difficult, not the split.

The students in this class were mainly from urban working-class families. There were students from single-parent homes as well as intact family homes, foster homes, divorced and shared-custody homes. There were homes that took an interest in their child's work and homes where no one was able to assist the child in learning. There were homes where a variety of books could be found and others where there was no printed material at all.

Initially, I wanted to use trade books as the text for reading, but I found that I did not have the fingertip familiarity with enough books at each of the different student levels. I didn't know what to recommend to everyone and many of the students seemed to be floundering, unable to make choices and in need of direction. I observed some students reading books well below their level and others reading books that were far too difficult for them. I became concerned at the prospect of the students not progressing. I was also getting looks from the other teachers, my colleagues. When they would ask me what basal I was using and what story I was on, I would answer that I wasn't using a basal. I got lots of surprised looks, as if to say, "What are you doing, lady?" I had no one in the school to collaborate with, although I was able to discuss some thoughts and ideas while riding to school with one of my colleagues who taught the fifth grade.

Teachers in the primary grades are usually given some basal readers, accompanying workbooks, phonics workbooks, science texts, and social studies texts along with all the accompanying teacher's manuals. How one uses these materials is not mandated, but most of the teachers use the texts in the most traditional way. At this time, my school was slowly switching from one set of basals to another. I stayed with the old basal because I was more familiar with this series and I was already anticipating making major changes in my teaching. I felt this would make my life a little easier.

I became insecure about what I was doing and began using the basal during reading workshop. I rationalized to myself that maybe it was okay to use the basal as long as they were reading other books in class and trade books during independent reading time and their free class time.

The children were reading from six different basals. Only one reading group existed and that was because they needed to learn some reading strategies before they could read on their own. I was not fond of reading groups because I felt the students did not spend enough time actually reading. The good readers were held back and the slower readers usually had difficulty keeping up. In my plan, the students would be able to go at their own pace; those who needed to go slowly could do so and those who could go faster would not be held back.

Due to the number of students, I found that I was not able to monitor their reading as much as I had hoped. For the group that still needed more help, I tried to initiate peer tutoring from the students in the classroom, but I found that it took too much time away from their own reading to ask them to do it on a regular basis, so I matched these children up with students in the highest-level self-contained learning disabled (LD) class. The tutoring was a success; the students were able to go at their own rate and they did more reading than they would have done had they been in a group setting. The other students were more independent and read by themselves or in pairs. Periodically, they read a story together as a group. Some enjoyed working with another student on a worksheet pertaining to the story better than working alone whereas some preferred to do their work by themselves.

As a recipient of the Rochelle Lee Grant that provides trade book libraries in the classroom, I knew how important it was for children to have an acquaintanceship with books. I also knew the benefits of "read aloud" to the students. The general feeling among most of the teachers is that read aloud is fine for a fill-in, but how can you take time from the regular subjects and read out loud? Read aloud took place twice a day. In the morning, I read a short trade book and in the afternoon I would read a chapter book. I wanted them to try to stretch their thinking and be able to carry over a thought from one day to the next. The books I read served as a stimulus for the students to reread the books on their own. Some students followed along in the chapter books as I read. These students were able to visibly see the modeling of reading with inflection and the use of punctuation.

Is there a natural connection between reading and writing, and is there an effect that each of these disciplines has upon the other? "All language processes develop concurrently in a related manner. Each process informs and supports the other" (Strickland & Morrow, 1988, p. 70). Graves and Stuart (1985) supported this same idea. They said, "as children become better writers, they also improve their reading skill" (p. 116). Goodman and Goodman (1983) said that it is not necessary for readers to write during reading, but writers must read and reread during writing. In my own mind I became more and more convinced of the connection and saw that connection made in my action research. Writing is powerful. Through writing, it is possible to know what students are aware of in their reading as well as to know what they have learned. Here, their knowledge of the letter–sound relationship, which is applicable to reading is evident. Students write what they know; that is why writing is so revealing.

One of the most important parts of my action research was the journal writing that took place first thing in the morning. This activity turned out to be a most profound experience for me. Students were given free expression in whatever they wrote; I continued to reassure them that this would not be graded and they should write without being burdened by formal constraints. I even encouraged them to begin by drawing and then add some words to tell about their drawing and what came to mind. What struck me about this whole process of journaling was that the thoughts were all coming from them and they were writing from the heart. Each piece of writing had its own "voice." They chose their own words to convey the uniqueness of an experience, thus giving meaning to the words and personality to the writing (Graves & Stuart, 1985).

The writing was, in a sense, cathartic for them and so revealing to me. Neither show and tell, nor being given subjects to write about in a composition, nor prompts could possibly have evoked such natural, flowing thoughts. I provided them with the permission, in a sense, and they took off. I wrote back to the students, providing them with a dialogue; I wanted them to know that someone was listening but not judging. Sometimes their classmates became their audience and asked them questions about their piece. As they gained trust in me and the other students, the juices began flowing and the thoughts, words, and feelings began to pour out on the pages. Their feelings could now be expressed knowing that they will be accepted and not evaluated. After all, feelings are neither right nor wrong; they just are.

Their progress in writing was readily visible by the documentation of the date on each piece of writing. There was no formula to the order of progress. Each child progressed in his or her own way and at his or her own rate. I was in awe of the whole process. The content of their pieces gave a glimpse into the things that were on their minds. When children are given carte blanche to write, they reveal their real feelings and concerns, hopes and wishes, likes and dislikes.

I was surprised to find that the children who have difficulty reading texts generally do not have difficulty reading their own writing. It seems that what they write they can read, but what comes in print is more difficult for them, unless they are familiar with the storyline and can use context clues or other reading strategies. For some children, their best reading is their journal reading.

Little Marisa was going through a most difficult time in her life when she came into my class. She and her family had just come from Romania and within a year her mother died, leaving her and five other siblings alone with their father. Marisa did not talk much in class, she kept to herself. She first mentioned her mother and father in her journal about mid-September. From the end of September until the end of November the subject of her mother's death was repeated over and over and over again. "My mother died when I was asleep," is what she kept writing. That sentence kept appearing in her writing. Almost every day, that sentence was found somewhere in her journal writing. Once she wrote "I don't have a birthday after mother died." From the end of November until February she moved on to talk about her family, her brothers and sisters and what she liked to do. Then in February she began to allow herself to write about and seek the friendship of others. After that, she was ready to reach out and accept the friendship of her classmates.

Journal writing has been one of the most positive experiences for me and for the children. It is hard to believe the kind of growth that takes place through this very simple medium. I feel badly that I was not able to keep up a dialogue with the students. Most of the time I used my preparation time to write back to the students. As much as I wanted to do it every day, and I had the best of intentions, the logistics of it never seemed to work out. Being alone in the classroom with 36 students made it much too difficult to do.

It is difficult to be the only one in the workplace trying out new ideas. Even though I felt what I was doing was right, it still didn't make the task any easier. What did keep me going was the support and encouragement of a group of teacher researchers from the suburbs that I met with once a month. Many of these teachers had new ideas and were also trying out different methods in their teaching, and they too were confronted by the traditional teachers who fought change. Being able to share my feelings of frustration and receive support from other colleagues was most important for me. Another important factor for me was the reinforcement I received from attending workshops. At workshops, one usually finds like-minded teachers and that gave me encouragement. The workshops confirmed to me that I was on the right track and that my frustration was just a matter of working out the logistics.

Without learning there can be no growth, and without growth there can be no change. This holds true for both the student and the teacher. I see myself more now as a facilitator rather than the purveyor of knowledge. I am constantly collecting data in my classroom while I analyze my own teaching and learning. I view children in a more holistic and developmental way than I did previously. I am more conscious of "process" and see "product" as being multidimensional and multifaceted. I am not the same as I was before.

Change is not easy. It is lonely being a majority of one and it is hard working against the grain. The need to connect with other educators is essential for me, and unfortunately there is no time in the school day to talk to colleagues. (Twenty minutes of lunchtime does not allow for any exchange of ideas!) It is difficult not to do what I believe; for to do otherwise, I would not be true to myself. I look forward to more growth and new challenges as a teacher researcher in the future.

REFERENCES

Bettelheim, B., & Zelan, B. (1982). *On learning to read: The child's fascination with meaning.* New York: Alfred A. Knopf.

Cramer, R. L. (1978). *Children's writing and language growth.* Columbus, OH: Charles E. Merrill.

Goodman, K., & Goodman, Y. (1983). Reading and writing relationship: Pragmatic functions. *Language Arts, 60*(5), 590–599.

Graves, D., & Stuart, V. (1985). *Write from the start: Tapping your child's natural writing ability.* New York: New American Library.

Strickland, D. S., & Morrow, L. M. (1988). Emerging readers and writers: New perspectives on young children learning to read and write. *Reading Teacher, 42*(1), 70–72.

Piecing Our Past Through Artistic Inquiry: Students and Teachers as Co-Researchers in an Urban Elementary School

Jackie Samuel
Bethel Cultural Arts Center

Susan Sheldon
Washington Irving School
Chicago Public Schools

As part of a DeWitt Wallace Readers Digest-funded project called Chicago Students at the Center, a teacher and an artist set out to see how the prescribed curriculum could be more student-centered and focused on inquiry. They planned curriculum, collected data from students, kept journals, and discussed what they had learned as beginning researchers exploring a new way of teaching.

A FIRST-YEAR TEACHER SPEAKS

Susan. As a first-year teacher, the subject I dreaded teaching the most was social studies. Come to think of it, I truly was afraid of it. How was I, with a bachelor's degree in finance and a minor in German, going to teach fifth graders about American history? I felt unprepared for the task at hand. I also didn't have any positive recollections of my own of social studies in either high school or elementary school. The only vivid memory I had was of my flamboyant U.S. history teacher flailing his arms so passionately as he sang the praises of Thomas Jefferson that his watch

261

flew across the classroom. I definitely knew Thomas Jefferson as a result, but his presidency would probably only take up one week of the entire school year of fifth-grade history!

I took a deep breath and reflected on what my cooperating teacher told me during my student teaching at Washington Irving School. History is simply a collection of people's stories—hence, the word "history." The more I investigated this perspective, the more it made sense to me, especially in my own life. I realized that historical events remained with me more as I was more able to connect the events with my own personal story. For instance, World War II never became a part of my own schema as a child until I made the connection of the war with my family. My great-grandparents and grandparents spoke German and lived here in the United States. However, my mother was never taught German. My grandparents only spoke English to her. This never made sense to me, until I realized that my mother was born in 1945, and no American wanted to be known as a German during this time period. Consequently, the German language ceased in my mother's household, and the pronunciation and spelling of her last name changed from Muller to Mueller (pronounced Miller). "Ah ha." It all came together for me at that moment. I made a personal connection with history.

I desired my students to have this same feeling of "Ah ha," as they made personal connections with history. As a result, we embarked on the project of investigating their own families and connecting their history to the bigger picture of themselves in the world. The students examined how the world events affected their lives and the decisions their families made. The family history quilt was only a by-product of this research and captured the images the children had of their families. This history project was the beginning of my students' historical journey, but, hopefully, it was the springboard for them to experience a countless number of "Ah ha's" in their study of history throughout their lives. As one of my students, Melvin Nix, so eloquently put it on the completion of our project, "I think this is just the beginning of our history quilt."

AN ARTIST SPEAKS

Jackie. I am a theater artist and arts education consultant for the Chicago Arts Partnership in Education (CAPE). I help teachers learn how to integrate the arts into their school curriculum. This is how I met Susan

Sheldon. I visited her for 20 weeks at her school. She would tell me what she was trying to accomplish, and I would help her find the resources she needed, in addition to finding links between the arts and what she was teaching. First, we started with a couple of small units in order to learn each other's work styles. Afterward, we decided to embark on a larger project, in order to "piece our past through artistic inquiry."

This quilt project was successful for a couple of reasons. First, this was Susan's first year of teaching. She brought the passion that most new teachers bring to their first classroom, but she also possessed an unyielding ability to be open to new ideas with the greatest commitment and ownership of the project. She also had a theater background and flexibility to trust her students to make choices in their learning.

Another wonderful aspect was the cultural diversity of her class. It was quite insightful to observe communication between students who could see differences but never had questioned them before. They shared and compared family life-styles, engaged their parents and siblings in the project, and compared American history and the effects it had on their ancestry, in addition to exhibiting their thoughts to the entire school. This had a tremendous impact on us all.

An unexpected success was how far this project took us. We started the school year wanting students to feel comfortable in articulating their thoughts and feelings through drama and ended up discovering how to research and utilize those thoughts and ideas in a multidisciplinary way. The students left this project with a sense of confidence and pride that one textbook or standardized test cannot give. When you read this, I hope that you can see the bond that happened between a teacher, her students, and parents. I learned much in this process about the power of the arts in a student-centered classroom.

DESIGNING CURRICULUM: STUDENTS AND TEACHERS AS CO-RESEARCHERS

[Because Susan was present throughout this project as the teacher, the story is told in her voice.] Because I was teaching fifth grade, I knew I had to teach U.S. history. I wanted my students to understand why their families came to the United States. If I could get them to understand why they came, then I knew they would more likely understand other people's immigration stories. Realizing I learned about history through my family, I figured that this is how my students probably would learn history, too.

In order to direct my students' thinking about their own histories, I decided to share some of my own. I told my students how my mother's last name changed over time because my family didn't want anyone to know we were German. I knew about World War II, so I told them what it was like in Germany and how it affected my family. As I revealed my stories, I asked them to start thinking about how their families may have been affected by events in history.

As I was beginning to embark on this history project, I met Jackie Samuel, an arts consultant specializing in creative drama. I mentioned that I wanted to make a quilt with my students that told their family histories. Jackie said she was willing to try a quilt project, because she had recent experience teaching storytelling to students, and a quilt project would be a great way to expand the storytelling process.

GETTING STARTED: TEACHER AND STUDENT BRAINSTORMING

Because Jackie was flexible enough to try it, we agreed to do the project. I began by simply brainstorming all the ideas I had about this project (see Fig. 1). I wasn't certain that I would implement all these ideas; I just wanted to get them all down on paper. I desired to start with a family timeline, researched back three generations. We could research when the students' grandparents and great-grandparents were born and where they came from. We could learn when and why their families moved to Chicago. Then we could make a class timeline. My students could write their family information along the top of the class timeline. Afterward, they could make a world and national timeline along the bottom of the paper. The timeline would hang on the wall so that they could see what was happening in the world as they looked at their own lives. That way they could see how world events might have had an impact on their families.

I also took a look at my students. I had students from Belize, Haiti, Mexico, Bangladesh, and other cultural backgrounds. My students were a wealth of information, and we needed to learn from each other. The children could present their cultures, traditions, and family histories to the class. I wanted them to talk about their differences and think about what happened in their families in comparison to their fellow

Teacher Brainstorming	Student Brainstorming
Individual timelines	Tape coverage of past events
Family timelines	Timelines
Class timeline	Autobiographies
Historical timeline	Art paintings
Interview family members	Historical fiction
Look at cultural heritage and traditions	Historical documents
Look at events in the world on a timeline	Interviews/oral histories
Look at effects of world events on family events	Photographs
	Journals from people of the past
	Family trees
	Old newspapers/magazines
	Legislation/government
	Documentaries

FIG. 1. Brainstorming: the first step in studying history and our personal connections.

classmates. I also wanted them to have discussions about their cultures and what happened in history that caused them to make the choices that they made. All of this did not happen, but something spectacular did.

To start off this unit, we looked at chronological timelines. We referred to a timeline in the textbook as an example and created one as a class based on our readings of historical fiction, our historical figure research, and our textbook readings. Students listed in their notebooks 10 significant events in their lives. Each student created a timeline of his or her own history based on those 10 events. Jackie and I created timelines, too. Students shared their timelines with the class.

Next, I wanted them to think about images. I did this by showing slides purchased for a field trip to the Art Institute of Chicago. We looked at portraits and paintings of different time periods, people, and places. This was done in order for them to think about what images they wanted to create on their quilt. We looked at clothes and objects in each painting. I asked the student what clothes they would be wearing in their quilt image. I pointed out special activities happening in the paintings. I asked the students what they enjoyed doing and reminded them that they could include this in their quilt image.

I also used these paintings to help students see the differences between the city and the country. This helped the students choose whether the setting for their image was going to be urban or rural. I asked the students about the different places where their family had lived. We discussed the country in the famous painting, "American Gothic" by Grant Wood. We discussed how we knew this painting was set in the country. I asked what they would put in their image in order to show that they lived in the country. In "Nighthawks" by Edward Hopper, we discussed urban life. I asked them to name their favorite restaurant or community store and to decide whether they would include this in their images on their square to represent their family.

THE FIELD TRIP TO THE ART INSTITUTE OF CHICAGO

The field trip to the Art Institute provided the students with an opportunity to see the slides that we had viewed in our classroom for this project to come to life. They also discovered the history behind the art pieces. They learned how the artists incorporated parts of themselves in their work, just as I wanted my students to do with their quilt images. Additionally, the students were surrounded by incredible pieces of art that inspired them and gave them ideas for their own work in the classroom.

Personally experiencing the artwork for themselves caused more creative juices to flow than any slides that we could have shown in the classroom. Lastly, the students were able to see how art changes to represent the time in which it was created. As a result, the students walked away from this trip thinking about what they could create in their quilt squares to represent themselves and the time in which they lived.

INTERVIEWING: A PART OF THE RESEARCH

As part of this project, the students needed to interview their relatives to discover their family histories. I created a list of questions that would hopefully generate some historical discussion. However, I did not share my questions with the students. I wanted them to create their own (see Fig. 2 for teacher- and student-generated interview questions).

Teacher's Questions

1. How did your family end up in Chicago?
2. Why did your family come to Chicago?
3. Why did your family come to America?
4. Who is in your family, back two generations?
5. Where did your family come from?
6. Did your family find what they were looking for here? If not, what did they find?
7. What type of education did your family members have?
8. How did your parents meet?
9. What are some significant events in the family that could be included on a family timeline?
10. What family stories could your mom, dad, grandpa, or grandma share?
11. What relatives should appear on your family tree?
12. What are the nationalities of your relatives?

Students' Questions

1. When were you born?
2. What kinds of clothes did you wear when you were young?
3. When were you married?
4. What type of music did you listen to when you were young?
5. What was school like when you were young?
6. What kind of jobs did you have growing up?
7. When did your family come to Chicago? Why did they come?
8. When did your family come to the United States? Why did they come?
9. What was the world like when you were growing up? What was happening?
10. What was the most important thing that happened when you were young?
11. Who did you live with when you were young?
12. Were you ever in the war and what was it like?
13. When and how did you meet your spouse (husband or wife)? How old were you?
14. Where does your family originally come from?
15. Where were your parents born?
16. What was your favorite sport?
17. Where did you live growing up?
18. What were your first words?
19. What was your favorite book growing up?
20. Do you have any brothers or sisters?
21. Who was the President of the United States when you were growing up?
22. Did your mother work when she had her children?
23. How old were your parents when you were born?
24. What is your favorite family story?
25. What are the names of your parents?

FIG. 2. Teacher- and student-generated interview questions.

The students worked together in groups and compared their questions; then each group made a group list of the most relevant and open-ended questions. Once the groups created their group list, we created a class list from the group list that would be used to interview as many family members as possible. They used their own questions and felt like they were a part of the process. Jackie came into the classroom and introduced my students to basic creative drama skills, such as diction, body language, and improvisation. After warming them up with drama, we introduced them to interviewing techniques. We talked about things like dressing neatly, being prepared to take notes, listening skills, and how to conclude an interview. We followed through with integrating drama by doing mock interviews together.

It took about 2 weeks to gather information. Some children chose to use a tape recorder. So we listened to audiotapes. We discussed what we heard on the audiotape. In addition to critiquing the interview, we also discussed their experience.

FAMILY TREES AND STORIES: MAKING A FAMILY ALBUM

We proceeded with creating family trees from interview notes. I exhibited a family tree of mine to discuss and modeled for students how to create one. Students then created their own family trees. In class, we read some examples of family stories from my own journal and using children's literature, such as Faith Ringgold's *Dinner at Aunt Connie's House* (1993). Students wrote family stories based on the family interviews that they conducted. They had to write at least one story for each generation interviewed. We practiced proofreading our stories by writing them on transparencies and sharing them with the class (see Fig. 3 for family stories written by the children; spelling as written by the students).

These stories helped the students better understand what family decisions had great effects in their household. They became great stories of survival. We developed a family album, including the family stories, the timelines, family trees, and any photos that the students brought to school. It was sometimes difficult for families to part with photos. I promised to laminate them to keep them protected. The students created an assessment for the work they had completed. They listed re-

Story 1: *Whean my grandmother was born she was only child that my great Grand-mother had. My great grandmother was really consent about her only child because villiger want to kill her. If the villiger can kill my grandmother they can take the land and every thing that my great grand parents own. That was Bangladesh rule, if you don't have any child and you don't give to some one it will belong to villiger. That time my great grandfather was at British. He was a business at that time with British. But my great grand mother was to smart for the villiger, she use to put light in the house and at night she will bundle my grandmother and took to her friend house everyday that is how villiger could not hurt my grandmother. After my great grand mother father died, British came and took many goods from my grandmother and father. Then my grandparent became poor. But now we are middiam family. We also give people some food to farm by theirself. Some people feel sorry now because they and their parents did not let my great grandparents and grandparents stay happy for what they did.*

Story 2: *Ones upon time long long in the 1950s. There a boy who born September 27, 1951. His name was Maxan. His mother and father was happe to see him. His brothers and sister were happe to see him home from the hospitail. As he grow biggar and biggar people and his country would wear shorts and sandles everyday or they would be so so hot. As he got biggar and biggar he met his young lady named Aldia. They went out together and had a great time. They had my big brother, my other brother, then my sister, then my sister and then me. Then my little brother was born.*

FIG. 3. Two family stories.

quirements and a simple rubric to use. This was all so personal that everything could not be graded.

CREATING THE QUILT

Now that we had our timelines, interviews, stories, and family albums, it was time to create the quilt. The children looked over their research and decided which images they would use on their individual quilt squares. We reviewed the images we had seen at the Art Institute and talked about how images represent stories, feelings, and ideas.

We used instructions and materials ideas from the book by Faith Ringgold called *Tar Beach* (1991). The book recommended using pillowcases for the actual squares. We cut individual rectangles out of cardboard for each student and taped each one's pillowcase square to the cardboard. Each student sketched his or her image on the pillowcase first. We posted family images in the classroom to help stimulate ideas.

Jackie brought in fabrics and materials like buttons and miscellaneous objects from a recycling center (see Fig. 4). An art teacher helped me with the paint type selection of acrylic paint. The students

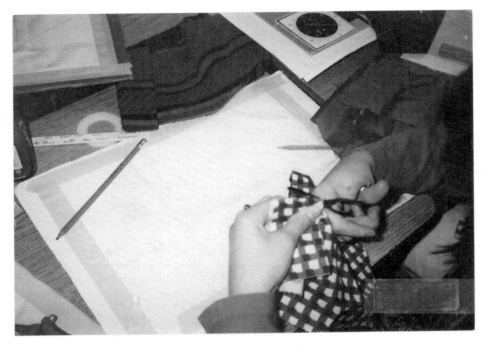

FIG. 4. Student working on quilt square.

added the material appliqués. I just gave them materials, not really knowing what they would do with them. All of a sudden they started telling me what they wanted. We used acrylic paint, on a paper plate as a palette, so they could mix the colors. When they finished, we spread the squares on the floor and played with the arrangement to make it more visually pleasing to the eye. We asked them to write their quilt square, responding to these questions:

1. What does the square represent about your family?
2. Why did you choose to design this image to represent your family?
3. Why did you include each item in your quilt square? (See Fig. 5.)

EXPANDING THE PROJECT TO THE WORLD: THE PERSONAL CONNECTION TO HISTORY

Student groups were assigned 20-year time periods and researched what happened in America during that period. Students placed the events that occurred during these periods on chart paper, as well as

I drew a house because it represents my family and it brings all the memories I had. I drew trees and a picnic because almost every week my family goes outside and we have a picnic. I drew flowers all over because it's like a garden. I drew this picture because my family and I always have memories of this house. This image is special to me, and it means a lot because I miss my country.

My quilt takes place in Haiti. And it takes place in 1994. The two house—the one in the left is for my mom. The in the right is for my mom sister. The coconut tree is for my mom and my aunts. An those letle flower is me and my cousin that plant it. And my mom house it was only me and her. Because in Haiti I use to live with my mom. My mom only had me. She didn't have any other babies. And the airplane represent me and my family that we have a dream that we coming in Chicago. We didn't know if any of us was coming in Chicago. And my mom's sister is cooking in her kichen. And my aunt's husband was on top of the house fixcing the top of the house and the black thing represent my whole family.

Why I created this quilt is because I like my country a lot. And I like my family a lot. And my family likes me to. All my family thats in Haiti I can't wait to go to Haiti to see my family. And I know they can't wait to see me to. I put my mom sister in the quilt because she is the one that live right by my mom house. Anyway in our country we only have letle houses. We don't have big building. This image means a lot to me because this is the one I really want to put in my quilt. I was about to put all my family in the quilt but I didn't have enough place to put all my family. My family come to America because there was a big war and they were shouting. My family love spending time together. We love picnic. At picnic day we all get together. We invite our neighbors and friends. They come at picnic day at morning. Then all people get together and start the picnic day with happy face. The boys play soccer. Girls play with Picnic Toys. I like helping my little sister walk. She liked walking on the grass. She and I use to catch butterflys from the flowers. I also loved to catch the green parrot from our starfruit tree. If I couldn't catch parrot, I'll start to yall at them. No matter what I did I never catch one green parrot. Coconut is the most importint thing in the family. If we need water clean water to drink, we can't have clean water from any ware. We only can drink water from the coconut because it is safe. I loved living in my own house. Where a lot of space to hide from mom. Mom use to make mud stove for outside and for day time. Mom always like to sit under tree to get some warm air. Mom is good cook, She is cook in my family. Four hearts stand for three of my brother and sister and one for me. I picked these items because that what my family do look like. They also do those things. I picked picnic day because I like picnic. It my favorite day. That day I don't have to go to school. I pick my brother and friend are playing soccer because they always do.

The quilt means what my family like to do with the people we care. It mean place where I like living where I liked living where I had my grandfather and people who knew me. It a place where I was raised. I never thought to leave the place where I was raised. My family moved to America for better life. They were told that America have better education. Good teachers they just take care of the children and educate children like their own children. Thats why my family came to America for education. My family came to Chicago. They thought that Chicago is the better city than New York City. My dad also was told that Chicago will be safe too. We came to Chicago because dad had friend to Chicago. Thats why my family came to Chicago.

FIG. 5. Children's comments on their quilt squares.

along the bottom half of the class timeline. Students then organized the events chronologically. Each group then presented its 20-year time period by explaining each significant event the group selected. These events were added to the bottom of our timeline. As a class we analyzed the events on our American history timeline and our class timeline. We discussed whether our family choices and decisions were influenced by what was happening in the world during these 20-year periods. The quilt, their family stories, and their written comments on their quilt square images helped the students to reflect on how American and world events impacted their own family's lives.

The project didn't seem to fully impress the students until they saw the whole quilt sewn together (see Fig. 6). Their mouths dropped. After we saw the quilt, I asked the students to write reflections on the work they did. I didn't read them. I was so tired at the end of the school year. It was a very difficult first year for me and I thought I did not have any kind of impact on my students. Jackie read the reflections and showed them to me. "Did you see this?" she asked. After I read them, I cried. I realized that although students don't always verbalize their feelings,

FIG. 6. The quilt.

they always find a way to show them. Their reflections showed me more than their feelings. One student wrote:

> The way I feel about the quilt is I really like it because the way we made it was team work. I see that it is beautiful. I love it when we made it was worth it. Now it is complete and I have a smile on my face because of the good work my whole class did.

Another wrote:

> Dear Journal, I loved doing the quilts. Mine especially. It was the most beautiful quilt in the world. I know I'm exaggerating but I can't help it— that quilt is beautiful.

And another:

> I felt good because I got closer to my family.

They demonstrated that this quilt project had truly had a positive effect on their personal, home, and school lives. They learned something about me, each other, their families, and the world in which they live. It took 9 weeks but it was worth it! Melvin said it best: "This is just the beginning of our history quilt."

Jackie's Reflections. One thing that I loved the most about this project was the bonding between everyone that occurred. It confirmed what I learned. Whether it is a field trip, family participation, group or shared learning, a true authentic experience enhances and educates us all.

Susan's Reflections. As I reflect on the quilt project with my students, I have a deep sense of satisfaction as a witness to an idea becoming a reality. The students created a quilt that was beyond what I had envisioned. They certainly rose to the occasion. I am uncertain as to whether or not they truly made the personal connections with history that I intended and hoped for them to make. This is something I may never know. I won't be around for the moments as my students sigh those "Ah ha's" when they make personal connections with history, and as they become more aware of themselves and the world in the years to come. I can only hope that this project planted a seed.

WEB SITES

http://www.pbs.org/americaquilts/classroom/index.html Resources for quiltmaking in the classroom.

http://members.aol.com/mathquilt/index.html Resources for integrating math and quiltmaking.

http://aep-arts.org Arts Education Partnership.

www.vsarts.org Goals 2000 Arts Education Partnership.

bcob@worldnet.att.net Learning to Read Through the Arts.

http://artsedge.kennedy-center.org ArtsEdge.

RESOURCES FOR TEACHERS AND ARTISTS

Flournoy, V. (1985). *The patchwork quilt*. New York: Dial Books.

Freedman, A. (1994). *A cloak for the dreamer*. New York: Scholastic.

Johnston, T., & DePaola, T. (1985). *The quilt story*. New York: G. P. Putnam & Sons.

Ringgold, F. (1991). *Tar beach*. New York: Crown.

Ringgold, F. (1993). *Dinner at Aunt Connie's house*. New York: Hyperion Press.

Saldana, J. (1995). *Drama of color*. Portsmouth, NH: Heinemann.

Scher, A., & Verall, C. (1992). *200+ Ideas for drama*. Portsmouth, NH: Heinemann.

Whitsord, P. (1991). *Eight hands round: A patchwork alphabet*. San Francisco: HarperCollins.

LEADING A SCHOOL-BASED STUDY GROUP: MY PERSONAL PATH TO RENEWAL

Kelli Visconti
Jane Stenson School

I would like to discuss my journey of initiating and leading a study group in the elementary building in which I teach fifth grade. I touch on my own feelings as I started this group and took it through its first 2 years at Jane Stenson School in Skokie, Illinois.

My inquiry into the teaching profession began with my field-based master's thesis on teacher burnout. Surprisingly, I was feeling burned out after only 4 years of teaching. I wanted to know why. My curiosity continued even after I finished my master's program. I contributed a chapter to the first edition of this text, again restating my inquiry in the teaching profession. Here's a quote from my teacher story, entitled, "Stay In or Get Out? A 'Twenty-Something' Teacher Looks at the Profession":

> Even though I am a young teacher, I learned that I too am responsible for continuing my own learning in my profession. . . . The four themes—(a) I'm not alone, (b) teachers are experts and deserve respect, (c) renewal comes from experimenting, and (d) renewal comes from dialogue with other teachers—that emerged from my research revealed action plans for my own professional development.
>
> The focus for growth seemed to be in collaboration and the willingness to take risks. . . . It seemed to me that burnout could be avoided if teachers work together, creating a community and a climate in a school where

each teacher can be an individual, and yet, have colleagues for support and encouragement. (Burnaford, Fischer, & Hobson, 1996, p. 154)

I am no longer a twenty-something teacher who has only been teaching for 4 years. I am now a thirty-something teacher who has been teaching for 11 years. I still feel that I am responsible for my own learning in my profession, which is why I continued searching for new ways to find renewal.

My vision of what a study group would accomplish had been formed by attending the International Conference on Teacher Research (ICTR) in Evanston, Illinois, in 1997. I came away feeling renewed and hopeful that starting a teacher research group in my building would help others, along with me, feel continually renewed in the profession. The questions and issues that have been raised in my own mind as a result of this group have been centered around the parameters of my role as a leader of this group. Having never been in the position of a leader that was so vaguely defined, I struggled greatly with wanting the group to take certain paths, but I also did not want to dominate the group too much. The journey of leading this group has prompted me to search further for the answers of how to continue to fill the gaps within our group today in its functioning and its purpose.

FALL 1997

In the fall of 1997, I asked Sue O'Neil, our principal, if I could run an idea past her. We scheduled a meeting and I told her all about the conference I'd been to in the spring. She loved the idea of starting a group here, and she told me that I had her full support.

I spoke at our first faculty meeting in September about my plans to start a group of teacher researchers. I mentioned all of the fascinating things I had seen, heard, and read at ICTR in the spring. I said that anyone was welcome to be a part of the group, and that I'd like to meet on a regular basis. Several of my colleagues came to me later and told me that they would love to be a part of the group I was starting. We were on our way!

"This is going to be great!" I thought to myself. "I can't believe some of my colleagues are actually interested." But how was I going to *lead* such a group? My excitement soon led to apprehension. On one hand, I felt very capable of handling the role of leader. On the other hand, I also felt nervous and ill-equipped to do the job. Was I such a fabulous teacher to be telling the members of our group about the latest research topics? Was I competent enough in my teaching methods to be focusing on something else after school? I have struggled with these feelings throughout the 2 years that our group has been in operation.

OUR FIRST MEETING

When the seven of us met for our first teacher research (TR) meeting in my fifth grade classroom, I brought snacks, I provided coffee, I had classical music playing in the background; it was a pleasing atmosphere to attend after teaching all day long. I was nervous about our meeting. How would I entice my colleagues into realizing the value of teacher research? I didn't want our group to sound like too much work. I mentioned that I thought we'd be meeting once or twice a month for an hour and a half to two hours.

When our meeting began, we discussed what teacher research is; I talked again about the conference I'd been to, and I showed them papers that I had read and had heard presented. The women who were there seemed a bit confused, and I wasn't doing a very good job of explaining what this whole thing was about. I think I was trying to cram an entire 3-day conference into a 15-minute explanation. It wasn't working.

Luckily, the conversation swung to topics for research. I was thinking that we'd all choose our own topics and come together at each meeting to discuss our findings. I had never done research any other way, and I couldn't imagine how we'd all be able to work on the same topic at the same time. The others felt differently. They felt strongly about coming up with a topic for all of us to work on together. They wanted us to focus on something that would benefit the entire school. We finally agreed on the topic of writing because we all seem to be extremely frustrated with the progress, or lack thereof, our students were making. We had the feeling that the students should come into our grade levels knowing more than they do.

"Yes! It's working," I thought to myself. "They don't really understand the process, but they're willing to give it a try. I'm not crazy about the idea of focusing on one topic for all of us, but we'll find a way to make it work."

At the end of our meeting, we agreed on our next meeting date and time. One of the women who had expressed an interest in coming had waited to see who else would sign up before committing to the task. She caught me in the hallway the next day and told me that she'd rather not participate. I completely understood.

KEEPING THE STAFF AND ADMINISTRATION INFORMED

After I wrote a proposal to our administration (Appendix A) and then a revised proposal (Appendix B), the administration agreed to funding up to $20 per member of the group for the year. I kept the faculty and administration informed about our group by giving a copy of the minutes of each of our meetings to all of them (Appendix C). Eventually, I began e-mailing our minutes to everyone to save paper. Occasionally I would get responses from my colleagues who received it but who were not a part of our group. They'd say things like, "Sounds like you're having some good discussions!" or "Keep up the good work!" Our principal approached me after a few of our meetings about whether or not she could join the group. I was delighted to have her support, and I told her that she could certainly be a part of it.

OVERCOMING OBSTACLES AS A LEADER

We began having monthly meetings with an agenda (Appendix D). I continued to provide snacks and atmosphere, and we were really moving quickly ahead toward getting ready to gather information from articles and books. At that time, I became very confused about my role as "the leader." I didn't want the other teachers to feel that our group was too time-consuming or too much of a hassle. No one else was jumping at the chance to skim articles at the university library, so I said that I would do it. Boy was that a mistake! I spent hours at two university libraries trying to find articles that would comply with our topic. Was I taking the whole thing too far? Why was I doing all this work? Was I expecting too much from myself and the group?

When I brought the articles back to the group, I felt uncomfortable asking the teachers to do extra reading for our group. I wanted the group to take more ownership for what we all wanted to accomplish, but I didn't know how to instill that. I felt then, and I still feel now that I am "selling" this group.

When I e-mailed the members about setting up meetings, it was very difficult to find a time when everyone was free. When other meetings needed to be scheduled or rescheduled, ours would be the first to be canceled. It was extremely frustrating.

I was also unsure about how to convey information about teacher research to the other group members. Do I "lecture" on TR every time I read more articles or books on the topic? How do I instill my passion for research in others? Was the traditional theory that elementary school teachers teach and university professors do research getting in our way? I didn't know.

I do know that if I weren't leading this group, I might feel the same as the others do, or I'm assuming they do. I might feel that it's last on my list of priorities. If I hadn't gone to the ICTR in 1997 and seen teacher research in action for myself, I might not feel as much passion for it as I do.

Conversely, I can't say that I'm the *only* one who's truly vested in this endeavor. Our principal has been nothing but supportive throughout this process. She has been a wonderful source of advocacy for the group and me whenever we needed advice on where to go with a concern or question. Individually, each member of the group has done something significant to contribute to our task, which I feel lucky for. They are definitely very hard-working, dedicated teachers who have a curiosity for learning.

THE VALUE OF TEACHER RESEARCH

I don't want our group to be just like another committee. I want it to be an opportunity to search for answers to areas of our teaching that we're confused about. I want it to be a chance for all of us to feel validated in our profession. I want it to be an opportunity to prevent feelings of burnout. Teacher research is a chance to focus on a topic of our own, without the administration telling us to do it. It is an opportunity for teachers to receive recognition within themselves and within the community for going above and beyond what happens in the classroom, but it includes and integrates what happens there. Through my research on teacher burnout, I found that unless teachers talk about teaching, and share their feelings with other teachers, they can be sucked into the vicious cycle of planning, teaching, grading, and reporting. That's not all that teaching is. Teaching is a learning experience for students *and* teachers. We are lifelong learners, and it is so important for us to make time to continue to validate that idea.

PRESENTING OUR RESEARCH

At the end of our first year, as a result of our research, we presented our findings to the staff at our last faculty meeting (Appendix E). One of the ways of gathering information for us had been to have every teacher give students the same writing prompt (Appendix F). Many of the teachers were very impressed with what we had discovered. Our research had actually provided valuable information for the teachers at every grade level. It felt great to have accomplished something in the short time that we had been together as a group. I was excited about our progress, and I foresaw a productive future for our group.

I think perhaps only time will tell whether our group will be able to withstand the pressures of other commitments, other district committees, and other personal issues that may prevent us from staying together. I continued to gather feedback from the other members to find out what value they see in teacher research, and what effect, if any, it has had on their teaching.

FEEDBACK FROM GROUP MEMBERS

At the end of our second year together, I asked the members of the group to reflect on some questions I had for them to answer: What feelings do you have about our meetings, discussions, and findings? What effect do you feel our group has on your own teaching? What effect do you feel the group has had on our staff? What do you feel the overall value of the group has been?

Here are some of their comments:

> I think it has lessened the feeling of "isolation" teachers often feel. The communication between teachers, grade levels, special ed. teachers, and principal has all been very positive. It helps build a collaborative feeling to work on a project together, i.e. the writing skills list for this year. I think it

has good possibilities to tie into staff development plans for coming years since the district is developing goals.

I think the group is worthwhile. I think we have had some great conversations, and produced some fine products (like the writing overview). My main concern is TIME. It doesn't seem like we ever have enough time to really finish anything. I don't think we should be having more meetings, because it is always hard to fit them in. I don't know what the answer is—maybe working over the summer.

I also have a problem with not seeing immediate results. I know there is nothing we can do to change this because this is a research committee and research does not foster immediate change. When I go to other meetings such as grade level meetings or institute day presentations, I often get ideas that I can use in my classroom the next day. When I go to these meetings I leave with food for thought, but nothing concrete. This is also typical of research, but rather frustrating. When we do get an idea of what we want to do, like making a checklist to put in the folders, it seems too overwhelming. I keep thinking, "Now when are we going to get the time to do that?" I just don't know if what we are doing is making a difference, and that is rather frustrating. Maybe I should just appreciate that we do have good conversations and it is fun to get together with you guys, and this process is slow moving.

I think the teacher research group has helped motivate me in all areas of teaching. It helps me formulate and solidify ideas I have been "kicking around" in my head while teaching. It also helps me feel more professional as an educator. Talking with other teachers about problems, successes, and goals for the future makes me feel as though I am continuing to be the "lifelong" learner we challenge our students to become. I love the informal/non-pressured setting Kelli sets up for the group. Being flexible, and having the understanding that this is part of a long-term study makes this a nice, casual, yet informative group to be part of.

GOALS FOR THE FUTURE OF THIS GROUP

In the future I would like to change or improve the following things within our teacher research group:

1. Read more on how to have a successful teacher research group.
2. Try to communicate more often and more comprehensibly to my staff about the current models and approaches for doing teacher research.

3. Visit some schools that are using teacher research as a means of staff development.

4. Ask one of the members of our group to colead the group with me.

5. Have guest appearances by other teacher researchers at our meetings next year.

6. Set up regular days and times for our meetings so that scheduling won't become an issue anymore.

After 2 years of being together, I would like to see our group learn more about teacher research in general. I also feel that all the teachers in our building would benefit from a conference or observation or speaker on this topic.

I would like to see our group branch out into more groups within the building and perhaps within the district. The more advocates for teacher research we have, the stronger a component it can become within our professional development program.

I would like our group to continue to meet on a regular basis, but perhaps in a more scheduled fashion: every other Tuesday from 3:15 to 5:00, or every third Thursday at the same time. Perhaps we should take our meetings to a coffee shop occasionally just to get the group out of the school setting.

SPEAKING AT AERA

In April 1999, Nancy Hubbard, David Hobson, Gail Burnaford, and I presented an interactive symposium at the American Education Research Association conference in Montreal, Canada. Our presentation was entitled "Teacher Action Research as Professional Development in Schools: Four Paths Toward Change," and my paper was titled, "A Teacher Researcher Gets a Group Going: A Self-Study of a Teacher Leader."

In preparing for this presentation, I wrote my story of initiating a teacher research group, and the trials and tribulations of getting the group started. Preparing the paper was the easy part. Figuring out what to say in front of a room full of university professors and classroom teachers from all over the world was the hard part. We had no idea how many people would attend our session, or how big our room for the presentation would be. The four of us got together before the conference on several occasions to go over what each of us would cover, and the possible questions that some of the audience members might ask. My school district gave me 4 days of release time to attend the conference.

Our presentation went quite well. We were pleased with the number of people who attended and with the quality of questions that were asked and comments that were made. We had a large number of people request copies of our papers.

Attending and speaking at AERA was a phenomenal experience for me. It not only provided a milestone of professional growth for me, but it has supported my passion for teacher research and has given me the strength to try to expand our group in the fall to include other clusters in our school.

RELEASE TIME FOR RESEARCH

After I attended AERA, our teacher research group needed to find time to do more work on our research about writing. One of the tasks we needed to accomplish was to design a checklist for teachers that would go into each student's cumulative folder. The checklist would be a tool for teachers to use to determine the individual progress of each child's writing ability. It would be much more detailed than our current report card, and it would also serve as a way for teachers to modify their language arts curriculum to meet the needs of the individual students.

Because we were coming to the close of the school year, and most after-school meeting times were filled with other committee meetings, our principal arranged for each member of the teacher research group to have release time from our classrooms so that we could collaborate on this checklist. I was thrilled to have this kind of validation from Sue. It meant a lot to me.

We spent an entire afternoon designing the checklist for each grade level. We were not able to completely finish it, but we were able to agree on the check points for all criteria for kindergarten through fourth grade. We agreed that we would reconvene in the fall to finish and refine the list so that it could be used by teachers in the spring of 2000.

FINAL THOUGHTS

Teacher research has been a valuable source of professional growth for me for the past 2 years. It has kept me alive in the area of teaching, and has protected me from the potential monotony of planning, teaching, grading, and reporting. It has bridged relationships for me across grade levels. It has helped me communicate my needs to the administration. It has boosted my self-esteem as I met the challenge of starting a group by myself in my own school district and carrying it through 2 full years of study. I hope that we are able to continue to grow together as a group, and that we can show other teachers the intrinsic value we have found in teacher research.

ACKNOWLEDGMENT

Special thanks to Sue E. O'Neil, principal at Jane Stenson School, Skokie, Illinois.

REFERENCE

Burnaford, G., Fischer, J., & Hobson, D. (1996). *Teachers doing research: Practical possibilities*. Mahwah, NJ: Lawrence Erlbaum Associates.

APPENDIXES

Appendix A: Proposal for Teacher Research Group, Jane Stenson School, by Kelli Visconti

Objectives: We hope to achieve the establishment of a teacher research group at Jane Stenson School for the purpose of investigating a variety of topics. At this point we would like to look at one of the following topics: "Inclusion vs. Pull-Out Models in Special Education and/or Advanced Studies," "What Do Children Really Come to School Knowing? Do We Assume They Know More Than They Actually Know?," or "How Much Emphasis Should Be Placed on Self-Esteem in the Classroom? Does It Vary from Grade-Level to Grade-Level?"

Time-line: September–June. We will be meeting once a month for approximately two hours.

Resource materials needed: Books, articles, magazines, as defined by the group, including a copy of *Class Acts: Teachers Reflect on Their*

Own Classroom Practice reprinted by Harvard Educational Review, plus 2–3 more professional books for reference.

Funding: We will need $20.00 per person for these materials. Stipend for facilitator: $50.00 per month, which includes the supervision of a two hour meeting once a month and taking the role of liaison between administrators, university professors, guest speakers, and the faculty and staff who will be participating in the research.

Total Amount Requested: $120.00 for materials

$$\frac{+\ \$50.00 \quad 9\,\text{months} = \$450.00\ \text{for Stipend}}{\$570.00}$$

Teacher researchers: Kelli Visconti, Kathe Biondi, Ellen Gruenberg, Barbara Greenberg, Lisa Nimz, Kathy Fergus, Sharon Delevitt.

Appendix B: Revised Proposal for Teacher Research Group, Jane Stenson School, by Kelli Visconti

Objectives: We hope to achieve the establishment of a teacher research group at Jane Stenson School, and later possibly district-wide, for the purpose of investigating a variety of topics. At this point, we have decided upon a topic as a focus for our research for this year: "Misconceptions and Assumptions Teachers Have of Their Students' Writing Abilities."

Time-line: We will be meeting once a month for approximately one and a half hours.

Facilitator: Kelli Visconti, to be in charge of the supervision and minutes of each meeting; acting as liaison between the administration and the members of the group; and acting as a leader towards a common goal. She will be responsible for helping teachers within our district get teacher research groups started at their own schools. The facilitator will be paid $50.00 per month.

Members of the group: The following people have shown great interest in being a part of this group: Kathe Biondi, Kathy Fergus, Ellen Gruenberg, Lisa Nimz, Barbara Greenberg, Kelli Visconti, and Sue O'Neil. They will each require $20.00 for resource materials as defined by the group: magazines, articles, teacher research books, including a copy of *Class Acts: Teachers Reflect on Their Own Classroom Practice*, reprinted by the Harvard Educational Review, plus two to three other professional books for reference.

University liaison: Dr. Gail Burnaford, National-Louis University, Project Director. Her role is to act as a resource and mentor for our group. No stipend is requested.

Teacher research group district-wide: Presently we would like to meet within our own group until January. At that time, we would like to invite other interested teachers within our district to attend a meeting as an informational session to discuss what teacher research is all about, and how they can start their own groups within their own buildings. Kelli Visconti will ultimately be responsible for helping other groups get started.

Outcomes of the teacher research group:

1. Submission to *In Brief*, the district newsletter.
2. Sharing of research findings formally and informally with other faculty members, administrators, and teachers within our district.
3. Possible publication of research findings.
4. Solving problems within our school through research and discussion.
5. Increasing effectiveness of teaching abilities through acquired knowledge, collaboration, and practice of new techniques.

District rewards through research:

1. Teachers will be modeling lifelong learning for children.
2. Teachers will be alleviating burnout through communication, discussion, and investment in their teaching.
3. The district will receive recognition through local and national publication of our findings.
4. Our district will be considered to be on the "cutting edge" of teacher research, along with surrounding suburban schools in Mundelein, Highland Park, Deerfield, and Winnetka.
5. We will be building cooperation and collaboration among faculty members.
6. We will be providing a systematic way to build in sharing among teachers.

7. We will be building a framework for staff development by providing relevance for new and better ideas for inservice.

Appendix C: Minutes of Teacher Research Group

To: STENSON; Katie D; Tom; Roger; Jason P
From: Kelli Visconti
Subject: TR Meeting
CC:
Date Sent: January 6, 3:59 P.M.

Minutes for Teacher Research Meeting 1/5/99
Present: Sue O'Neil, Kathe Biondi, Kathy Fergus, Ellen Gruenberg, Barb Greenberg, Kelli Visconti

We began the meeting with a discussion of our research from last year, "Assumptions that Teachers Make About Their Students' Writing Abilities." We talked about how it prompted an awareness to all members of our staff regarding the topic of writing. We reviewed our findings from the surveys we collected from the staff about our expectations at the beginning and at the end of each grade level. We decided collectively that we would like to continue on our path of exploring the area of writing in our building. We would like to finish our task of designing a checklist for each child's cum folder that his/her teacher could fill out at the end of every year. The checklist will include topics relevant to the writing curriculum for their grade level. It will include words such as "introduced, mastered," etc. We hope it will serve as a launching pad for that child's goals for the following year in the area of writing.

The next topic we discussed was the area of grammar. We feel that we need to somehow incorporate grammatical expectations in our checklist. We may need to do another survey of our teachers to find out what their beginning of the year and end of the year expectations are for grammar. We noted that even though there are grammatical lessons within the spelling and reading basals, we would like to provide teachers with specific areas to cover for each grade level. The need will then arise for adequate resources to cover these topics in each grade level. We feel that we can deal with those needs through investigation of a variety of resources.

Ellen asked if what we are doing falls under the heading of "Teacher Research." It was a good question, and one that I had been wondering myself. I told the group that I had discussed our group with Gail Burnaford, previously of NLU, and now of NU. She said that it definitely falls under that heading, and that just because we are not presenting at conferences and publishing our work at this time, it does not mean that we are not researching. I have been doing some reading on this topic, and many sources illustrate formal dialogue that goes on among teachers, which eventually contributes to a change in one's teaching or in a school's curriculum qualifies as Action or Teacher Research. Because we have met as a group on a regular basis and kept track of our findings and grown professionally as a result of our work, we are teacher researchers.

We thought of another topic in the near future that we would like to study: "The Effect of the Use of Math Manipulatives in Various Grade Levels" or something along those lines.

Recorder: Kelli Visconti.

Appendix D: Sample Agenda for Teacher Research Meeting, February 9

Topics to be discussed:

1. Critiquing each other's writing?
2. Barb G. reports on developmental spelling document presented by Ellen from her Gifted Ed. class.
3. Kelli reports on ERIC search ... needs help putting time into xeroxing microfiche articles (13 more need to be copied.
4. Reporting on articles from the ERIC search (Kathe, Kelli, Ellen).
5. Reacting to articles through writing ... we need to start gathering our thoughts on paper for future presentations, sharing, and/or publishing.
6. What are our own assumptions and misconceptions of students' writing abilities? Do we need to start journaling about this? Should we interview other teachers to find out what their assumptions are?
7. Checklist of high-frequency words, language mechanics topics, paragraph structure for cum folder. Now or later?
8. Sue—writing samples from other grade levels? (Sorry we threw this at you when you weren't here.)

9. Acquiring writing samples from other schools?
10. Another look at our goals for this year . . . are we progressing? Fast enough? Do we want to invite other schools? Try to have something written for *In Brief* by the end of the school year? Formal or informal sharing with faculty, administrators . . . when? With what?
11. International Conference of Teacher Researchers, San Diego, CA, April 17–18, 1998; Montreal, Canada, 1999.

Appendix E: Findings from Writing Assumptions Teacher Survey

Kindergarten, beginning of year assumptions:

1. Enjoys listening to stories.
2. Recognizes reading their name.
3. Knows nursery rhymes.
4. Recognizes upper case letters.

Kindergarten, end of year assumptions:

1. Knows all sounds of the alphabet.
2. Recognizes all upper and lower case letters.
3. Knows all phonetic sounds of letters.
4. Starting to do journal writing and inventive spelling, and feels confident and not threatened: starts to string together sounds.

First grade, beginning of year assumptions:

1. No assumptions. Wait and see attitude. (One teacher)
2. Knows how to write all letters, capital and small.
3. Can identify ABC's.
4. Knows most beginning sounds.

First grade, end of year assumptions:

1. Can construct simple sentences.
2. Understands sentences begin with upper case letters and end with a period or question mark.

3. Can blend letter sounds together to spell new words (including inventive spelling).
4. Understands sentences or writing needs to make sense.

Second grade, beginning of year assumptions:

1. Can write a complete sentence, beginning with a capital letter and ending with correct punctuation.
2. Knows how to decode one-syllable words with long and short vowels.
3. Spell phonetically.

Second grade, end of year assumptions:

1. Can write 4–5 sentences on a given subject.
2. Knows periods, capitals, question marks.
3. Is aware of run-on sentences.
4. Reads fluently and with expression.
5. Can comprehend at an inferential level.
6. Reads chapter books.

Third grade, beginning of year assumptions:

1. Use of capitalization, punctuation (periods), and complete sentences.
2. Hopefully can indent and be able to write a simple paragraph so we can expand writing from there.

Third grade, end of year assumptions:

1. Be able to write and express themselves by using beginning, middle, and endings to their writing.
2. Can use transition words (hopefully).
3. Can remember to indent and write complete sentences and good paragraphs since we stress it greatly.

Fourth grade, beginning of year assumptions:

1. Use periods at the end of sentences, capital letters at the beginning.

2. Basic literacy items: alphabet, print goes left to right, experience with books, how to handle them, etc.
3. Knows that there are different genres.
4. Can demonstrate an understanding of what he/she reads either orally or in written form.
5. Can communicate ideas clearly, orally.
6. Can communicate ideas clearly in writing, the majority of which (80–90%) is standard English and spelling.

Fourth grade, end of year assumptions

1. Be able to form cohesive, coherent paragraphs.
2. Be aware that communication style and media changes depending upon intended audience.
3. Is able to identify pronouns, nouns, and verbs.

Fifth grade, beginning of year assumptions

1. Can write the whole alphabet in cursive: capitals and lower case.
2. Uses punctuation at the end of every sentence.
3. Uses a capital letter at the beginning of every sentence.
4. May be able to proofread their own papers for spelling mistakes, except for some words.
5. Be able to use a dictionary to look up the correct spelling of a word.
6. Have some knowledge of the use of conjunctions.
7. May have an idea of usage of colons and semicolons.
9. May know how to use quotation marks.
10. May know when to underline or use quotation marks for titles of books, magazines, songs, poems, etc.
11. Usually knows when to begin a new paragraph.
12. Indents for new paragraphs.
13. May be able to do some note taking if modeled.

Fifth grade, end of year assumptions

1. Can write an essay in rough draft, and then in final form.
2. Correct paragraph structure.

3. Capitals, periods, commas, and quotation marks are used correctly.
4. Cursive writing is completely mastered, in pen.
5. Can write a narrative essay.
6. Can write a persuasive essay.
7. Can write a summary of a story, for the most part, without adding too many details.
8. Can alphabetize a list of words.
9. Knows when to underline or use quotation marks for a title.
10. Can look up the definition of a word in the dictionary.

Appendix F: Data Collection: The Writing Prompt

April 1, 1998

Teachers:

As I mentioned in the Teacher Research Minutes from March 23rd, we will be asking all classroom teachers to give an informal writing prompt to their class. As a favor to the research group, we would *really* appreciate it if you could give this prompt to your class sometime before April 27th. This is in no way a test, but simply a way for us to look at writing samples from each grade level using the same topic for everyone.

Please encourage your students to do their best on it. You don't need to give them a time limit, but we would like them to complete it in school.

After everyone in your class has completed it, we would like you to choose three samples: one high ability essay, one average ability essay, and one low ability essay for your particular grade level. (We would like three samples from each *teacher*, not from each grade level.) Please do not write any corrections on the samples.

When you are finished, please put the three samples in my box on or before April 27th. If you have any questions, or if any of this is unclear, please e-mail me.

Thank you, sincerely, in advance,
Kelli Visconti, and the Teacher Research Group

* *

The Writing Prompt

Directions: Write an essay about the topic listed below on a separate sheet of paper. Do your best, use your best handwriting, and try to remember to use the things you've learned about writing a good essay. You may use pen or pencil.

Topic: If you could do anything over summer vacation, what would you do?

THREE CONTEXTS FOR EXPLORING TEACHER RESEARCH: LESSONS ABOUT TRUST, POWER, AND RISK

Nancy Hubbard
McWayne Elementary School

Like all teachers, I have always done action research, even before I knew what action research was. Every day, as I tried new ideas and new practices, I went through the process of acting, reflecting, adapting, and acting again. Throughout the last 10 years of my teaching, I have been involved in doing both formal and informal teacher action research in various contexts. In my first study, I explored the field of physics in my whole-language second-grade classroom. In my second action research study, I examined the personal intelligences with three first-year teachers. The third experience was teaching action research to other teachers. As I looked back at the past decade, I realized that those three studies were significant to my growth as a teacher. What I found within those three experiences was an intertwining of common threads and connections.

RESEARCH STUDY 1: TRUSTING IN STUDENTS' ABILITIES—CAN I LET THEM BE IN CHARGE OF THEIR OWN LEARNING?

My second-grade classroom in 1990 existed within the whole-language philosophy. My students and I worked together as a group. They told me what they really wanted to learn about, and then they did the learning, as I facilitated the opportunities for that learning. Sometimes they would wonder about bats or frogs. At other times they would wonder about Japan or dinosaurs or the human body. But they didn't wonder about the way things worked. Although they were engaged in a society of fast-paced technology, I didn't hear them wonder about machines, inventions, or technology. In their homes, in their school, and in their play, technology had already made an enormous impact in their lives, but it was commonplace to them, as mundane as eating and sleeping, and they took it for granted.

The teacher research study came about one day as we read a book. From one event in the story, they suddenly wanted to know about how pulleys worked. That interest grew into elevators. How did they work? Their wonderings multiplied quickly. It grew to wondering about levers and fulcrums, wedges, and gravity. Unfortunately, I really didn't know anything about physics. And so I began to research. I decided to explore how physics and whole language could be merged in my second-grade classroom. Books were helpful, but what helped me the most were those I searched out for assistance in the science and technology fields. A Nobel Prize winner for physics, Dr. Leon Lederman, shared with me:

> Seven year olds scare me. They are always asking questions about how and why things work. And what do we do? We tell them to shut up. From then on they lose interest. We take naturally curious, natural scientists and manage to "beat" the curiosity right out of them. (Lederman, personal communication, October 25, 1990)

He went on to tell me that children learn physics by observing, estimating, and guessing. They need to get a feel for it even though they can't understand why it works. William Hall, a research engineer for Amoco Research Center and father of five, confirmed this same idea:

> Most of the principles of physics are easy enough to be intuitive for primary school children. Our worst sin is to muddle their minds with the "formulas and math" of physics. Our greatest challenge is to understand a given principle so completely and firmly, that we can teach it in its beautiful simplicity. (Hall, personal communication, 1990)

I researched and studied all that I could, and although I tried to plan the lessons, I found that it was the children who were the best planners. Ideas evolved from toys, literature, trips, or the personal experiences of the children. When they wanted to know about elevators, they proceeded to ask questions as well as read books, observe, experiment, and build. They were most excited about what they had planned themselves. And they learned. Our classroom became more and more child centered. Their questions and interests guided the direction of the curriculum. They posed the questions, stated the problems, and solved those problems together. At the same time, as I circulated through the room, I asked them questions that provoked them to ask even more questions of each other. They were learning, as I had learned in my own continuing education experience, that solving problems and doing difficult tasks and experiments were easier to do collaboratively.

My role in the learning process became significantly different from any way I had known in the past. Throughout the projects and activities, I visited work stations and small conversational groups. The children were sometimes frustrated and had many difficult questions. I desperately wanted to answer their questions, and yet I knew that it would be more beneficial if they could find the answers through their own discovery. I found myself answering their questions by asking more questions of them. In constructivist settings, the students are involved in a discovery process. They are discovering and inventing, while at the same time negotiating solutions, sharing supplies, explanations, and ideas, and continually evaluating. Students use the tasks proposed by the teacher in order to allow their own thinking to become more powerful, more abstract (Clements & Battista, 1990).

The students are constructing their own knowledge while engaging in social talk and activity about problems or tasks that they share. Making meaning becomes a process that involves persons-in-conversation. The more experienced members can help by structuring tasks in order to enable the less skilled members to perform and internalize the process. The critical feature, though, is the nature of the dialogue between the students and teachers. The teacher must be an excellent listener. When teachers listen to what their students say, they can interpret what they understand, and then guide the students into further dialogue, action, and understanding (Driver, Asoko, Leach, Mortimer, & Scott, 1994).

My research revealed that student-created ideas were as valid as, if not more valid than, my own plans and ideas. Because I was not consumed with thoughts of executing lessons exactly as planned, I became a keen observer of children. However, in order for this to happen, several other things had to be in place. The first was that it was necessary for me to have a trusting relationship with my students. I had to believe in their ability to take charge of their own learning and had to know them well enough as learners to realize their potential.

The second thing that had to happen was the surrendering of some of my own power. Although I knew they were capable of doing their own learning, I then learned that I had to step back and allow them to do that learning. I found that I would need to take on a new role, not one of planning and directing exactly what was to be done, but one of facilitating. This is difficult for many teachers, for they are used to being in charge, running things exactly as they have planned.

The next piece that had to be in place was my own willingness to be a risk taker. My principal was more instrumental in this research than he had ever realized. He not only endorsed the changes that were taking place, but also ignited new ideas, encouraging them to materialize. When administrators empower teachers, giving them the freedom to take risks in the classroom and try new and innovative ideas, tremendous events ensue. This "permission" is extremely important to classroom teachers. For too long, the publishers, the administrators, and the school boards have been the experts, with the teachers delivering their message of "the right way to do things." Teachers have accepted these ways as being not only the right way, but also the best way, even though they do not always believe it in their hearts and minds. Too often, teachers do not realize that they are also the experts, that they can think for themselves, doing what they know is best for their students. Teacher leaders who encourage risking taking will promote teachers' professional growth, supporting change in education.

I continued to be an observer and a researcher well after that action research project was over. I found myself watching and thinking more about children's learning as well as my own learning. Through this watching and learning had come a great deal of questioning, and further research has come from it. This questioning, along with the elements of trust, giving up of power, and risk taking, became important themes not only in this piece of teacher research, but also in subsequent research projects.

RESEARCH STUDY 2: GIVING UP POWER—
CAN I ALLOW STUDENTS TO EMPOWER
THEMSELVES?

For the past 7 years I have been in a school where I collaboratively teach 47 children, ages 7 to 10, in two connecting multiage classrooms. The school is one of open enrollment, a school that bases its teaching, learning, and assessment on the theory of multiple intelligences, a theory developed by Howard Gardner of Harvard University (1983). Action research has been a significant part of our daily routine. Vicky, my teaching partner, and I are constantly trying new techniques and practices. We reflect regularly on our accomplishments and those processes that we used to get where we are. We often have a video camera on a tripod in our room, ready to capture what is happening for later reflection. Because we team teach, we are constantly available to each other for comments on the day's activities, and sometimes reflect on the process as it has developed. I don't recall that we have ever talked about what we do as action research. It had simply has become a normal part of our daily routine of teaching.

Our open-enrollment school bases its teaching, learning, and assessment on the theory of multiple intelligences. Gardner's (1983) theory states that intelligence is more than the traditional view of verbal and logical intelligences. In this theory, he has now identified eight intelligences, but states that there may very well be more than those eight. He defines intelligence as the ability to solve problems or create a product that is valued within a culture. Both solving a problem and creating a product are broad domains, and can be much more than solving a math computation problem or creating a sculpture. It can also be working with others to complete a perplexing task, or envisioning and executing a new dance.

In the book *Celebrating Multiple Intelligences: Teaching for Success* (New City School, 1994), the faculty at New City School, a private school in St. Louis, Missouri, that bases its teaching and learning on the multiple intelligences theory, described seven of the intelligences:

Bodily kinesthetic: Using one's body, or part of it, to solve problems and communicate.

Verbal-linguistic: Having the ability to use words and language in many different forms.

Musical-rhythmic: Being sensitive to nonverbal sounds in the environments, such as pitch, tone, and tonal patterns.

Visual-spatial: Having the ability to form a mental model and to be able to maneuver and operate using that model.

Logical-mathematical: Having the ability to discern patterns and approach situations logically.

Interpersonal: Being able to assess and respond appropriately to the moods, temperaments, motivations, and desires of others.

Intrapersonal: Being sensitive to one's inner feelings, knowing one's own strengths and weaknesses.

An eighth intelligence later named by Gardner in 1994 was described by Shores (1995) as *naturalistic*, meaning having the ability to recognize important distinctions in the natural world.

At the beginning of the 1998–1999 school year, in addition to doing informal action research in the classroom, I began working on a dissertation, which was also a teacher research piece. But rather than doing research with children, I chose to do the project with adults. Currently, educators are looking at the multiple intelligences in terms of the teaching, learning, and assessment of their students. However, I had not found literature that addressed teachers applying the multiple intelligences theory to their own thinking and teaching. I decided to explore this with respect to first-year teachers.

I focused on the personal intelligences, interpersonal and intrapersonal, which rely on all the other intelligences to express themselves. These personal intelligences are of particular importance to teachers. Not only does teaching require strong intrapersonal skills, which include reflection and metacognition, but it also requires ongoing interactions with others, the interpersonal intelligence. In my study, I looked at the particular skills that were within the personal intelligences, such as showing concern and empathy, demonstrating cooperation and collegiality with peers, and working effectively at conflict resolution (New City School, 1994).

Although success in school depends a great deal upon strength in verbal-linguistic and logical-mathematical domains, success in life relies heavily on successful relationships with others: partners, children, other family members, friends, peers, colleagues, neighbors, and many others. When teachers are strong in their interpersonal skills, they are able to work with students, colleagues, parents, administrators, and community leaders for greater mutual benefit, greater ease, and greater individual development (Lazear, 1991).

The intrapersonal intelligence, on the other hand, concerns an intelligence that is inwardly directed. It is dedicated to knowing one's self rather than those people around us. Within the intrapersonal realm lie skills such as reflectivity, higher order thinking and reasoning, and metacognition (Lazear, 1991).

This research stemmed not only from my interest in multiple intelligences theory, but also from my own disastrous first year of teaching. I was 20 years old and had a class of 41 eighth graders in a Catholic school. Four of my boys were old enough to drive to school. Classroom management was definitely not my strength. I found that my communication skills with parents were poor. The textbooks were older than I was, and I made $4,800 a year. I felt very alone. It was horrible, and I swore I'd never teach again.

Eventually, I did return to teaching again, but it didn't happen until 12 years later. Unfortunately, my story is not unusual. Each year, new teachers experience their first year as a classroom teacher in a variety of ways. Some abandon the profession as I did. I found, as other researchers have, that many first-year teachers find they have unrealistic expectations about teaching. They feel isolated from their colleagues and are often afraid to ask others questions for fear of appearing inadequate. Many have trouble with classroom management and feel overwhelmed. Others have difficulty talking with parents and understanding their perspectives (Kestner, 1994). These are all areas that relate to the interpersonal and intrapersonal skills.

I conducted this research study to respond to this research question: How does first-year teachers' understanding of their personal intelligences interact with the issues and the challenges that they face during their initial year of teaching? As a result of this study, I also learned some important things about myself as an experienced teacher leader. I learned some ways in which I could work more effectively with first-year teachers in order to enrich their understanding of their own personal (interpersonal and intrapersonal) intelligences.

I selected three of the participants, two grade school teachers and a middle school teacher. At the beginning of the year I met with the three teachers and we talked about the eight intelligences, particularly the personal intelligences. Each month after that, from October through February, we met both individually and as a group, having conversations about the issues and challenges that emerged in their teaching.

The sessions didn't go as I had planned. Perhaps I thought that I would be able to "fix" their problems and ease their burden during that first year. I had planned so many questions to ask them, but it didn't happen that way. Instead, they told their stories, often over and over again. They questioned themselves. They questioned each other. They wondered and they worried. Could I give up my power? Could I give up that need that I had to fix it all for them? I finally realized that if they were to be successful, they would have to create their own success. So I listened. And listened more. Sometimes we celebrated successes.

Sometimes we shared the hurt and the devastation. Sometimes we got angry together. Occasionally I related similar personal stories from my own first teaching year. As I shared my own stories, they felt more at ease, knowing that I had been in their shoes. But most of the time, especially at the beginning, I just listened.

As time went on, I began to ask more questions, the kind of questions that made them realize they could empower themselves to face their own challenges, and solve their own problems. Through those conversations and questioning, they raised their own consciousness, in constructing and using their own knowledge for the improvement of their practice. They also helped each other clarify their questions, and they challenged each other to think carefully through their problems as they compared stories within the group. I found that I didn't have to use my power to fix anything. Neither did I have to empower them, for they began to empower themselves.

The new teachers learned much about teaching in those 6 months, but I think I learned even more during those conversations. Through the process of collecting rich data and writing thick descriptions, I learned how I could work more effectively with beginning teachers in order to help make their first teaching experiences more successful.

In this study I learned four ways that I could work more effectively with first-year teachers:

1. To teach them about the personal intelligences and how those intelligence skills can be used to learn the process of dealing with the issues and challenges within their first year.
2. To make certain that they understand that they are free to express their feelings and needs as well as learn how to express them to those with whom they work.
3. To help them discover the perspectives of other stakeholders in education in order to bring about the best possible solutions within their educational settings.
4. To listen carefully to their stories so that both the teachers and listeners are able to understand more thoroughly their own perspectives.

I believe that my work enabled the new teachers to better understand their own thinking and reasoning as well as to better understand their communications with others. We identified the issues and challenges they faced as beginning teachers, and we learned more about how their intelligences impacted the ways in which they dealt with those issues and challenges.

Doing research with the first-year teachers was a bit more difficult than it was with children. It was the first time I had worked in a research setting with adults, and it was very different from doing research with children. When I worked with children, I did much of my classroom research by observing children and observing their work. When I did this work with adults, I was engaged in conversations either within the setting of personal interviews or in focus-group interviews. I was treading on new ground, just as I had in my first teaching experience. But again, as in my first study with second graders, I found that there were certain elements that had to be in place.

I first had to build a trusting relationship with my participants. We did this mainly through conversation and sharing. Because I was interviewing teachers, I became an essential listener. I could have told my participants what to do and how to say things. Perhaps I could have solved, or at least tried to solve, their problems. Again, as in my first study, giving up the power to control was difficult. I found myself once more being the facilitator. I began to ask the questions that would help the participants discover for themselves what they needed to do in their own teaching.

Risk taking was also in important issue for both the participants and for me as the researcher. None of us knew what the outcome would be, but the novice teachers knew that they needed all the help they could get, and I felt that I this study was very important to improving the success of teachers everywhere. And so we embarked on a study in which we had no assurance of success. Risk taking was crucial in order to travel these new paths.

RESEARCH STUDY 3: TAKING A RISK— HOW WILL I SURVIVE BEING A FIRST-YEAR TEACHER FOR THE SECOND TIME?

The third context in which I dealt with action research was the most challenging for me. I began to teach a graduate class in the master's of education program at National-Louis University. This group of 16 teachers from a variety of grade levels remained together for 22 months.

Their most significant assignment was an action research project that they were to do in their classrooms with their students. As the group's instructor, I was going to teach them about action research.

What I found that helped me the most was something that had been in front of me all year long. Like the three young teachers I had been working with, I, too, was a first-year teacher, but in a new context. Although I was 25 years older than most of these new teacher researchers, I too needed to be more cognizant of using the skills within the personal and interpersonal intelligences. I had never thought much about it before. Because of my age and my life experience, those skills had come more automatically to me in the elementary classroom. They didn't come automatically to me in this new situation, however. Being on the other side of the desk was an entirely new perspective.

Doing action research is one thing; teaching it is another. Action research sees its participants as cocreators of their reality through practice, experience, and action. It was my job to teach teachers how to produce knowledge and action that is directly useful to the participants via research, education, and action. I was learning to discover how I could teach teachers to empower themselves to construct deeper knowledge and use that knowledge to raise their own consciousness through self-inquiry and reflection.

I wondered what I would need to do to successfully make it through this group I was teaching for the first time. I had to do some questioning: What is it that I do in teacher research that I can teach someone else to do? How was I going to communicate this to someone else? Is action research something that I can *tell* somebody how to do, or can I only set up the situation for them where they empower themselves to do it?

Because I have always worked with children, I had to think of teaching in another context when working with adults. I asked myself more questions: How can I teach action research to a group of very diverse teachers? What do I need to do, to know, to teach them to do better work in their classrooms, to grow as teachers? How can I use my own personal intelligence skills to teach my group more effectively?

As I struggled through the first few weeks, I realized that I was now the first-year teacher, and what I had just done with first-year teachers, I would have to do with myself. I found that I often had to remind myself of the personal intelligences, using cooperation, collegiality, metacognition, and reflection. I reflected on what I was to do in this role. I also used metacognitive skills, "thinking about my thinking," as I planned and carried out each class session. While I was teaching, I realized that I had to be very mindful of what it was I was saying, every step that I was taking. I had to be mindful and concentrate on what my group members were saying. Through this, I realized that all the intrapersonal and interpersonal skills aren't for just first-year teachers; they are for everyone. I started making a connection between what I was doing with the new teachers in my multiple-intelligences work and this graduate class of experienced teachers.

As with the first two research settings, I found common threads running throughout this teaching of action research. Even in teaching action research, it was critical that I establish trust with this group of students. In order for my teaching to be effective, we all had to learn to know each other through our conversations and our journaling. As Driver et al. (1994) stated, making meaning became a process that involved persons-in-conversation.

As before, I had to give up power to the learners. As an experienced teacher, it was not my job to tell them what to do, but rather to be the facilitator for their own learning. But this was risky for me as one who also played the role of a "first-year" teacher. What if they didn't learn? What if they learned it wrong? I knew I needed to let go, but it was difficult. Taking a risk to allow them to be in charge of their own learning was scary to me, but turned out to be very empowering to them.

As with my first two studies, this exploration of my practice showed me new ways of being a facilitator of learning. I could not choose their topics or do the research for them, but I could inform them about action research. Although difficult, they had to come to their own understanding of what action research meant within their own study, just as I had to do when my second-grade students began learning about physics. Similarly, the first-year teachers in my multiple intelligences study needed to explore their own skills using the personal intelligences, as I was learning to use those same skills in my new role as graduate school instructor.

I have done three action research studies involving my own practice. I have learned to use research methods to enhance what I do in my classrooms of children and adults. Teacher action research has become a way of being a professional for me.

WEB SITES

http://www.iwaynet.net/~ankhe/multiple.htm Multiple intelligences in the classroom.

http://www.lee.k12.fl.us/schools/gty/mi.htm Multiple intelligences.

REFERENCES

Clements, D., & Battista, M. (1990). Constructivist learning and teaching. *Arithmetic Teacher, 38*(1), 34–37.

Driver, R., Asoko, H., Leach, J., Mortimer, E., & Scott, P. (1994). Constructing scientific knowledge in the classroom. *Educational Researcher, 23*(7), 5–12.

Gardner, H. (1983). *Frames of mind.* New York: Basic Books.

Kestner, J. (1994). New teacher induction: Findings of the research. *Journal of Teacher Education, 45*(1), 39–45.

Lazear, D. (1991). *Seven ways of knowing.* Palatine, IL: Skylight.

New City School. (1994). *Multiple intelligences: Teaching for success.* St. Louis, MO: Author.

Shores, E. (1995). Interview with Howard Gardner. *Dimensions of Early Childhood, 23*(4), 5–7.

THE ACTION RESEARCH LABORATORY AS A VEHICLE FOR SCHOOL CHANGE

Joseph C. Senese
Highland Park High School

Although action research can be pursued at any level of schooling, it is not typically part of the culture of schools as we know them. Schools are not usually places of inquiry. Action research is not merely a planning process distinct from change; it *is* change, and as such, is difficult to implement in school systems. (Burnaford, 1996, p. 138)

The Action Research Laboratory (ARL) at Highland Park High School was created and designed to provide teachers the means and encouragement to make substantive changes in their classroom practices that would increase student learning. As an assistant principal at the high school, I wanted to test my belief that a small group of teachers conducting collaborative action research can have a significant impact on the school culture and help to improve the school. Initiated in 1995, the ARL currently contains six teams, each consisting of three high school teachers and/or administrators from seven different disciplines in a cooperative venture to apply current research in education to their classrooms and jobs. Although only 10% of the faculty belong to it, the Action Research Laboratory offers the promise of becoming a practical vehicle for generating all-school change.

The action research that ARL teachers conduct propels them into areas of personal and professional interest. ARL teachers have experi-

TABLE 1
Action Research Interests

Team	Areas of Inquiry
ARL Team 1	Project-based learning; assessment; gender-based learning
ARL Team 2	Deemphasizing grades; ethical problem solving; problem-based learning
ARL Team 3	Creating community in the classroom; looping
ARL Team 4	Engaging senior students for the entire year; community building; applications of learning
ARL Team 5	Creating a sense of belonging for students
ARL Team 7	Creating flow for others; writing to learn

mented with curriculum, instruction, and assessment in ever-evolving ways (see Table 1). Highland Park High School now has the results of on-site research about the following areas:

1. The effectiveness of classes that have supplemented instruction with projects and experiential learning.
2. Classes in which no number or letter grades are assigned.
3. Ways to improve a sense of community in the classroom.
4. Ways to engage seniors in their final year of high school.
5. How to instill in students a sense of belonging.
6. How administrators can help others to be open to change.

These topics of inquiry evolve naturally from the teachers' experiences in conducting action research, creating a flow of experimentation derived from their own teaching and their students' learning. Their stories are the legacy of the ARL. From their ventures, these teachers have developed their thinking about and their skills in effective educational practices. They have affected the thinking and practices of their peers and have become a force for systemic change within the school.

GOALS OF THE PROGRAM

The Action Research Laboratory was designed to provide a system for school improvement through coordinated professional development activities based on theories of learning and organizational behavior. Teachers in the ARL investigate and experiment with curriculum and alternative learning opportunities for students. This, in turn, gives rise to restructuring academic disciplines and their relationships with each other, a step crucial to reinventing the school. The four goals of the Action Research Laboratory support these aims.

- *Collaboration*: To provide teachers sufficient time to be able to reflect on their classroom experiences and to consult with and share with other teaching professionals.
- *Experimentation*: To provide teachers with the ways and means in which to entertain new ideas of instruction, curriculum development, and assessment.
- *Research base*: To provide teachers with the support to put into practice what educational research says will best help all students learn.
- *Teacher empowerment/school change*: To provide the ARL teachers, their department members, and the faculty at large a living laboratory that proves that best practices can and will make a "successful" high school better.

In meeting these goals, the ARL teachers are truly researchers in charge of their own professional growth. They organize and reorganize themselves as their understandings emerge, making the program fluid and adaptable to changing experiences and needs. The activities they create in performing collaborative action research are varied and deep, giving rise to meaningful changes.

PROGRAM DESCRIPTION

Teachers in the Action Research Laboratory meet on a regular basis to discuss, design, and refine classroom practices. Each team of three, led by a facilitator, concentrates on a common, general area, but individual teachers develop plans for their classes independently. Each ARL team acts as a sounding board for ideas. Additionally, ARL teachers must observe the other teachers on their team. The facilitator provides ARL teachers the time to develop and carry out action research and the structures with which to share their progress with others. The facilitator also provides organization and support for the teachers while offering ways to expand the teachers' horizons through opportunities for attendance at workshops and conferences as well as through support materials.

In order to create opportunities for fresh discussion and novel approaches, I have insisted that the teachers on a team must be from different disciplines. This construct promotes insightful questioning while requiring teachers to reconsider and support commonly held beliefs and practices about the structure, organization, and methods of their own disciplines and of the school. Few things can be assumed when only one teacher in each ARL team is a resident content-area "expert." Consequently, team members ask each other fundamental and essential questions; answers delve into *why* and *how* to teach rather than *what* to teach.

Because the program is a laboratory, ARL teachers are expected to share a working model of these educational applications so that the entire staff of the high school can benefit from this action research. By the end of each year of participation in the ARL, all teachers and facilitators have documented their professional growth and action research by a record-keeping method of choice and by either a paper suitable for publication or another means of sharing their work.

As each team grows in its chosen direction, I have noted that cross-pollination among teams has occurred. Meetings of various ARL teachers have always proven to be spirited and informative as teachers share the experiences of their action research. These meetings among teams have become a regular part of the ARL. ARL teachers are truly a community of teacher researchers.

For the first 2 years of the program, I acted as facilitator for each team. As the program expanded, I soon realized that the program's potential would be limited by the amount of time I could devote to meeting with teams of teachers. Therefore, when ARL participants have completed 2 or 3 years of conducting their own collaborative action research, they are asked to facilitate other ARL teams. Consequently, the numbers of teachers directly participating in the Action Research Laboratory was able to increase from 3 teachers the first year, to 6 the second year, 12 the third year, and 19 in the fourth year. Teachers are truly facilitating their colleagues' professional growth, an exciting element of the program.

A CONSTRUCTIVIST APPROACH TO PROFESSIONAL DEVELOPMENT

Participants in the ARL have what has become a predictable reaction to the program after they have been involved in it for about 2 months: panic. Every ARL team has expressed frustration, sometimes even anger, that the members have not been given the answers to their research inquiry. They, just like students, expect that someone possesses the answer and that they will find this answer in the facilitator's knowledge or in the literature. That they have to construct their own answers to their own questions is a rude awakening. However, the program would not have the impact or the significance that it does without the teachers constructing their own meaning. Constructivism, especially in the structure of the meetings as well as in the leadership of the ARL, is essential to the growth and success of the program to make deep change. Wheatley (1992) explained it this way:

> We know that the best way to build ownership is to give over the creation process to those who will be charged with its implementation. We are never successful if we merely present a plan in finished form to employees. It doesn't work to just ask people to sign on when they haven't been involved in the design process, when they haven't experienced the plan as a living, breathing thing. (p. 66)

Only when teachers learn that their experiences are worth something, that they can shape their own futures and influence the system as a whole, do they take on a new role, that of leader. In a "leaderful" organization, everyone is given the latitude to construct meaning and apply that meaning to his or her situation. In testing out these mental models, these theories, teachers not only interact with the system, they change the system, because they *are* the system. They have made the system what it is; therefore, any changes in their own beliefs and practices necessarily impact the system as a whole.

Wheatley's (1992) explanation of this paradoxical situation is especially effective (p. 112). She likened the system to a hologram in which each piece of the hologram contains the whole picture. Consequently, any change in a piece is a change in the whole. The new science has given us a more complete understanding of how systemic change happens even when only a few participants seem to be making changes. We are the system; it does not exist outside of us.

DEEP TARGET OUTCOMES

As with any professional development program, the immediate goal of the ARL is to support teacher growth. But teacher growth in and of itself is fairly meaningless if it does not increase student learning. Therefore, expanded student learning is the ultimate goal of the program. At the same time, a long-term goal of the ARL is school change. School change—that is, the deep modifications in the structure, relationships, and meaning of a school—captures the essence of what the ARL is intended to accomplish over the course of time: To meet the challenges of the postmodern age, schools, just like the teachers in the ARL, need to be reinvented.

Brown and Moffett (1999) recognized the importance of the teacher researcher in efforts to reinvent schools: "The literature of school reform constantly affirms the powerful role of the teacher as the heart of the reform process in schools today. External authority and wisdom figures, it turns out, have significantly less effect on the restructuring process than site-based teacher leaders" (p. 108).

I have been intrigued by how this can work in a large school system when only a fraction of the teachers are part of the ARL. Wheatley (1992) offered a way of thinking about this. She explained how a system can be provoked into a response by even a slight fluctuation in its equilibrium. She noted, "In a dynamic, changing system, the *slightest* variation can have explosive results" (p. 126). This premise of how change occurs is the cornerstone of the ARL. The ARL has been that slight fluctuation that was dynamic enough to have the power to disturb the system and force it to change. The change is not planned or orchestrated. The system itself adjusts to the fluctuations, and something new and persuasive develops out of these natural occurrences.

The ARL is proving to be a fruitful way to make this change occur in a heavily entrenched institution such as a school system. Because deep change, the kind described here, needs time to take hold, early indications are that something radical (referring to the original meaning of the word: "at the root") and profound is happening at the high school. The indications that Highland Park High School is moving in this direction encourage the efforts of those involved in the program. The ARL has begun transforming the high school in important ways so that in the coming years it will be substantially and elementally different from what was before the initiation of the ARL.

The road of change has had its bumps too. Other teachers in the school have perceived that ARL teachers have a "favored" status because of their participation in this program. Three years after the founding of the ARL, the faculty finally was ready as a whole to consult with ARL teachers on how to conduct action research. Not all teachers found ARL teachers' work suspect or threatening, but some teachers felt challenged by the work of the teacher researchers. Ironically, the perception that ARL teachers have been favored with school funding has always been a misperception. To avoid that very criticism, I only used grant money from state and private sources to fund the fledgling program in the first 3 years. My experiences with teacher researchers in other schools, districts, and countries constantly uncover peers' cries of elitism. Teacher researchers declare that fear of criticism is the number one impediment to conducting action research. Teacher researchers do not want to appear critical of their colleagues by questioning revered educational traditions such as grading practices, competition among students, and long-standing instruction or assessment beliefs and practices. Yet the teacher researchers are the pioneers who take a risk to examine their beliefs, to put their own practices on the line, and to document their results. Once teacher researchers have amassed data to support changes in instruction, curriculum, assessment, and even organizational structures, fresh and revolutionary conversations invariably arise. No wonder some find teacher research threatening!

Five sources of data, related to the deep target outcomes of the Action Research Laboratory, have provided evidence of the program's influences on the development of the school as a learning organization. Each piece of data, in and of itself, holds limited capacity to change the system, but when multiple data sources are taken together, the evidence to change becomes persuasive and dynamic. Multiple sources of evidence and consistent results over time reveal the power inherent in a small group of teacher researchers working together at Highland Park High School. Consequences of the ARL include teachers developing points of view about the systems in which they work, acquiring perceptions of teaching as a true profession, influencing education beyond the school doors, garnering support for action research, and expanding teacher leadership.

DEVELOPING POINTS OF VIEW ABOUT SYSTEMS IN SCHOOL

Teachers do not join the ARL to make systemic changes. They join to improve their own practices. In a short time, however, researchers begin to realize that systems must change in order for them to reach their goals. This is a critical element to effecting school change through the commitment of small groups of collaborative action researchers.

For example, after only 1 year on an ARL team, Cathy Abreu, a Spanish teacher who is a member of ARL Team 4, commented: "You can't always look at yourself in isolation. You're always considered a part of that whole and how you can affect the whole when your organization is like a dinosaur. It's hard to pull together." The importance of this comment is twofold. First, Cathy's thinking about the entire system is exciting if the objective has been to uncover evidence of the initiation of deep change. Second, even if Cathy was a big-picture person before her ARL experiences, through her participation in the ARL she now has systemic ways of dealing with what she dubbed the "dinosaur" of the organization. The ARL has become the conduit through which she and other teacher researchers can effect school change.

In interviews from the second year of the ARL, teachers vocalized their emerging ability to look at the larger picture, to see the relationships among their own work and the work of the school in general, and to approach issues with a wider perspective. Christine Hill, a science teacher from ARL Team 1, noted: "I think [the ARL is] like the spokes on a wheel. It's not like it has one isolated effect. It has several effects in many different areas, implicit and explicit, actually." This observation points to a change in the customary thinking of classroom teachers. It represents the kernel of a slight perturbation that is necessary to disturb and reorganize the larger system, a concept at the core of self-organization (Wheatley, 1992).

ARL Team 2 health teacher John Gorleski remarked on how participation in the ARL has broadened his horizons:

> It's forced us once a month to get together with other professionals and talk about education. I mean I wouldn't have done that on my own. I wouldn't have sat down with [the other two team members] and said, "Let's talk about education and the state of our school." I mean, that has been so refreshing to have had that opportunity to do that.

Paul Swanson, ARL Team 2 English teacher, even went so far as to characterize his role in effecting change in the school system as a revolutionary: "I often think that I'm the person who has to go around and be subversive against the system." Strong but not surprising words for one whose eyes have perceived the importance of his daily work!

ACQUIRING PERCEPTIONS OF TEACHING
AS A TRUE PROFESSION

The yearly reports written by ARL teachers provide a rich source of information that supports the effects that they are having in changing the school system. What comes through in these documents is the clear resolve and direction that these teachers have developed, because they have had evidence of the worth of what they do in the classroom. Their work has been affirmed by research that they themselves have conducted. In addition, they have listened to and read work by some of the most influential thinkers in education today. These experiences have provided them with the ability to write and speak with significant weight and authority. This comment by Paul Swanson is typical: "Some [faculty members] suggested I was playing games because I was not eliminating grades but only delaying them. Later in the year through a series of semi-formal conversations, I tried to combat my colleagues' oversimplified reactions to this experiment." Most teachers would not venture to confront their peers. This teacher has been empowered to do that because of the surety he has realized from his own action research.

This professionalizing of teaching has made a difference in how parents are understanding the idea of "school" as perhaps something different from their own educational experiences. Robin Rogus, ARL Team 1 mathematics teacher, documented the importance to her of reaching out and involving parents, a much larger picture than most classroom teachers consider:

> I feel that the parental feedback helps in substantiating my efforts to provide alternative forms of assessment and project-based learning in a predominantly textbook-driven course. I also feel that my clear communication of the course's objectives that I presented at last year's Parent Open House led to the greater parental awareness of my ARL work.

Almost every ARL teacher has communicated in fresh ways with parents, either through letters home at the beginning of or during the semester, by asking for feedback through surveys, or by informal parent contacts. These changes in school–home communication, multiplied by the number of ARL participants, can have nothing but a significant impact on the school system. As a matter of fact, parents are now seeking to find out if their children's teachers are a part of the ARL.

The commitment that these teachers have developed as a result of their ARL experience echoes in health teacher John Gorleski's comments:

> Last year I set as a goal ". . . to be an advocate for the effectiveness of de-emphasizing grades in the classroom, both inside and outside the walls of [the district]." In addition to "preaching the gospel of de-emphasizing grades," I have been a vocal supporter of action research as a whole.

Teachers with this kind of commitment and passion cannot but disturb the school system in such ways that it will have to make adjustments to accommodate the changes that the action research is bringing about.

If enhancing a teacher researcher's ability to question and improve his or her practice is an indication of a change in teacher self-perception, then Bryan Ott, ARL Team 1 social studies teacher, offered ample evidence that change is happening:

> [Because of my participation in the ARL,] I am more highly concerned with issues of fair standards versus high standards, student standards versus teacher standards, and differences between standards and expectations from one teacher to the next than at any time in my career. If anything, I have learned that I have much more to learn. I am conscious, and thankful, of the fact that those of my colleagues conducting action research have become my best resource for learning what I need to continue to improve my classes.

Teachers have also documented the interrelationships among ARL teachers and their influences on each other. Within a team, one teacher's successes and even failures touch the other two members. Year-end written reports by teachers for the 1997–1998 school year showed the influences that ARL teachers have had on each other. In these reports, at least one member of every ARL team has considered the action research being done by other teams, and, more significantly, how that action research has influenced his or her own work. The sharing of rubric formation, interviewing techniques, assessment practices, deemphasis of grades, ways to create community—all of these ARL projects have found their way into other ARL teachers' work.

In like manner, teacher interviews supply evidence of how the ARL gives teachers the support to take risks to improve their practices and student learning. Typical of their comments is this one:

By far, the most rewarding part of working on an ARL team was the opportunity to learn and grow with a small group of teachers. I found that the two teachers and one assistant principal were just as committed to my learning and growth as I was to theirs. This feeling of mutual commitment provided a wonderful staff development experience; by working with these colleagues on a consistent basis throughout the year, I was able to explore new ideas and take risks in the classroom, with a type of "safety net" in place. For that reason, as well as my desire to explore my remaining questions, I will continue to conduct action research. (Lauren Fagel, social studies teacher, ARL Team #2)

When only a fraction of the faculty is engaged in the ARL, how can it help to change the school for better? Because the ARL focuses the professional development of a committed group of teacher-researchers, even a relatively small part of the faculty, it possess the power to move the system forward. Wheatley (1992) explained how this type of thing holds tremendous power to change an organization:

It is not the law of large numbers, of favorable averages, that creates change, but the presence of a lone fluctuation that gets amplified by the system. Through the process of autocatalysis, where a small disturbance is fed back on itself, changing and growing, exponential effects can result. (pp. 95–96)

The ARL honors the individual's importance in creating his own patterns of meaning, patterns that return to the organization and create new and exciting variations that then become part of the larger system. And multiple sources of evidence suggest that the high school will be a changed place given sufficient time.

INFLUENCING EDUCATION BEYOND
THE SCHOOL DOORS

The effects of the ARL have not halted at the doors of the Highland Park High School. The number of articles published by ARL participants, the number of presentations being made by ARL teachers, and the number of articles written about the ARL have all provided a rich vein of evidence that the work of the ARL extends beyond the doors of Highland Park High School. (See Appendix A). Articles by ARL participants have been published in education journals, in books, and on Internet sites. (See Appendix B).

These examples give only a flavor of the breadth and depth of the efforts by ARL teachers to "get the word out." The enthusiasm, professionalism, and dedication they have shown in writing articles, in making presentations, and in talking to other teachers and reporters, have imbued significance to their efforts and the ways in which the ARL has changed how they think about themselves, their work, and their school. These teachers have repeatedly commented that the ARL has made them see themselves as professionals.

GARNERING SUPPORT FOR ACTION RESEARCH

Administrators in the high school as well as in the district office have endorsed the efforts of the ARL and helped to promote its goals. Linda Hanson, the district superintendent and a member of ARL Team #7, requested that I present the Action Research Laboratory program to all the administrators in the district and to the school board. Janell Cleland, the Director of Learning, (and also a member of ARL Team #7) has called collaborative action research the "preferred method of professional development" for the district. The ARL went from an innovation to institutionalization in 3 years. It has become part of my job description, and school professional development funds have now been set aside to finance some of its activities.

Karen Harris, the chair of the Social Studies Department, noted the positive effects of having four ARL teachers in her department:

> Innovative and growth promoting describe a variety of interdepartmental efforts undertaken by social studies teachers this year. [They] participated in Action Research [Laboratory] teams, each with two colleagues from other departments. Topics addressed include assessment of projects and performances, the relationship between grades and student learning, the effects of building community on student achievement and strategies to engage seniors in their learning. Through professional talk and collaborative efforts, the work of these individuals has had a positive effect on the practices of others in the department. (Highland Park High School Annual Report, 1997–1998, Highlights and Accomplishments)

EXPANDING TEACHER LEADERSHIP

Teachers, through their years of participation in the ARL, have now started to comment on the broader goals of the program. They speak freely about "getting the word out," about where they might get published, and about which conferences they might attend. Their conversations have been larger than the individual action research that they are conducting. They talk about a commitment to the larger education community. Teachers are developing their own web of relationships.

Two ARL teachers who took on the role of cofacilitators for a new team also noted that their role as leaders had been developed, a sure sign of the staying power of the ARL. John Gorleski commented:

> The biggest thing that I've gotten out of this is to have more faith in my colleagues. If something has to be done and I have a choice between letting you do it and hoping it gets done like I like it to be done, often I do it myself. This experience [of facilitating another ARL team] has forced me to allow other people to do the work and have faith that it's going to get done. That has been a change that I think has been very positive for me this year, being a facilitator.

Paul Swanson, another cofacilitator, expressed similar thoughts about his role:

> I really learned a great deal from the three members of [ARL] Team #3. I saw a great deal of enthusiasm, a great deal of willingness to look at systems of doing things. And, a persistence. I think all three are artists as teachers in different ways and I learned so much from their strengths.

The attention that ARL teachers have garnered through their work demonstrates a new leadership role. The awards bestowed on the program are testimony to the power of the ARL to sustain itself over time, make significant changes, and affect education outside of the high school. All in all, the ARL has applied for 18 awards/grants, mostly to help pay for its operating costs. A side benefit of this has been the recognition that the ARL has earned outside of the school. Even when the ARL does not receive the grant or the award, the action research network has noted its accomplishments and has called on ARL teachers to participate in fresh ventures. Some of the speaking engagements by ARL teachers and all of the articles written about the ARL can trace their origin to these beginnings. For example, at an Illinois Association for Supervision and Curriculum Development conference in October 1998, 4 ARL participants presented their findings in a poster session. The ARL teachers were asked to present at that conference because I had made a presentation about the ARL at the National Staff Development Council Conference the year before. From their colleagues' participation in the IASCD Conference the year before, 5 more Highland Park High School teachers presented at the same conference in 1999. One of those presenters was not even an ARL teacher but has used the process of action research in his own classroom. As the ARL becomes better known in the wider school community, this unpredictable web of relationships will position the ARL to make deep and lasting changes.

In the fall of 1998, the ARL had the honor of being recognized as a program of excellence in the team category of the Illinois State Board of Education's recognition program called Those Who Excel. Significantly, the award was not for individual teachers' action research but for the program as a whole. The momentum that has propelled the ARL into the spotlight where it can cause the most change has been forceful and consistent.

Brown and Moffett (1999) noted that teachers who see themselves as part of a professional community like the ARL have the best chances of making meaningful changes in their practices. Because the ARL has modeled the process of collaborative action research, the faculty of the high school has been able to move forward in its two school improvement initiatives: to actively engage students and to enhance relationships. At the start of the 1998–1999 school year, as the entire faculty organized into action research teams centered on these initiatives, the ARL teachers instructed the faculty in the processes of collaborative action research. In addition, I led the faculty in exercises to help them organize around important action research topics of their own choosing. During a fall inservice this year, the entire faculty shared the work they have done in the Learning Teams for the last two years. In lectures, roundtable discussions, poster sessions, demonstrations, and performances, teachers talking to teachers about their work created a powerful venue, not only for sharing their progress but also for institutionalizing the impressive things they learned about how to help students learn better.

Two other examples of the school-wide effects of the ARL teachers' research readily come to mind. Because of the work that Christine Hill did in the ARL with the freshman physical science curriculum, the entire freshman science program embraced more authentic assessment techniques including student, self, and peer assessments. Similarly, because of her association in the ARL, Robin Rogus has worked to make the geometry curriculum more hands-on and interactive. Her research has resulted in a revamping of the curriculum for all students taking geometry.

Other indications of the influence of the ARL at the high school exist in addition to these more dramatic examples in curriculum. Cross-disciplinary discussions are now commonplace. All teachers now regularly participate in "professional sharings," informal conversations during a lunch period to share where they are in their research or what they have learned at a conference. Teachers readily take on leadership in their own and their colleagues growth.

Evidence of the efficacy of the ARL has come from unexpected places, too. Geneva High School in Geneva, Ohio, found the structure of the ARL compelling and is in the process of forming its own ARL. Twelve teachers under the leadership of guidance counselor Roger Smith are working on exciting collaborative action research projects in order to improve instruction and learning. The actualization and experiences of the ARL in another school system will be an important indication of the effectiveness of this professional development model as a vehicle for school change. The exchange between teachers and researchers from Geneva High School and Highland Park High School should prove to be yet another avenue for growth and change.

The ARL gives teacher researchers freedom, freedom to decide with whom they will work, what they will work on, and how they will do that work. The freedom, as a matter of fact, is overwhelming at times. Teachers, just like students, are not used to making some of these decisions about their own learning. They need the support and encouragement of a program like the ARL to give them permission to take bold action, to act on their beliefs, and to make a difference. They then begin to see themselves very differently.

Although they were excellent teachers before their participation in the ARL, these teachers are now changed in elemental ways. Time and again in interviews and at meetings, each ARL teacher speaks to the difference in their lives that the ARL has made. Deep change like that comes only with the processes of sustained, job-embedded professional development.

Real work for real people with real consequences in real time make the experiences of the ARL authentic to the participants. Wohlstatter, Van Kirk, Robertson, and Mohrman (1997):

Considerable agreement is emerging about the nature of organizational learning and the dynamics that must be established in order for an organization to learn. Seven dynamics appear repeatedly in this literature: dialogue about purpose, rich connectedness among participants, holistic thinking, learning from experience, connection to external environment, personal mastery, and involvement of all participants in learning processes. These dynamics enable organizational members to think out of the box and make changes in the organizational system that allow it to better achieve its mission. The dynamics also allow participants to make ongoing incremental changes that have systemic impact. (p. 47)

A WORD OF ADVICE

A belief in the goodness of the intentions of the teachers in a school, a belief in each teacher's desire to produce better lessons, to become a better teacher, and to create a better school experience for all students secures the promise of significant change emerging from the ARL. Wagner (1998) predicted this result when the work of teachers is truly collaborative and when teachers are allowed to direct their own work in significant ways:

> Over time, the constant interaction in such a collaborative change process creates a different set of work incentives—just as it does in a constructivist classroom. As people begin to share ideas and develop common aspirations, the goal is no longer simply to do only what is necessary to comply with the demands of the boss. Rather, people begin to work to earn the respect of their colleagues and to create something truly worthwhile together. (p. 517)

Accepting the significance of this belief and what it requires schools to do is not as easy as it may appear. My conversations with administrators who express interest in establishing collaborative action research teams in their own schools or districts indicate that the most formidable aspect of the ARL for administrators is not being able to let go of the process. Administrators eagerly express a willingness to provide teachers with the support, the means, and the resources to conduct action research, but they often have difficulty in letting teachers supervise themselves and take responsibility for their own growth and learning. As an experienced school administrator, I know that as a group we tend to do what comes naturally to us. We want to institutionalize initiatives, to structure teacher research, and to supervise the process. My experience in the Action Research Laboratory indicates that we should do exactly the opposite. If administrators are truly earnest about consequential, nonpoliticized teacher research, they must allow the process to develop in its own unique, unpredictable ways. Once in place, the program self-organizes, and that organization is unique to the participants and to the system in which it exists. The irony is that no one actually "controls" the program. It truly takes on a life of its own. It becomes another entity within the organization, and therein lies its power to change the organization. Administrators need to be aware that teacher research may take the organization in directions that no one can predict. The great promise and the great excitement of collaborative action research as a vehicle for positive school change emerge only if schools can trust the people in the organization and trust the process of collaborative action research (Senese, 1998).

REFERENCES

Brown, J. L., & Moffett, C. A. (1999). *The hero's journey: How educators can transform schools and improve learning.* Alexandria, VA: Association for Supervision and Curriculum Development.

Burnaford, G. (1996). Supporting teacher research: Professional development and the reality of schools. In G. Burnaford, J. Fischer, & D. Hobson (Eds.), *Teachers doing research: Practical possibilities* (pp. 137–150). Mahwah, NJ: Lawrence Erlbaum Associates.

Senese, J. (1998). Action! *Journal of Staff Development, 19*(3), 33–37.

Wagner, T. (1988). Change as collaborative inquiry: A "constructivist" methodology for reinventing schools. *Phi Delta Kappan, 79*(7), 512–517.

Wheatley, M. J. (1992). *Leadership and the new science.* San Francisco: Berrett-Koehler.

Wohlstetter, P., Van Kirk, A. N., Robertson, P., & Mohrman, S. (1997). *Organizing for successful school-based management.* Alexandria, VA: Association for Supervision and Curriculum Development.

APPENDIXES

Appendix A

Publications by Members of the Action Research Laboratory

Fagel, L., Gorleski, J., Senese, J., & Swanson, P. (June 1998). *Classroom practitioners' perspectives on the merits of the Action Research Laboratory experience.* Paper presented at Herstmonceux II Conference, S-STEP, a special interest group of the American Educational Research Association, East Sussex, England. Available at http://educ.queensu. ca/~ar/sstep2/highland.htm

Fagel, L., Gorleski, J., Senese, J., & Swanson, P. (1998, August). Emphasizing learning by deemphasizing grades. In G. Mills (Ed.), *Action research: A guide for the teacher researcher* (pp. 94–97). Upper Saddle River, NJ: Merrill.

Gorleski, J. (1998, Spring). What good are grades? *Teaching and Learning* (pp. 21–24). (Springfield, IL: Illinois State Board of Education)

Gorleski, J. (1999, August). *The results of de-emphasizing grades in the secondary health classroom.* Available at http://www.parnet.org/parchive/bibliodetail.cfm?id=526

McDaniel (Hill), C. (1998, Spring). Interviews as an assessment tool in an Action Research Lab. *Teaching and Learning* (pp. 33–34). (Springfield, IL: Illinois State Board of Education)

Senese, J., McDaniel (Hill), C., & Rogus, R. (1998, December). *The Action Research Laboratory: Applying the principles of constructivism to staff development* [Cassette Recording]. Cassette No. 8040-C12. Washington, DC: National Staff Development Council.

Senese, J. (1998, Summer). Action! *Journal of Staff Development*, pp. 33–37.

Senese, J. (1999, December). Data can help teachers to stand tall. *Journal of Staff Development*, p. 84.

Presentations by Members of the Action Research Laboratory

Abreu, C., Elman, J., & Witt, J. (1999, December). *Engaging high school seniors in their own learning.* Presented at the Ontario Educational Research Council Conference, Toronto, Ontario, Canada.

Abreu, C., Elman, J., & Witt, J. (1999, April). *Engaging high school seniors in their own learning.* Presented at the Greater Chicago Teacher Research Conference, National-Louis University, Evanston, IL.

Brejcha, D., Gray (Levin), L., & Johnson, W. (1999, April). *Building communities to enhance learning.* Presented at the International Conference on Teacher Research, Lennoxville, Quebec, Canada.

Brejcha, D., Gray (Levin), L., & Johnson, W. (1999, October). *Building communities to enhance learning.* Presented at the Illinois Association for Supervision and Curriculum Development Research Conference, Naperville, IL.

Fagel, L. (1999, October). *What do I need for an "A"?: Teaching values by de-emphasizing grades in the social studies classroom.* Presented at the Illinois Council for the Social Studies, Illinois Council of Social Studies Conference, Chicago.

Gorleski, J. (1998, October). *Emphasizing learning by de-emphasizing grading practices in the health classroom.* Presented at the Illinois Association for Health, Physical Education, Recreation, and Dance Conference, Chicago.

Gorleski, J. (1999, October). *Emphasizing learning by de-emphasizing traditional grading practices.* Presented at the Illinois Association for Supervision and Curriculum Development, Naperville, IL.

Rogus, R. (1999, October). *Making geometry meaningful through technology and projects.* Presented at the Illinois Council of Teachers of Mathematics Conference, Springfield, IL.

Rogus, R. (2000, April). *Making geometry meaningful through technology and projects*. Presented at the National Council of Teachers of Mathematics, Chicago.

Senese, J., Fagel, L., Gorleski, J., & Swanson, P. (1998, August). *Classroom practitioners' perspectives on the merits of the Action Research Laboratory experience*. Presented at the Herstmonceux II Conference, Bath, England.

Senese, J., McDaniel (Hill), C., & Rogus, R. (1998, December). *The Action Research Laboratory: Applying the principles of constructivism to staff development*. Presented at the National Staff Development Council Conference, Washington, DC.

Senese, J. (1999, April). *The Action Research Laboratory as a vehicle for school change*. Presented at the Annual Meeting of the American Educational Research Association, Montreal, Quebec, Canada.

Senese, J. (1999, April). *The Action Research Laboratory as a model of staff development*. Presented at the International Conference on Teacher Research, Lennoxville, Quebec, Canada.

Senese, J. (1999, July). *Evidence of success in the school change process: What kinds are needed and how much is enough?* Presented at the Action Learning, Action Research and Process Management Association Conference, Brisbane, Australia.

Senese, J. (1999, July). *The Action Research Laboratory: An American PEEL*. Presented at the Project for Enhancing Effective Learning Conference, Melbourne, Australia.

Senese, J. (1999, December). *Supporting teacher research at the school level*. Presented at the Ontario Educational Research Council Conference, Toronto, Ontario, Canada.

Senese, J. (1999, December). *The paradox of staff development*. Presented at the National Staff Development Council Conference, Dallas, TX.

Senese, J. (2000, April). *Initiating and supporting teacher research*. Presented at the Annual Meeting of the American Educational Research Association, New Orleans, LA.

Senese, J. (2000, April). *The effects of being a teacher researcher on student learning*. American Educational Research Association Annual Conference, New Orleans, LA.

Appendix B: Internet Resources for School-Based Action Research

http://educ.queensu.ca/~ar/sstep2/highland.htm Teacher Self-Study: Classroom Practitioners' Perspectives on the Merits of the Action Research Laboratory Experience.

http://www.d113.lake.k12.il.us/hphs/action/page1.htm The Action Research Laboratory: A Model of Professional Development for Teachers At Highland Park High School.

http://www.mcrrel.org/resources/links/action.asp Education Resources: Action Research/Teacher as Researcher.

http://www.triangle.co.uk/ear/index.htm *Educational Action Research*—A refereed international journal.

http://educ.queensu.ca/~ar/aera2000/ Initiating and Supporting Teacher Research.

THE LARGER ARENA

8

How Does it Matter?
Teacher Inquiry in the Traditions
of Social Science Research

Susan Jungck
National-Louis University

"What terms and images come to mind when you hear *research* and, specifically, *research in education*?" Perhaps you, like most of the teachers and administrators in my introductory research courses, associate research with:

- Large, national-type studies that involve statistics; usually (always?) these studies attempt to prove something.
- A lot of data.
- Comparison groups.
- Boring.
- Quantitative is all I know—factual type.
- Control groups.
- Objectivity.
- Facts, figures.
- Lots of jargon.
- Experimenting.
- Validating hypotheses.
- Theories.

- Cut-and-dry conclusions.
- Statistics.
- Boring reading.
- Dusty-shelf material.
- Library research.
- Testing ideas.
- Very involved, a rather awesome task.
- Fact finding.
- No practical application to classroom.
- Sometimes makes me feel stupid because I can't comprehend [and] knowing and understanding certain ed. research makes me feel smart, superior with it.
- It is done by professional scholars (researchers) scientists, etc.—in other words—experts.
- Not relevant to me.
- Something I would never do!
- Evaluation of teachers (Jungck, 1987).

Overwhelmingly, these responses correspond to what Agar (1986) and Guba and Lincoln (1994) referred to as the "received view" of the natural and social sciences that has dominated our language for nearly 400 years. Indeed, it is the conception of science and research that most of us "received" in elementary school when we memorized what was called "the scientific method." This "received view" is a philosophical paradigm; it is a worldview consisting of basic beliefs that guide action. A paradigm, according to Guba and Lincoln (1994), "defines, for its holder, the nature of the 'world', the individual's place in it, and the range of possible relationships to that world and its parts. The beliefs are basic . . . accepted on faith . . . there is no way to establish their ultimate truthfulness" (p. 107). They went on to say that paradigmatic beliefs are implicit responses to three fundamental questions: (a) What is the form and nature of reality? (b) What is the nature of the relationship between the knower or would-be-knower and what can be known? and (c) How can the inquirer (would-be knower) go about finding out whatever he or she believes can be known? (p. 108)? Thus, paradigms are not just philosophical abstractions; in very direct ways they reflect and construct our perceptions of the world and dominate our language.

They significantly and holistically influence, according to Eisner (1991, p. 8), the very basis of "what we are likely to experience."[1]

Although there probably exists no single definition of positivism, even among adherents, Francis Schrag (1992) claimed that the following prototype represents what most would consider positivistic research in education:

> Individuals are selected and allocated to treatment and control groups; the two or more groups are provided alternative "treatments" and their progress (or decline) on one or more "dependent variables" is recorded; finally, a statistical evaluation of the results is conducted aimed at assessing whether a difference between the results in the two groups may be caused by chance (see Wulff, chap. 10). (p. 5)

Many of these positivistic assumptions and values are reflected in the teachers' responses just listed. For them, research is done by "experts" and is "something I would never do." Knowledge is investigated by those "professional scholars (researchers)," who as objective investigators are capable of not influencing the objects of their study. Reality is reduced to relationships between precise variables, those "cut-and-dry conclusions" that, as context-free generalizations, are seen as "not relevant to me." The neat and tidy worlds and results of this ap-

---

[1]The "received view" of research reflected in the preceding teachers' comments reflects a positivist philosophy, a belief system that Guba and Lincoln (1994, pp. 109, 110) describe as:

(Realism) An apprehendable reality is assumed to exist, driven by immutable natural laws and mechanisms. Knowledge of the "way things are" is conventionally summarized in the form of time- and context-free generalizations, some of which take the form of cause–effect laws. Research can, in principle, converge on the "true" state of affairs. The basic posture of the paradigm is argued to be both reductionistic and deterministic (Hesse, 1980).

(Objectivist) The investigator and the investigated "object" are assumed to be independent entities, and the investigator to be capable of studying the object without influencing it or being influenced by it. When influence in either direction . . . is recognized, or even suspected, various strategies are followed to reduce or eliminate it. Inquiry takes place as through a one-way mirror. Values and biases are prevented from influencing outcomes.

(Experimental and manipulative) Questions and/or hypotheses are stated in propositional form and subjected to empirical test to verify them; possible confounding conditions must be carefully controlled (manipulated) to prevent outcomes from being improperly influenced.

proach to research seem apparently irrelevant, "boring," and "dusty-shelf material" to many teachers! Although I have overly simplified the nature of positivism as contemporary philosophers might describe it, this general conception has dominated the popular language and practice of education research through most of this century.[2]

The significance of this dominant language should not be underestimated. Patti Lather (1991) emphasized the power and significance of language in shaping "our experience of 'the real.' " Essentially, "the way we speak and write reflect the structures of power in our society ... language is a productive, constitutive force as opposed to a transparent reflection of some reality" (p. 25). Most recently, Coulter (1999) wrote of the subjectivity of all language:

> The many different ways of speaking result from different values, and different assumptions. Professions, classes, regions ... have distinct languages which are more than jargons, but reflect particular ways of organizing experience and contingent historical and social forces. (p. 6)

In historical context, however, the emergence of this positivistic tradition represented a progressive gain over prior traditions that rested knowledge in theological, mythological, and metaphysical systems of thought.[3]

---

[2]Karl Popper's (1968) influential elaboration of a contemporary postpositivistic conception of the "received view" qualified the notion of verifiable certainty, the "cut-and-dryness" of positivism, and describes more what science and scientists can and actually do. Reality or knowledge can never be proved or verified; we can only get closer to understanding it through approximating it by a process he described as falsifying versus verifying hypotheses. In this view, researchers individually are not assumed to be completely objective either; that is an ideal and responsibility shared by the larger collective community of researchers and critics.

[3]Beginning in the mid-17th century, a philosophical shift referred to as the Age of Reason and the Enlightenment ushered in a new faith based in the potential of science, reason, rationality, and logic as the basis of knowledge and truth claims. Prior to claims that knowledge was based on science and rationality, knowledge construction and legitimation were limited to those who through divine right and religious ordination had the authority. With the advent of this scientific revolution, these parochial sources of knowledge were challenged, and a confidence developed that truth claims could be empirically based and thus verifiable. Knowledge so constructed became more tentative, and thereby open to modification and development through rationality and logic. Knowledge production became the legitimate purview of a more broad-based community of researchers, less vulnerable to the edicts and self-interests of religious and secular elites (Bredo & Feinberg, 1982, pp. 13–14). This confidence in science and reason persists today, enhanced by the

However, I believe that there have been negative consequences and actual losses due to the continued dominance of this scientistic worldview: What and whose knowledge, voices, experiences, and research have been generally ignored, marginalized, or missing within the profession? In general, the domination of positivistic research limits participation in the community of researchers and the generation of knowledge in our field. As an approach to knowledge, it glosses the complexity and contextuality of teachers' knowledges and ignores the cultural and personal realms of their professional experiences and understandings.

The dominant perception of what is considered "real" or legitimate research has functioned to artificially separate teachers from researchers, teaching from researching, and theorizing from practicing. Thus, it should not be surprising that so many teachers reflect detachment from the dominant "received view" of research.

The current teacher researcher movement potentially redresses much of this. Because it stems from an alternative philosophy, communicates through different languages, and uses different methodologies, it can broaden our dialogues and understandings about education and schooling. In order for research of any type to matter, the borders that separate different discourse and research communities have to be crossed (Walker, 1997). Somekh (1994) said that academics and teacher researchers need to "inhabit each other's castles." More specifically, Coulter (1999) argued

> that for these two solitudes to meet, the discussion needs to move from focusing on the generation of knowledge necessary for scholarly dialogue to examining the dialogue itself. This means a shift . . . to a consideration of the justification of what counts as appropriate and useful knowledge. (p. 5)

Teachers are in a position to produce particular kinds of "appropriate and useful knowledge," but the production and legitimation of this knowledge is not without contradictions and paradoxes (see chap. 6).

---

more precise postpositivistic methods and sophisticated quantitative languages. We see this in our field's emphasis on measures of IQs, academic achievement, standardized tests, learning styles, and risk factors, all of which are assumed to be scientifically based and objective descriptions of something real. As such, they are used to make and defend decisions about the ability, readiness, appropriate labeling, grading, promotion, and tracking/grouping of students. The models and methods of scientific rationality are typically used to justify our practices, thereby avoiding, sometimes even denying, the role of subjectivity and values in these often controversial and contested decisions.

THE PARADOX OF TEACHER RESEARCH:
IS IT REAL? HOW DOES IT MATTER?

A contemporary paradox bothers me and stimulates the remaining focus of this chapter. During the last 10 years, more and more teachers
have been encouraged and supported for conducting and publishing
research. Advocates for action research in education and cases of
teachers doing research go back more than 50 years. Recently however, there has been a surge of activity in this area. In part, this is at-
tributable to what Cochran-Smith and Lytle (1993, p. 11) referred to as
the emergence of more "supportive structures" that value teacher research. Professional organizations like the American Educational Research Association (AERA) and the National Council of Teachers of
English (NCTE), graduate programs in education, school-based professional development activities, computer listservs and web sites, and
government funding sources, as well as local, national, and international teacher-research conferences, are increasingly focusing on action research and supporting teacher researchers.

The kind of research that teachers have been doing, however, as illustrated so well in this volume, does not typically reside within a
positivistic prototype, but in what Cochran-Smith and Lytle (1993, p. 13)
referred to as "new paradigms and alternative kinds of discourse and
analysis." Based on my experience in working with teacher researchers
who are enrolled in my university's master's of education program, and
the accounts of teacher research appearing in this volume and numerous other recent publications (see Cochran-Smith & Lytle, 1993; Hollingsworth, 1997; Hollingsworth & Sockett, 1994; McTaggart, 1997; Newman, 1990; and journals such as *Teaching and Change*, *Educational
Action Research: An International Journal*, and *Teacher Research: The
Journal of Classroom Inquiry*), I am struck by the insight and skills that
current teacher researchers have to understand, inform, and narrate
the actions that guide their practices. Obviously, good teachers teach
themselves through re-searching themselves very well! Paradoxically,
however, teachers tend to have less familiarity with the philosophical
tradition and language of the "new paradigms and alternative kinds of
discourse and analysis" that informs and legitimates their research.
Consequently, they often appear rather conflicted about whether what
they are doing is "real research."

Pat, a former graduate student of mine, illustrated the paradox, a
philosophical insecurity that seemingly lingered along side her experi-

ential expertise, accomplishments, and confidence. Pat was narrating, to a group of teacher colleagues, a very detailed and reflective account of how her understanding of language development had deepened through the process of developing a writing workshop in her second-grade classroom that year. She talked about how her own ideas and practices had been developed, changed, and shaped by her experiences. She talked about "the" current theories of language and writing development and how her own research both resonated with and challenged them. She had the rapt attention of her colleagues, I was inspired, and we were all in the process of celebrating the completion of this research, when she abruptly stopped. She looked at her newly published book and said, "My husband was disappointed when he read this, he said it didn't sound like research because it was so personal, so subjective. He said, 'Researchers don't use 'I.' " She asked us, "Is this real research?" Although confident in the knowledge she had produced, she appeared less confident in the legitimacy of her way of knowing. Her colleagues, experienced teachers and newly published researchers themselves, were not so sure either.

Pat, like the rabbit in Margery Williams's book *The Velveteen Rabbit* (1983), sought to know the "magic called real." In Williams's story, the other toys in the nursery act superior and pretend to be "real"; they were after all, models of things, mechanical in nature, full of "modern ideas" and users of "technical terms" (p. 10). Comparatively, the rabbit feels "insignificant and commonplace," far from what others considered "real" (p. 12). He learns, instead, that "Real isn't how you are made" or an inherent quality, but "it's a thing that happens to you," explains the Skin Horse. "As when a child loves you for a long, long time, not just to play with, but really loves you, then you become real" (p. 12). Through use and through being valued, "reality" is always contingent, constructed, and described from a point of view.

As "insignificant and commonplace" as the story of the velveteen rabbit might seem, Williams was reflecting a philosophical belief system that emerged in the late 19th century as a critique of positivism. In general, this paradigm reflects those who adhere to constructivist and phenomenological belief systems and employ interpretive approaches to research. During the last 25 years or so, academic researchers in education have increasingly worked within this paradigm; they have helped to broaden our perceptions, methods, and languages for what is considered "real" research and in our field. At the 1994 AERA Conference, Eugene E. Garcia, then director of the U.S. Department of Bilingual Education and Minority Language Affairs, referenced this growing influence:

> The biggest shift in social sciences methodology over the past twenty-five years has been the increased emphasis on qualitative, ethnographic, participant-observer approaches. This shift has been supported at the philosophy of science level by the discrediting of the logical positivist's goal of "decontextualized" general law, substituting a recognition of the context-dependence of all scientific statements, and the essential role that quality research must invest in the high costs of providing contextual knowledge. (Garcia, 1994, p. 8)

Garcia referred here to the constructivist philosophy, interpretive purpose, and qualitative data that characterize this approach to research. Much of the action research in education conducted today is done within this framework (Noffke, 1997, p. 12), especially the action research that teachers like Pat are conducting. Basically, a constructivist paradigm differs from positivism by assuming that reality and knowledge is situated, created, and constructed, not fixed and discovered.[4]

Fred Erickson (1986) characterized the methods and theories of interpretive research with an illustrative prototype that stands in marked contrast to positivistic research:

> Interpretive research is concerned with the specifics of meaning and action in social life that takes place in concrete scenes of face-to-face interaction and that takes place in the wider society surrounding the scene of action. The conduct of interpretive research on teaching involves intense and ideally long-term participant observation in an educational setting

---

[4]Guba and Lincoln (1994, pp. 110–111) described the constructivist paradigm as:

(Relativist) Multiple, apprehendable and sometimes conflicting social realities that are the products of human intellects, but that may change as their constructors become more informed and sophisticated.

(Transactional and subjectivist) The investigator and the object of investigation are assumed to be interactively linked so that the "findings" are literally created as the investigation proceeds.

The variable and personal . . . nature of social constructions suggest that individual constructions can be elicited and refined only through interaction between and among investigator and respondents.

The inquirer's voice is that of the "passionate participant" actively engaged in facilitating the "multivoice" reconstruction of his or her own construction as well as those of all other participants.

followed by deliberate and long-term reflection on what was seen there. That reflection entails the observer's deliberate scrutiny of his or her own interpretive point of view, and of its sources in formal theory, culturally learned ways of seeing, and personal value commitments. As the participant observer learns more about the world out there he or she learns more about himself or herself. (p. 156)

When Erickson wrote this in 1986, interpretive research was still largely the domain of outside, academic researchers, and the idea of teacher researchers was still emergent. Erickson's article, appearing in the respected *Handbook of Research on Teaching*, largely functioned to explain and legitimate this paradigm to educators. Moreover, significantly, Erickson recognized its logical appropriateness for teacher researchers as well:

It is a few steps beyond this for the classroom teacher to become the researcher in his or her own right. As Hymes notes (1982), interpretive research methods are intrinsically democratic: one does not need special training to be able to understand the results of such research, nor does one need arcane skills in order to conduct it. Fieldwork research requires skills of observation, comparison, contrast, and reflection that all humans possess. In order to get through life we must all do interpretive fieldwork. What professional interpretive researchers do is to make use of the ordinary skills of observation and reflection in especially systematic and deliberate ways. Classroom teachers can do this as well, by reflecting on their own practice. Their role is not that of the participant observer who comes from the outside world to visit, but that of an unusually observant participant who deliberates inside the scene of action. (p. 157)

Essentially, Erickson foreshadowed and made a case for an interpretively based teacher researcher movement as a political and professional imperative:

If classroom teaching in elementary and secondary schools is to come of age as a profession—if the role of teacher is not to continue to be institutionally infantilized—then teachers need to take the adult responsibility of investigating their own practice systematically and critically by methods that are appropriate to their practice.... Anything less than that basic kind of institutional change is to perpetuate the passivity that has characterized the teaching profession in its relations with administrative supervisors and the public at large. (p. 157)

I have quoted Erickson's work at length because, early on, he associated the shift in education to the inclusion of more constructivist and interpretive research with the emergence of the teacher researcher movement. During the 1980s, these two movements rapidly developed in tandem and, increasingly, in conjunction with each other. However, this confluence is not to suggest that the increasing use of interpretive research approaches by academic researchers caused teachers to suddenly become researchers. More likely, constructivist frameworks provided a new lens through which to recognize and legitimate alternative ways of knowing. Having new lenses, we were better positioned to "see" the kinds of inquiry and knowledge production that good teachers had always been doing, and begin to legitimate it as research.

I believe that good teachers *have always* conducted this kind of research, not as a systematic and explicit research protocol, but more as a natural and necessary process of their own learning. For example, in 1963 in *Teacher* (1963/1986), Sylvia Ashton-Warner wrote about her teaching experiences in New Zealand during the 1930s. It was a personal, narrative, and interpretive account of problems (as she saw them), observations (as she interpreted them), and solutions (as she tried them). She used the first person "I" throughout. Her style was reflective, analytical, passionate, action oriented, and very subjective. Her methods were not sophisticated, complex, or unbiased. She observed and listened to her students, interpreted her situation, kept a reflective diary, and theoretically related her work to that of Plato, Pythagoras, T. S. Eliot, Fromm, Jung, and others. She planned, implemented, observed, modified, and published her teaching approaches. We are told on the book jacket of the latest publication that "Today her findings are strikingly relevant to the teaching of socially disadvantaged and non-English-speaking students." Is this real research? Does it matter?

TEACHER RESEARCH

"If you want to understand what a science is . . . you should look at what the practitioners of it do" (Geertz, 1973, p. 5). Here, Geertz assumed a common phenomenological value and research strategy, "which tries to stay close to the phenomena by avoiding as much as possible all abstraction and imposition of constructs, and by relating always the object of study to the experiences of the subject who does the studying" (Eger, 1993). I too prefer staying close to the phenomena when discussing some of the methods that teachers use in conducting their research. So teacher researchers themselves, in observing, describing, and understanding their students, classes, colleagues, and curriculum, tend to stay "close to the phenomena" through focusing on particular people, stories, and situations, and interpreting them through context and narratives of their own personal professional experience. In constructivist and interpretive research, the active role of the researcher is assumed and valued; methods and data are not seen as independent of researchers. In contrast, by framing issues, selecting and implementing methods, and interpreting data, the researcher's personal involvement is so integral to the process and outcomes that the researcher (vs. the methods) becomes the key instrument.

When we observe teachers as they do research, and read accounts of their research such as those that appear in this volume, we tend to notice, among the diversity of methods, some common themes characterizing their work. In doing research, teachers tend to be, as Clandinin and Connelly (1994) described the process, "simultaneously focused in four directions: inward and outward, backward and forward":

> By inward we mean the internal conditions of feelings, hopes, aesthetic reactions, moral dispositions. . . . By outward we mean existential conditions, that is, the environment or what E. M. Bruner (1986) calls reality. By backward and forward we are referring to temporality, past, present and future. To experience an experience is to experience it simultaneously in these four ways and to ask questions pointing in each way. (p. 417)

We see examples in this volume of teacher research accounts that move back and forth between these dimensions of experience. They do so through inner reflection and meaning construction, outer observations and activity, and contextualized accounts analyzed through perspectives of time and space.

Differences, however, exist in the degree to which teacher researchers focus in any of these directions, or assume these perspectives, either in the course of conducting their research, or in the outcomes they envision. Any particular project might, for example, focus more outwardly than inwardly, more on understanding a situation than on changing it, more intently on the present and future than on the past, or more based on narrative reflection and understanding than on outward expressions of change. Although teachers don't tend to equally or explicitly address all these dimensions of experience in any one project, what is important to note here is the richness and power of research contributions from teachers, who are well positioned to draw on dimensional and contextualized ways of knowing. Consequently, particular research methods that capture and enhance these multidimensional ways of knowing and "staying close to the phenomena" have emerged as particularly relevant to teacher researchers. I note three of them here.

HOW METHODS MATTER

Three research methods, emergent from or consistent with interpretive/constructivist philosophy, that have been utilized in much of the recent teacher research are *action research*, *personal experience/accounts*, and *narrative genres*. Collectively, these methods focus the research endeavor on utilizing the power of the subjective involvement of the researcher; interpreting and constructing nuanced knowledge within a context; understanding the conditions, processes, and effects of change within a context; and valuing multiple voices and perspectives (Reason, 1994).

Action research in the United States is a 50-year-old tradition associated with social change efforts. Historical accounts, definitions, and interpretations of action research are varied (Noffke, 1994), but Elliott (1991) captured what is central in most, "the study of a social situation with a view to improving the quality of action within it" (p. 69). Central to action research is the aim of understanding and improving practice. In the 1940s, Kurt Lewin developed a research model that, although modified a bit, persists today in many teacher research projects. The model orients "outwardly" and "forwardly" by focusing research attention on observing, understanding, and changing a situation in a particular context. The model, described in more detail in other chapters of this volume, consists of identifying a general idea or goal, information gathering, general planning, developing related actions, implementing and evaluating those actions, and then reassessing and perhaps even revising the initial ideas or goals. Researchers spiral through ongoing cycles of these, essentially researching in action. Data-gathering techniques tend to focus on collecting evidence about the effectiveness of new strategies and perspectives of the various stakeholders. They might include things like interviewing; reflective teacher memos and field notes; checklists, questionnaires, surveys; observing, photographing, videotaping, tape recording; and document analysis. In action research, researcher reflection and interpretation tend to be more rational and instrumental to the primary goals of the action research project: understanding, developing, and evaluating changes in the social environment. As a valued research strategy of teachers, action research honors their keen observational skills, their inclination (indeed obligation) to influence their own environment with an aim toward improving it, and their skill at developing, observing, and modifying simultaneously, on the spot! The model formalizes and systematizes what good teachers tend to do naturally (see chap. 3).

Throughout this volume, we see not only references to the importance of action research as a dynamic model of change, but the realization of the model in the form of newly developed insights and practices. In recent years, action research has become so associated with teacher research that we are increasingly seeing it incorporated in formal degree work, certification programs, professional development, and education reform efforts (Noffke, 1994). Action and teacher research is becoming so linked that, as in this text, we are seeing the combination referred to as *teacher action research* (see Preface).

If we consider action research as one methodological strand of teacher research, like the warp in a weaving, then the "personal accounts" (Lancy & Kinkead, 1993) or "personal experience" (Clandinin & Connelly, 1994) methods of interpretive research, like the weft in a weaving, are its complement. Personal accounts or personal experience methods, which emphasize the inner and subjective dimensions of understanding, experiencing, and interpreting events, are either the oldest or the newest forms of research in education!

In a recent book devoted to describing qualitative (interpretive) research traditions in education, Lancy and Kinkead (1993) devoted only a brief section in their chapter on personal accounts research to the subgenre of "self-generated case-study" research by teachers. For them, this method is so new as to not yet be a tradition, to be in a state of "flux" (p. 169). Although I agree that this is probably the most recent genre of education research to gain legitimation and visibility in our field, it is actually emergent philosophically and substantively from one of the oldest notions of how humans come to know and understand their world: narrative.

What is central to personal accounts methods is the construction and rendering of meaning through narrative devices, and what weaves this method so well into teacher action research projects is its directional focus "inward" and on creating understanding through the temporality of past, present, and future. Bruner (1986, p. 11) described narrative as one of the two fundamental modes (the other being the positivistic, logico-scientific mode) through which humans order their experiences and construct reality. Similarly, Polkinghorne (1988) asserted how fundamental narrative is: "Human beings exist in three realms—the material realm, the organic realm, and the realm of meaning. The realm of meaning is structured according to linguistic forms, and one of the most important forms for creating meaning in human existence is the narrative" (p. 183).

Narrative modes of knowing and the methods of personal experience research focus on interpreting what events mean to the participants involved. Personal experience methods, when used multidimensional ways as Clandinin and Connelly (1994, p. 417) described, generate holistic and contextual understandings. Whether through self-generated case studies or personal narratives and stories, personal accounts methods enable researchers to reflect on, integrate, and convey multidimensional ways of knowing. When teachers focus on their experiences through narrative, they tend to interpret and reinterpret those experiences. When teachers seek to understand the narratives of others (their students, colleagues, etc.), they introduce more voices and perspectives into their research projects. Thus, positioned and inclined as they are to "stay close to the phenomena," teacher researchers can introduce more polyvocality and perspectivity into our professional knowledge base. One should not underestimate the potential of narrative understanding, in particular, to promote growth and change. "Therefore, difficult as it may be to tell a story, the more difficult but important task in narrative is the retelling of stories that allow for growth and change" (Clandinin & Connelly, 1994, p. 418).

The methods of personal accounts research (like narrative, autobiography, and personal case studies) necessitate the active presence of a first person researcher, an "I" in the research. The constructivist renderings of these methods reflect the contexts and social interactions through which current understandings were derived and are sensible. As products of research, they offer us " 'a plurality of independent and unmerged voices and consiousnesses, a genuine polyphony of fully valid voices', Bakhtin, 1963/1984a, p. 6. The result is no final, complete truth, but unfinalizable, partial truths generated from the interaction among characters" (Coulter, 1999, p. 7).

Thus, we tend to see that teacher research is characterized by a selecting and blending of methods, such as those described here, that collectively enable the teacher researcher to draw on, question, integrate, and develop dimensionally nuanced understandings. Additionally, teacher researchers, as insiders, are most likely to have the personal investments and incentives to initiate, inform, and sustain long-term community dialogue around local issues that matter (Coulter, 1999, pp. 11, 12). And it will be teachers who necessarily continue to develop these methods.

CONCLUDING REAL QUESTIONS

Is teacher research real research? Does it matter that we have this kind of knowledge available in our profession? How? When teachers as researchers are affirmed, when teacher knowledge counts, when we find ways to support, feature, and utilize the knowledge they produce within the broader forums and communities of formal research in education, when researchers occasion more border crossings enabling them to "dialogue about knowledge and its relationship to practice" (Coulter, 1999), who really benefits?

REFERENCES

Agar, M. H. (1986). *Speaking of ethnography.* Newbury Park, CA: Sage.

Ashton-Warner, S. (1986). *Teacher.* New York: Simon & Schuster. (Original work published 1963)

Bredo, E., & Feinberg, W. (Eds.). (1982). *Knowledge and values insocial and educational research.* Philadelphia: Temple University Press.

Bruner, J. (1986). *Actual minds, possible worlds.* Cambridge, MA: Harvard University Press.

Clandinin, D. J., & Connelly, F. M. (1994). Personal experience methods. In N. K. Denzin & Y. S. Lincoln (Eds.), *Handbook of qualitative research* (pp. 413–427). Thousand Oaks, CA: Sage.

Cochran-Smith, M., & Lytle, S. L. (1993). *Inside outside: Teacher research and knowledge.* New York: Teachers College Press.

Coulter, C. (1999). The epic and the novel: Dialogism and teacher research. *Educational Researcher, 28*(3), 4–13.

Eger, M. (1993). Hermeneutics as an approach to science: Part II. *Science & Education, 2*, 303–328.

Eisner, E. (1991). *The enlightened eye: Qualitative inquiry and the enhancement of educational practices.* New York: Macmillan.

Elliott, J. (1991). *Action research for educational change*. Philadelphia: Open University Press.

Erickson, F. (1986). Qualitative methods in research on teaching. In M. Wittrock (Ed.), *Handbook of research on teaching* (3rd ed., pp. 119–161). New York: Macmillan.

Garcia, E. E. (1994, Summer). *Newsletter of Division G: The Social Context of Education*. (Available from American Educational Research Association, Washington, DC)

Geertz, C. (1973). *The interpretation of cultures: Selected essays*. New York: Basic Books.

Guba, E. G., & Lincoln, Y. S. (1994). Competing paradigms in qualitative research. In N. K. Denzin & Y. S. Lincoln (Eds.), *Handbook of qualitative research* (pp. 105–117). Thousand Oaks, CA: Sage.

Hollingsworth, S., & Sockett, H. (Eds.). (1994). *Teacher research and educational reform: Ninety-third yearbook of the National Society for the Study of Education*. Chicago: University of Chicago Press.

Hollingsworth, S. (Ed.). (1997). *International action research: A casebook for educational reform*. Washington, DC: Falmer.

Jungck, S. (1987, November). *Alternatives for curriculum inquiry in teacher education*. Paper presented at the meeting of the American Educational Studies Association, Chicago.

Lancy, D. F., & Kinkead, J. (1993). Personal accounts. In D. F. Lancy (Ed.), *Qualitative research in education: An introduction to the major traditions* (pp. 168–207). New York: Longman.

Lather, P. (1991). *Getting smart: Feminist research and pedagogy with/in the postmodern*. New York: Routledge, Chapman and Hall.

McTaggart, R. (Ed.). (1997). *Participatory action research:International contexts and consequences*. Albany: SUNY Press.

Newman, J. M. (1990). *Finding our own way*. Portsmouth, NH: Heinemann.

Noffke, S. (1994). Action research: Towards the next generation. *Educational Action Research, 2*(1), 9–21.

Noffke, S. (1997). Themes and tensions in US action research: Towards historical analysis. In S. Hollingsworth (Ed.), *International action research: A casebook for educational reform* (pp. 2–16). Washington, DC: Falmer.

Polkinghorne, D. E. (1988). *Narrative knowing and the human sciences*. Albany, NY: SUNY Press.

Popper, K. (1968). *Conjectures and refutations*. New York: Harper & Row.

Reason, P. (1994). Three approaches to participative inquiry. In N. K. Denzin & Y. S. Lincoln (Eds.), *Handbook of qualitative research* (pp. 324–339). Thousand Oaks, CA: Sage.

Schrag, F. (1992). In defense of positivist research paradigms. *Educational Researcher, 21*(5), 5–7.

Somekh, B. (1994). Inhabiting each other's castles: Towards knowledge and mutual growth through collaboration. *Educational Action Research, 2*(3), 357–380.

Walker, M. (1997). Transgressing boundaries: Everyday/academic discourses. In S. Hollingsworth (Ed.), *International action research: A casebook for educational reform* (pp. 2–16). Washington, DC: Falmer.

Williams, M. (1983). *The velveteen rabbit*. New York: Alfred A. Knopf. (Original work published 1922)

9

TEACHER RESEARCH AND SCHOOL REFORM: LESSONS FROM CHICAGO, CURITIBA, AND SANTIAGO

Joseph C. Fischer

Norman Weston
National-Louis University

> Democracy and democratic education are founded on faith in people, on the belief that they not only can but should discuss the problems of their country, . . . the problems of democracy itself. Education is an act of love, and thus an act of courage. It cannot fear the analysis of reality or, under pain of revealing itself as a farce, avoid creative discussion. (Freire, 1981, p. 38)

In many countries of the world today, the hope is that school reforms will help ameliorate a wide range of social problems, build more civil and democratic societies, and advocate for social justice and human rights. Schools are asked to help young people find meaning in their lives and at the same time help them prepare for a future in a world that is consumer oriented, with increasing disparities in income levels, and a growing economic underclass excluded from global prosperity. The return of democratic governments, after long years of dictatorship, in Chile, Brazil, and Eastern Europe, for example, poses great challenges to educators on how to teach democracy, social justice, and human rights (Havel, 1997). As they try to teach recent history, teachers in these countries are perplexed about dealing with painful memories of fear, missing families, exile, torture, and bloodshed. However, these are not merely issues for distant countries.

If humans are to live together in a more peaceful and interdependent world, people everywhere need to better understand each other, build more just and caring communities, and address the systemic global problems of economic disparities, violence, and racial hatred. Accordingly, school reform programs, both at the local and national level, must be framed within larger social, economic, and moral agendas that address the central questions of our day, including, how are we creating more peaceful, civil, democratic and just societies? No one is left out of this work.

As we examine school reform programs in the United States and around the world, we are struck by their remarkable similarity in purposes and implementation strategies. Most reform plans tend to outline ambitious and often conflicting goals for schooling. These generally include: (a) preparation for work in a global market economy, (b) citizenship and democratic participation in society, (c) skills in critical thinking, decision making, and life-long learning, (d) moral development and value education, and (e) appreciation for diversity and inter cultural understanding.

We are equally impressed with the wide agreement, among local and national reform programs, advocating changes in instructional and learning strategies. For example, reform agendas are nearly unanimous in emphasizing active discovery and interest-based learning. Almost across the board, there are calls for integrated curriculum, thematic learning, and interdisciplinary studies. Students are expected to "learn how to learn," collaborate with others, participate in setting learning goals, and evaluate their performance. Schools are being asked to be more relevant by organizing curriculum around social, economic, cultural, and political issues and realities. Most reform agendas hold that students need to construct rather than merely receive knowledge, and expect teachers and students to effectively use educational technology across content areas. Nearly all reform plans emphasize greater local school control over curriculum and better accountability for teaching and learning. Increasingly, teachers are asked to critically examine their practice, engage in research, and share experiences and insights with colleagues.

Accompanying these sweeping calls for change, we also note a striking commonality of tensions and contradictions in reform agendas across different societies, mostly having to do with issues related to ownership and control. For example, the tension between individual school needs and interests and the pervasive demands of central bureaucracies and authorities is universally felt. Although time for planning among teachers is recognized as a vital part of educational renewal, existing school structures and curriculum requirements provide few opportunities for teachers to plan together and share discoveries, concerns, and practices. Although research concludes that teacher ownership is crucial to reform agendas and professional renewal, top-down approaches and deficit models of professional development continue to stifle teacher initiative, enthusiasm, and professionalism. Such approaches tend not to view teachers as capable of authoring school renewal projects, and, unfortunately, make little use of teacher experience, initiative, and insight. School-based improvement projects developed by faculty and students are a rarity. This is regrettable, for planning and self-study are essential in helping schools envision who they want to be, how they want to change, and what they are striving toward. Our conclusions echo Kenneth Sirotnik's research findings:

> School improvement must take place in schools by and for the people in them; description, judgment, decision making, and action taking regarding improvement efforts require informed inquiry and critical thinking; this evaluative process includes multiple perspectives on what constitutes appropriate knowledge and information; and this process is not a one-shot deal but an ongoing part of the daily work life of professionals involved in their own school improvement efforts. (Sirotnik, 1987, p. 41)

Our purpose in this chapter is to discuss lessons learned from experiences with teacher research conducted within the context of school reform programs in three large cities: Chicago in the United States, Curitiba, Brazil, and Santiago, Chile. By describing important insights teachers gained from doing action research within local and national school reform programs, we hope to provide a glimpse of the potential both for critical analysis of curriculum and for supporting "best practices" in schools. We do this by examining a commonality of issues and concerns that all teachers face as they conduct research. Finally, we explore how teacher research can contribute to school reform within the larger perspective of social change. We focus on three themes that we believe lie at the heart of the work that teacher researchers face in Chicago, Curitiba, and Santiago, and are relevant to school reform agendas in most countries today: (a) honoring teacher wisdom, (b) teacher ownership of school improvement plans, and (c) creating schools for democratic living.

Examples cited are from the authors' long-term participation in school reform and teacher research projects in these three cities. Norman Weston is the main consultant on teacher action research for an Annenberg Project, "Illinois Alliance for Achievement Network," being carried out in three inner-city Chicago elementary public schools: Bethune, Piccolo, and Spry. Joseph Fischer, program evaluator for the project, has also worked in Curitiba, Brazil, as a consultant for a secondary school reform project, and taught action research classes at the Pontificia Universidade Catolica do Parana. He continues to work in Santiago, Chile, on a teacher education improvement project with the Universidad Metropolitana de Ciencias de la Educacion. Visiting Chile several times a year, he teaches action research courses and collaborates with university faculty on school-based research.

We begin with a reform initiative in Chicago, having teacher research at the core. It reveals what can happen when the knowledge and experience of teachers are recognized and honored. The project began by building bridges between National-Louis University and three inner-city schools, and focused on creating community through democratic participation in teacher action research.

HONORING TEACHER WISDOM: VOICES FROM CHICAGO

In the fall of 1997, three Chicago elementary schools (Bethune, 560 students, 98% African American; Piccolo, 930 students, primarily Latino and African American; and Spry, 850 students, predominately Latino), all members of the Illinois Alliance for Achievement Network, set out on the first year of a 3-year Annenberg-funded project with the vision of uniting everyone into a community of inquiring learners (Weston, 1998). Teacher action research was built in as one of the components of the community building process. Due to low test scores, two of the schools were on probation. As part of Chicago school reform, if test scores do not improve over a probationary period, a school can be "reconstituted"—that is, shut down. Needless to say, teachers in these schools feel that they are under a lot of pressure. As outside university consultants to the project, our immediate problem became: How can we present the fairly radical idea of action research to a group of teachers, already overwhelmed and feeling under siege, as something more than "just another thing to do"? We knew we would have to begin by winning the teachers' trust and confidence. It was not until later, however, that we discovered that the answer to our question was to trust in the action research process itself.

Whose Research Is It? Defining the Problem

To help the 90 participating teachers in these three Chicago schools collectively identify those areas or situations they felt were problems, or in need of improvement, and that could be the focus of their action research projects, we adopted a democratic approach by David Forward (1989). To begin, we asked volunteer leaders to put forth the following questions to their groups of four to eight teachers:

1. What is happening now?
2. How is this a problem?
3. Imagine some solutions.
4. What resources do we already have?
5. What are our boundaries and limitations?
6. What do we need?
7. How can we begin?

As a problem-defining session, beginning the dialogue was most important. We offered the following advice to the group leaders: Do not "shortchange" the discussion at these first sessions. It is important that people have their say. If not, they will not take ownership of the problem, nor of any possible solutions. A good rule of thumb, we have learned, is listen, respect, and affirm. This is not always easy to do, as one group leader recalled: "I learned that you have to be a good delegator. I got overwhelmed at times, but I finally learned to turn things over. I didn't have to control everything. It got easier after that."

Our approach was to let the teachers decide on research topics; these were to be their projects—not ours, not the Board of Education's. However, the fact that two schools in the Chicago Annenberg/Alliance project were on probation for having low test scores could not be ignored. So we addressed the problem head on. "How can you do action research when you have to be concerned about raising test scores?" we asked. "Well, all this sounds good," one teacher replied, "but the reality is we have to raise those scores." In the end, although they felt pressure to do research directly related to improving test scores, most teachers opted to do projects that they felt had the greatest merit for students (e.g., writers' workshop, buddy reading, learning centers). One group, however, did do a well-documented 2-year study on the effectiveness of test-preparation materials. They concluded that the materials were worthwhile for their students, that they were not a waste of time, and would be used again next year. What this reaffirmed for us was that teachers must play a major role in selecting topics for their research.

A particular value of research done by teachers is that projects are often conceived of in ways imagined or seen only by classroom practitioners. Thus, they have the potential to identify problems, or illuminate instructional areas, that normally do not draw the attention of educational researchers from the outside. A Chicago project entitled "Centro de Escritura" (The Writing Center) is a good example. Seeing that their children did not enjoy writing, two first-grade teachers—one special education, the other bilingual—combined their classrooms in a project designed to improve the children's writing skills by enticing them to become young authors. Another project investigated relaxation and visualization techniques with elementary school children in hopes of increasing retention, listening skills, and self-esteem. The teachers saw imagery as a springboard to reading, writing, literature groups, and dramatic expression. Soon they realized that other important benefits resulted from their study: "Having to traverse some pretty rough streets on their way to school, inner-city children often show up in the morning hurt, angry, or distressed. Helping them get ready to learn has turned negativity into something positive."

Chicago teachers came to appreciate that action research encouraged them to work together as well as with their students. "It was beneficial to collaborate with peers and to let the students know that they were participating in research," said one. Another added, "I learned that cooperating with other teachers can be very rewarding, and that if I let children make some key choices, peace and calm result, not mayhem. That interchanges between classrooms are very beneficial to the kids." The power and value of working with other teachers can be extended through action research to include students as well. Then the impact tends to become school-wide.

The Moral Dimension of Action Research

Our experience with action research in Chicago has taught us that when you trust teachers to identify and discuss their own problems and reflect on educational practices, things happen that can propel curriculum outward to transcend school and classroom boundaries. Because there is a moral (and hence political) dimension to action research, questions like "What is the best thing to do in this situation?" often lead to, "What is the right thing to do?" A research project by Chicago teachers entitled "Homelessness: The Problem of Transience" is an example of the moral dimension that action research can take. Noting that a significant number of their K–8 students were periodically living in neighborhood homeless shelters, coming to school in unwashed clothes, and being made fun of by other students, a group of teachers decided that their project would be to investigate and try to rectify the situation. After visiting a number of shelters near the school, the teachers succeeded in having washing machines installed so that the children could have a clean uniform to wear each day. They also set up small study spaces in the shelters, and equipped them with pencils, paper, books, and other supplies, so that the children might have their own place to read, study, and do homework. Who else, except teachers working with children who are periodically homeless, would even conceive of such a project? In their caretaker's role, these teachers identified and acted on a problem having far deeper significance than attempts to reform city schools by only focusing on raising test scores. They began with the basics—safety, shelter, and security.

Combining skill development with increasing social awareness, teachers at the Unity/Umoja/Unidos "small school" of Brian Piccolo School in Chicago focused an entire school year on increasing awareness about diversity in their school, community, and the world outside. The Piccolo teachers noted:

> When this project started, we did not expect, as a group, that these activities were going to have the impact they had on students. We concluded that students who get involved in activities where they could see themselves as part of a whole, participating hand-in-hand with students of other cultures did undoubtedly increase self-esteem, break language barriers and racial taboos, and were better prepared for reading and writing at the same time.

For each of the last 2 years, in mid June, Chicago Alliance teachers have gathered together for an annual Research Forum to celebrate and share their work as teacher researchers. Many projects have focused on community building, intercultural understanding, and democratic living, whereas others came to the same place through projects de-

voted to skill development. "Kids You Want to Know" was a biography
writing project for sixth-grade students. Teachers concluded: "We believe this project helped students to develop peer relationships, which
is something we never even considered, and yet is such a critical element in personal success." To personalize their work with computers
and practice keyboarding skills, seventh- and eighth-grade students at
Spry Community School in Chicago began by writing personal letters to
family and friends, and then to students at Bethune School, thus cross-
ing an imaginary boundary line between Chicago's primarily Latino and
African-American neighborhoods of North and South Lawndale.

Trusting Teachers

Commenting on how action research was different from other reform
programs, one teacher participating in the Alliance Network program
said:

> Having the teachers first come up with a dilemma . . . I think that is a won-
> derful component of this project. The freedom of the teacher to select
> something they want to do individually or shared expands the teacher.
> You don't always have to succeed, so there is no fear of failure.

We asked another teacher what she thought about action research as a
vehicle for school reform. "Well, it is one of the few things I have experienced—with all the new programs and so forth—that allows teachers to
have a say in things. It respects what teachers know. You can see that
here today." Being recognized and respected can lead to feelings of efficacy and empowerment. "I had never heard about empowerment before this project," said one of the younger teachers, "but I see action research as empowering the teacher and the student. We so seldom have
a chance to talk about our own teaching. I discovered a lot of expertise
out there!"

Having teachers take responsibility and ownership of the process
from the very beginning, we believe, was crucial to the project's success. Paradoxically, what had at one point appeared to be a problem
turned out to be a necessary element at the very core of the process.
Trusting the teachers to go through the research process was essential
to realizing the product.

Honoring teachers' wisdom means including teacher voices in designing school reform programs. From our work with teachers in Chi-

cago, and also in Curitiba and Santiago, we believe there is a huge thirst for more collaboration, recognition, and honest discussion among teachers of all ages. The more teachers do research and document what they are doing in a systematic fashion, the more we are going to have a better understanding about what good teaching is, what practice works, and how children learn. Moreover, doing action research contributes to a teacher's sense of efficacy and professional development. "Dedicating all my efforts to my project gave a lot of rewards when I saw other teachers interested in my work," said one Chicago teacher. Taking the risk to become a better teacher and to share her research in a public forum paid off in increased professional esteem for this teacher.

TEACHER OWNERSHIP OF SCHOOL IMPROVEMENT: VOICES FROM CURITIBA AND SANTIAGO

Having teachers take responsibility and ownership of the action research process from the very beginning, we believe, is crucial to any effort at school reform and curriculum innovation. Moreover, from our experience in Chicago, Curitiba, and Santiago, we have found that trusting teachers to take a central role in action research is essential to realizing democratically based efforts at school improvement. Basically, this begins with inviting teachers to play a leading role in school reform planning and designing curriculum reforms. The examples cited here are from Brazil and Chile, but are equally relevant to the school reform context in Chicago.

School Action Plans and Teacher Research in Curitiba, Parana

In Brazil, each school is asked to develop a specific action plan to address how it will implement the national school reform agenda. The Ministry of Education sees these school-based action plans as evidence of commitment to ongoing improvement and renewal. In helping schools develop their action plans, education professor, Carmen de Castro Neves advised: "Action plans illuminate philosophical principles, define policies, organize strategies, optimize resources, and mobilize different sectors of the community, and because they are public permit constant monitoring and evaluation" (Fischer, 1998a, p. 33). Action plans, when supported by teacher action research, give direction to school reform visions and are effective tools for implementing and evaluating reform agendas.

Brazilian educational leaders argue that school action plans are powerful ways to promote democratic participation in educational change, to help schools develop a sense of identity and mission, and to raise consciousness of the social and political realities that influence schools. Moreover, in analyzing a sample of these action plans, one is struck by the wide range of curriculum and instructional strategies that teachers proposed. The action plans provide a rich mosaic of practical ways to implement the complex and comprehensive national school reform program. The challenge for Brazil's educational system is to provide assistance to schools resisting needed reforms, while giving freedom to more reform-minded schools to carry out their own plans.

During 1997, teams of Brazilian teachers in Curitiba and throughout the state of Parana met to write guidelines based on the goals of the national reform plan. These curriculum guidelines were meant to provide an orientation to individual schools as they developed their action plans. Important themes and issues emerged from this crucial work that helped support the work of implementing the sweeping reform agenda. The teams of teachers from different parts of the state tended to articulate similar priorities for schooling:

1. Schools needed to provide opportunities for self-actualization and self-learning through critical reflection.
2. Students must develop skills in math, science, and technology to prepare for work in a global economy.
3. Students had to develop citizenship and collaboration skills to participate in building a more democratic society.

What was most remarkable about the teachers' proposals was the extensive number and quality of suggestions of instructional strategies offered to carry out the extensive reform agenda.

In addition to calls for resources to improve instructional practices, teachers called for changes in how schools are organized, supported, and financed. They also argued that school reforms must address social and economic problems:

> This is a critical time in which education can and must contribute to bettering our human condition, where people live together with pluralism of

ideas, respect for the environment, and participate actively and critically in society. Schools must be agents of social transformation, capable of un-derstanding and participating critically in a world in constant evolution. (Fischer, 1998a, p. 22)

It soon became obvious in Curitiba, Parana, however, that it is one thing to write curriculum proposals and quite another to implement the comprehensive reform agenda. In spite of calls for participation of teachers in the reform plan, state-sponsored professional development programs continue to be "top-down." In spite of the reform, the state-run school bureaucracy of Parana mainly retains its traditional orienta-tion to schools through mandates, regulations, and monitoring. The idea of tapping teachers' experience and wisdom is not part of the cul-ture of the bureaucracy. Teachers noted with dismay the contradiction between calls for democratic school planning and the top-down man-dates that continued to be sent to them.

Nonetheless, throughout the state of Parana, there are many posi-tive examples of change and innovation as schools, teachers, and uni-versities carry out the goals of the school reform. For example, during a graduate research course at the Pontifical Universidade Catolien do Parana, in Curitiba, secondary school teachers discussed how action research might play a central role in setting up and evaluating their school improvement plans. Teachers found a great affinity between the nature of action research and the goals of the Brazilian reform, espe-cially the emphasis on students constructing knowledge, teachers re-flecting on practice, participation in active and integrated learning, and schools working to create democratic communities of learning and in-quiry. A main assignment of the course was to have teachers design an action research project that would help their school implement its ac-tion plan. Several teachers described ongoing projects their schools had started to implement. Examples of these projects include:

1. Improving discipline through creating a democratic school commu-nity.
2. An interdisciplinary studies program at Colegio Estadual do Parana.
3. Values education programa at Col. Est. Maria Aguiar Teixeira.
4. Quality of life through curriculum integration at Col. Est. Jose Guimaraes.

In discussing their learning experiences at the end of the course, one group of teachers told the class: "During this course, we became acutely aware that we need to be more appreciative of our teaching practices, which have evolved through living them with our students and colleagues. We can be creators of new practices and school improvement plans based on our critical reflection, research, and dialogue with colleagues." Another group reported: "A grateful surprise was to discover that action research is not alien to teaching practice. On the contrary, classrooms and schools are an immense field for research and study." Other teachers added: "Methods used in this course, such as the reflection journal, writing our career lifeline, brainstorming, and group discussions, liberated us to express new ideas and consider possible reform actions in our schools" (Fischer, 1998a).

School Reform and "Best Practice" in Santiago de Chile

A goal of the Chilean educational reform is to provide time in schools for teachers to reflect on their practice and share insights and experiences with colleagues. The idea is that by sharing education practices, teachers will find ways to improve opportunities for student learning. In addition, curriculum improvement through democratic participation in school action plans is a stated aim of the educational reform agenda. Unfortunately, most schools have insufficient resources for releasing teachers for such discussion and planning, and most Chilean teachers work two shifts in different schools. Moreover, the school reform agenda tends to emphasize what needs to be changed, rather than building on the experiences, insights, and good educational practices of teachers.

Speaking at a conference on Chilean school reform held in Santiago de Chile during March 1999, Fischer noted:

> School reforms need not start from zero. All during their career, teachers experiment with new ideas and strategies, and continue to develop a repertoire of good practices. Our challenge is to document, analyze and share these practices so that they can provide a framework for school reform.

Most Chilean universities do not have a tradition of school-based research to study and evaluate effective educational practices. Thus, few case studies exist to guide teacher preparation programs and course work. Fortunately, Chilean universities have recognized this shortcoming and are developing incentives and professional development programs to encourage and support their faculty who want to engage in school-based action research.

La Legua is one of the poorest and most dangerous neighborhoods of Santiago, Chile. Nevertheless, one of its public elementary schools, Escuela 480, Su Santidad Juan XXIII, is a bright oasis of school reform and renewal. On most Saturday mornings teachers work on new curriculum ideas, usually culminating in an "almuerzo con musica" (lunch with live music). Faculty, parents, and students painted the school, built a modest outdoor theater for performing plays the children create, and continue to raise money to buy computers and supplies. Visiting the classrooms, one is struck by the activities students are organizing, how engaged they are in their learning, and how in each classroom students are working in groups. All this is an individual school effort, with minimal funding from the Ministry of Education. The principal, Oscar Rivera Godoy, noted that their school's improvement plan focuses on writing across the curriculum and involves all thirty teachers and 640 students. It aims to "develop language, thinking, creativity and personal development of students," he said enthusiastically.

In its funding proposal to the Ministry of Education, the school outlined specific objectives to:

1. Promote dialogue as a permanent source of communication.
2. Develop critical thinking and self-analysis.
3. Foster awareness of social reality through action research.
4. Express opinions, ideas, feelings.
5. Creatively resolve problems.
6. Develop personal initiative and participate in group work (School Action Plan, Escuela 480, La Legua).

This is a remarkable list of objectives that the school, with its modest budget and resources, hopes to carry out. The school is clearly dedicated to the spirit of the reform—of creating a participatory community of learning, advocating for all its students, and preparing them for responsible citizenship and employment. Escuela Juan XXIII faces many challenges as it tries to educate children from impoverished homes, but its teachers continue to be dedicated fully to their vision of creating a quality school of learning, caring, and inquiry.

Many Chilean teachers, studying for their master's of education degree in Santiago, are conducting action research projects on educational practices that foster more active, participatory, and integrated learning. In Chilean universities, qualitative and action research projects on school-based practices are now acceptable requirements for the Master of Education degree. Teacher educators are beginning to believe that action research is a way to help schools carry out the goals of the national school reform and meet particular needs of the local school community. A glance at a list of recent master's projects at one university in Santiago, is illustrative of this trend:

Critical Curriculum Intervention During Preservice Education.

Conversation Circles: Critical Pedagogy and Improving Teacher Education.

Inclusive Education: Revision of Aesthetic and Creative Education.

Profound Learning: A Form of Discovery in Mathematics Education.

Curriculum Integration in Preservice Education of Chemistry and Natural Science Teachers.

It is significant to note that these action research studies have been undertaken following a 17-year dictatorship in which teacher participation in school change and curriculum reform was limited. Today, many teacher researchers are trying to recover lost time, noting the gap in their professional development under the dictatorship, and the severe restrictions on what they could study and publish. With the restoration of democratic government in Chile, the idea of teacher-led curriculum making is again capturing the hearts and minds of Chilean educators.

There is still much work to be done. Governments, school systems, and universities need to trust teachers as instructional leaders who are willing to take a more decisive role in Chile's school reform agenda. The challenge for the Ministry of Education is to find adequate resources to support teachers as they implement school action plans. Incentives and opportunities for teachers to engage in action research would be a good investment. When more teachers are involved in reflection and inquiry about their work, there is an increased likelihood of implementing the goals of Chile's educational reform.

CREATING SCHOOLS FOR DEMOCRATIC LIVING: VOICES FROM SANTIAGO AND CURITIBA

Paulo Freire and John Dewey challenge us to see schools as places for democratic living, where all teachers and students participate in decision making, create communities of active learners, and define school goals. Democratic education is not merely a matter of taking civic classes; it is a way of life in which we constantly renew our dedication to freedom of speech and work to build a more just and civil society. Moreover, in Freire's (1981) view, democratic education is "founded on faith in people, on the belief that they not only can but should discuss the problems of their country, . . . the problems of democracy itself" (p. 39)

Many would argue that the central challenge for postdictatorship Chile and Brazil still remains: to engage in discussions about democratic education, build a civil society, and work for social justice. Most Chileans and Brazilians admit that democracy in their country is still fragile, and that people have to learn to trust each other again. Perhaps the most perplexing question teachers must face in their work with students is, how can we talk about democracy, civility, and social justice while trying to deal with memories of our painful past?

"Now, After So Many Years of Silence, We Can Speak"

During November 1998, in Santiago, Chile, teachers and students followed closely the British House of Lords decision to uphold Spain's request to extradite ex-dictator General Pinochet to stand trial for crimes against humanity. On the evening of the decision, during a graduate course on curriculum development at a university in Santiago, students discussed the House of Lords' ruling. They also heard how their older classmates had been arrested and tortured during the dictatorship. The younger students (who were children during the September 1973 coup) asked, "How could our country let this happen?" Other classmates noted, "The whole country was like a prison, and neighbors informed on neighbors." They talked about how the secret police sat in classes and how they could not freely express their points of view. "Even a hint of criticism of the government or its policies could get you arrested. We lost our voice." With the restoration of democracy, students remembered their relief and gratitude that they were free again to express themselves. One said, "Now, after so many years of silence, we can speak again."

Many Chilean students and faculty are trying to find ways to restore democratic education, but realize that there is much denial of their painful past, making this work problematic. Moulian (1997) held that a decisive element of the Chilean reality today "is the compulsion to forget, and that this . . . blocking of memory is a situation repeated in societies that lived experiences on the edge. This negation with respect to the past means the loss of discourse, the difficulty to talk." Different names are used to express the past: For some it was "trauma," for others it was "victory" (p. 31). Chileans recognize that they live in a divided country with an enormous gap between those who supported the dictatorship and those who opposed it. Some educational leaders argue that to teach civility and create democratic schools, Chileans must find the courage to face painful memories and to talk openly about the past. Others believe there has been enough suffering.

At Chilean universities, faculty members are beginning to ask students to face difficult questions about their responsibilities as future teachers: How can teachers in Chile talk about the past with their students to teach about civility and social justice? What can we say about what it was like to live under the dictatorship? Do we talk about violence, disappeared family members, exile? What lessons can we find in our past? What do we want to find? How can we build a better future, one that is more open, less divided? During the coup on September 11, 1993, soldiers sacked Pablo Neruda's home in Santiago and burned his books. Twelve days later Neruda, the Nobel Prize winner poet of Chile, died. In literature classes, students read his poetry: "Tyranny cuts off the singer's head, but the voice at the bottom of the well returns to the secret springs of the earth and rises from darkness through the mouth of the people. . . . There's no forgetting, there's no winter that will wipe your name, shining brother, from the lips of the people" (quoted in Poirot, 1990, pp. 68–72).

During March 1999, at a school reform conference of school principals in Puente Alto, Santiago, one participant concluded, "We need to learn how to lead democratically. We don't know how to live participatory leadership." When asked to share examples of democratic and collaborative classroom practices they had recently seen, the principals were pleasantly surprised at the number and extent of them. They wondered if these might serve as a possible guide for reform: "We need to document, celebrate, and affirm these collaborative practices. They could be the beginnings of more participatory and democratic leadership for school change." Another offered, "These examples of participation and collaborative learning can serve as a hopeful guide as we continue to struggle to build democratic schools."

During their graduate work at Chilean universities, more and more teachers are beginning to do action research projects that directly address some of the difficult issues of building democratic schools and dealing with painful memories of the past. In August 1999, at the closing of a graduate course that Fischer taught in Santiago, teacher leaders talked about how doing action research had influenced their professional work in schools. Francisco Ochoa Neira told us: "I see my role as a supervisor in a much different way now. I was reluctant to stop and talk to teachers about their concerns, focusing more on monitoring instruction. I am much more willing to listen, to appreciate where teachers are coming from." Another supervisor, Silvia Quinteros Munox, added:

> I can look at the faces of teachers now with much more confidence. Now, I am able to invite them to reflect upon their work, because I have become more comfortable reflecting upon my own. It is not easy to be self-critical and to look at your professional work. Because of critical self-study, I am much closer to the teachers I work with now.

At the beginning of the course, teachers were asked to think about the kind of schools in which they would want to work, where they could grow professionally, and where students come to learn. Looking back at this challenge, teacher Carmen Donaso said:

> I was bored with my work, stressed out, frustrated. I thought this was an unrealistic question. I did not feel I could influence anything. Now I know this question prompted us to look inside, to begin with ourselves, to find ways to struggle with our own feelings of doubt, inadequacy, fear. Working with a group of colleagues in this course, I learned not to be afraid to get to know myself and to work toward improving my professional environment.

In talking about what role action research might have played in his professional growth, Santiago Aranzaes Hernandez said:

At first, it was difficult to enter a school and begin to note what was happening. Soon, I began to observe things I had not noticed before during my routine work of supervision. My research project forced me to write down my feelings and observations. The writing helped me clarify things, to see connections, to appreciate the bigger picture. I was able to deal with problems better and not get so overwhelmed with them.

Nancy Quiroga Diaz related how she worked with students who were abused and formed a discussion group of parents to try to deal with the problem. She told us, "The parents began to understand that they must break the vicious circle of abuse by treating their children with love." Jorge Ibarra Sandoval, her colleague, added:

Few things have affected me so much as working with Nancy during this course. I have learned not to run away from my feelings. I study my emotions to help me understand my colleagues and students better. I feel liberated and gained more professional satisfaction.

These comments are powerful testimonials that it is possible to deal with painful memories and face difficult situations in schools. What influenced these open and frank dialogues? We believe these teachers were able to deal with the many difficult events in their professional lives because they had built a high level of trust among themselves by working in small groups during their 6 months together. All kept a journal of reflections, noting their responses and feelings during their work in schools. They came to see their writings as a means to better understand the complex and often overwhelming challenges of their work. Perhaps there is another lesson at work here as well. As teachers are supported in reflecting upon their work, within a supportive collaborative setting, they are better able to address the larger questions of democratic education. They can begin to talk about how schools can help build a more peaceful society. For these teachers, dealing with painful memories became liberating.

Jose Guimares School: Working for Social Transformation

We close this chapter by briefly describing the experiences of Jose Guimares School in Curitiba, Brazil, which faced some painful realities and set out to build a democratic community of learning. Jose Guimares School serves mainly a poor and working class neighborhood of Curitiba. The principal, Candida de Carvalho Junqueira, talked about her teachers, students and parents attending workshops on Saturdays that they have organized, "in order to build a sense of community, to foster a culture that this is their school and they are responsible for it." She talked about how they had a serious discipline and motivation problem, and how the faculty and student body got involved in discussing ways to address it. The group discussed imposing strict discipline and having clear rules and punishment for those who did not follow them. The faculty met in groups to study methods of discipline, origins of the students' concerns, and problems of the school community. Gradually, the faculty began to focus on how to build a democratic culture for learning.

The faculty had been reading the works of Paulo Freire and started to quote him frequently:

> We need to create a school which is an adventure, which advances, and which is not fearful of taking risks. . . . A school in which everyone is a thinker, acts, creates, speaks, loves. A school which believes that knowledge is an instrument for social transformation, and which is passionately dedicated to life.

They had come to see themselves not as enforcers of discipline, but as educators who needed to invite their students to participate with them in building a democratic school (Fischer, 1998a, p. 25).

CONCLUSIONS

A study of reform activity in 57 urban school districts from 1992 to 1995 found that the apparent failure of reform in these districts was due not to too little reform, but to too much (Hess, 1998). The frenetic pace at which new reform programs and curricula have come and gone over the last 10 years have left even the most dedicated teachers and principals tired, worn out, and cynical about the "next big thing coming down from above." The fact that almost all reform activity has come from sources outside of the school and classroom (from corporate advisory panels, state and federal government commissions, and university educational consortia) has not gone unnoticed by teachers. As a profession, the collective voice of teachers (and their students) has been unsolicited and largely ignored in broad-based school and curricular reform. As primary stakeholders, the insiders' perspective is missing. The political reality is that whoever has the power to name the problem, and to frame the solution, ultimately controls both the content and the scope of school curriculum. Having little or no voice in the reform debate, teachers often do not feel ownership of newly mandated reform curricula.

Today, action research is being increasingly touted and used for district, state, and national school reform initiatives (Caro-Bruce & McCreadie, 1995; Heckman, 1996). Unfortunately, the focus often is not to improve practice, or to increase understanding, but to assess the effectiveness of a particular intervention, typically not of the teachers' choosing. Feldman (1995, p. 190) termed this the "institutionalization" of action research. Herein lies the dilemma: How can teacher action research, essentially a "bottom-up" democratic means of renewal and reform, be employed from the top down in the name of school reform?

We believe that increased teacher autonomy has a major role to play in creating and sustaining long-term educational improvement. Participating with teachers on research projects across three different school reform settings, we came to similar conclusions:

1. Teacher research can play an important role in identifying relevant school improvement goals and in ascertaining the effectiveness of reform programs.
2. To maximize school reform efforts, teachers need freedom and support in choosing research questions and pursuing ideas for improving learning and teaching.
3. There is an affinity between developing good teaching practices and engaging in action research, and both are vital for successful school reform and renewal programs.
4. University and school collaboration is needed to maximize benefits of teacher research that supports school reforms (see chap. 6).

The bigger picture of what kind of society we want to create must guide educational reform efforts. Teacher research, school reform, and social action rest on moral choices and commitments. Ultimately, school reforms must support the universal quest of all people for social justice, democracy, civility, and human rights. The challenge is to create democratic schools that can help transform society, support enlightened citizens, and help students participate in the work of justice, peace, and cultural understanding.

WEB SITES

www.cps.k12.il.us Chicago Public Schools web site.

Democratic Education

www.civiced.org
www.edudemo.org
http://civnet.org/civitas

Human Rights

www.ehrfoundation.org
www.unhchr.ch
http://shr.aaas.org
www.un.org/overview/rights.html

Social Justice

www.ccseb.com/ddl
www.justpeace.org
www.igc.org
www.lib.jjay.cuny.edu
www.amnesty.org
www.smplanet.com/kids/peace

REFERENCES

Caro-Bruce, C., & McCreadie, J. (1995). What happens when a school district supports action research? In S. Noffke & R. B. Stevenson (Eds.), *Educational action research: Becoming practically critical* (pp. 154–164). New York: Teachers College Press.

Feldman, A. (1995). The institutionalization of action research: The California "100 Schools" Project. In S. Noffke & R. B. Stevenson (Eds.), *Educational action research: Becoming practically critical* (pp. 180–196). New York: Teachers College Press.

Fischer, J. (1998). *Estudando e Valorizando as Boas Practicas Educativas na Escola.* Curitiba, Brazil: SEED/DESG/PROEM.

Fischer, J. (1999). Investigacion-accion y desarrollo professional. In *Horizontes educacionales* (pp. 9–11). Chillan, Chile: Universidad del Bio-Bio.

Forward, D. (1989). A guide to action research. In P. Lomax (Ed.), *The management of change: Increasing school effectiveness and facilitating staff development through action research* (pp. 29–39). Avon, England: Clevedon.

Freire, P. (1981). *Education for critical consciousness.* New York: Continuum.

Havel, V. (1997). *The art of the impossible: Politics as morality in practice.* New York: Knopf.

Heckman, P. E. (1996). *The courage to change: Stories from successful school reform.* Thousand Oaks, CA: Corwin.

Hess, F. M. (1998). The urban reform paradox: Maybe the real problem in city school districts is not too little reform but too much. *American School Board Journal, 185*(2), 24–27.

Moulian, T. (1997). *Chile Actual, Anatomia de un mito.* Santiago: Arlcis.

Poirot, L. (1990). *Pablo Neruda, Absence and presence.* New York: W. W. Norton.

Sirotnik, K. (1987). Evaluation in the ecology of schooling: The process of school renewal. In J. Goodlad (Ed.), *The ecology of school renewal: Eighty-sixth yearbook of the National Society for the Study of Education* (pp. 41–62). Chicago: University of Chicago Press.

Weston, N. (1998). Building a learning community through teacher action research: Honoring teacher wisdom in three Chicago Public Schools. *School Community Journal, 8*(1), 57–71.

In Practice—Part III

1. Visit the human rights and school reform websites noted at the end of Chapter Nine. Discuss how teacher action research could play a political role in challenging the status quo and working for social justice. Describe how your action research initiatives might become political tools that address inequities and contribute to social justice.

2. Prepare an explanation for why teacher action research is "real" research. Include the historical context for such research and contrast this paradigm with other perspectives on research.

3. Read Sylvia Ashton-Warner's book *Teacher* and discuss how her work can be and cannot be characterized as teacher research.

4. Write about how your research would be different if an outside ethnographic researcher conducted it. How would your role be affected? How would the methods for collecting and interpreting data be different?

Afterword: The Three P's in Teacher Research: Reflecting on Action Research From Personal, Professional, and Political Perspectives

Owen van den Berg
National-Louis University

As you have seen in this book, there are many different views about what action research is and how one might go about doing it. Many of them emphasize the notion that the purpose of action research is to improve educational action or practice. For instance, one of the founders of action research, Stephen Corey, said that the value of action research is determined primarily by the extent to which findings lead to improvement in the practices of the people engaged in the research (Corey, 1953, p. 13). Similarly, John Elliott, the doyen of action researchers in England, argued that the central distinguishing feature and function of the action research movement is to improve practice rather than to produce knowledge (Elliott, 1989, p. 4).

So, action research can be viewed as, simply, research into action. If *you* are doing action research, it is research into *your* action, and so you have to research what *you* are doing! This might sound very obvious, but in both South Africa and the United States, the two countries where I have worked with teachers doing action research since 1986, I have been struck by the number of people who seem to struggle with the idea that, in action research, they will have to look at what they are doing, and very closely, in order to change it for the better.

I can only speculate on the reasons for this. One might be that at the universities we are still tempted, as students, to formulate our research questions in pseudo-scientific terms, such as, What effect does cooperative learning have on the motivation of seventh grade mathematics students?—as if we teacher researchers could *possibly* answer such a universal question on the basis of our single experience with one class of students in one small corner of the globe! We shouldn't create false expectations on the cover pages of our writings.

Another reason might be that we think that it is the Method or Strategy that makes the difference, uninfluenced by who is using it, or attempting to use it. It is as if we think that Ms. Cooperative Learning arrives at our door, knocks politely, and then proceeds to teach our students for the next 10 or 15 weeks! Perhaps it is because every few months we hear about a new miracle method for all our educational ills that we develop this touching faith in a new technique to solve all our problems—a belief in practopia, perhaps. The point, of course, is that we mediate and interpret, even distort a teaching strategy when we seek to use it. For instance, my understanding and use of, say, a Multiple Intelligences approach might be very different from that of another teacher, even if it looked on the surface as if we intended to do the same things.

Whatever the reasons, I need to reemphasize that it is crucial for us to recognize that if action research is research into action, or practice, then to be action researchers we have to look—seriously, systematically, critically—at our own action, if we are to have any hope of improving it. We might *think* we know how we teach, but until we actually collect data on our teaching and reflect on what that data might mean, we often are ignorant of many of our real strengths and real failings as teachers. My view, then, is that if an action research plan does not include getting direct feedback on the planner's teaching, then that person cannot claim to be engaged in action research. Collaboration is key.

In my work as a teacher educator, the first task I typically give to my graduate students is to have them tape-record a lesson or two that they teach, to listen to the tapes, and to select a 2-minute passage for transcription and discussion. Almost without exception, their initial reactions to these tapes are entirely negative: They are horrified to see how they repeat certain phrases over and over again; they are surprised by their tone of voice; they are shocked to see that they asked questions of only the boys or the girls in the class; and so on. If you had asked them if they did those things before listening to the tapes, they would very likely have denied them. Interestingly, though, the section of the tape they choose to transcribe for discussion in the class is typically not one of the segments that initially shocks them, but rather some other aspect of the lesson dynamics that strikes them as intriguing. Also, when their graduate class colleagues hear the segment of the tapes while reading the transcript, they invariably offer comments that go beyond the individual teacher's thoughts about what is happening in that segment. Collaborative action research offers us the opportunity to see ourselves anew, to make the commonplace strange, as one anthropologist once put it.

When we have designed an action research project—that is, a plan for something *new* that we would like to see happen in our classroom, or a plan for a brand new look at what we are doing—we add another level of complexity to the challenge of researching our own actions. The reason for this is that now we are no longer simply trying to find out more about how we presently teach, but we are researching our first efforts at doing something different, something new, in our teaching. Action research is often research into an attempt to innovate—an important point, to which I shall return in a moment.

When one gathers information about one's teaching and reflects on it, the questions that one has to ask are not simply what am I doing and what alternatives are there, but also, why am I doing what I am doing? Smith and his colleagues commented of teachers:

> The individual's perspective, that is his or her definition of the situation, depends on a complicated belief structure or system, which, in turn, arises from the accumulated life experience. . . . Innovation is not just a technical problem, not just a political problem, nor just a cultural problem. . . . In our view, innovation is also a person problem. (Smith, Prunty, Dwyer, & Kleine, 1986, pp. 86, 224)

When we teach, or innovate, or research our teaching or innovations, we are also exploring our own complicated backgrounds and view of the world. We are not simply looking at what methods or strategies we use or should use; we are raising questions about the values we hold and about our own self-image. When this starts to happen, action research becomes for us an exploration of who we are and what we stand for. It is at this stage of one's action research that, I believe, it is useful to think of one's actions in terms of three metaphors or perspectives—the personal, the professional, and the political.

THE PERSONAL DIMENSION

When I teach, and research my teaching, I bring my whole accumulated past, and my present view of it, to bear on those actions and my attempts to make sense of them. And so it might well be that I like or dislike some of my students for reasons that have to do with my own upbringing; or that I might prefer certain teaching strategies to others because they fit in with my own psychological levels of comfort; or that I might prefer and demand certain student behaviors over others because they resemble those I grew up with (such as my extended family's view about what it meant to be polite or rude). So when I research my teaching, I need to be prepared to confront these personal or individual dimensions of my work. I am not a neutral participant, and not all of my decisions in the classroom are based simply on educational principles. Much of what I am and do is wrapped up in my past, and my perception of myself that emerges from that past.

There are two central points here. The first is that we probably know ourselves less well than we think. My South African colleague Sue Davidoff (1993) argued in this regard that:

> How we experience ourselves consciously in the world, I believe, is actually only a small part of who we really are. Buried under this conscious self-experience is a world of unconscious feelings and responses to the world which profoundly affect the way in which we perceive and respond to our environment. (pp. 60–61)

The second point is that any self-discovery that results from a systematic and critical look at one's teaching can be very threatening—in fact, our very willingness to engage in such risk taking might be significantly influenced by aspects of our world of unconscious feelings and responses. Dadds (1992) provided a powerful statement of this risk and its potential consequences:

> Studying one's own professional work is no straightforward matter and adopting the reflective mode is not simply a cerebral activity. As we study our teaching, we are studying the images we hold of ourselves as teachers. Where these established self-images are challenged, questioned and perhaps threatened in the learning process, we may experience feelings of instability, anxiety, negativitiy, even depression. This is especially so if the self we come to see in self-study is not the self we think we are, or the self we would like to be. Thinking about our work in self-evaluation can,

thus, be a highly charged emotional experience, one from which we may be tempted to retreat, thus endangering future learning. (p. 1)

When we engage in systematic and critical action research, the chances are good that we will learn to know ourselves, and the reasons for our behavior patterns, better than was the case before. If we wish to transform our teaching, the learning of our students, and the way our schools function, I believe that we are going to have to transform ourselves and our knowledge of ourselves.

Let me leave the last word on this topic to Anne Wilson Schaef, who, in a book of meditations, wrote, "Probably the most important journey we will ever take is the journey inward. Unless we know who we are, how can we possibly offer what we have?" (Schaef, 1990, p.).

THE PROFESSIONAL DIMENSION

When we teach, we become part of a much larger group of people engaged in the same enterprise. Our image of teaching as a profession, and whether we fit into that image, is another important part of our makeup as people. We have been socialized, as school students, subsequently as students of education, and finally as teachers, into particular beliefs about what the profession stands for and what sorts of behavior count as professional. Often we are even nervous about trying out different teaching strategies in our classrooms because of what our fellow teachers might think. Sarason (1990) illustrated this with respect to the medical profession:

> The opposition and controversy regarding change [in medical circles] cannot be understood in terms of an individual psychology, that is, the personalities of individual physicians. What one has to comprehend is the professional education and indoctrination of these individuals into their specialties and the ways in which that education and that indoctrination were mightily reinforced once their professional training was over. We use terms like stubbornness, resistance, opposition, and smugness to describe individuals . . . [but] one must, at the very least, look into the institutional contexts in which they grew up, as well as the contexts in which as individuals they do what they do. (pp. 107–108)

Interestingly, however, when teachers talk about their action research and what they have tried to do in their classrooms, they often do not make explicit these tensions between their desire to bring about change and their concern that this might be viewed as problematic by other professionals. As action researchers we need, I believe, to make our hopes and fears about our *professional* role and location clearer in our thinking and writing. I stated earlier that we need to understand our whole accumulated past if we are to understand why we do what we do, and also why we have the hopes and fears that we do. Understanding that whole accumulated past does not simply include our family upbringing; it includes the way we have been socialized in every sphere of life that has touched us, including our professional socialization. The personal self-discovery that helps us to understand why we teach the way we do needs to be informed as well by a fuller understanding of our hopes and fears about our status as professionals.

The issue of professionalism goes beyond the personal dimension of how I fit into the profession, however, to include a consideration of how the profession is treated within the public realm at large. It is ironic, perhaps, in a country that argues that local control of education is essential for the maintenance of democracy, that so many teachers feel so very constrained by the local tyrannies of school superintendents, principals, and other officials. In South Africa under apartheid, many teachers were arrested and lost their jobs—but, ironically, the South African teachers I worked with did not seem to suffer from the collective paralysis of fear that many American teachers I have worked with seem to demonstrate in regard to their superiors. I suspect that it has something to do with the perceived proximity of the authoritarianism and not with the authoritarianism itself.

The notion of a profession as a collectivity of autonomous, responsible practitioners is consistently undermined in the United States by the tendency of senior administrators in American local authorities and state bureaucracies to issue instructions that they expect to be carried out without question or consideration of context. Teachers struggle to resist that authority, or even to write about its existence in the action research reflections.

Action research, however, seems to be based on the notion that local conditions vary widely, and that the solution to many problems is not to be found by the handing down of universal solutions—which seldom work! The proposed solutions usually take no account of local conditions, which Schon (1983, pp. 15–16) described as problematic situations characterized by uncertainty, disorder, and indeterminacy. Herbert Altrichter's view (1993) was that action research should be based on a concept of a socially responsible professionalism and so be "biased towards decentralist decisions, local developments, open schools, flat networks of professionals and clients instead of hierarchies, responsible professionals negotiating qualitative accountability with clients instead of formal accountability" (p. 53).

If action research is concerned first with local research into local problems in search of local solutions, which may very well also be useful for practitioners elsewhere, then the top-down undermining of the teaching profession by senior administrators has to be challenged. Failing the emergence of significant numbers of senior administrators who exercise leadership in the direction of the empowerment of teachers and the shedding of their own administrative power, our work will have to challenge the existing power relations within school systems. That brings us explicitly to the realm of the political, to which I now turn.

THE POLITICAL DIMENSION

Many people are distinctly uncomfortable when one talks about education as an essentially political undertaking; they would prefer a situation in which politics is kept out of education.

Unfortunately, the only way a teacher can keep politics out of education is by giving up the job of teaching. Teaching and education are profoundly political. They have to do with the type of citizens we want the society to produce, and with what sort of society we want. These are profoundly political questions that *should* be the topic of major, ongoing public debates and actions. Questions about the nature of schooling should not be left to teachers to decide, any more than we would be well served if it were left to lawyers to decide what laws or legal system we should have, or if it were left to physicians to decide on the health care system. On the other hand, teachers (or lawyers, or doctors, as the case may be) should also not be excluded from these debates and simply be told to implement decisions taken by others.

The politics of education has to do with more than decisions about the governance and organization of schools and the content of the curriculum. When I teach, I emphasize certain things and deemphasize others; I promote certain attitudes and counteract others; I reward certain behaviors while resisting others. For instance, one teacher might reward obedience and conformity, whereas another might encourage students to exhibit inquiring and critical habits. Paolo Freire and Ira Shor (1987) put it very well, if somewhat too neatly, when they said:

> This is a great discovery; education is politics! After that, when a teacher discovers that he or she is a politician, too, the teacher has to ask, What kind of politics am I doing in the classroom? That is, in favor of whom am I being a teacher? By asking in favor of whom am I educating, the teacher must also ask against whom am I educating. (p. 46)

We need to ask similar questions about our research as well: For instance, whose problems am I trying to understand by my research? And whose purposes are being served by my work? In working with South African teachers who typically were very radical in wanting political change, I was aways struck by the fact that they were very authoritarian when it came to their own preferred teaching styles. I used to challenge them by saying that, although they were staunch democrats at the political rallies on Saturday night, they were to the right of Genghis Khan when they walked into their classrooms on Monday morning! Given the overtly charged political environment in South Africa at the time, they usually had little trouble acknowledging that they were political agents, that their work had political consequences.

In the United States, many teachers seem satisfied with the notion that the country is the world's greatest democracy and so struggle to come to terms with the political role they play as teachers. Gore and Zeichner (1990) argued, however, that reflective teaching should be politically sophisticated and stress reflection about the social and political context of schooling and the assessment of classroom actions for their ability to contribute toward greater equity, social justice, and humane conditions in schooling and society (pp. 6–7). Certainly we are not acting as informed citizens if we continue to teach without questioning the perpetuation of inequality and injustice within the educational and social systems of which we are a part as teachers and citizens.

As action researchers intent on improving our own action, we need to understand our whole accumulated past if we are to understand why we do what we do, and why we have the hopes and fears that we do. Understanding that whole accumulated past does not simply include our family upbringing; it includes the way we have been socialized in every sphere of life, including our professional and political socialization. The personal self-discovery that helps us to understand why we teach the way we do needs to be informed as well by a fuller understanding of our hopes and fears about our status as professionals and as citizens who are striving for some or other vision of the society (a vision that is often hotly contested by other teachers and citizens).

Action research is the study of our own practice with the intention of improving it. Arriving at alternative and hopefully better ways to teach is a complex activity that brings us face to face with our own values. In exploring our values, we—and our students—will benefit enormously from our thorough reflection on our own taken-for-granted assumptions and on our own deep-seated attitudes, beliefs, and habits that have arisen from the ways we have been socialized by our families and by the great institutions of society. By the end of our action research projects, we may not have answered the question of what method works best, but we should certainly have come to a fuller and deeper understanding of the setting within which we and our students work, and of what makes us tick. As teachers with a heightened sense of who we are personally, professionally, and politically, we are likely to be better able to enrich and empower all the students with whom we work.

REFERENCES

Altrichter, H. (1993). The concept of quality in action research: Giving practitioners a voice in educational research. In M. Schratz (Ed.), *Qualitative voices in educational research* (pp. 40–55). Washington, DC: Falmer Press.

Corey, S. M. (1953). *Action research to improve school practices.* New York: Teachers College, Columbia University Bureau of Publications.

Dadds, M. (1992, September). *The feeling of thinking in professional self-study.* Paper presented at the CARN Conference, Worcester, England.

Davidoff, S. M. (1993). *Reflections on facilitating action research.* Unpublished master's thesis, University of the Western Cape, Cape Town, South Africa.

Elliott, J. (1989, December). *Studying the school curriculum through insider research: Some dilemmas.* Paper presented at the International Conference of School-Based Innovations, Hong Kong.

Freire, P., & Shor, I. (1987). *A pedagogy for liberation.* London: Macmillan.

Gore, J., & Zeichner, K. (1990, September). *Action research and reflective teaching in practice.* Paper presented at the CARN Conference, Worcester, England.

Sarason, S. B. (1990). *The predictable failure of educational reform.* San Francisco: Jossey-Bass.

Schaef, A. W. (1990). *Meditations for women who do too much.* New York: HarperCollins.

Schon, D. A. (1983). *The reflective practitioner.* London: Maurice Temple Smith.

Smith, L. M., Prunty, J. P., Dwyer, D. C., & Kleine, P. F. (1986). *Educational innovators, then and now.* New York: Falmer Press.

Author Index

SUBJECT INDEX